The
Paradise

Bobos in Paradise

and

On Paradise Drive

Simon & Schuster

Suite

David Brooks

NEW YORK   LONDON   TORONTO   SYDNEY   NEW DELHI

Simon & Schuster
1230 Avenue of the Americas
New York, NY 10020

Bobos in Paradise copyright © 2000 by David Brooks

On Paradise Drive copyright © 2004 by David Brooks

This Simon & Schuster hardcover edition October 2011

SIMON & SCHUSTER and colophon are registered trademarks
of Simon & Schuster, Inc.

For information about special discounts for bulk purchases,
please contact Simon & Schuster Special Sales at 1-866-506-1949
or business@simonandschuster.com.

The Simon & Schuster Speakers Bureau can bring authors to your
live event. For more information or to book an event contact the
Simon & Schuster Speakers Bureau at 1-866-248-3049
or visit our website at www.simonspeakers.com.

Manufactured in the United States of America

10   9   8   7   6   5   4   3   2   1

Library of Congress Cataloging-in-Publication Data is available.

ISBN: 978-1-4516-4315-2
ISBN: 978-1-4516-4917-8 (ebook)

These titles were previously published individually.

Introduction to
The Paradise Suite

Bobos in Paradise was published in 2000, at the height of the dot-com boom. *On Paradise Drive* was published in 2004 and was written in the shadow of September 11. Since then, the world has seen a bloody war in Iraq, a global financial crisis, the rise of Barack Obama, various tsunamis and other disasters, a Tea Party movement, and an Arab spring sweeping across the Middle East. It is fair to ask: Are these books still relevant?

My answer would be that yes, they are still relevant, but in the years since a series of darker, troubling questions about their subjects have come to the fore that need to be asked and addressed.

Bobos in Paradise is frustratingly relevant. I would like to write another sociological survey like *Bobos,* and I have waited for a new and different culture to replace the culture of Whole Foods, Restoration Hardware, and locally grown, thick-textured breads that I wrote about in that book.

Alas, this new replacement culture has not yet come. There is clearly the beginning of a new mentality in the world of Twitter and social media, but these mental glimmerings have not yet materialized into a new sort of lifestyle or a new living environment. Instead, the people at Google still dress and act the way they did when I wrote *Bobos*, the retail environment in upscale America is still the same, as are the beliefs and behaviors in educated circles.

In fact, the trends I described in that book have only deepened. It is still basically true that people who are good at manipulating ideas are still likely to make a lot of money. It is still true that they are ambivalent about success, and they clothe their affluence in moral, organic, and environmental drapery. It is still true that the upscale culture continues to be a mixture of the bourgeois and the bohemian, though the bohemian patina does seem to get thinner every year. The financial crisis did very little to change Wayne, Pennsylvania, or Palo Alto, California, or Bethesda, Maryland, or Burlington, Vermont, or Austin, Texas, or Winnetka, Illinois, or any of the other outposts of Bobo culture.

If anything, these places have thrived and become more like themselves. Once a WASP bastion, Wayne, Pennsylvania, which plays a large role in that book, has become a culinary bastion. There are more restaurants than Protestants there now, and it is exceedingly hard to park.

It has also become ever more clear that the revolutions of the 1960s and the 1980s, which were once thought to be opposites, were really complimentary parts of the same thing. They were both revolts against the supposed conformity and group/other orientation of the 1950s. In the 1960s, boomers staged a cultural revolution that emphasized individual freedom. In the 1980s, boomers staged an economic revolution that emphasized economic freedom. But as I intimated in that book and as writers ranging from Mark Lilla to Phillip Blond have made explicit since, both those revolutions had a lot in common, even though the hippies and the yuppies supposedly hated one another. Both had the effect of celebrating individual choice and weakening civic bonds. Now that the culture wars have cooled, the synthesis between the two movements is all we have left.

On Paradise Drive is still relevant, too, though events have been less kind to that book's subjects. That book was an attempt to connect some long-running motifs in American history to the way Americans live today. It was an attempt to show how the moral materialism of the Puritans, for example, still influences everyday life, even in the supposedly soulless suburbs. One of the points in the book is that Americans are driven by an eschatological drive that is half-real and half-fantasy. As a result, Americans are energetic and manic, but they also have a tendency to be dangerous to themselves and to take every ambition beyond its logical extreme.

That tendency has been borne out in the years since. Parts of the book describe the rise of fast-growing suburbs, in places like Arizona and Nevada, as modern examples of Americans' horniness for the future. Well, the excess of that horniness has now been exposed, the gigantic overbuilding, the horrible overborrowing, the enthusiastic excess in all directions.

On a more positive note, the underlying dynamism of the country has been on display as well. In the book I tried to point out that the America Alexis de Tocqueville wrote about in the 1830s is still the America we see and feel around us today. The Paradise Spell creates problems, but also helps us overcome them because the energy and the longing for a future wonderland never lets us rest.

In the years since I wrote these books, though, a large anxiety has risen and clouded over the national mind: the question of whether America is in decline. Since 2004,

China, India, and other emerging economies have gone from strength to strength. People in America, Europe, Japan, and other affluent countries have been given more reason to doubt themselves. In the United States, as I write in 2011, 70 percent of voters believe the country is headed in the wrong direction. Two-thirds believe the country is on the way down.

Neither book directly addresses the gloomy questions that surround anxieties of decline, but both help us think about the problems.

Bobos is a book about the transformation of elite culture. It describes how the American elite moved from a system that rewarded WASP bloodlines and social connections to a system that rewarded SAT scores, grades, skills, and complacence. It describes how the meritocracy has become more open, more competitive, and more fair.

Yet here is the paradox: As the meritocracy has become more diverse and more fair, trust in elite institutions has declined. Moreover, the performance of those elite institutions may have declined, too. Banks were once run by the scions of old families. Now they are run by the cream of the straight-A/perfect SATs set. And yet would we say that banks are performing more ably than they were, or that they are more deserving of our respect?

Government was once home to rampant cronyism, staffed by party hacks. Today it is staffed by sophisticated people from public policy schools. Would we say that government performs its job more ably than it did?

Journalism was once a profession for working stiffs who drank a lot. Now it attracts very bright people from Stanford, Williams, and even the University of Chicago. Would we say that the media is more respected than it was in the days of Murrow and Cronkite?

These questions answer themselves. The promise of the meritocracy has not been fulfilled. The talent level is higher but the reputation is lower.

Why? Well, I can think of a few reasons. The current meritocracy is based on an overly narrow definition of talent. Between the ages of sixteen and twenty-four, students advance by pleasing adults, getting fancy degrees, and making good connections. But the traits that really lead to accomplishment are hard to measure and are developed both earlier and later in life—skills related to wisdom, empathy, courage, and character.

The members of the current elite may think too highly of themselves. They may be too easy on themselves, too self-indulgent as they angle for promotion and profile. They may have less of a self-effacing sense of service to a larger cause.

Public trust in elites may have declined because the current meritocratic system has opened up wider chasms than even the old one. The WASP banker in a small Tennessee city may have belonged to a restricted country club, but at least he lived in a small Tennessee city. Now top bankers live in New York, Charlotte, or LA and have much less contact with people down the income and educational scale.

Finally, leadership class solidarity is weaker. The Protestant establishment was inbred, but its Republican and Democratic members still felt cross-partisan loyalties. They were imbued with an aristocratic sense of service to the nation. Those loyalties have weakened, the curriculum of service has been neglected, and the war between rival factions within the elite—Republicans versus Democrats, corporate types versus professional types—has grown more vicious and dismaying.

When I wrote *Bobos* I had some qualms about the new upper class. Now I have more. It is not behaving as a leadership class should. It is nether humble and deferential to the voices of the wider public nor is it able to take upon those duties that inevitably fall upon elites in all societies and all times. In fact, today's elites can't even acknowledge they are elites and thus assume their responsibilities.

The events of the past few years have also caused me to take a more skeptical view of the suburbs than I did in *On Paradise Drive*. In that book I celebrated the energy that propels people farther and farther out, in search of a paradise.

But in the years since, there has been ample evidence to suggest that people develop most amid cities. Some of this evidence has been gathered by Edward Glaeser of Harvard. People who live in cities and dense suburbs benefit from closer and more regular face-to-face contacts. Their productivity levels rise faster than those of people who live in sprawling and rural parts of the country. They are more creative and more inventive. Groups that meet face-to-face perform much better than groups that communicate electronically. In a study of patent applications, researchers found that an astonishing share of the inventors who contributed to a breakthrough lived within a few miles of each other. Proximity matters.

Some people are skeptical of sprawl for environmental reasons. I've become a bit more skeptical of sprawl for human capital reasons. People learn from people they love, and for that you need to be face-to-face.

If I were to write these books today, I'd spend more ink expressing anxiety about the state of the society. That said, not much else would change. These books are meant to describe American society at the start of the twenty-first century. They are meant to describe how people act, the categories in their heads, the source of their motivations, and how they fashion their dreams.

These deeply ingrained beliefs and aspirations do not change quickly. America, thank heaven, is still America, and it is still, overall, a sweet place to be.

Bobos in Paradise

*The New Upper Class and
How They Got There*

To Sarah

Contents

Introduction

THIS BOOK started with a series of observations. After four and a half years abroad, I returned to the United States with fresh eyes and was confronted by a series of peculiar juxtapositions. WASPy upscale suburbs were suddenly dotted with arty coffeehouses where people drank little European coffees and listened to alternative music. Meanwhile, the bohemian downtown neighborhoods were packed with multimillion-dollar lofts and those upscale gardening stores where you can buy a faux-authentic trowel for $35.99. Suddenly massive corporations like Microsoft and the Gap were on the scene, citing Gandhi and Jack Kerouac in their advertisements. And the status rules seemed to be turned upside down. Hip lawyers were wearing those teeny tiny steel-framed glasses because now it was apparently more prestigious to look like Franz Kafka than Paul Newman.

The thing that struck me as oddest was the way the

old categories no longer made sense. Throughout the twentieth century it's been pretty easy to distinguish between the bourgeois world of capitalism and the bohemian counterculture. The bourgeoisie were the square, practical ones. They defended tradition and middle-class morality. They worked for corporations, lived in suburbs, and went to church. Meanwhile, the bohemians were the free spirits who flouted convention. They were the artists and the intellectuals—the hippies and the Beats. In the old schema the bohemians championed the values of the radical 1960s and the bourgeois were the enterprising yuppies of the 1980s.

But I returned to an America in which the bohemian and the bourgeois were all mixed up. It was now impossible to tell an espresso-sipping artist from a cappuccino-gulping banker. And this wasn't just a matter of fashion accessories. I found that if you investigated people's attitudes toward sex, morality, leisure time, and work, it was getting harder and harder to separate the antiestablishment renegade from the pro-establishment company man. Most people, at least among the college-educated set, seemed to have rebel attitudes and social-climbing attitudes all scrambled together. Defying expectations and maybe logic, people seemed to have combined the countercultural sixties and the achieving eighties into one social ethos.

After a lot of further reporting and reading, it became clear that what I was observing is a cultural consequence of the information age. In this era ideas and knowledge are at least as vital to economic success as natural resources and finance capital. The intangible world of information merges with the material world of money, and new phrases that combine the two, such as "intellectual capital" and "the culture industry," come into vogue. So the people who thrive in this period are the ones who can turn ideas and emotions into products. These are highly educated folk who have one foot in the bohemian world of creativity and another foot in the bourgeois realm of ambition and worldly success. The members of the new information age elite are bourgeois bohemians. Or, to take the first two letters of each word, they are Bobos.

These Bobos define our age. They are the new establishment. Their hybrid culture is the atmosphere we all breathe. Their status codes now govern social life. Their moral codes give structure to our personal lives. When I use the word *establishment,* it sounds sinister and elitist. Let me say first, I'm a member of this class, as, I suspect, are most readers of this book. We're not so bad. All societies have elites, and our educated elite is a lot more enlightened than some of the older elites, which were based on blood or wealth or military valor. Wherever we educated elites settle, we make life more interesting, diverse, and edifying.

This book is a description of the ideology, manners, and morals of this elite. I start with the superficial things and work my way to the more profound. After a chapter tracing the origins of the affluent educated class, I describe its shopping habits, its business culture, its intellectual, social, and spiritual life. Finally, I try to figure out where the Bobo elite is headed. Where will we turn our attention next? Throughout the book I often go back to the world and ideas of the mid-1950s. That's because the fifties were the final decade of the industrial age, and the contrast between the upscale culture of that time and the upscale culture of today is stark and illuminating. Furthermore, I found that many of the books that really helped me understand the current educated class were written between 1955 and 1965, when the explosion in college enrollments, so crucial to many of these trends, was just beginning. Books like *The Organization Man, The Death and Life of Great American Cities, The Affluent Society, The Status Seekers,* and *The Protestant Establishment* were the first expressions of the new educated class ethos, and while the fever and froth of the 1960s have largely burned away, the ideas of these 1950s intellectuals continue to resonate.

Finally, a word about the tone of this book. There aren't a lot of statistics in these pages. There's not much theory. Max Weber has nothing to worry about from me. I just went out and tried to describe how people are living, using a method that might best be described as comic sociology. The idea is to get at the essence of cultural patterns, getting the flavor of the times without trying to pin it down with meticulous exactitude. Often I make fun of the social manners of my class (I sometimes think I've made a whole career out of self-loathing), but on balance I emerge as a defender of the Bobo culture. In any case, this new establishment is going to be setting the tone for a long time to come, so we might as well understand it and deal with it.

1

The Rise of the Educated Class

I'M NOT SURE I'd like to be one of the people featured on the *New York Times* weddings page, but I know I'd like to be the father of one of them. Imagine how happy Stanley J. Kogan must have been, for example, when his daughter Jamie was admitted to Yale. Then imagine his pride when Jamie made Phi Beta Kappa and graduated summa cum laude. Stanley himself is no slouch in the brains department: he's a pediatric urologist in Croton-on-Hudson, with teaching positions at the Cornell Medical Center and the New York Medical College. Still, he must have enjoyed a gloat or two when his daughter put on that cap and gown.

And things only got better. Jamie breezed through Stanford Law School. And then she met a man—Thomas Arena—who appeared to be exactly the sort of son-in-law that pediatric urologists dream about. He did his undergraduate work at Princeton, where he, too, made Phi Beta

Kappa and graduated summa cum laude. And he, too, went to law school, at Yale. After school they both went to work as assistant U.S. attorneys for the mighty Southern District of New York.

These two awesome résumés collided at a wedding ceremony in Manhattan, and given all the school chums who must have attended, the combined tuition bills in that room must have been staggering. The rest of us got to read about it on the *New York Times* weddings page. The page is a weekly obsession for hundreds of thousands of *Times* readers and aspiring Balzacs. Unabashedly elitist, secretive, and totally honest, the "mergers and acquisitions page" (as some of its devotees call it) has always provided an accurate look at at least a chunk of the American ruling class. And over the years it has reflected the changing ingredients of elite status.

When America had a pedigreed elite, the page emphasized noble birth and breeding. But in America today it's genius and geniality that enable you to join the elect. And when you look at the *Times* weddings page, you can almost feel the force of the mingling SAT scores. It's Dartmouth marries Berkeley, MBA weds Ph.D., Fulbright hitches with Rhodes, Lazard Frères joins with CBS, and summa cum laude embraces summa cum laude (you rarely see a summa settling for a magna—the tension in such a marriage would be too great). The *Times* emphasizes four things about a person—college degrees, graduate degrees, career path, and parents' profession—for these are the markers of upscale Americans today.

Even though you want to hate them, it's hard not to feel a small tug of approval at the sight of these Résumé Gods. Their expressions are so open and confident; their teeth are a tribute to the magnificence of American orthodonture; and since the *Times* will only print photographs in which the eyebrows of the bride and groom are at the same level, the couples always look so evenly matched.

These are the kids who spent the crucial years between ages 16 and 24 winning the approval of their elders. Others may have been rebelling at that age or feeling alienated or just basically exploring their baser natures. But the people who made it to this page controlled their hormonal urges and spent their adolescence impressing teachers, preparing for the next debate tournament, committing themselves to hours of extracurricular and volunteer work, and doing everything else that we as a society want teenagers to do. The admissions officer deep down in all of us wants to reward these mentor magnets with bright futures, and the real admissions officers did, accepting them into the right colleges and graduate schools and thus turbocharging them into adulthood.

The overwhelming majority of them were born into upper-middle-class households. In 84 percent of the weddings, both the bride and the groom have a parent who is a business executive, professor, lawyer, or who otherwise belongs to the professional class. You've heard of old money; now we see old brains. And they tend to marry late—the average age for brides is 29 and for grooms is 32. They also divide pretty neatly into two large subgroups: nurturers and predators. Predators are the lawyers, traders, marketers—the folk who deal with money or who spend their professional lives negotiating or competing or otherwise being tough and screwing others. Nurturers tend to be liberal arts majors. They become academics, foundation officials, journalists, activists, and artists—people who deal with ideas or who spend their time cooperating with others or facilitating something. About half the marriages consist of two predators marrying each other: a Duke MBA who works at NationsBank marrying a Michigan Law grad who works at Winston & Strawn. About a fifth of the marriages on the page consist of two nurturers marrying each other: a Fulbright scholar who teaches humanities at Stanford marrying a Rhodes scholar who teaches philosophy there. The remaining marriages on the page are mixed marriages in which a predator marries a nurturer. In this group the predator is usually the groom. A male financial consultant with an MBA from Chicago may marry an elementary school teacher at a progressive school who received her master's in social work from Columbia.

These meritocrats devote monstrous hours to their career and derive enormous satisfaction from their success, but the *Times* wants you to know they are actually not consumed by ambition. Each week the paper describes a particular wedding in great detail, and the subtext of each of these reports is that all this humongous accomplishment is a mere fluke of chance. These people are actually spunky free spirits who just like to have fun. The weekly "Vows" column lovingly details each of the wedding's quirky elements: a bride took her bridesmaids to get drunk at a Russian bathhouse; a couple hired a former member of the band Devo to play the *Jeopardy* theme song at the reception; another read A. A. Milne's Christopher Robin poems at a ceremony in a former du Pont mansion. The *Times* article is inevitably studded with quotations from friends who describe the bride and groom as enchanting paradoxes: they are said to be grounded but berserk, daring yet traditional, high-flying yet down to earth, disheveled yet elegant, sensible yet spontaneous. Either only paradoxical people get married these days, or people in this class like to see themselves and their friends as balancing opposites.

The couples tell a little of their own story in these articles. An amazing number of them seem to have first met while recovering from marathons or searching for the remnants of Pleistocene man while on archeological digs in Eritrea. They usually enjoyed a long and careful romance, including joint vacations in obscure but educational places like Myanmar and Minsk. But many of the

couples broke up for a time, as one or both partners panicked at the thought of losing his or her independence.
Then there was a lonely period apart while one member,
say, arranged the largest merger in Wall Street history
while the other settled for neurosurgery after dropping out
of sommelier school. But they finally got back together
again (sometimes while taking a beach vacation at a group
home with a bunch of people with cheekbones similar to
their own). And eventually they decided to share an apartment. We don't know what their sex lives are like because
the *Times* does not yet have a fornication page ("John
Grind, a lawyer at Skadden Arps with a degree from
Northwestern, has begun copulating with Sarah Smith, a
cardiologist at Sloan-Kettering with an undergraduate degree from Emory"). But we presume intimate relations are
suitably paradoxical: rough yet soft, adventurous yet intimate. Sometimes we get to read about modern couples
who propose to each other simultaneously, but most of
the time the groom does it the old-fashioned way—often,
it seems, while hot-air ballooning above the Napa Valley
or by letting the woman find a diamond engagement ring
in her scuba mask while they are exploring endangered
coral reefs near the Seychelles.

Many of these are trans-conference marriages—an
Ivy League graduate will be marrying a Big Ten graduate—so the ceremony has to be designed to respect everybody's sensibilities. Subdued innovation is the rule. If you
are a member of an elite based on blood and breeding, you
don't need to carefully design a marriage ceremony that
expresses your individual self. Your high status is made
impervious by your ancestry, so you can just repeat the
same ceremony generation after generation. But if you are
in an elite based on brainpower, like today's elite, you
need to come up with the subtle signifiers that will display
your own spiritual and intellectual identity—your qualifi-
cation for being in the elite in the first place. You need in-

vitations on handmade paper but with a traditional type-
face. Selecting music, you need Patsy Cline songs mixed in
with the Mendelssohn. You need a 1950s gown, but done
up so retro it has invisible quotation marks around it. You
need a wedding cake designed to look like a baroque
church. You need to exchange meaningful objects with
each other, like a snowboard engraved with your favorite
Schiller quotation or the childhood rubber ducky that you
used to cradle during the first dark days of your Supreme
Court clerkship. It's difficult to come up with your own
nuptial wrinkle, which will be distinctive without being
daring. But self-actualization is what educated existence is
all about. For members of the educated class, life is one
long graduate school. When they die, God meets them at
the gates of heaven, totes up how many fields of self-
expression they have mastered, and then hands them a divine diploma and lets them in.

The Fifties

The *Times* weddings page didn't always pulse with
the accomplishments of the Résumé Gods. In the late
1950s, the page projected a calm and more stately ethos.
The wedding accounts of that era didn't emphasize jobs or
advanced degrees. The profession of the groom was only
sometimes mentioned, while the profession of the bride
was almost never listed (and on the rare occasions when
the bride's profession was noted, it was in the past tense,
as if the marriage would obviously end her career). Instead, the *Times* listed pedigree and connections. Ancestors were frequently mentioned. The ushers were listed, as
were the bridesmaids. Prep schools were invariably mentioned, along with colleges. The *Times* was also careful to
list the groom's clubs—the Union League, the Cosmopolitan Club. It also ran down the bride's debutante history,

where she came out, and whatever women's clubs she might be a member of, such as the Junior League. In short, the page was a galaxy of restricted organizations. A description of the gown took up a good portion of the article, and the description of the floral arrangements was also exhaustive.

As you read through the weddings page of that time, sentences jump out at you that would never be found on today's weddings page: "She is descended from Richard Warren, who came to Brookhaven in 1664. Her husband, a descendant of Dr. Benjamin Treadwell, who settled in Old Westbury in 1767, is an alumnus of Gunnery School and a senior at Colgate University." Or "Mrs. Williams is an alumna of Ashley Hall and Smith College. A provisional member of the Junior League of New York, she was presented to society in 1952 at the Debutante Cotillion and Christmas Ball." Even the captions would be unthinkable today: "Mrs. Peter J. Belton, who was Nancy Stevens." (The *Times* would only use that past tense caption today for people who have had sex change operations.)

The paper, more reticent, did not list ages in those days, but the couples were clearly much younger; many of the grooms were still in college. A significant portion of the men had attended West Point or Annapolis, for this was a time when the military academies were still enmeshed in the East Coast establishment, and military service was still something that elite young men did. The section itself was huge in the late fifties. On a June Sunday it could stretch over 28 pages and cover 158 weddings. The ceremonies were much more likely then than now to have taken place in old-line suburbs—such towns as Bryn Mawr on Philadelphia's Main Line or Greenwich in Connecticut, Princeton in New Jersey, or the haughtier towns around Chicago, Atlanta, San Francisco, and elsewhere across the nation. The section was also, predictably, WASPier. About half the couples who were featured in the

late fifties were married in an Episcopal ceremony. Today
fewer than one in five of the marriages on the *Times* page
are Episcopalian, while around 40 percent are Jewish, and
there are many more Asian names. It's hard to directly
measure the rise of different religious groups, because in
the 1950s Jewish weddings were listed separately on
Mondays, but it's pretty clear the trends of the last 40
years have been bad for the Episcopalians and good for
the Jews.

Looking at the faces and the descriptions of the wedding section of the 1950s is like looking into a different
world, and yet it's not really been so long—most of the
people on those yellowing pages are still alive, and a siz-
able portion of the brides on those pages are young
enough that they haven't yet been dumped for trophy
spouses. The section from the late fifties evokes an entire
milieu that was then so powerful and is now so dated: the
network of men's clubs, country clubs, white-shoe law
firms, oak-paneled Wall Street firms, and WASP patri-
archs. Everybody has his or her own mental images of
the old Protestant Establishment: lockjaw accents, the Social Register, fraternity jocks passing through Ivy League
schools, constant rounds of martinis and highballs,
bankers' hours, starched old men like Averell Harriman,
Dean Acheson, and John J. McCloy, the local bigwigs that
appear in John Cheever and John O'Hara stories. Of
course, no era is as simple as its clichés—John J. McCloy,
the quintessential East Coast patrician, was actually a self-
made man—but the sociological evidence from the period
does generally support the stereotypes.

There was a strong sense of inherited European culture. "Have John learn Greek," McCloy's father rasped
on his deathbed. Young girls still cared about the aristocratic Coming Out rituals, which were measured by gradations that are now long forgotten. Christmas season
was the busiest time to debut, while the Thanksgiving pe-

riod was the briefer but more socially select time. Mainline Protestant denominations were thriving in those days. Three-quarters of the political, business, and military elites were Protestant, according to studies done at the time. It really was possible to talk about an aristocratic ruling class in the fifties and early sixties, a national elite populated by men who had gone to northeastern prep schools like Groton, Andover, Exeter, and St. Paul's and then ascended through old-line firms on Wall Street into the boardrooms of the Fortune 500 corporations and into the halls of Washington power. The WASPs didn't have total control of the country or anything like it, but they did have the hypnotic magic of prestige. As Richard Rovere wrote in a famous 1962 essay entitled "The American Establishment," "It has very nearly unchallenged power in deciding what is and what is not respectable opinion in this country." If you look at the news photographs from *Time* or *Newsweek* in those days, you see one sixtyish white male after another. Among other things, this elite had the power to drive the ambitious climbers who lacked the proper breeding—like Lyndon Johnson and Richard Nixon—nearly crazy with resentment.

Meanwhile, every affluent town in America had its own establishment that aped the manners and attitudes of the national one. There were local clubs where town fathers gathered to exchange ethnic jokes and dine on lamb chops topped with canned sauces—cream of mushroom, cream of asparagus, cream of leek. (People didn't worry about cholesterol then, since it had not yet become unfashionable to get sick and die.) The WASP aesthetic sense was generally lamentable—Mencken said Protestant elites had a "libido for the ugly"—and their conversation, by all accounts, did not sparkle with wit and intelligence. They tortured their young girls by allowing them to take horseback riding lessons but then forcing them to compete in dressage competitions, where they mastered all the virtues that were characteristic of the WASP elite and that are so uncharacteristic of today's educated elite: good posture, genteel manners, extreme personal hygiene, pointless discipline, the ability to sit still for long periods of time.

This was the last great age of socially acceptable boozing. It was still an era when fox hunting and polo didn't seem antiquarian. But the two characteristics of that world that strike us forcefully today are its unabashed elitism and its segregation. Though this elite was nowhere near as restrictive as earlier elites—World War II had exerted its leveling influence—the 1950s establishment was still based on casual anti-Semitism, racism, sexism, and a thousand other silent barriers that blocked entry for those without the correct pedigree. Wealthy Jewish and Protestant boys who had been playing together from childhood were forced to endure "The Great Division" at age 17, when Jewish and Gentile society parted into two entirely separate orbits, with separate debutante seasons, dance schools, and social secretaries. A Protestant business executive may have spent his professional hours working intimately with his Jewish colleague, but he never would have dreamed of putting him up for membership in his club. When Senator Barry Goldwater attempted to play golf at the restricted Chevy Chase Club, he was told the club was restricted. "I'm only half Jewish, so can't I play nine holes?" he is said to have replied.

The WASP elite was also genially anti-intellectual. Its members often spoke of "eggheads" and "highbrows" with polite disdain. Instead, their status, as F. Scott Fitzgerald had pointed out a few decades before, derived from "animal magnetism and money." By contrast with today's ruling class, they had relatively uncomplicated attitudes about their wealth. They knew it was vulgar to be gaudy, they tended toward thriftiness, but they seem not to have seen their own money as an affront to American principles of equality. On the contrary, most took their elite status for granted, assuming that such position was simply part of the natural and beneficent order of the universe. There was always going to be an aristocracy, and so for the people who happened to be born into it, the task was to accept the duties that came along with its privileges. At their best they lived up to the aristocratic code. They believed in duty, service, and honor, and more than just as words. The best of them still subscribed to the code of the natural aristocracy that one of their heroes, Edmund Burke, had included in *An Appeal from the New to the Old Whigs*. Burke's sentence is worth quoting in full because it captures a set of ideals that serve as an interesting foil to those of our own age:

> To be bred in a place of estimation; to see nothing low and sordid from one's infancy; to be taught to respect one's self; to be habituated to the censorial inspection of the public eye; to look early to public opinion; to stand upon such elevated ground as to be enabled to take a large view of the widespread and infinitely diversified combinations of men and affairs in a large society; to have leisure to read, to reflect, to converse; to be enabled to draw the court and attention of the wise and learned, wherever they are to be found; to be habituated in armies to command and to obey; to be taught to despise danger in the pursuit of honor and duty; to be formed to the greatest degree of vigilance, foresight, and circumspection, in a state of things in which no fault is committed with impunity and the slightest mistakes draw on the most ruinous consequences; to be led to a guarded and regulated conduct, from a sense that you are considered as an instructor of your fellow citizens in their highest concerns, and that you act as a reconciler between God and man; to be employed as an administrator of law and justice, and to be thereby among the first benefactors to mankind; to be a

professor of high science, or of liberal and ingenuous art; to be amongst rich traders, who from their
success are presumed to have sharp and vigorous
understandings, and to possess the virtues of diligence, order, constancy, and regularity, and to have
cultivated an habitual regard to commutative justice: these are the circumstances of men that form
what I should call a *natural* aristocracy, without
which there is no nation.

There are parts of this code that barely touch our
own—the emphasis on the military virtues, the sense that
one is an elevated instructor to one's fellow men, the sense
that one should act as a reconciler between God and man.
And while nobody has written to lament the decline of the
WASP as beautifully as Giuseppe Tomasi di Lampedusa
lamented the declining of the old Sicilian aristocracy in
The Leopard, or as elegantly as Evelyn Waugh lamented
the British aristocracy in *Brideshead Revisited,* it is still
possible to look back with some admiration at the Protestant elite, despite the racism, anti-Semitism, and rigidity
that were its fatal flaws.

At its best, the WASP establishment had a public service ethic that remains unmatched. Its members may have
been uncomfortable with ambition, but they were acutely
aware of obligation. They cared about good manners and
self-control, and looking back on them, they sometimes
seem weightier than we who have succeeded them, perhaps because they sacrificed more. Young gentlemen like
George Bush volunteered to fight in World War II without
a second thought, and a disproportionate number of
young men from the privileged WASP families lost their
lives in the world wars. They were a reticent bunch, without the restless rebelliousness of later generations. Com-
paratively, they had little weakness for narcissism. "You're
talking about yourself too much, George," Bush's mother

told him amidst the 1988 presidential campaign. Most important, of course, they led America during the American Century, and they built many of the institutions that the educated elites now happily occupy.

The Hinge Years

But even as those Episcopal brides with early settler ancestors, cotillion memories, and upper-class husbands were staring out from the pages of the 1959 weddings page, their world had already been fatally undermined. The earth-shaking decisions had been made, as many crucial decisions are made, by a college admissions committee. Without much fuss or public discussion, the admissions officers wrecked the WASP establishment. The story at Harvard, told by Richard Herrnstein and Charles Murray in the relatively uncontroversial first chapter of *The Bell Curve,* epitomizes the tale. In 1952 most freshmen at Harvard were products of the same WASP bastions that popped up on the *Times* weddings page: the prep schools in New England (Andover and Exeter alone contributed 10 percent of the class), the East Side of Manhattan, the Main Line of Philadelphia, Shaker Heights in Ohio, the Gold Coast of Chicago, Grosse Pointe of Detroit, Nob Hill in San Francisco, and so on. Two-thirds of all applicants were admitted. Applicants whose fathers had gone to Harvard had a 90 percent admission rate. The average verbal SAT score for the incoming men was 583, good but not stratospheric. The average score across the Ivy League was closer to 500 at the time.

Then came the change. By 1960 the average verbal SAT score for incoming freshmen at Harvard was 678, and the math score was 695—these are stratospheric scores. The average Harvard freshman in 1952 would have placed in the bottom 10 percent of the Harvard freshman class of 1960. Moreover, the 1960 class was drawn from a much wider socioeconomic pool. Smart kids from Queens or Iowa or California, who wouldn't have thought of applying to Harvard a decade earlier, were applying and getting accepted. Harvard had transformed itself from a school catering mostly to the northeastern social elite to a high-powered school reaching more of the brightest kids around the country. And this transformation was replicated in almost all elite schools. At Princeton in 1962, for example, only 10 members of the 62-man football team had attended private prep schools. Three decades earlier every member of the Princeton team was a prep school boy.

Why did this happen? Nicholas Lemann provides the guts of the answer in his book *The Big Test*. It's a remarkable story, because in many ways the WASP elite destroyed itself, and did so for the highest of motives. James Bryant Conant was president of Harvard after World War II, and so sat at the pinnacle of the Protestant Establishment. Nonetheless, Conant was alarmed by the thought that America might develop a hereditary aristocracy consisting of exactly the sort of well-bred young men he was training in Cambridge. Conant dreamed of replacing this elite with a new elite, which would be based on merit. He didn't envision a broad educated populace making democratic decisions. Rather, he hoped to select out a small class of Platonic guardians who would be trained at elite universities and who would then devote themselves selflessly to public service.

To help find these new guardians, Conant enlisted Henry Chauncey, a graduate of Groton and Harvard, an Episcopalian, a descendant of Puritan stock. Chauncey didn't have Conant's grand vision of what society should look like, but he did have a more distilled passion—for standardized tests and the glorious promise of social science. Chauncey was an enthusiast for tests the way other technoenthusiasts have fallen in love with the railroad, or nuclear power, or the Internet. He believed tests were a magnificent tool that would enable experts to measure people's abilities and manage society on a more just and rational basis. Chauncey went on to become the head of the Educational Testing Service, which created the Scholastic Aptitude Test. And so to a degree rare among social engineers, he was actually able to put his enthusiasm into practice. As Lemann observes, we are now living in a world created by Conant and Chauncey's campaign to replace their own elite with an elite based on merit, at least as measured by aptitude tests.

Conant and Chauncey came along during an era uniquely receptive to their message. The American intellectual class has probably never been so sure of itself, before or since. Sociologists, psychologists, and macroeconomists thought they had discovered the tools to solve personal and social problems. Freud's writings, which promised to explain the inner workings of the human mind, were at their peak of his influence. The McCarthy controversy mobilized segments of the intellectual class. The launching of Sputnik made educational rigor seem vital to the national interest. Finally, John F. Kennedy brought intellectuals into the White House, elevating intellectuals into the social stratosphere (at least many of them thought so). As we'll see in Chapter 4, intellectuals began to take themselves (even) more seriously in these years, often with good reason.

Conant and Chauncey were not the only academics who rose up to assert intellectual values against those of the WASP Establishment. In 1956 C. Wright Mills wrote *The Power Elite,* a direct assault on the establishment if ever there was one. In 1959 Jacques Barzun wrote *The House of Intellect.* In 1963 Richard Hofstadter wrote *Anti-Intellectualism in American Life,* a sprawling, confident broadside by an academic superstar against the "practical" classes, both rich and poor. In 1964 Digby Baltzell, of the University of Pennsylvania, wrote *The Protestant Establishment,* a book that introduced the term *WASP* and detailed the establishment's intellectual and moral failings. Though largely sympathetic to WASP ideals, he argued that the WASP elite had become a self-satisfied caste that was unwilling to bring in enough new talent to replenish the ranks. By and large, these academics wanted the universities to serve as meritocratic and intellectual hothouses, not as finishing schools for the social elite. Faculty members demanded that admissions officers look at the legacy applications more critically.

The WASPs had fended off challenges to their cultural hegemony before, either by simply ignoring them or by counterattacking. The first half of the century brought what historian Michael Knox Beran calls the "risorgimento of the well-to-do." Families like the Roosevelts adopted a tough, manly ethos in order to restore vigor and self-confidence to the East Coast elite and so preserve its place atop the power structure. In the 1920s, sensing a threat to the "character" of their institutions, Ivy League administrators tightened their official or unofficial Jewish quotas. Nicholas Murray Butler at Columbia reduced the proportion of Jews at his school from 40 to 20 percent in two years. At Harvard, President A. Lawrence Lowell diagnosed a "Jewish Problem" and also enforced quotas to help solve it. But by the late fifties and early sixties, the WASPs could no longer justify such discrimination to others or to themselves. John F. Kennedy's chief of protocol, Angier Biddle Duke, was forced to resign from his favorite men's club, the Metropolitan Club in Washington, because it was restricted.

History, as Pareto once remarked, is the graveyard of aristocracies, and by the late fifties and early sixties the WASP Establishment had no faith in the code—and the social restrictions—that had sustained it. Maybe its members just lost the will to fight for their privileges. As the writer David Frum theorizes, it had been half a century since the last great age of fortune making. The great families were into at least their third genteel generation. Perhaps by then there wasn't much vigor left. Or perhaps it was the Holocaust that altered the landscape by discrediting the sort of racial restrictions that the Protestant Establishment was built on.

In any case, in 1964 Digby Baltzell astutely perceived the crucial trends. "What seems to be happening," he wrote in *The Protestant Establishment,* "is that a scholarly hierarchy of campus communities governed by the values of admissions committees is gradually supplanting the class hierarchies of local communities which are still governed by the values of parents. . . . Just as the hierarchy of the Church was the main avenue of advancement for the talented and ambitious youth from the lower orders during the medieval period, and just as the business enterprise was responsible for the nineteenth century rags-to-riches dream (when we were predominantly an Anglo-Saxon country), so the campus community has now become the principal guardian of our traditional opportunitarian ideals."

The campus gates were thus thrown open on the basis of brains rather than blood, and within a few short years the university landscape was transformed. Harvard, as we've seen, was changed from a school for the well-connected to a school for brainy strivers. The remaining top schools eliminated their Jewish quotas and eventually dropped their restrictions on women. Furthermore, the sheer numbers of educated Americans exploded. The portion of Americans going to college had been rising steadily throughout the 20th century, but between 1955 and 1974 the growth rate was off the charts. Many of the new students were women. Between 1950 and 1960 the number of female students increased by 47 percent. It then jumped by an additional 168 percent between 1960 and 1970. Over the following decades the student population kept growing and growing. In 1960 there were about 2,000 institutions of higher learning. By 1980 there were 3,200. In 1960 there were 235,000 professors in the United States. By 1980 there were 685,000.

Before this period, in other words, the WASP elites dominated prestige education and made up a significant chunk of all the college-educated population. By the end of this period, the well-bred WASPs no longer dominated the prestige schools and they made up just an infinitesimal slice of the educated class. The elite schools had preserved their status. The proportion of Ivy League graduates in *Who's Who* has remained virtually constant throughout the past 40 years. But the schools maintained their dominance by throwing over the mediocrities from the old WASP families and bringing in less well connected meritocrats.

The rapid expansion of the educated class was bound to have as profound an impact on America as rapid urbanization has had on other countries at other moments in history. By the mid-1960s the middle-aged WASPs still wielded some authority in the corporate world. They still possessed enormous social and political prestige, not to mention financial capital. But on campus they had been overrun. Imagine now you are a young meritocrat, the child of, say, a pharmacist and an elementary school teacher, accepted to a prestigious university in the mid-sixties. You are part of a huge cohort of education arrivistes. Your campus still has some of the aristocratic trappings of the WASP culture, though it is by now a little embarrassed by them. And as you look out into the world, you see the last generation of the Old Guard—the people we recognize from the 1950s weddings pages—still holding key jobs and social authority. They are in the positions of power and prestige you hope to occupy. But they are still living by an ethos you consider obsolete, stifling, and prejudiced. Among other things, that ethos, which emphasizes birth and connections, blocks your ascent. Naturally, you and your many peers, even if you do not think about it deliberately, are going to try to finish off the old regime. You are going to try to destroy what is left of the WASP ethos and replace it with your own ethos, which is based on individual merit.

More broadly, you are going to try to change the social character of the nation. The rise of the meritocrats produced a classic revolution of rising expectations. Tocqueville's principle of revolutions proved true: as social success seems more possible for a rising group, the remaining hindrances seem more and more intolerable. The social revolution of the late sixties was not a miracle or a natural disaster, the way it is sometimes treated by writers on the left and right. It was a logical response to the trends of the crucial years between 1955 and 1965. The components of elite status were due to change. The culture of upscale America was due for a revolution.

The Sixties

"How's our award-winning scholar?" one of the overbearing adults asks the Dustin Hoffman character, Ben, as he comes downstairs in the first scene in *The Graduate*. Mike Nichols's movie, which was the top money-making film of 1968, is about an introspective college graduate who has just come back to a rich white suburb in California after finishing a lavishly successful stint at an East Coast school. He realizes, to his horror, the immense cultural gulf between his parents and himself. As Baltzell had anticipated, campus values displaced parental values. In that famous first scene, Ben is cooed over and passed around like a conquering hero by a group of glad-handing, loud-talking WASP elders. Hoffman's face is an oasis of calm amid a riot of Dale Carnegie bonhomie. There's plenty of cocktail party jollity. His mother starts reading out his college accomplishments from the class yearbook. And one of the smug moguls pulls him out to the pool, extends a cloak of self-importance, and tells him that the future is in plastics—a scene that brutally exemplifies the cultural decay of the old order. Millionaire moviemakers tend to be merciless when depicting millionaire businessmen and lawyers, and *The Graduate* casts an unpitying eye on the life of the Protestant elite: the lavish wet bars, the monogrammed golf clothes, the gold watches, the white furniture against white walls, the shallowness and hypocrisy, and in the form of Mrs. Robinson, their lives of cocktail-soaked desperation. Ben doesn't know what he wants out of life, but he is certain he doesn't want *that*.

In Charles Webb's original novel, the character of Ben Braddock is a six-foot-tall, blue-eyed blond. Mike Nichols first imagined Robert Redford in the role. That casting would have better explained why Mrs. Robinson is sexually attracted to Ben, but it probably would have ruined the picture's prospects. Who wants to identify with a mopey, blue-eyed, blond Adonis? But Hoffman is a sensitive soul, not a Aryan Dick Diver type. So he perfectly represented all the new ethnic strivers who were suddenly pouring through the colleges, facing life in the affluent suburbs, and finding it arid and stifling.

The educated-class rebellion we call "the sixties" was about many things, some of them important and related to the Civil Rights movement and Vietnam, some of them entirely silly, and others, like the sexual revolution, overblown (actual sexual behavior was affected far more by the world wars than by the Woodstock era). But at its core the cultural radicalism of the sixties was a challenge to conventional notions of success. It was not only a political effort to dislodge the establishment from the seats of power. It was a cultural effort by the rising members of the privileged classes to destroy whatever prestige still attached to the WASP lifestyle and the WASP moral code, and to replace the old order with a new social code that would celebrate spiritual and intellectual ideals. The sixties radicals rejected the prevailing definition of accomplishment, the desire to keep up with the Joneses, the prevailing idea of social respectability, the idea that a successful life could be measured by income, manners, and possessions. The educated baby boomers of the 1960s wanted to take the things the Protestant elite regarded as high status and make them low status. The demographic shifts of the 1950s led to the cultural conflicts of the 1960s. Or, as the endlessly impressive Digby Baltzell prophesied in *The Protestant Establishment:* "The economic reforms of one generation tend to produce status conflicts in the next."

What exactly would the sixties student leaders hate about the *New York Times* weddings page of 1959? The specific cultural changes the educated class heralded will be treated in later chapters. But it's worth making a short list here because the habits of thought that were established when the educated class was in its radical stage continue to influence its thinking now in its hour of supremacy. The student radicals would have detested the couples displayed on the weddings page for what was *perceived* to be their conformity, their formality, their traditionalism, their carefully defined gender roles, their ancestor worship, their privilege, their unabashed elitism, their unreflective lives, their self-satisfaction, their reticence, their contented affluence, their coldness.

We'll go into greater detail about all these cultural shifts in the pages that follow, but to put it bluntly, the radicals of the 1960s favored bohemian self-expression and despised the earlier elite for its arid self-control. And their effort to tear down the old customs and habits of the previous elite was not achieved without social cost. Old authorities and restraints were delegitimized. There was a real, and to millions of people catastrophic, breakdown in social order, which can be measured in the stunning rise in divorce, crime, drug use, and illegitimacy rates.

The *New York Times* weddings pages of the late sixties and early seventies reflect the conflicts and contrasts of that confrontational age. The section was smaller, to start with. While there might be 158 marriages listed in the typical June section in 1959, there were closer to 35 in a typical June section in the late sixties and early seventies. Hip couples didn't want to post their nuptials on a page that was a bastion of ritual and elitism. Among the couples who did send in their announcements, there is a striking dichotomy. Some couples seem oblivious to the turmoil all around them. Their entries are still loaded down with Junior League memberships, prep school affiliations, ancestor name-dropping, and debutante histories. These marriages are seemingly indistinguishable from the 1950s ones. But a few columns over there will be a wedding in which everybody is barefoot and in which the ceremony was performed in the manner of a pagan spring ritual. Another announcement will describe a couple that dispensed with traditional language, wrote their own vows, and hired a rock band for the reception. The new practice of writing your own vows really did mark a historic turning point. The people who used the traditional vows were making a connection to the generations that had come before, taking their place in a great chain of custom. The people who wrote their own vows were expressing their individuality and their desire to shape institutions to meet individual needs. They were more interested in seeing themselves as creators rather than inheritors. They were adopting the prime directive of the educated class: Thou shalt construct thine own identity.

The most famous wedding moment of the period, of course, was the one that took place in the last scene of *The Graduate*. Elaine, the Katharine Ross character, is going through a conventional, if rushed, wedding ceremony in a modern Presbyterian church in Santa Barbara, with a starched blond doctor of the WASP variety. We know he's retrograde because he proposed by suggesting, "We'd make a great team"—a phrase that captures the supposed emotional coldness of the WASP culture, as well as its insistent sportiness. Disheveled Ben rushes into the church just as the ceremony is ending, pounds on the glass on the balcony overlooking the nave, and calls out Elaine's name. Elaine looks up, sees the vicious expressions on her parents' and her husband's faces, and decides to run off with Ben. Elaine's mother, Mrs. Robinson, hisses, "It's too late," and Elaine shouts back, "Not for me." Ben and Elaine ward off the family and the rest of the crowd and dash onto a public bus. The long final scene shows them sitting side by side on that bus, Elaine in her torn wedding dress. At first they look elated, but then they become more and more sober, and finally they look a little terrified. They've emancipated themselves from a certain sort of WASP success, but it dawns on them that they haven't figured out what sort of successful life they would like to lead instead.

And Then Comes Money

The hardest of the hard-core sixties radicals believed the only honest way out was to reject the notion of success altogether: drop out of the rat race, retreat to small communities where real human relationships would flourish. But that sort of utopianism was never going to be very popular, especially among college grads. Members of the educated class prize human relationships and social equality, but as for so many generations of Americans before them, achievement was really at the core of the sixties grads' value system. They were meritocrats, after all, and so tended to define themselves by their accomplishments. Most of them were never going to drop out or sit around in communes smelling flowers, raising pigs, and contemplating poetry. Moreover, as time went by, they discovered that the riches of the universe were lying at their feet.

At first, when the great hump of baby boom college graduates entered the workforce, having a college degree brought few financial rewards or dramatic life changes. As late as 1976, the labor economist Richard Freeman could write a book called *The Overeducated American,* arguing that higher education didn't seem to be paying off in the marketplace. But the information age kicked in, and the rewards for education grew and grew. In 1980, according to labor market specialist Kevin Murphy of the University of Chicago, college graduates earned roughly 35 percent more than high school graduates. But by the mid-1990s, college graduates were earning 70 percent more than high school graduates, and those with graduate degrees were earning 90 percent more. The wage value of a college degree had doubled in 15 years.

The rewards for intellectual capital have increased while the rewards for physical capital have not. That means that even liberal arts majors can wake up one day and find themselves suddenly members of the top-income brackets. A full professor at Yale who renounced the capitalist rat race finds himself making, as of 1999, $113,100, while a professor at Rutgers pulls in $103,700 and superstar professors, who become the object of academic bidding wars, now can rake in more than $300,000 a year. Congressional and presidential staffers top out at $125,000 (before quintupling that when they enter the private sector), and the journalists at national publications can now count on six-figure salaries when they hit middle age, not including lecture fees. Philosophy and math majors head for Wall Street and can make tens of millions of dollars from their quantitative models. America has always had a lot of lawyers, and now the median income for that burgeoning group is $72,500, while income for the big-city legal grinds can reach seven figures. And super-students still flood into medicine—three-quarters of private practitioners net more than $100,000. Meanwhile, in Silicon Valley there are more millionaires than people. In Hollywood television scriptwriters make $11,000 to $13,000 a week. And in New York top magazine editors, like Anna Wintour of *Vogue,* make $1 million a year, which is slightly more than the head of the Ford Foundation. And these dazzling incomes flow not only to the baby boomers, who might still find them surprising, but to all the subsequent generations of college graduates as well, most of whom have never known a world without $4 million artists' lofts, $350-a-night edgy hotels, avant-garde summer homes, and the rest of the accoutrements of the countercultural plutocracy.

The information age has produced entirely new job categories, some of which seem like practical jokes, though you wouldn't know it from the salaries: creativity officer, chief knowledge officer, team spirit coordinator. Then there are the jobs that nobody dreamed of in high school: Web page designer, patent agent, continuity writer, foundation program officer, talk show booker, and on and on. The economy in this era is such that oddballs like Oliver Stone become multimillionaire moguls and slouchy dropouts like Bill Gates get to run the world. Needless to say, there are still gypsy scholars scraping by while looking for a tenure-track position, and there are still poor saps in the publishing industry parlaying their intelligence into obscenely small paychecks. But the whole thrust of the information age has been to reward education and widen the income gap between the educated and the uneducated. Moreover, the upper middle class has grown from a small appendage of the middle class into a distinct demographic hump populated largely by people with fancy degrees. Within a few years, barring a severe economic downturn, there will be 10 million American households with incomes over $100,000 a year, up from only 2 million in 1982. Consider the cultural and financial capital of that large group, and you begin to appreciate the social power of the upper middle class. Many of the members of the educated elite didn't go out hungry for money. But money found them. And subtly, against their will, it began to work its way into their mentality.

The members of the educated elite find they must change their entire attitude first toward money itself. When they were poor students, money was a solid. It came in a chunk with every paycheck, and they would gradually chip little bits off to pay the bills. They could sort of feel how much money they had in their bank account, the way you can feel a pile of change in your pocket. But as they became more affluent, money turned into a liquid. It flows into the bank account in a prodigious stream. And it flows out just as quickly. The earner is reduced to spectator status and is vaguely horrified by how quickly the money is flowing through. He or she may try to stem the outward flow in order to do more saving. But it's hard to know where to erect the dam. The money just flows on its own. And after a while one's ability to stay afloat through all the ebbs and flows becomes a sign of accomplishment in itself. The big money stream is another aptitude test. Far from being a source of corruption, money turns into a sign of mastery. It begins to seem deserved, natural. So even former student radicals begin to twist the old left-wing slogan so that it becomes: From each according to his abilities, to each according to his abilities.

The educated elites not only earn far more money than they ever thought they would but now occupy positions of enormous responsibility. We're by now all familiar with modern-day executives who have moved from SDS to CEO, from LSD to IPO. Indeed, sometimes you get the impression the Free Speech movement produced more corporate executives than Harvard Business School.

What's more amazing is the growth of lucrative industries in which everybody involved is a member of the educated class. Only about 20 percent of the adult population of America possesses a college degree, but in many large cities and suburban office parks, you can walk from office to office, for mile upon mile, and almost everybody in the place will have a sheepskin in the drawer. Educated elites have taken over much of the power that used to accrue to sedate old WASPs with dominating chins. Economists at the International Monetary Fund jet around the world reshaping macroeconomic policies. Brainiacs at McKinsey & Company swoop down on corporate offices run by former college quarterbacks and issue reports on how to merge or restructure.

The educated elites have even taken over professions that used to be working class. The days of the hard-drinking blue-collar journalist, for example, are gone forever. Now if you cast your eye down a row at a Washington press conference, it's: Yale, Yale, Stanford, Emory, Yale, and Harvard. Political parties, which were once run by immigrant hacks, are now dominated by communications analysts with Ph.D.s. If you drive around the old suburbs and follow the collarless-shirt bohemians home from their organic fruit stands, you notice they have literally moved into the houses of the old stockbroker elite. They are sleeping in the old elite's beds. They are swamping the old elite's institutions. As the novelist Louis Auchincloss summarized it, "The old society has given way to the society of accomplishment." Dumb good-looking people with great parents have been displaced by smart, ambitious, educated, and antiestablishment people with scuffed shoes.

The Anxieties of Abundance

Over the past 30 years, in short, the educated class has gone from triumph to triumph. They have crushed the old WASP elite culture, thrived in an economy that lavishly rewards their particular skills, and now sit atop many of the same institutions they once railed against. But all this has created a gnawing problem. How do they make sure they haven't themselves become self-satisfied replicas of the WASP elite they still so forcefully denounce?

Those who want to win educated-class approval must confront the anxieties of abundance: how to show—not least to themselves—that even while climbing toward the top of the ladder they have not become all the things they still profess to hold in contempt. How to navigate the shoals between their affluence and their self-respect. How to reconcile their success with their spirituality, their elite status with their egalitarian ideals. Socially enlightened members of the educated elite tend to be disturbed by the widening gap between rich and poor and are therefore made somewhat uncomfortable by the fact that their own family income now tops $80,000. Some of them dream of social justice yet went to a college where the tuition costs could feed an entire village in Rwanda for a year. Some once had "Question Authority" bumper stickers on their cars but now find themselves heading start-up software companies with 200 people reporting to them. The sociologists they read in college taught that consumerism is a disease, and yet now they find themselves shopping for $3,000 refrigerators. They took to heart the lessons of *Death of a Salesman,* yet now find themselves directing a sales force. They laughed at the plastics scene in *The Graduate* but now they work for a company that manufactures . . . plastic. Suddenly they find themselves moving into a suburban house with a pool and uncomfortable about admitting it to their bohemian friends still living downtown.

Though they admire art and intellect, they find themselves living amidst commerce, or at least in that weird hybrid zone where creativity and commerce intersect. This class is responsible for more yards of built-in bookshelf space than any group in history. And yet sometimes you look at their shelves and notice deluxe leather-bound editions of all those books arguing that success and affluence is a sham: *Babbitt, The Great Gatsby, The Power Elite, The Theory of the Leisure Class.* This is an elite that has been raised to oppose elites. They are affluent yet opposed to materialism. They may spend their lives selling yet worry about selling out. They are by instinct antiestablishmentarian yet somehow sense they have become a new establishment.

The members of this class are divided against themselves, and one is struck by how much of their time is spent earnestly wrestling with the conflict between their reality and their ideals. They grapple with the trade-offs between equality and privilege ("I believe in public schooling, but the private school just seems better for my kids"), between convenience and social responsibility ("These disposable diapers are an incredible waste of resources, but they are so easy"), between rebellion and convention ("I know I did plenty of drugs in high school, but I tell my kids to Just Say No").

But the biggest tension, to put it in the grandest terms, is between worldly success and inner virtue. How do you move ahead in life without letting ambition wither your soul? How do you accumulate the resources you need to do the things you want without becoming a slave to material things? How do you build a comfortable and stable life for your family without getting bogged down in stultifying routine? How do you live at the top of society without becoming an insufferable snob?

The Reconcilers

These educated elites don't despair in the face of such challenges. They are the Résumé Gods. They're the ones who aced their SATs and succeeded in giving up Merlot during pregnancy. If they are not well equipped to handle the big challenges, no one is. When faced with a tension between competing values, they do what any smart privileged person bursting with cultural capital would do. They find a way to have both. They reconcile opposites.

The grand achievement of the educated elites in the 1990s was to create a way of living that lets you be an affluent success and at the same time a free-spirit rebel. Founding design firms, they find a way to be an artist and still qualify for stock options. Building gourmet companies like Ben & Jerry's or Nantucket Nectars, they've found a way to be dippy hippies and multinational corporate fat cats. Using William S. Burroughs in ads for Nike sneakers and incorporating Rolling Stones anthems into their marketing campaigns, they've reconciled the antiestablishment style with the corporate imperative. Listening to management gurus who tell them to thrive on chaos and unleash their creative potential, they've reconciled the spirit of the imagination with service to the bottom line. Turning university towns like Princeton and Palo Alto into entrepreneurial centers, they have reconciled the highbrow with the high tax bracket. Dressing like Bill Gates in worn chinos on his way to a stockholders' meeting, they've reconciled undergraduate fashion with upper-crust occupations. Going on eco-adventure vacations, they've reconciled aristocratic thrill-seeking with social concern. Shopping at Benetton or the Body Shop, they've brought together consciousness-raising and cost control.

When you are amidst the educated upscalers, you can never be sure if you're living in a world of hippies or stockbrokers. In reality you have entered the hybrid world in which everybody is a little of both.

Marx told us that classes inevitably conflict, but sometimes they just blur. The values of the bourgeois mainstream culture and the values of the 1960s counterculture have merged. That culture war has ended, at least within the educated class. In its place that class has created a third culture, which is a reconciliation between the previous two. The educated elites didn't set out to create this reconciliation. It is the product of millions of individual efforts to have things both ways. But it is now the dominant tone of our age. In the resolution between the culture and the counterculture, it is impossible to tell who co-opted whom, because in reality the bohemians and the bourgeois co-opted each other. They emerge from this process as bourgeois bohemians, or Bobos.

The New Establishment

Today the *New York Times* weddings section is huge once again. In the early 1970s the young rebels didn't want to appear there, but now that their own kids are in college and getting married, they are proud to see their offspring in the Sunday paper. For a fee the *Times* will send you a reproduction of your listing, suitable for framing.

And the young people, the second-generation Bobos, are willing to see their nuptials recorded. Look at the newlyweds on any given Sunday morning, beaming out at you from the pages of the *Times*. Their smiles seem so genuine. They all look so nice and approachable, not dignified or fearsome, the way some of the brides on the 1950s pages did. Things are different but somehow similar. For example, a reader opening the weddings section on May 23, 1999, would have learned that Stuart Anthony Kingsley was getting married. Mr. Kingsley graduated magna cum

laude from Dartmouth and got an MBA at Harvard before
going on to become a partner at McKinsey & Company.
His father is a trustee of the National Trust for Historic
Preservation, and his mother is an overseer of the Boston
Symphony Orchestra and a trustee of the Society for the
Preservation of New England Antiquities. Those sorts of
affiliations would have set off approving nods from the old
WASP dowagers of the 1950s era. But look who Mr. Kings-
ley is marrying—Sara Perry, whose father is coordinator of
Judaic Studies at Southern Connecticut State University
and whose mother is associate executive director of the
New Haven Jewish Federation, which might not have met
with approving nods from the dowagers.

But nowadays such an alliance blends right in. We
don't even raise an eyebrow when Mr. New England Antiquities marries Ms. Judaic Studies because we know how
much the bride and groom have in common: Ms. Perry
graduated from her college magna cum laude, just as her
husband did (except hers was Yale, not Dartmouth). She,
too, got her MBA from Harvard (and she earned a
master's degree in public administration besides). She, too,
has become a financial consultant (except she is a senior
vice president at Community Wealth Ventures, which
works with foundations). The ancient enmities between
class and ethnic groups have been overcome by the common bond of meritocratic ascent. They were married by
the mayor of New Haven, John DeStefano, Jr., in the
home of Ms. Perry's maternal grandparents, Lucille and
Arnold Alderman.

Today's establishment is structured differently. It is
not a small conspiracy of well-bred men with interlocking
family and school ties who have enormous influence on
the levers of power. Instead, this establishment is a large,
amorphous group of meritocrats who share a consciousness and who unself-consciously reshape institutions to
accord with their values. They are not confined to a few

East Coast institutions. In 1962, Richard Rovere could write, "Nor has the Establishment ever made much headway in such fields as advertising, television or motion pictures." Today's establishment is everywhere. It exercises its power subtly, over ideas and concepts, and therefore pervasively. There are no sure-fire demographic markers to tell who is a member of this establishment. Members tend to have gone to competitive colleges, but not all have. They tend to live in upscale neighborhoods, such as Los Altos, California, and Bloomfield, Michigan, and Lincoln Park, Illinois, but not all do. What unites them is their shared commitment to the Bobo reconciliation. People gain entry into the establishment by performing a series of delicate cultural tasks: they are prosperous without seeming greedy; they have pleased their elders without seeming conformist; they have risen toward the top without too obviously looking down on those below; they have achieved success without committing certain socially sanctioned affronts to the ideal of social equality; they have constructed a prosperous lifestyle while avoiding the old clichés of conspicuous consumption (it's OK to hew to the new clichés).

Obviously, none of this is to suggest that all members of the new Bobo establishment think alike, any more than it's true to say that all members of any establishment think alike. Some of the bourgeois bohemians are more on the bourgeois side; they are stockbrokers who happen to like artists' lofts. Some are on the bohemian side; they are art professors who dabble in the market. Nonetheless, if you look at some quintessential figures of the new establishment—such as Henry Louis Gates, Charlie Rose, Steven Jobs, Doris Kearns Goodwin, David Geffen, Tina Brown, Maureen Dowd, Jerry Seinfeld, Stephen Jay Gould, Lou Reed, Tim Russert, Steve Case, Ken Burns, Al Gore, Bill Bradley, John McCain, George W. Bush—you can begin to sense a common ethos that mingles 1960s rebellion with

1980s achievement. You can feel the Bobo ethos, too, in the old institutions that have been taken over by the new establishment, such as the *New Yorker,* Yale University, the American Academy of Arts and Letters (which now includes people like Toni Morrison, Jules Feiffer, and Kurt Vonnegut among its members), or the *New York Times* (which now runs editorials entitled "In Praise of the Counterculture"). You can sense the ethos with special force in the new establishment institutions that would have been alien to the old elite: NPR, DreamWorks, Microsoft, AOL, Starbucks, Yahoo, Barnes & Noble, Amazon, and Borders.

And over the past few years, this new educated establishment has begun to assume the necessary role of an establishment. That is to say, it has begun to create a set of social codes that give coherent structure to national life. Today, America once again has a dominant class that defines the parameters of respectable opinion and taste—a class that determines conventional wisdom, that promulgates a code of good manners, that establishes a pecking order to give shape to society, that excludes those who violate its codes, that transmits its moral and etiquette codes down to its children, that imposes social discipline on the rest of society so as to improve the "quality of life," to use the contemporary phrase.

The new establishment has assumed this role hesitantly. It hasn't become a technocratic elite with a strong sense of public service, as many of the early champions of the meritocracy envisioned. It hasn't established clear lines of authority, since it still has trouble coming to terms with authority. Instead, it has exercised its influence through a million and one private channels, reforming society through culture more than through politics. Its efforts to establish order have been spotty and often clumsy—all the political correctness codes, the speech codes on campuses, the sexual harassment rules. But gradually a shared set of understandings and practices has cohered into a widely accepted set of social norms. Thirty years ago, when tearing down the established structure was the order of the day, civility was not a cherished value, especially on campuses. But now that a new civil order has come into being, the word *civility* is again heard on nearly every educated person's tongue. And somehow some sort of looser social peace is in the process of being restored. Many of the social indicators that skyrocketed during the age of transition, the 1960s and 1970s, have begun to drop: crime rates, abortion rates, teen births, illegitimacy, divorce rates, teenage drinking.

Most of this book is a description of these new codes of etiquette and morality. If you do not share the ethos of the Bobo class, you will probably not get hired by establishment institutions. You will probably not get promoted. For example, early in this century it was perfectly acceptable to be racist and anti-Semitic or homophobic. Today those beliefs automatically banish a person from educated circles. Earlier this century social climbers built ornate castles, aping the manners of the European aristocracy. Today a vice president at Microsoft might build a huge modern mansion, but if he built a house like J. P. Morgan's he'd be regarded as a pompous crank. Forty years ago grandees could still hang the pelts of the wild animals they had killed upon their walls. In today's educated class that would be considered an affront to humane values.

Today's educated elites tend not to bar entire groups, but like any establishment, they do have their boundary markers. You will be shunned if you embrace glitzy materialism. You will be shunned if you are overtly snobbish. You will be shunned if you are anti-intellectual. For one reason or another the following people and institutions fall outside the ranks of Bobo respectability: Donald Trump, Pat Robertson, Louis Farrakhan, Bob Guccione, Wayne Newton, Nancy Reagan, Adnan Khashoggi, Jesse Helms,

Jerry Springer, Mike Tyson, Rush Limbaugh, Philip Morris, developers, loggers, Hallmark greeting cards, the National Rifle Association, Hooters.

The New Pecking Order

So when the Protestant Establishment collapsed, it is not as if America became a magical place without elites, without hierarchies, without etiquette and social distinctions. That may have been true during the age of transition. In the 1970s and through part of the 1980s, it really was difficult to pick out a coherent social order. But that fluidity couldn't last—and it's probably a good thing too. Countries need to achieve new states of social equilibrium, and that has now happened to America. New codes are in place that are different from the old codes but serve many of the same social functions of giving order and coherence to life.

American social life, for example, is just as hierarchical as it was in the 1950s, maybe more so. Hierarchies based on connections have given way. Under the code of the meritocrats, people are more likely to be judged by their posts. Invitations to Renaissance weekends, Aspen Institute seminars, Esther Dyson technology conferences, and exclusive private dinners are all determined by what job you have. If you have a prestigious position, your social life is secure. You will find constant validation by surrounding yourself with people as accomplished as or even more accomplished than you are, and you will come to relish what might be called the joy of summits. If you do not, your social life will always have those awkward moments when someone next to you at dinner turns and asks, "What do you do?"

If you are a visiting name professor from Yale freshly arrived on a small campus to give a guest lecture, you will be taken to dinner at the finest restaurant the town has to offer. But if you are a faculty member at Colgate invited to be a guest lecturer, you'll be dining at the home of your host with her kids. If you are an undersecretary in the Justice Department, you will be the keynote lunchtime speaker at various bar association conferences, but if you move on to some lucrative law firm, you will be lucky to serve on one of the end-of-the-day panel discussions. According to the *New York Observer,* former *New Yorker* editor Tina Brown used to throw parties at which top-rank writers and editors were invited to arrive at eight and lower-ranked writers and editors were told to show up at nine-thirty.

Of course, this does not mean those with the biggest offices automatically earn the highest rank. Your career choice has to reflect the twisting demands of the Bobo ethos. In the 1950s the best kind of money to have was inherited money. Today in the Bobo establishment the best kind of money is incidental money. It's the kind of money you just happen to earn while you are pursuing your creative vision. That means the most prestigious professions involve artistic self-expression as well as big bucks. A novelist who makes $1 million a year is far more prestigious than a banker who makes $50 million. A software designer who has stock options in the millions is more prestigious than a real estate developer with holdings in the tens of millions. A newspaper columnist who makes $150,000 a year will get his calls returned more quickly than a lawyer who makes six times that. A restaurant owner with one successful nightspot will be on the receiving end of more cocktail party fawning than a shopping center owner with six huge malls.

This is the age of discretionary income. People are supposed to forgo earnings opportunities in order to lead richer lives. If you have not forgone any earnings, you just can't expect your status to be very high, no matter how much money you've got in the bank. Professors who are good-looking enough to have become newscasters but chose not to are admired and envied more than professors who had no alternative but to go into the academy. People who have made $100 million with purportedly anticommercial independent movies are more prestigious than people who have made $150 million studio movies. A rock star who goes platinum with a sensitive acoustic album is more admired (and in the long run therefore more bankable) than a rock star who goes double platinum with a regular headbanging album. Media people like Christiane Amanpour and James Rubin will have their wedding featured at the top spot of the *New York Times* weddings page, whereas ordinary financial analysts will be reduced to paragraph status down below. The guy who dropped out of Harvard to start a software company is asked to give the dinner speech at a grand affair, and sitting next to him will be the Vanderbilt heir who eagerly solicits his attention and has to pay for the dinner.

To calculate a person's status, you take his net worth and multiply it by his antimaterialistic attitudes. A zero in either column means no prestige, but high numbers in both rocket you to the top of the heap. Thus, to be treated well in this world, not only do you have to show some income results; you have to perform a series of feints to show how little your worldly success means to you. You always want to dress one notch lower than those around you. You may want to wear a tattoo or drive a pickup truck or somehow perform some other socially approved act of antistatus deviance. You will devote your conversational time to mocking your own success in a manner that simultaneously displays your accomplishments and your ironic distance from them. You will ceaselessly bash yuppies in order to show that you yourself have not become one. You will talk about your nanny as if she were your close personal friend, as if it were just a weird triviality that you happen to live in a $900,000 Santa Monica house and she takes the bus two hours each day to the barrio. You will want to perfect a code to subtly downplay your academic credentials. If asked where you went to school, you will reply "Harvard?" with a little upward lilt at the end of your pronunciation, as if to imply, "Have you ever heard of it?" When referring to your stint as a Rhodes scholar, you will say, "While I was in England on a program . . ." In Washington I once asked a transplanted Englishman where he went to school and he replied, "A little school near Slough." The village of Slough is a modest little place west of London. The next town over is called Eton.

Class Rank

Nor is it true that the decline of the old WASP code of morality has left America in a moral vacuum. Some people see the decline of the old Protestant Establishment and mourn our losses: no more chivalry, no more of that keen sense of duty and public service, no more gravitas and deference to authority, no more reticence and self-effacement, no more chastity or decorum, no more gentlemen, no more ladies, no more honor and valor. They see the codes and rules that have fallen away and too quickly assume that we have entered a nihilistic age.

In fact, our morals have followed the same cycle of decay and regeneration as our manners. The old Protestant Establishment and its ethical system faded. There was a period of anarchy. But more recently the new educated establishment has imposed its one set of rules. And as we shall see in Chapter 5, it is not clear, especially at first glance, which moral framework is more restrictive, the old WASP ethos or the new Bobo one.

These topics are all in front of us. Suffice it to say, this has got to be one of the most anxious social elites ever. We Bobos are not anxious because there is an angry mob outside the gates threatening to send us to the guillotine. There isn't. The educated elite is anxious because its members are torn between their drive to succeed and their fear of turning into sellouts. Furthermore, we are anxious because we do not award ourselves status sinecures. Previous establishments erected social institutions that would give their members security. In the first part of the 20th century, once your family made it into the upper echelons of society, it was relatively easy to stay there. You were invited on the basis of your connections to the right affairs. You were admitted, nearly automatically, to the right schools and considered appropriate for the right spouses. The pertinent question in those circles was not what do you do, but who are you. Once you were established as a Biddle or an Auchincloss or a Venderlip, your way was clear. But members of today's educated class can never be secure about their own future. A career crash could be just around the corner. In the educated class even social life is a series of aptitude tests; we all must perpetually perform in accordance with the shifting norms of propriety, ever advancing signals of cultivation. Reputations can be destroyed by a disgraceful sentence, a lewd act, a run of bad press, or a terrible speech at the financial summit at Davos.

And more important, members of the educated class can never be secure about their children's future. The kids have some domestic and educational advantages—all those tutors and developmental toys—but they still have to work through school and ace the SATs just to achieve the same social rank as their parents. Compared to past elites, little is guaranteed.

The irony is that all this status insecurity only makes the educated class stronger. Its members and their children must constantly be alert, working and achieving. Moreover, the educated class is in no danger of becoming a self-contained caste. Anybody with the right degree, job, and cultural competencies can join. Marx warned that "the more a ruling class is able to assimilate the most prominent men [or women] of the dominated classes, the more stable and dangerous its rule." And in truth it is hard to see how the rule of the meritocrats could ever come to an end. The WASP Establishment fell pretty easily in the 1960s. It surrendered almost without a shot. But the meritocratic Bobo class is rich with the spirit of self-criticism. It is flexible and amorphous enough to co-opt that which it does not already command. The Bobo meritocracy will not be easily toppled, even if some group of people were to rise up and conclude that it should be. So let's go off and survey the manners and mores of today's dominant social class.

2

Consumption

WAYNE, PENNSYLVANIA, used to be such a square town. It's 13 miles west of Philadelphia, and while other Main Line communities, like Bryn Mawr and Haverford, have always had a little cosmopolitan flair to go with their dense concentrations of country club grandees, Wayne was strictly a white bread kind of place. *Mary Poppins* played in the town cinema for an entire summer when it was rereleased a few years ago. Dusty apothecaries lingered on the main shopping street, delivering remedies to the old Main Line widows who owned mansions at the southern end of the township. *The Philadelphia Story* was set here; *The Preppy Handbook* might as well have been. Of all the zip codes in the country, Wayne ranked eighth in the United States in total number of families listed in the Social Register (the local St. David's Episcopal Church figured prominently in the *New York Times* weddings page of the 1950s). The women called each other by those

weird nicknames WASPs used to go for, like Skimmy and
Binky, and competed for choice volunteering assignments
at the annual Devon Horse Show. The men could be seen
emerging from the train station at about six in their un-
memorable suits. Occasionally one would sport a tie
showing a flock of ducks, or if he was thinking of having
dinner at the Merion Cricket Club, he might browse on
his way home at the Tiger Shop men's clothiers for a pair
of green golf pants. For decades the local newspaper, creatively named the *Suburban,* reassured its serene commuter readers that nothing was happening in Wayne and
nothing was ever likely to happen.

But over the past six years or so, all that has changed.
A new culture has swept into town and overlaid itself onto
the Paisley Shop, the Neighborhood League Shop, and the
other traditional Main Line establishments. The town,
once an espresso desert, now has six gourmet coffeehouses. The Gryphon draws a sallow-eyed crowd of
teenage sophisticates and hosts poetry readings. Cafe Procopio is the one across from the train station, where hand-
some middle-aged couples come on Sunday morning,
swapping newspaper sections and comparing notes across
the tables on their kids' college admissions prospects. Upscale gathering places like this are filled with texts, and on
the side of the take-out coffee cups is a text that informs
you that Cafe Procopio is named after a left bank Parisian
cafe, founded in 1689, that became "a gathering place
where throughout the centuries intellectuals and artists
would meet for a good cup of coffee. At Cafe Procopio we
carry on the tradition of a true cafe, a natural meeting
place with a spirit all its own." There probably still aren't
a lot of artists and intellectuals in Wayne, but suddenly
there are a lot of people who want to drink coffee like one.

A fabulous independent bookstore named the
Reader's Forum has moved into town where the old drugstore used to be (it features literary biographies in the

front window), and there's a mammoth new Borders nearby where people can go and feel guilty that they are not patronizing the independent place. The artsy set can now go to a Made By You—one of those places where you pay six times more to decorate your own mugs and dishes than it would cost to buy flatware that other people have decorated—and to Studio B, a gift emporium that hosts creative birthday parties to ensure that self-esteeming kids get even more self-esteeming. There are several new food places in town. Sweet Daddy's sells gourmet jelly beans, spiced apple cider sorbet, and gelato in such flavors as Zuppa Inglese. There are now two stores that specialize in discriminating picnic baskets, in case you want to dine al fresco on sun-dried tomato cheese sticks and Marin County's Best Black Bean Dip, which is fat-free. For lunch Your Gourmet Kitchen sells crab panini and herb-grilled chicken breasts with sprouts on sourdough, and on Saturday mornings it hosts an omelet bar. Near the center of town, there's a new Los Angeles–style restaurant named Teresa's Cafe, which gets crowded and noisy at night, a little enclave of Santa Monica bustle in the midst of the Philadelphia suburbs.

In the old Wayne there weren't any interesting food stores. And there certainly weren't any restaurants with casual-sounding names like Teresa's; instead, they had imposing French names like L'Auberge. But now it is the formidable French places that have had to adjust. The restaurant La Fourchette has changed its name to the less pretentious Fourchette 110. It's traded in its French haute cuisine for more casual food. The menu looks like it was designed by a friendly Gérard Depardieu, not an imposing snob like Charles de Gaulle.

The Great Harvest Bread Company has opened up a franchise in town, one of those gourmet bread stores where they sell apricot almond or spinach feta loaf for $4.75 a pop. This particular store is owned by Ed and

Lori Kerpius. Ed got his MBA in 1987 and moved to Chicago, where he was a currency trader. Then, as if driven by the ineluctable winds of the zeitgeist, he gave up on the Decade of Greed stuff so he could spend more time with his family and community. So he and his wife opened this shop.

They greet you warmly as you walk in the door and hand you a sample slice (I chose Savannah dill) about the size of a coffee table book. A short lecture commences on the naturalness of the ingredients and the authenticity of the baking process, which, in fact, is being carried out right there in front of you. The store is spare so you won't think there is any salesmanship going on. Instead, there are teddy bears and children's books for the kids who hang around, and there's Starbucks coffee on sale for the adults. The Kerpiuses sponsor local arts activities—each kid who sends a drawing to the store gets a free loaf—so the walls of the store are covered with children's colorings alongside tokens of the store's generous participation in the local soccer league. If you ask them to slice the bread in the store, they look at you compassionately as one who has not yet risen to the higher realm of bread consciousness. But they hand you an information sheet for those who might want to slice the bread at home when it is at a more appropriate temperature (cut it in a herringbone pattern). The pamphlet lets you know that the integrity of the bread will not be damaged by freezing and reheating ("On ski trips we've wrapped ours in foil and put it on our engine").

To the west of town there is a Zany Brainy, one of those toy stores that pretends to be an educational institution. It sells lifelike figurines of endangered animals, and it's driven the old Wayne Toytown, which carried toys that didn't improve developmental skills, out of business. Farther down Lancaster Pike there is now a Fresh Fields supermarket. When the shoppers push a cart through the entrance, they are standing in an epicenter of the Upscale Suburban Hippiedom that is so characteristic of the new Wayne and so foreign to the old one. The visitor to Fresh Fields is confronted with a big sign that says "Organic Items today: 130." This is like a barometer of virtue. If you came in on a day when only 60 items were organic, you'd feel cheated. But when the number hits the three figures, you can walk through the aisles with moral confidence, glancing at an infinite variety of cabbage, like kale and bok choy, that the scions of the old Main Line families would never even have heard of.

Like so much else in this new cultural wave, Fresh Fields has taken the ethos of California in the 1960s and selectively updated it. Gone are the sixties-era things that were fun and of interest to teenagers, like Free Love, and retained are all the things that might be of interest to middle-aged hypochondriacs, like whole grains. So in the information age, suburban customers can stroll amidst the radish sprouts, the bins of brown and basmati rice, the jars of powdered fo-ti root, the Mayan Fungus Soap, the Light Mountain All Natural hair coloring, the tree-oil mouthwashes, and the vegetarian dog biscuits, basking in their reflected wholesomeness.

Finally, there is a batch of new home furnishings stores in Wayne. Within a few hundred feet of each other on Lancaster Pike there are three stores that make new furniture look old and another store that takes old lumber to make furniture that is actually new. They sort of meet in the middle to produce never-before-owned hand-me-downs.

These stores seem to be competing to see who can most enthusiastically produce the distressed look, and they've gone so far that sometimes the furniture doesn't look distressed; it looks like it's decomposing, with drawers scraped and hanging off, paint chipping on the floor. A store called the Painted Past sells hand-painted TV armoires, fat smelly candles, and a dented metal bedroom dresser on wheels. A store called Domicile sells hand-painted TV armoires, fat smelly candles, and a Provençal spaghetti strainer. The short-lived Somogyi Collection sold hand-painted TV armoires, no fat smelly candles, but it did have plenty of scratched dining room hutches made from excessively grained gourmet wood.

The apotheosis of this look is a company called Anthropologie, which has placed its flagship store in an old car dealership. It's odd enough for Wayne to have a store named after an academic discipline. The old crowd would have been deeply suspicious of such eggheadism (not to mention the French spelling). But the people in the forefront of this new culture seem to turn life into one long stint of graduate school. What's inside would really shock the old scions of the nearby riding clubs. For a while, there was a coffee shop within Anthropologie, so the shopper in Wayne was never more than 50 yards from a cappuccino and a French magazine to browse through. Second, the store always seems to have Louis Armstrong's "What a Wonderful World" playing on the sound system, not genteel Bach. But more surprisingly, there's not a Hepplewhite chair in sight. No eagle-clawed settees are featured in Anthropologie's showroom (George Washington would not feel at home). Furthermore, there is no Louis XIV furniture or Second Empire stuff. The old Wayne took its furniture cues from the European aristocrats. But the new Wayne, from the look of Anthropologie and its competitors, takes its cues from the European peasantry. The store—a vast open area under exposed beams—is a symphony of what fashion types call Bruise Tones—subdued blues, browns, blacks, and greens.

There are broad chinked floor planks and raw exposed trunks to support the ceiling. There is a section devoted to Provençal and another to Tuscan furnishings. In fact, the whole range of equatorial peasantry is represented. There are nooks that feature Moroccan crafts, Peruvian fabrics, and Indian chests. For the dining room there is an array of harvest tables, unvarnished and worn, so that the country table that was designed for the slaughtering of pigs now serves to show off delicate squash ravioli in $25 earthenware bowls.

Even the iconography is different. The old Wayne preferred images of hunt animals, like stags, hounds, ducks, and horses. The new-style Wayne consumer seems to prefer carvings and images of pacifistic or whimsical animals, like penguins, cows, cats, and frogs. The old-style Wayne matrons went in for floral prints, so when a bunch of them walked together down the street, they looked like a moving copse of hydrangea bushes. But the blouses and sweaters for sale at Anthropologie are monochromatic and muted. Taken in its entirety, the feel of the store says *A Year in Provence,* while the prices say Six Years out of Medical School.

The New Elite in the Old Ones' Beds

The fancy bread store, the artsy coffee shops, and the earthy furniture stores may seem like surface epiphenomena. But these institutions are not just arbitrary shifts in fashion—hemlines were up last decade, so they will probably be down the next. Rather, the kind of transformation we've seen in Wayne and in the rest of America's upscale neighborhoods is a symptom of a profound cultural shift. The demographic changes described in the last chapter have come to Wayne. The educated-class meritocrats have taken over the old Main Line suburb, just as they took over the elite colleges and the *New York Times* weddings page. The manor grounds have been broken up, and developers have put up $600,000 homes for the multidegreed professionals. The lawyers who bought five-bedroom Victorians in the 1990s have different attitudes than the lawyers who bought five-bedroom Victorians in the early sixties. And even the scions of the old WASP families have adapted to the new mode.

And so suddenly the streets of Wayne are dominated by the PBS-NPR cohort: vineyard-touring doctors, novel-writing lawyers, tenured gardening buffs, unusually literary realtors, dangly-earringed psychologists, and the rest of us information age burghers. These people have different aspirations than the old country club and martini suburban crowd, and naturally enough want their ideals reflected in the sort of things they buy and images they project. Shopping may not be the most intellectual exercise on earth, but it is one of the more culturally revealing. Indeed, one of the upshots of the new era is that Karl Marx may have had it exactly backward. He argued that classes are defined by their means of production. But it could be true that, in the information age at least, classes define themselves by their means of consumption.

The Historical Roots of Bobo Culture

The story of the educated class really begins in the first third of the 18th century. It's necessary to go that far back because, while demographically the educated class has only exploded in the past few decades, the values this class embodies are the culmination of a cultural struggle that began with the first glimmerings of the industrial age. It's necessary to revisit the birth of bourgeois ethos, to grasp the essence of that way of living. Then it's important to look back to the early bohemian rebellions, to understand the central bohemian ideals. It's only after reviewing these two rival cultural movements that we can grasp how different strains of the bourgeois and the bohemian world-views were woven together by the squads of biscotti-nibbling Bobos.

The first flowering of bourgeois tastes took place, in America at least, around 1720. That was the period when significant numbers of affluent Americans discovered gentility. After a few decades of struggle, many colonists could afford to live in a more comfortable style than the rough pioneers. American society had stabilized, and the successful merchants wanted their homes to reflect their interests in taste and culture. So they started building new houses and renovating old ones. They began raising the ceilings in their living rooms and covering over the exposed beams. They chose dainty, narrow floorboards instead of the broad sturdy ones of the pioneer era. They added cornices, paneling, plasterwork, and pediments to the walls to create an atmosphere of refined grace. They moved the kitchen and other utilitarian rooms to the back of the house, where visitors would not see them. They reduced the size of the fireplace openings in the front rooms so that what had become a gaping stove and furnace turned into a delicate warming area.

Most important, they began building parlors into their homes. The parlor was a room set apart from the functional uses of the house. It was used to entertain important guests or to conduct such genteel activities as reading, needlepoint, or music appreciation. Families kept their best furniture and most precious belongings in the parlor: brass andirons, gilt mirrors and clocks, the plushest rugs, upright-backed, claw-footed cherry chairs. Armies of craftsmen were employed to create the delicate porcelains, the dainty tea services, and the other gewgaws that the affluent colonials displayed in these salons. The idea was to create an elevated environment where people could cultivate delicate sensibilities and higher interests. It was also a place where people could show off their genteel manners and demonstrate their elite status. "Parlor people claimed to live on a higher plane than the vulgar and coarse populace, to excel them in their inner beings," writes Columbia historian Richard Bushman in *The Refinement of America,* his superb survey of this culture shift.

Most of America, Bushman emphasizes, was rugged and plain; "only a few privileged locales were properly adorned for the society of polished people who knew how to conduct themselves with genteel ease and grace." The new upper middle classes were building a social hierarchy that would allow them to distinguish themselves from the coarse masses. In parlor society, women were praised for having tiny hands and feet and for landing on the carpet like butterflies. Men in the 18th century were expected to wear snug waistcoats, which restricted movement and demanded formal posture. And while the rest of society had to be content with wooden boards for dining room tables and thick stools to sit on, the parlor aesthetic prized polish and smoothness. It was Edmund Burke who later articulated the general principles of this aesthetic: "I do not now recall any thing beautiful that is not smooth. . . . Take a beautiful object, and give it a broken rugged surface, and however well formed it may be in other respects, it pleases no longer."

The American elites may have been guided by European styles and manners, but they were not European aristocrats. Like their middle-class counterparts across the Atlantic, they were merchants, not lords. When courtly etiquette books were adopted by the merchant classes, some of the aristocratic theatrics were dropped, and wholesome manners came to the fore. And gradually the social ethic of the merchant class found its quintessential expression in the writings of Benjamin Franklin.

Franklin celebrated wholesome ambition. The central goal of life, he seemed to imply, is to improve yourself and thereby improve your station in life. Franklin celebrated a characteristically bourgeois set of virtues: frugality, honesty, order, moderation, prudence, industry, perseverance, temperance, chastity, cleanliness, tranquillity, punctuality, and humility. These are not heroic virtues. They don't fire the imagination or arouse the passions like the aristocratic love of honor. They are not particularly spiritual virtues. But they are practical and they are democratic. Anybody with the right work ethic can adopt them. "How little origin is to happiness, virtue or greatness," Franklin observed.

Franklin's ethos doesn't celebrate intellectual acrobatics: "Cunning proceeds from want of capacity." It doesn't endorse long periods of introspection or metaphysical contemplation: "I approved for my part the amusing one's self with poetry now and then, so far as to improve one's language, but no farther," he wrote. And Franklin's religious utterances tend to link the transcendent to the everyday: "God helps those who help themselves," he preached, watering down the Puritan concept that each person has two connected callings, one in this world and one in the next. It's impossible to imagine Franklin renouncing worldly achievement so he could go retire to a monastery to contemplate the eternal. Instead, he managed to place worldly ambition in a low but sturdy moral framework. Be honest. Work hard. Be straightforward. Focus on the concrete and immediate interests rather than the abstract and utopian visions. And he set the tone for a plain-talking style of American wisdom: "Fish and visitors stink in three days" was one of his characteristic sayings, which, like so many of his utterances, has become a truism.

And while Franklin was personally more flamboyant than any large group of people could ever be, his writings do capture the bourgeois values of parlor society. This was a class of people who believed in cultivation and self-improvement, at least so far as was socially or commercially useful. They went in for clean, classical styles, not gaudy baroque ones. Their manners were respectable, not decadent or florid. They were smart but not overly intellectual. Their clothes were well made, but they tended to favor modest hues. They believed in making money, but also in using wealth for self-improvement, not self-indulgence. They savored refinement, but were put off by grandeur and by the extravagant gesture. They wanted to appear more refined than the working masses, but not as flamboyant as the spendthrift and amoral European aristocrats. They were not called the middle classes for nothing. They were comfortable with prudent moderation and loathed extremes.

The Bohemian Revolt

Within half a century of Franklin's death in 1790, writers, artists, intellectuals, and radicals were in open rebellion against the growing dominance of the bourgeoisie and bourgeois tastes. The rebels congregated in the town that Franklin had conquered just a few decades before, Paris. In a world dominated by the merchant classes, these artists no longer had aristocratic sponsors to flatter, which was emancipating, but they had to fend for themselves in the marketplace, which brought its own traumas. To succeed, artists and writers had to appeal to an impersonalized audience, and many of these creative types came to resent their dependence on disembodied middle-class patrons, who never seemed to pay sufficient homage to genius. And as writers and artists felt more and more detached from the rest of society, they developed heroic images of their own importance.

One of the books that wonderfully captures the artistic revolt against the merchant class is César Graña's 1964 work, *Bohemian versus Bourgeois*. In the 1830s, Graña notes, pained abhorrence of the bourgeoisie became the official emotion of most writers and intellectuals. Flaubert, the most virulent of the rebels, signed some of his letters with the title "Bourgeoisophobus" and railed against the "stupid grocers and their ilk." Hatred of the bourgeoisie, he concluded, was "the beginning of all virtue." Stendhal dismissed Benjamin Franklin, "the Philadelphia artisan," as a pious bore. Poet and playwright Alfred de Musset hurled himself against the sacred institutions of the parlor crowd: "Damned Be the Family and Society. Cursed Be the Home and Cursed Be the City. Damnation upon the Motherland."

What, exactly, did the French literati find so appalling about the middle classes? In a word, their materialism. The bourgeois definition of success seemed all wrapped up with money and productivity. The artists, conversely, admired creativity, imagination, spirit. Therefore, the intellectuals found the bourgeois crass and pathetic. They castigated the bourgeois for being dull, joyless, unimaginative, conformist. Most damning of all, the bourgeois were unheroic. The old aristocrats had at least aspired to a certain grandeur. The peasants had a kiss of Christlike holiness. But these middle classes had no hint of the transcendent. They were prosaic and mediocre. There was nothing to spark the imagination, nothing loftier than their usefulness, their punctuality, their countinghouse concerns, their daily grind, their machines, their philistinism. Stendhal saw the bourgeois as "meticulous in advancing his own little schemes." They made him want "to weep and vomit at the same time." Flaubert saw the bourgeois as "plodding and avaricious." Zola later added, "The French bourgeoisie is too much the shopkeeper, too deeply sunk into its fat."

And most maddening of all, it was precisely the bourgeoisie's limitations that accounted for its tremendous worldly success. It was the merchants' petty-minded efficiency that allowed them to build successful companies and amass riches. It was their icy calculation that enabled them to devote themselves to the bottom line. It was their mechanical tinkering that enabled them to build the machines and factories and so displace the craftsmen and artisans. It was their concern for money that allowed them access to power and position. Nowadays we are used to the fact that sometimes the people who devote their lives to, say, marketing soap or shoes get to amass fortunes, live in big houses, and attract dinner party flattery, but in the 1830s all this was relatively new and shocking. It was the bourgeoisie's dullness that led to its power.

The intellectual set decided to hell with that, and they established their own alternative universe, which might forever be weak in economic terms but at least would be strong in the realm of spirit and the imagination. They considered it better, Graña notes, to be a regal outcast than an affluent worm. And so *la vie bohème* was born. Strictly speaking, bohemianism is only the social manifestation of the romantic spirit. But for clarity's sake, and because the word *romanticism* has been stretched in so many directions, in this book I mostly use the word *bohemian* to refer to both the spirit and the manners and mores it produces.

The French intellectuals set up ways of living that are by now familiar to us all. The sensitive souls flocked to run-down urban neighborhoods and created artistic communities and movements. In these places the poet and painter had higher status than the banker or president. And unable to ward off the growing strength of the bourgeoisie, the artists could at least shock them. After Flaubert finished *Salammbô,* his novel about Carthage, he predicted, "It will 1) annoy the bourgeois . . . ; 2) unnerve and shock sensitive people; 3) anger the archeologists; 4) be unintelligible to the ladies; 5) earn me a reputation as a pederast and a cannibal. Let us hope so." And so was born one of the war cries that was a hallmark of the bourgeois-bohemian feud: *Epater les bourgeois!*

The bohemian men grew their hair long and wore beards. They adopted flamboyant modes of dress by which they could easily be identified—red vests, Spanish cloaks. They celebrated youth culture and went in for provocations, whimsical humor, and practical jokes. The painter Emile Pelletier went on walks with his pet jackal. The poet Gérard de Nerval took a lobster on a leash on a walk through the Tuileries gardens. "It does not bark and it knows the secrets of the deep," he remarked. They developed a mordant fascination with the mystical and the macabre. They often wrote about suicide and sometimes performed it. They embraced novelty and sometimes applauded experimentation merely to demonstrate their contempt for the conservative middle classes.

The bohemians identified with others they saw as victims of the bourgeois order: the poor, the criminals, the ethnic and racial outcasts. They admired exotic cultures that were seemingly untouched by bourgeois mores. Many Parisians idealized Spain, which still seemed medieval. Flaubert marveled at the primitive way of life he found in Brittany. They idealized those they took to be noble savages, putting strange African artifacts in their bedrooms. They envied faraway societies, such as China, which seemed spiritually pure. They elevated sex to an art form (actually, they considered every aspect of life an art form) and scorned the prudery of the bourgeoisie. The more you read about the Parisian bohemians, the more you realize that they thought of everything. For the next 150 years rebels, intellectuals, and hippies could do little more than repeat their original rebellions.

Needless to say, in reality the conflict between the bourgeois and the bohemians was never as polarized as the polemics would indicate. The bourgeois were far more cultivated than Flaubert and his cronies gave them credit for. The Germans were sophisticated enough to distinguish between the property-owning bourgeoisie—*Besitzbuerger-tum*—and the cultivated bourgeoisie—*Bildungsbuerger-tum*. And the rebels were never as antimaterialistic as they pretended. Nonetheless, the mental categories entailed in this culture war did dominate people's thinking. The bourgeois prized materialism, order, regularity, custom, rational thinking, self-discipline, and productivity. The bohemians celebrated creativity, rebellion, novelty, self-expression, antimaterialism, and vivid experience. The bourgeois believed there was a natural order of things. They embraced rules and traditions. The bohemians believed there was no structured coherence to the universe. Reality could only be grasped in fragments, illusions, and intimations. So they adored rebellion and innovation.

The bourgeois realm was the realm of business and the market. The bohemian realm was art. The bourgeois preferred numerical and mechanistic modes of thought. The bohemians preferred intuitive and organic modes of thought. The bourgeois liked organizations. The bohemians valued autonomy and regarded the bourgeoisie as conformist herd animals. The bourgeois loved machines; the bohemians preferred the intimate humanism of the preindustrial craftsman. When it came to manners and consumption, the bourgeois admired poise and polish. The bohemians—with the exception of the Dandies, who came and went during the 19th century—admired authenticity and naturalness. The bourgeois worshiped success; the bohemians built a set of status symbols around antisuccess. The bourgeoisie sought tangible improvements. The great goal of the bohemian was the expansion of the self. Graña sums it up: "Romantic literature glorified strong passions, unique emotions, and special deeds. It despised normalcy, foresight, concern with customary affairs, and attention to feasible goals—everything of which the middle class was a daily example."

The Transcendentalists

The Parisian-style conflict between the Right and Left Banks would come to America soon enough. But the heyday of Greenwich Village bohemia—when it is possible to imagine flamboyant artists walking their lobsters through the park—was still at least 60 years away. In the mid-19th century the American artists and intellectuals who criticized bourgeois industrialism lacked the pranksterish humor and rebellious amoralism of their European counterparts. The American antimaterialists didn't seek to build a counterculture of urban rebels. They sought their alternative to the industrial economy amidst nature, in the simple life. Their aesthetic was more naturalist than artistic.

Richard Hofstadter called transcendentalism "the evangelicalism of the highbrows" because the transcendentalists always had enormous influence on the educated classes. They were mostly New England thinkers, writers, and reformers, such as Ralph Waldo Emerson, Henry David Thoreau, Bronson Alcott, and Margaret Fuller. They got their name because their goal was to transcend materialism and rationalism and so penetrate the inner spirituality that was at the core of each person. They began with the conviction, expressed by William Channing, that "there is something greater within [each individual] than in the whole material creation, than in all the worlds which press on the eye and ear; and that inward improvements have a worth and dignity in themselves."

The next step in this philosophy was to conclude that life is too precious to devote to money and things; material duties should be considered just a stepping stone to spiritual exploration. The transcendentalists did not totally reject the world. Emerson adopted a "gradational ethic" that held that people begin with their material needs and are meant to "ascend and ascend." In "The Young American" he wrote, "Trade is also but for a time, and must give way to somewhat broader and better, whose signs are already dawning in the sky." Thoreau bought and sold provisions but believed in living "simply and wisely" because "I wanted to live deep and suck out all the marrow of life, and to live so sturdily and Spartan-like as to put to rout all that was not life."

The transcendentalists lived in a bourgeois culture that was intoxicated by the possibilities of technology and by the "improvements," to use a popular word of the era, that would come with progress. The steam engine, the railway, the factory, scientific management—all of these things would eliminate distance, facilitate trade, and generate wealth. Man was on the verge of conquering nature, of redeeming the howling wilderness by making it productive. In his 1964 book, *The Machine in the Garden,* literary critic Leo Marx cites this quotation from an 1840s journalist named George Ripley as an example of what he calls the technological sublime:

> The age that is to witness a rail road between the Atlantic and the Pacific, as a grand material type of unity of nations, will also behold a social organization, productive of moral and spiritual results, whose sublime and beneficial character will eclipse even the glory of those colossal achievements which send messengers of fire over the mountain tops, and connect ocean with ocean by iron and granite bands.

Even Emerson was initially caught up in the excitement. But over time the transcendentalists concluded that while technology might bring material gain, it would also threaten nature and man's spiritual connection to nature.

"Things are in the saddle, / And ride mankind," Emerson famously complained. "We do not ride upon the railroad; it rides upon us," Thoreau echoed. Machines, wealth, and money, they believed, intercede between people and the experiences that really matter. The transcendentalists concluded that most of their fellow Americans worked too hard and too slavishly. They were able to calculate and measure but often did not take the time to sense and feel. Their middle-class neighbors were too concerned with their standard of living and not enough concerned with their reason for living.

The transcendentalists experienced their most vivid and profound experiences in the woods. Thoreau moved briefly to Walden Pond, where he lived "a border life" between the civilization of town life to his east and the primitivism of the frontier to the west. "The land," Emerson wrote, "is the appointed remedy for whatever is false and fantastic in our culture. The continent we inhabit is to be a physic and food for our mind, as well as our body. The land, with its tranquilizing, sanative influences, is to repair the errors of a scholastic and traditional education, and bring us into just relation with men and things." Striking a note that is the antithesis of the genteel culture of parlor society, Thoreau added, "Life consists with wildness. The most alive is the wildest." The civilization that erects barriers between man and nature can lead only to alienation and unhappiness.

It is a sign of the tremendous influence of the transcendentalists that the rhetorical flourishes of the 19th-century technologists now seem to us absurd, while the thoughts of the oddballs in the woods seem profound. They left a permanent imprint on American culture. Thanks in part to their influence, bohemia in America has usually been more naturalist, more devoted to the simple life, less nihilistic than its European counterpart.

The Culture War

The culture war between the bohemians and the bourgeoisie raged throughout the industrial age. It took different forms over time, and it was fought on different battlegrounds, but the main themes were pretty constant. There was always, in America, a bourgeois strain, materialist, rationalist, technological. It aspired to refined tastes and genteel manners. And there was always a bohemian strain, artistic, antirationalist, spiritual. It admired authentic furnishings, adventurous styles, naturalistic manners.

During the Gilded Age, for example, a bourgeois child would have read the *McGuffey Readers,* which contained moral tales for achievement-oriented kids, or Horatio Alger novels that had names like *Strive and Succeed, Luck and Pluck, Slow and Sure,* and *Fame and Fortune.* These books updated Benjamin Franklin's advice: work hard, be diligent, seize opportunities, be honest but not too intellectual, be pleasing to others, waste not want not. Such a child, if successful, would have grown up to live in a stately home, maybe on the hill above his town, or in one of the new commuter suburbs that were springing up. There, he might turn to Andrew Carnegie's essays, such as the hugely popular "Wealth," to take instruction in spending, giving, and getting.

But at the same time in another part of the country there would be writers like John Muir who rejected the "gobble gobble school" of bourgeois capitalism. There were furniture makers like Gustav Stickley who wanted to devise ways of living that would be comfortable and beautiful but that rejected the crass materialism of mainstream taste. Stickley was influenced by the Arts and Crafts movement that had been led in Britain by John Ruskin and

William Morris, who celebrated the simple virtues embodied in the preindustrial handicraft guild communities.

Stickley's magazine, the *Craftsman,* was the leading organ for their ideas. "We need to straighten out our standards," Stickley wrote, "and to get rid of a lot of rubbish that we have accumulated along with our wealth and commercial supremacy. It is not that we are too energetic, but that in many ways we have misused our energy precisely as we have wasted and misused so many of our wonderful natural resources." So the homes and furniture Stickley designed would not be mini-palaces for the aspiring bourgeoisie. They would encourage a simple and naturalist style of life. They would offer "an escape" from the "machine of commercial tyranny" where people could get their spiritual lives in balance. Stickley meant his Arts and Crafts and Mission styles to be a craftsmanlike alternative to the grandiose styles of the merchant princes, though, the bourgeoisie being the bourgeoisie, the merchants quickly co-opted his products. The Astors and the Rockefellers hired Stickley to furnish their country retreats. Henry Ford filled his Manhattan apartment with Mission furniture.

In the 1920s the bourgeois and the bohemian impulses took different forms. On the one hand, there were classic bourgeois presidents like Harding, Coolidge, and Hoover. There was a massive expansion of upscale suburbs; mansion after mansion sprung up in places like the Main Line outside Philadelphia and Westchester County near New York. There was an expanding class of petty bourgeoisie, who set up parlors in their small bungalows in Chicago, Los Angeles, and elsewhere. The members of the new parlor set might hardly ever use these rooms. Their homes were so small they really couldn't spare the space. Nonetheless, the parlors sat there, valued as symbols of newly earned, if slightly outdated, gentility. And there were millions of aspiring bourgeois buying books like Bruce Barton's *The Man Nobody Knows*. Barton argued that Jesus was actually best understood as a great business executive and a successful networker. "A kill-joy! He was the most popular dinner guest in Jerusalem!" Barton exclaimed. "A failure! He picked up twelve men from the bottom ranks of business and forced them into an organization that conquered the world." In 1926 bookstores sold more copies of *The Man Nobody Knows* than of any other nonfiction book.

On the other hand, there was a literary assault on bourgeois values and a flourishing bohemian alternative in Greenwich Village and elsewhere. During this period such writers as Sinclair Lewis, Thorstein Veblen, John O'Hara, John Dos Passos, Ernest Hemingway, and Gertrude Stein rejected bourgeois values, going off to Paris or Moscow, engaging in radical politics, or otherwise railing against the rise of provincial Babbittry. Malcolm Cowley, a Greenwich Village habitué who was also a writer and editor, summarized the priorities of early-20th-century American bohemians in his 1934 book, *Exile's Return*. The bohemians, he said, stood for the following ideas: "the salvation by the child"—each of us is born with special potentialities that are slowly crushed by society; "the idea of self-expression"—the purpose of life is to express the full individuality of one's inner being; "the idea of paganism"—the body is a temple, so there is nothing unclean about nudity and sex; "the idea of living for the moment"; "the idea of liberty"—every law and convention should be shattered; "the idea of female equality"; "the idea of psychological adjustment"—people are unhappy because they are repressed or maladjusted; "the idea of changing place"—truth could be found if one got on the road and moved to someplace new or vital.

Then came the 1950s, seemingly the high point of the bourgeois era but at the same time the moment when it was being undermined. It was the era of President Eisenhower, the Organization Man, Junior League clubs, and *Leave It to Beaver* television culture. On the other hand, there were squads of rebel bohemians hitting the road and smoking pot. Like their bohemian predecessors, the Beats celebrated spontaneity and sensation. They enjoyed shocking the bourgeoisie. They rejected money and comfort for the sake of liberation and freedom. And they despised what Allen Ginsberg called the "Moloch whose mind is pure machinery."

And there were writers and intellectuals who saw in the Beat styles the first glimmerings of a social revolution. In his 1960 book, *Growing Up Absurd,* Paul Goodman rhapsodized about the Beats: "Their main topic is the 'system' with which they refuse to cooperate. They will explain that 'good' jobs are frauds and sells, that it is intolerable to have one's style of life dictated by Personnel, that a man is a fool to work to pay installments on a useless refrigerator for his wife," and so on. Goodman's main assault was on "the organization," the great interlocking system of bureaucracies and structures, which Goodman and the Beats felt stifled autonomy and creativity. Society needed to be disrupted and disorganized. But Goodman was savvy enough to notice something else about the Beats. Though they were dissidents and though they rejected affluence and all that, the Beats actually lived pretty well. It was their spirit of pleasure that made them so attractive. In a passage that brilliantly anticipates the Bobo consumerism of today, Goodman observed, "The Beat subculture is not merely a reaction to the middle class or to the organized system. It is natural. Merging with the underprivileged, the Beats do not make a poor go of it. Their homes are often more livable than middle class homes; they often eat better, have good records, etc. Some of their habits, like being unscheduled, sloppy, communitarian, sexually easy-going and careless of reputation, go against the grain of the middle class, but they are motivated by good sense rather than resentment: They are probably natural ways that most people would choose if they got wise to themselves." This was a different notion: bohemia was a lifestyle most people would choose to live if they got wise to themselves. If you had taken that idea in 1960 and made it the cornerstone of your investment choices, you would be a billionaire today.

In the sixties, of course, the bohemian subculture turned into a mass movement, suitable for the covers of *Life* and *Look* magazines. The hippie assaults on the bourgeois lifestyle are so well known they don't really need to be summarized at great length here. But briefly, and leaving aside the civil rights movement and Vietnam and all the complex and substantive political turmoils of that decade, here are a few of the countercultural straws in the wind: In the realm of public theater, Abbie Hoffman threw dollar bills down on the traders of the New York Stock Exchange. The Diggers, a group of San Francisco performance artists, declared "The Death of Money and the Birth of the Free." In the literary realm, Norman Mailer explored what it meant to be a hipster. In his collection of essays, *Advertisements for Myself,* Mailer published, glossy-magazine style, a list of what was hip and what was square, and his list corresponds to the traditional split between the bohemian and the bourgeois. Night, he wrote, is hip, whereas day is square. Crooks are hip, whereas the police are square. The body is hip, whereas the mind is square. Questions are hip; answers are square. Induction, thinking intuitively, is hip; deduction, thinking more rationally, is square.

Theodore Roszak, the chronicler of the 1960s revolt, summarized the hippie critique of the middle classes in *The Making of a Counter Culture:* "The bourgeoisie is obsessed by greed; its sex life is insipid and prudish, its family patterns are debased; its slavish conformities of dress and grooming are degrading; its mercenary routinization of life is intolerable." The bourgeois floated on a swell of affluence, so the student leaders rejected materialism. The bourgeois admired politeness, elegance, and decorum, so the student leaders were raw. The bourgeois were neat, so the student leaders were haphazard. The bourgeois had short hair, so the student leaders had long hair. The bourgeois were technological, so the student leaders were natural. The bourgeois were career oriented, so the student leaders were experience oriented. The bourgeois pretended to be chaste, so the student leaders pretended to be promiscuous. The bourgeois practiced conspicuous consumption, so the students practiced conspicuous nonconsumption. The bourgeois celebrated work, so the students celebrated pleasure. The bourgeois ate meat and processed food, so the student leaders ate soybeans and other organic foods. In the 1960s millions of people figured out you could go up in your peers' estimation by going down in lifestyle and dress. And swelling with great numbers, the romantic counterculture actually overshadowed the bourgeois mainstream culture. More than a century after Flaubert and his Parisian cronies first raised the banner *"Epater les bourgeois,"* the bohemian movement had grown from a clique to a horde. For a time it seemed like the ideas of bohemia would actually rout what remained of Benjamin Franklin's bourgeois ethos.

The Bourgeois Counterattack

Then in the 1970s and 1980s, a funny thing happened. The bourgeois ethos began fighting back. For the previous century the argument between the bourgeois and the bohemians had been one-sided. The bohemians would launch their articulate attacks, but the bourgeoisie would just follow the advice of their throw pillows: Living well is the best revenge. They would just go on living their lives, semi-oblivious to the countercultural assault. They might sneer at the radicals or the eggheads, but they didn't produce a comprehensive critique of bohemianism. But after the sixties and seventies, the party of the bourgeoisie could not help but notice the party of bohemia. The counterculture was everywhere. The personal was political. The bourgeoisie had to respond.

Among those who formulated the response were the neoconservatives. These were writers and academics such as Irving Kristol, James Q. Wilson, Gertrude Himmelfarb, Norman Podhoretz, and Midge Decter, who, at least in the 1970s, still tended to accept the policies of the New Deal and the Great Society. Neoconservatism started as a movement dominated by social scientists. The journal *Public Interest* was founded in 1965 by Irving Kristol and Daniel Bell to publish cool-headed, technocratic analyses of public policies. The assumption was that the great ideological wars were over and that now policy disputes would be settled by hard-headed social science scrutiny. Daniel Patrick Moynihan wrote an essay in that first issue called "The Professionalization of Reform," which was a manifesto for rule by the intellectual class: "Men are learning to make an industrial economy work. . . . The ability to predict events, as against controlling them, has developed even more impressively." But like many successful magazines, *Public Interest* and its sister neocon publication, *Commentary,* found themselves engaged in a project totally antithetical to the one for which they had been created. The neoconservatives, mostly lower-middle-class kids, were appalled by the antibourgeois attitudes of the countercultural intellectuals and student radicals. And they produced something rare in the history of this dispute, an articulate defense of the bourgeoisie and a telling critique of bohemia.

The basic neoconservative argument started with a series of concessions. It acknowledged that the bourgeois lifestyle is not heroic or inspiring. "Bourgeois society is the

most prosaic of all possible societies. . . . It is a society
organized for the convenience and comfort of common
men and common women," Irving Kristol wrote in an
essay called "The Adversary Culture of the Intellectuals."
Therefore bourgeois society aims to improve material conditions; it does not devote huge energies to transcendence,
to classical virtue, to spiritual transfiguration. Bourgeois
societies produce happy civilizations but not grand and
immortal ones. What's more, Kristol wrote, an "amiable
philistinism" is inherent in bourgeois society. The high
arts are not accorded a lot of respect, but popular culture
flourishes (and every movie has a happy ending). Bourgeois societies are usually free societies, but they are not
always just societies. Often it is the narrow-minded brute
who ends up with the most money and success while the
truly wise person languishes unrewarded.

On the other hand, bourgeois culture does have one
massive historical accomplishment to its credit, the neoconservatives argued. It provides an effective moral context
for capitalism. With its emphasis on prudence, frugality,
punctuality, thrift, piety, neighborliness, responsibility, and
industry, it restrains some of the greedy passions that might
otherwise make a market economy barbaric. Moreover,
with its reverence for institutions such as family, organized
religion, manners, ceremonies, and community groups like
the Rotary Club or the PTA, bourgeois culture fosters institutions that keep a free society from descending into
amoralism. Furthermore, the neocons added, let's not underestimate the importance of material progress. The bourgeoisie's talent for wealth creation has made life longer and
more pleasant for billions of people around the world.
Technology has brought untold improvements to everybody's lives. The tinkering of the entrepreneur may not be
the stuff of grandeur, but commercial improvements produce real benefits. For instance, bourgeois capitalism leads
to unprecedented social mobility.

The bohemians may aspire to grand spiritual transcendence, the neocons continued, but what they often
end up with is self-indulgent nihilism. The neoconservatives disdained the perpetual rebelliousness of the counterculture. They were offended by what they took to be the
New Left's snobbery, its contempt for middle America.
The rejection of authority and custom doesn't lead to
blissful liberation, they argued; it leads to self-destructive
behavior. The romantic searchers throw off conventional
morality, but their antinomianism is subversive of all
morality, of all civil restraint. Egotism takes over. Pretty
soon fathers are abandoning their families, and the sanctity of the two-parent family is delegitimized. Children
raised without clear moral guideposts slip into criminality
and drug abuse. Popular culture becomes more vulgar.
People are recast as society's victims and so are not asked
to accept responsibility for themselves.

Neoconservatives like Gertrude Himmelfarb pointed
out that between 1860 and 1970—that is, through many
of the horrors of the industrial age—the divorce rate remained essentially constant in America and Britain. But
starting in 1970, when bohemianism became a mass
movement and bourgeois culture found itself in retreat, divorce rates skyrocketed and illegitimacy rose dramatically,
as did crime rates, drug use, and many other social
pathologies. The assault on bourgeois values was a social
disaster, the neoconservatives argued. The task ahead,
many neocons believed, was to restore bourgeois values to
their former influence.

The Dream of Reconciliation

Even while the bourgeois-bohemian clash was at its
height, people dreamed of finding some balance between
the two sides. In his 1915 book, *America's Coming-of-*

Age, Van Wyck Brooks complained of the social division between the "machinery of self-preservation and the mystery of life."

"We have in America," Brooks wrote, "two publics, the cultivated public and the business public, the public of theory and the public of activity, the public that reads Maeterlinck and the public that accumulates money: the one largely feminine, the other largely masculine." Brooks sought a "genial middle ground" between these two mentalities. He wanted to "bring the ideal into things," to make being good compatible with making good. Though some thinkers and writers might have longed for a reconciliation, the world was not, at least during the industrial age, ready for one. But in the information age, the world of ideas and the world of business have merged, and the much-longed-for reconciliation between the bourgeois and the bohemian has come to pass.

Look around America's upper-middle-class neighborhoods, like Wayne, Pennsylvania. A town like that certainly has its share of bourgeois elements. It's a suburb. It's affluent. There is obvious reverence for traditional bourgeois institutions like family and religion. But the new Wayne residents have adopted bohemian styles as well, the strong coffees, the grains, the casual manners. In his 1954 book, *The Tastemakers,* Russell Lynes could write of Gustav Stickley, "His name and his writings are now almost forgotten." But today you can't walk 15 feet in Wayne or in similar communities without stumbling across some bit of furniture inspired by the antimaterialist craftsman.

Indeed, one of the most interesting features of the town is the way the new educated-class consumers have taken the old styles of the genteel parlor society and stood them on their head. Everything the old gentry tried to make smooth, we in today's educated gentry try to make rough. They covered over ceiling beams. We expose them. They buried bulky stone chimneys in plaster and paint.

We unearth stone chimneys and admire massive rocky hearths. They prized delicate narrow floor planks. We like broad sturdy ones. They preferred marble. We prefer slate. They filled their homes with knock-off versions of high art. We like handicrafts. They covered their furniture in silk. We toss coarse Colombian throw rugs over our sofas, with maybe a few stray hairs from a long dead burro.

More broadly, they liked polish and high civilization. We like indigenous spirituality. They liked refined manners that demonstrated self-mastery. We like loose manners that demonstrate honesty. They made entertaining into a performance—the preparation was done by the servants somewhere in the dim recesses of the house. We invite our guests backstage into the kitchen and give them some veggies to chop. The old genteel style sprang from a belief that humankind is ascending from crude barbarism to a state of civilized grace. Members of today's affluent class are suspicious of refinement and genteel manners. So the new elite disdains all the words that were used as lavish compliments by the old gentry: delicate, dainty, respectable, decorous, opulent, luxurious, elegant, splendid, dignified, magnificent, and extravagant. Instead, the new elite prefers a different set of words, which exemplify a different temper and spirit: authentic, natural, warm, rustic, simple, honest, organic, comfortable, craftsmanlike, unique, sensible, sincere.

The Bobo class has moved into bourgeois haunts and infused them with bohemian sensibilities, at the same time watering down bohemian attitudes so they don't subvert bourgeois institutions. So today a "Days of Rage" T-shirt can be worn by health-conscious aerobicizers. The pseudo-transgressive photography of Robert Mapplethorpe can be hung in the guest bathroom of a weekend place, where people can gaze at it while soothing themselves in the oversized whirlpool. (And, as we'll see in the next chapter, the Bobos have moved into bohemian haunts and infused them with bourgeois sensibilities, similarly diluted.) Today it's almost impossible to divide towns along the old culture war lines. If you go to Berkeley or Greenwich Village, the old bohemian centers, you will find distressed-furniture boutiques that host workshops in cabinetry. There will be music stores with stacks of the local alternative weekly and yoga posters on the community bulletin board. But you will find these very same sorts of stores in Wayne, Pennsylvania, or Winnetka, Illinois, and the other epicenters of the old bourgeois elite. The educated class has conquered all and hegemonized its Bobo culture over affluent regions from coast to coast. Now the Babbitt lion can mingle with the beatnik lamb at a Pottery Barn, a Smith & Hawken, a Museum Shop, a Restoration Hardware, a Nature Company, a Starbucks, or any of the other zeitgeist-heavy institutions that cater to educated affluents. Today the culture war is over, at least in the realm of the affluent. The centuries-old conflict has been reconciled.

The Code of Financial Correctness

In its place we now have this third culture. And slowly, slowly a new set of rules and sumptuary codes is emerging to replace the competing codes of the bohemians and the bourgeoisie. This new set of codes organizes the consumption patterns of the educated class, encouraging some kinds of spending, which are deemed virtuous, and discouraging others that seem vulgar or elitist. They redefine what it means to be a cultured person.

Taken as a whole, this set of rules make it clear that the Thorstein Veblen era is over. Maybe off in Vegas there are still some rich peasants trying to conspicuously consume, buying big limousines, powerboats, and sports franchises and piling up possessions to demonstrate their net worth. But the Bobo renounces accumulation and embraces cultivation. He must show, in the way he spends his money, that he is conscientious and not crass. The emerging code of financial correctness allows Bobos to spend money without looking like one of the vulgar Yuppies they despise. It's a set of rules to help them convert their wealth into spiritually and intellectually uplifting experiences. A person who follows these precepts can dispose up to $4 or $5 million annually in a manner that demonstrates how little he or she cares about material things.

Rule 1. Only vulgarians spend lavish amounts of money on luxuries. Cultivated people restrict their lavish spending to necessities.

Aristotle made the ancient distinction between needs—objects we must have to survive, like shelter, food, clothing, and other essentials—and wants, which are those things we desire to make us feel superior to others. The Bobo elite has seized on this distinction to separate itself from past and rival elites. Specifically, the members of the educated-class elite feel free to invest huge amounts of capital in things that are categorized as needs, but it is not acceptable to spend on mere wants. For example, it's virtuous to spend $25,000 on your bathroom, but it's vulgar to spend $15,000 on a sound system and a wide-screen TV. It's decadent to spend $10,000 on an outdoor Jacuzzi, but if you're not spending twice that on an oversized slate shower stall, it's a sign that you probably haven't learned to appreciate the simple rhythms of life.

Similarly, it is acceptable to spend hundreds of dollars on top-of-the-line hiking boots, but it would be vulgar to buy top-of-the-line patent leather shoes to go with formal wear. It is acceptable to spend $4,400 on a Merlin XLM road bike because people must exercise, but it would be a sign of a superficial nature to buy a big, showy powerboat. Only a shallow person would spend hundreds of dollars on caviar, but a deep person would gladly shell out that much for top-of-the-line mulch.

You can spend as much as you want on anything that can be classified as a tool, such as a $65,000 Range Rover with plenty of storage space, but it would be vulgar to spend money on things that cannot be seen as tools, such as a $60,000 vintage Corvette. (I once thought of writing a screenplay called *Rebel Without a Camry,* about the social traumas a history professor suffered when he bought a Porsche.) In fact, the very phrase "sport utility vehicle" is testimony to the new way Bobos think about tools. Not long ago *sport* was the opposite of *utility.* You either played or you worked. But the information age keyboard jockeys who traffic in concepts and images all day like to dabble in physical labor during their leisure time, so hauling stuff around in their big mega-cruisers with the four-foot wheels turns into a kind of sport.

And when it comes to a room as utilitarian as the kitchen, the sky's the limit. Up until the Bobos came along, the kitchen was a reviled part of the house. The 19th-century architect Calvert Vaux, for example, was dismayed at people who would eat in the kitchen. "This habit marks the low state of civilization," he remarked. In his 1972 book, *Instant Status; or How to Become a Pillar of the Upper Middle Class,* Charles Merrill Smith noted, "Upper class women never go into the kitchen. . . . Upper middle class women, of necessity, do go into the kitchen from time to time but wish to leave the impression they do not. A true upper middle class house, then, de-emphasizes domestic convenience." At the same time, but at the opposite end of the cultural continuum, Betty Friedan and her fellow feminists were also urging their sisters to get out of the kitchen. But today in the age of Bobo reconciliation, everybody is back in the kitchen, albeit on his or her own terms. Indeed, in today's educated-class homes, the kitchen has become the symbol of domestic bliss, the way the hearth used to be for the bourgeoisie.

That's why when you walk into a newly renovated upscale home owned by nice, caring people, you will likely find a kitchen so large it puts you in mind of an aircraft hangar with plumbing. The perimeter walls of the old kitchen will have been obliterated, and the new kitchen will have swallowed up several adjacent rooms, just as the old Soviet Union used to do with its neighbors. It's hard to tell where one of today's mega-kitchens ends. You think you see the far wall of some distant great room shimmering in the distance, but it could be a mirage reflected off the acres and acres of Corian countertop. And then when you turn into the pantry, you observe that it is larger than the entire apartment the owner lived in while in graduate school.

Kitchens this big require strategizing. The architects brag about how brilliantly they have designed their kitchens into "work triangles" to minimize the number of steps between, say, stove, dishwasher, and sink. In the old kitchens you didn't need work triangles because taking steps was not a kitchen activity. You just turned around, and whatever you needed, there it was. But today's infinite kitchens have lunch counters and stools and built-in televisions and bookshelves and computer areas and probably little "You Are Here" maps for guests who get lost on their way to the drink station.

As for kitchen equipment, today's Bobo kitchen is like a culinary playground providing its owners with a series of top-of-the-line peak experiences. The first thing you see, covering yards and yards of one wall, is an object that looks like a nickel-plated nuclear reactor but is really the stove. No more flimsy cooking cans with glorified Bunsen burners on top for today's domestic enthusiasts. Today's gourmet Bobos want a 48-inch-wide, six-burner, dual-fuel, 20,000 Btu range that sends up heat like a space shuttle rocket booster turned upside down. Furthermore, they want cool gizmos, like a lava-rock grill, a built-in 30,000 Btu wok burner, brass burner igniters (only philistines have aluminum ones), and a ½-inch-thick steel griddle. They want an oven capacity of 8 cubic feet minimum, just to show they are the sort of people who could roast a bison if necessary. And they want the whole awesome package covered in metal with such a high nickel-to-chromium content that magnets won't stick. That's how you know you have purchased the sort of utilitarian gear your family deserves. La Cornue makes an adequate stove with gas and electric simmer plates for about $23,500. The AGA 59-inch cooker, patented in 1922, has the unadorned sturdiness that suggests it was once used to recycle horses into glue, but it also features such conveniences as a warming plate, a simmering plate, a baking oven, a roasting oven, and an infinite supply of burners. It uses no direct heat, only radiant surfaces, and thus expresses a gentle philosophy of life. It costs only $10,000.

Presiding over the nearby quadrants of the kitchen will be the refrigeration complex. The central theme of this section is that freezing isn't cold enough; the machinery should be able to reach temperatures approaching absolute zero, at which all molecular motion stops. The refrigerator itself should be the size of a minivan stood on end. It should have at least two doors, one for the freezer section and one for the in-law suite, in case you want to rent out rooms inside. In addition, there should be through-the-door delivery systems for water (carbon filtered), ice (cubes, crushed, or alphabet style to help the toddlers with their letter recognition), and perhaps assorted microbrews. There should be gallon door bins, spillproof split shelves, sealed snack pans, full extension slides, and scratchproof bin windows, and the front doors should not be white, like those regular refrigerators they sell at Sears, but stainless steel—the texture of culinary machismo.

A capacious kitchen with durable appliances is a sign that you do your own chores, sharing the gritty reality of everyday life, just as Gandhi and Karl Marx would have wanted you to. It means you've got equipment with more power than all but six of the NATO nations. It means that when you throw those fish sticks into the oven, you know they will be browned evenly, and you could boil the water for the macaroni and cheese in eight seconds if you really turned the thing up full blast. It means that you have concentrated your spending power on where it matters, on the everyday places you and your family actually use. Spending on conspicuous display is evil, but it's egalitarian to spend money on parts of the house that would previously have been used by the servants.

Rule 2. It is perfectly acceptable to spend lots of money on anything that is of "professional quality," even if it has nothing to do with your profession.

Very few of us are actually professional sherpas, leading parties up Mount Everest, but that doesn't mean an expedition-weight three-layer Gore-Tex Alpenglow reinforced Marmot Thunderlight jacket is not a reasonable purchase. Just because you don't actually own a bagel shop doesn't mean you have to settle for a flimsy $29 toaster when you could select a $300 multipurpose industrial-strength toasting system that will be browning breakfast breads well into the 23rd century. Similarly, the fact that you are a only a part-time gardener doesn't mean you should settle for a $6 hoe when there are $55 ones at the gourmet gardening stores. Because while cultivated people would never judge each other on the costliness of their jewelry, they do judge each other on the costliness of their gear. When buying gear, you have to prove you are serious enough to appreciate durability and craftsmanship. You have to show you are smart enough to spend the very most.

To cater to this sentiment, upscale stores have adopted a set of clever disguises. They pretend to be selling hard gear-type stuff when they are actually selling soft boring stuff like clothing. The REI outdoor store will advertise its ice axes, knowing that they will make you feel virtuous as you walk by them up to the sweater section. Restoration Hardware trumpets its hardware, but it actually earns far more revenue from selling couches and chairs. The Lands' End company sells a lot of socks, but on their catalogue cover they will show a picture of hikers walking along the crest of Mount Everest.

One of the results of this trend is that there is an adventure gap opening up between members of the educated class and their belongings. The things they own were designed for more dangerous activities than any they actually perform. The hiking boots that were designed for the Andes spend most of their time in the farmer's market. The top-of-the-line fleece outergarments are used for nothing more strenuous than traversing the refrigerated aisle in the Safeway. The four-wheel-drive vehicles are never asked to perform any ordeal more treacherous than a bumpy road in the slush. But just as in the age of gentility hypocrisy was vice paying homage to virtue, so today among the Bobos rugged gear is comfort paying homage to adventure.

Rule 3. You must practice the perfectionism of small things.

It's kind of pretentious to build yourself a big estate with magnificently manicured grounds. But nobody can accuse you of getting too big for your britches if you devote fanatical attention to small household items, like selecting exactly the right pasta strainer, the distinctive doorknob, or one of those ingeniously designed corkscrews. Bobos practice what journalist Richard Starr calls the perfectionism of small things. They might line their bread drawer with terra-cotta; a small thing but it enhances breathability. They might spend hours contemplating backsplashes, devoting their massive powers of contemplation to finding one that is protective yet unobtrusive. They might dedicate their evenings so they can become insulation connoisseurs. They might scour the hardware catalogues until they find the Swiss-made KWC faucet, which many believe to be the world's finest pullout spray head. The idea behind all this effort is to show that you have so much brainpower to spare, you can even be thoughtful about your water flow.

The mental powers that were once devoted to organic chemistry finals and metaphysics term papers can now be lavished on appliance garages (it's important to get the ones with tambour doors). Bobos don't want gaudy possessions that make extravagant statements. That would make it look like they are trying to impress. They want rare gadgets that have not yet been discovered by the masses but are cleverly designed to make life more convenient or unusual. It's a sign you have mastered the art of living if you've built in a raised dishwasher so you don't have to stoop while unloading. It's a testimony to your commitment to your kids if your bathroom cabinet has view-at-a-glance, childproof plastic medicine containers. A person with an elevated sensibility gets a life-affirming rush while opening soup with a particularly brilliant can opener. If your Christmas tree lights are vintage 1933 with the slightly larger bulbs, your sophisticated guests will appreciate your nose for old-fashioned workmanship. Nobody wants to talk about a diamond necklace over dinner, but it's charming to start a conversation about the host's African-inspired salad serving forks. The smaller an item is, the more praiseworthy it is to have thought deeply about its purchase.

Rule 4. *You can never have too much texture.*

Smoothness may have been pleasing to Edmund Burke. And high-achieving but grasping yuppies of the 1980s may have surrounded themselves with smooth surfaces—matte black furniture, polished lacquer floors, and sleek faux-marbleized walls. But to demonstrate their superiority to such people, the educated elites prefer to build environments full of natural irregularities. For the Bobos, roughness connotes authenticity and virtue.

So the educated elites love texture. They prefer rough area rugs woven from obscure grasses over shiny wall-to-wall carpets, bumpy wooden toys over smooth plastic ones, thick and textured ceramics over smooth and dainty porcelain, crinkly and idiosyncratic wildflowers over smooth tulips. In accordance with our impasto longings, we in the educated class savor pummeled antique doorknobs, lichenous stone walls, scarred provincial cabinets, rough-hewn beams, weathered slates, raw Tibetan fabrics, and rammed-earth interiors. Really rich Bobos will hire squads of workmen with ball-peen hammers to pound some rustic wear into their broad floor planks. They'll import craftsmen from Umbria to create the look of crumbling frescoed plaster in their foyer. They'll want foundations built from craggy stones that look as if they could withstand a catapult assault, and interior beams built from logs that look as if they've been chipped by Paul Bunyan.

Any unreflective currency trader can choose clothing on the basis of pattern, but it takes an elevated sensibility to design a wardrobe by mixing textures. So Bobo shirts are flannel, not silk. Our collars are relaxed and folded, not starched and metallic. We will complement our linen slacks with a marled blouse, a Salvadoran folk-art fleece sweater, a hemp baseball cap, and, as it comes on the market, sisal underwear. When a group of Bobos stand together, observers will be awed by the subtle symphony of fabrics. Their mouths will hang open and they will think to themselves, "Wow, there goes a cloud of nubby people. I wonder if they know where I can get some fresh fava beans."

The texture principle applies to comestibles too. Everything the educated person drinks will leave sediment in the bottom of the glass: yeasty microbrews, unfiltered fruit juices, organic coffees. Bobo breads are thick and grainy, the way wholesome peasants like it, not thin and airy, as the old shallow suburbanites prefer. Even our condiments will be admirably coarse; rough, unrefined sugar is considered by many to be the height of refinement.

Rule 5. The educated elites are expected to practice one-downmanship.

Cultivated people are repelled by the idea of keeping up with the Joneses. Nothing is more disreputable than competing with your neighbors by trying to more effectively mimic the style of the social class just above you. Instead, as members of the educated class, you reject status symbols in order to raise your status with your equally cultivated peers. Everything about you must be slightly more casual than your neighbor. Your furnishings must be slightly more peasanty. Your lives should have a greater patina of simplicity. So your dinnerware will not have the sort of regal designs they use at Buckingham Palace. It will be basic white, like what they sell at Pottery Barn. Your shoes won't be snazzy pumps; they'll be simple but expensive penny loafers from Prada. Ostentation is a disgrace, but anything unadorned is a sign of refreshing honesty. You must learn to keep down with the Joneses.

The educated class pioneered this form of status inversion back in the 1960s when some anonymous genius discovered that you could sell faded blue jeans at a higher price than new blue jeans. Suddenly there was a class of consumers that wanted to reject the cult of newness that had hitherto been the guiding mode of consumerism. This taste for the faux archaic has now spread across the upscale marketplace. So now fancy furniture stores sell steamer trunks that are newly made but stained to look old, complete with torn destination stickers. Across the developing world there are factory workers busy beating up the goods they have just made in order to please American consumers, and one can only imagine what they think of us. But for us the payoff is clear. If your furniture is distressed, your conscience needn't be.

In the 1950s and 1960s the smart set wanted to appear relentlessly modern. A 1958 advertisement for the Invincible furniture company featured "Modernaire desks, modular Modernettes and Modernease chairs." Today these same styles are fashionable precisely because they are archaic. Being truly modern is out of date. Instead, restaurants splatter paint on their floors and dent their tables with hammers to exude a lived-in feel. The sales of self-consciously old-fashioned push lawn mowers skyrocket by 20 to 30 percent annually, catering to retro-chic professionals who could easily afford motor mowers. Meanwhile, roller-skate revivalists are powering a surge back to four-wheel skates and away from in-line models.

The course of status inversion is both back and down. It is not sufficient to buy stuff that is old. It is necessary in addition to go down the social scale and purchase objects that once belonged to persons much poorer than yourself. The aim is to surround yourself with products that purport to have no social status significance because they were once owned by people who were so simple and virtuous they didn't realize how fashionable they were. That is why the richer Bobos get, the more they live like Shakers. If you go into a Bobo home, you will possibly find Shaker-inspired stereo consoles and Shaker-inspired workstations. Bobo cabinets will have been converted from homely typesetting shops. Old closet doors will have been salvaged from an old sausage factory. The baby gates on the stairs will have been converted from 19th-century rabbit hutches. There will be ancient farm implements hanging from the wall as decorative devices. The tables will be arrayed with general store objets d'art, such as old cans of liniment salve, biscuit tins, kitchen utensils, and beat-up spice containers. Upending the hierarchies of the *ancien régime,* we want people to think we spent less on our stuff than we actually did.

We prize old things whose virtues have been rendered timeless by their obsolescence: turn-of-the-century carpentry tools, whaling equipment, butter churns, typesetting trays, gas lamps, and hand-operated coffee grinders. Lightship baskets made from rattan with oak bottoms now sell for between $1,000 and $118,000. We can appreciate the innate wisdom of the unlettered seaman and the objects he created. He saw his objects as tools, but we appreciate them as works of art.

Another essential element of one-downmanship is the co-optation of oppressed cultures. The old elite may have copied the styles of the European aristocrats or the colonial masters, but Bobos prefer the colonial victims. In fact, if you tour a super-sophisticated home, you will see an odd mélange of artifacts that have nothing in common except for the shared victimization of their creators. An African mask will sit next to an Incan statue atop a tablecloth fashioned from Samoan, Brazilian, Moroccan, or Tibetan cloth. Even some European cultures, such as the Celts, qualify for one-downmanship—they have been oppressed enough that an educated person can feel a sense of benevolence while appreciating the beauty of their iconography. Sometimes it will be the religious objects of an oppressed culture that will be displayed in an educated home: Amazonian figures, Native American totems, Egyptian deities, animistic shells, or Shinto statuettes. It is acceptable to display sacred items in an educated person's home so long as they are from a religion neither the host nor any of his or her guests is likely to profess.

We educated elites surround ourselves with the motifs of lives we have chosen not to live. We are busy meritocrats, but we choose goods that radiate pre-meritocratic calm. We march into the future with our Palm Pilots and cell phones, but we surround ourselves with rootsy stuff, the reactionary and the archaic. We guiltily acknowledge our privileges but surround ourselves with artifacts from the less privileged. It's not that we're hypocrites. It's just that we're seeking balance. Affluent, we're trying not to become materialists. Busy, we're trying not to lose sight of the timeless essentials. So we go around frantically shopping for the accoutrements of calm. We dream of building a home where we can finally sit still and relax, a place we can go where our ambition won't follow.

In this spirit we sometimes even reintroduce the old WASP styles into our eclecticism. The WASPs may have been racist and elitist. They may have been the establishment that we Bobos destroyed. But at least they weren't consumed by ambition. So when we look at those calm beautiful faces in the Ralph Lauren ads, we can't help feeling that they have something we long for. And so mixed in with our multicultural decor may be an item or two that could have come right out of the New York Yacht Club, maybe a faded leather chair or a dark wooden desk. The WASP Establishment is dead, and irony of ironies, the Protestant Establishment has been transmogrified into one of those extinct cultures destroyed by the march of technology and progress.

Rule 6. Educated elites are expected to spend huge amounts of money on things that used to be cheap.

As part of our effort to free ourselves from the corruptions of money, we in the educated elite spend a lot of time distancing ourselves from the moneyed elite, the people who are richer than us but less well educated. The members of the money class pour resources into big luxury items, like yachts and jewelry. They go in for products the lower classes could never purchase, such as foie gras, caviar, and truffles. But we in the educated elite go in for products the money classes would never purchase. We prefer to buy the same items as the proletariat—it's just that we buy rarefied versions of these items that the members of the working class would consider preposterous. So we will buy chicken legs, just like everybody else, but they'll likely be free-range chickens that in life were treated better than Elizabeth Taylor at a health spa. We'll buy potatoes, but we won't buy an Idaho spud. We'll select one of those miniature potatoes of distinction that grow only in certain soils of northern France. When we need lettuce, we will choose only from among those flimsy cognoscenti lettuces that taste so bad on sandwiches. The beauty of such a strategy is that it allows us to be egalitarian and pretentious at the same time.

Accordingly, we end up paying hugely inflated prices for all sorts of things that used to be cheap: coffee at $3.75 a cup, water at $5 a bottle, hemp clogs at $59 from Smith & Hawken, a bar of soap at $12, an Italian biscuit for $1.50, a box of gourmet noodles for $9.95, a bottle of juice for $1.75, and lemongrass at a few bucks a stalk.

Even our white T-shirts can run to $50 or more. We spend our money on peasant goods that are created in upscale versions of themselves. We are able to cultivate ever finer tastes about ever more simple things.

Rule 7. Members of the educated elite prefer stores that give them more product choices than they could ever want but which don't dwell on anything so vulgar as prices.

Members of the educated class are distinguished not only by what they buy but by how they buy. It's commonly observed, for example, that almost nobody in an upscale coffeehouse orders just a cup of coffee. Instead, one of us will order a double espresso, half decaf–half caffeinated, with mocha and room for milk. Another will order a vente almond Frappuccino made from the Angolan blend with raw sugar and a hint of cinnamon. We don't just ask for a beer. We order one of 16,000 microbrews, picking our way through winter ales, Belgian lagers, and blended wheats. Thanks to our influence on the market, all the things that used to come in just a few varieties now come in at least a dozen: rice, milk, tomatoes, mushrooms, hot sauces, breads, beans, and even iced tea (there are now at least 50 flavors of Snapple).

This is because educated people refuse to be merely pawns in a mass consumer society. Others may buy machine-made products or live in identical suburban tract homes or buy vulgar replicas of earlier vulgar mansions or eat conventional apples. But members of the educated elite do not want to be found to be derivative in their shopping oeuvre. We do not plagiarize our purchases. Shopping for us isn't just about picking up some stuff at the store. Rather, it is precisely by selecting just the right pasta bowls (hearty, not delicate; muted, not cute; Sienese, not Wedgwood) that an educated person can develop his or her own taste. In the realm of the Bobos, you become the curator of your possessions. You can, for example, be the Bernard Berenson of the mantelpiece, exercising your exquisite judgment in the realm of living room decor. You can choose candlesticks and picture frames that are eclectic and subversive—an array of statuettes and clocks that is at once daring and spontaneous yet also reflects an elegant unity of thought. You can push the boundaries of fireplace discourse, experimenting with new andirons and firewood formations. Each item you display will be understood to have been a rare "find." You will have picked it out from one of those new stores that organize themselves like flea markets. Thousands of less cultivated shoppers will have gone over it before but lacked the wit to stop and appreciate its ironic emanations. But there it sits on your mantel, a lasting tribute to your taste and slight eccentricity. If T. S. Eliot were alive today and of a mind, he'd open a chain of home furnishings stores called Objective Correlatives, and each object in them would be the physical expression of some metaphysical sentiment.

Nor is it ever enough just to buy something; one has to be able to discourse upon it. That is why, for example, the Lands' End catalogue doesn't just show off, say, a nice tweed jacket. It has little bits of text all around describing the Celtic roots of tweed, relating an interesting 14th-century legend about tweed, explaining why the best lambswool is sheared in the first six months of a lamb's life, and noting that the jacket is made by adorable old men with lined faces. The Lands' End people surround their advertisement with edifying articles by such writers as Garrison Keillor to let us know that the document we hold in our hands is not merely a catalogue but is actually more like one of those money-losing highbrow magazines.

In this and myriad other ways, the companies that sell to us have developed careful marketing strategies for people who disdain marketing. They help make shopping seem a bit like an honors project at Bennington College. We don't just look for a toothpaste. We assign ourselves a curriculum in toothpaste-ology. We learn about all the different options: whitening (we feel guilty that we are vain), gum protection (which is responsible), baking soda (organic and virtuous sounding, if perhaps a bit rough on the enamel). Then we study the brand names, musing over the big corporate brands, like Crest and Colgate, and the charming and socially conscious brands, like Tom's of Maine, which seems to be made by such nice, unpretentious people. And it's only when we are feeling tired and lazy at the airport store that we just go ahead and pick the toothpaste that has the nicest box.

The companies that appeal to educated consumers not only are informing us about things but are providing a philosophic context for their product. Coffee shops like Starbucks decorate their wall trim with texts—the apt Emersonian maxim or the ironic comment from Napoleon. Grocery stores provide brochures delineating the company's notions about community. Ice cream companies now possess their own foreign policy doctrines. These stores offend us if they dwell overmuch on utilitarian concerns—such as what a great bargain we are getting—but they win our loyalty if they appeal to our idealistic hopes. Volvo advertises a "car that can not only help save your life, but help save your soul as well." Toyota counters with a slogan for its line of trucks that reads, "Haul some concrete. Move some lumber. Save the world." Johnnie Walker Scotch announces, "In a Crass and Insincere World, Something That Isn't." The ABC Carpet & Home store on 19th Street and Broadway in New York endorses Keats's dictum "I am certain of nothing but of the holiness of the heart's affections and the truth of the imagination." I don't know what that means, but it sounds elevated.

The Rowenta company doesn't just try to persuade us that its irons really press out wrinkles. It sends out little catalogues called "The Feng Shui of Ironing." "In Feng Shui terms," the literature informs us, "a wrinkle is actually 'tension' in the fabric. Releasing the tension by removing the wrinkle improves the flow of ch'i." Similarly, the enlightened Williams-Sonoma catalogue doesn't try to flog us morally neutral sausages. The sausage links it advertises derive, the catalogue informs us, from the secrets of curing that Native Americans taught the first European settlers in Virginia (the mention of Native Americans gives the product six moral points right off the bat). The "sausages are made from pure pork and natural spices, using family recipes passed down through the generations." This is not some Upton Sinclair jungle but a noble lineage of craftsman sausage makers, and we members of the educated elite are willing to pay $29.50 for 24 little links in order to tap in to this heritage. Shopping, like everything else, has become a means of self-exploration and self-expression. "Happiness," as Wallace Stevens wrote, "is an acquisition."

Nor is it only our own selfish interests that we care about on our shopping forays. We want our material things to be bridges that will allow us to effect positive social change. We select our items from catalogues that have plain models in free-flowing dresses. It is by choosing just the right organic fiber shirt in the perfect tone of earth brown (the production of which involved no animal testing) that we use our consumption power to altruistically improve the world. We dine at restaurants that support endive cooperatives, and browse through department stores that have been endorsed by size-rights activists. We have put our Visa cards at the service of environmental concerns and so created a cleansing consumerism. And we put them away for the same reason. Some members of the educated elite can categorize their friends on the basis of which reason they give for boycotting tuna.

We members of the educated elite attach more spiritual weight to the purity of our food than to five of the Ten Commandments. And so we insist upon natural ingredients made by pesticide-averse farmers who think globally and act locally.

Midas in Reverse

Marx once wrote that the bourgeois takes all that is sacred and makes it profane. The Bobos take everything that is profane and make it sacred. We have taken something that might have been grubby and materialistic and turned it into something elevated. We take the quintessential bourgeois activity, shopping, and turn it into quintessential bohemian activities: art, philosophy, social action. Bobos possess the Midas touch in reverse. Everything we handle turns into soul.

3

Business Life

I'M HOLDING up traffic. I'm walking down the street in Burlington, Vermont, and I come to a corner and see a car approaching, so I stop. The car stops. Meanwhile, I've been distracted by some hippies playing Frisbee in the park, and I stand there daydreaming for what must be 15 or 20 seconds. The car waits.

In a normal city cars roll through these situations; if they see an opening, they take it. But this is Burlington, one of the most socially enlightened cities in America, and drivers here are aware that America has degenerated into a car-obsessed culture where driving threatens to crush the natural rhythms of foot traffic and local face-to-face community, where fossil-fuel-burning machines choke the air and displace the renewable energy sources of human loco-motion. This driver knows that while sitting behind the wheel, he is ethically inferior to a pedestrian like me. And to demonstrate his civic ideals, he is going to make damn sure that I get the right of way. No matter how long it takes.

Finally he honks politely and I wake up from my reverie and belatedly cross the street. But by the time I reach the next corner, I'm lost in my thoughts again, and seeing a car coming, I stop. This car stops too. And waits. I have to go through this embarrassing ritual about a dozen times before I finally adapt to local mores and trudge straight into the intersections. In Burlington we pedestrians have inherited the earth. Social enlightenment rules.

Burlington is a Latte Town.

Latte Towns are upscale liberal communities, often in magnificent natural settings, often university based, that have become crucial gestation centers for America's new upscale culture. They tend to be the birthplaces of the upscale retailers, gourmet bread stores, handmade furniture outlets, organic grocery stores, and the rest of the uplifting enterprises that make up Bobo consumer culture. Boulder, Colorado, is a Latte Town, as are Madison, Wisconsin; Northampton, Massachusetts; Missoula, Montana; Wilmington, North Carolina; and half of the towns in northern California, Oregon, and Washington state. There are, all told, hundreds of Latte Towns in America, and even in non-Latte Towns there are often Latte Neighborhoods. You know you're in a Latte Town when you can hop right off a bike path, browse in a used bookstore with shelves and shelves of books on Marxism that the owner can no longer get rid of, and then drink coffee at a place with a punnish name before sauntering through an African drum store or a feminist lingerie shop.

The ideal Latte Town has a Swedish-style government, German-style pedestrian malls, Victorian houses, Native American crafts, Italian coffee, Berkeley human rights groups, and Beverly Hills income levels. There should be some abandoned industrial mills that can be converted into lofts, software workstations, and organic brownie factories. And in utopia a Latte Town would have Rocky Mountain views to the west, redwood forests downtown, a New England lake along the waterfront, and a major city with a really good alternative weekly within a few hours' drive.

For most of this century, literary types have portrayed small towns as stifling enclaves of Babbittry and reaction, but today these micro-cities are seen as refreshing oases from mass society and as potential centers of community and local activism. To take a stroll down the pedestrian mall in Burlington, for example, you start at Leunig's, the indoor/outdoor bistro where some of the local business-men gather for breakfast each morning, wearing Timber-lands, no socks, collarless shirts, and jeans. An executive with flowing gray hair will be chatting amiably with an-other who sports a Jerry Garcia beard, their cell phones tucked into their black canvas briefcases. The Birkenstock sandal store around the corner will have a sign in the win-dow pointing out that its wares make nice corporate gifts.

As you stroll up the street, you see young parents pushing those all-terrain baby carriages that are popular with the outdoors set. The high-end fashion chain Ann Taylor has its Burlington outlet cheek by jowl with the Peace and Justice Store, nicely showing how haute couture now cohabits effortlessly with hippie thrift-shop eclecti-cism. The pedestrian mall is lined with upscale candy, muf-fin, and ice cream stores. There are any number of stores with playful names like Madhatter and Muddy Waters. Ironic allusions and oppressive wordplay are key ingredi-ents to the Latte Town sensibility, where people are not shy about showing off the cultural literacy (the University of Vermont sits up on the hill in Burlington, looking down on the commercial center and Lake Champlain beyond.) There are several fine bookstores in Burlington, of course. You can't get the *New Republic* or any magazine to its right, but you can browse through *Curve,* the wonderfully titled lesbian magazine, or any number of French glamour journals while listening to World Music or New Age disks like *Wolf Solitudes* on the headphones. The bookstores do carry some books on politics, but the current affairs sections tend to be tucked away in the back. The sections that are featured right at the front of the store, and that presumably do the most business, are the sex section, the psychology section, the cooking section, the ethnic studies section (which is mostly books about women), and the alternative lifestyle section (which is 80 percent about gay issues). And this does seem to be a pretty accurate reflection of local priorities.

Burlington boasts a phenomenally busy public square. There are kite festivals and yoga festivals and eating festivals. There are arts councils, school-to-work collaboratives, environmental groups, preservation groups, community-supported agriculture, antidevelopment groups, and ad hoc activist groups. The result is an interesting mixture of liberal social concern and old-fashioned preservation efforts to ward off encroaching modernism and, most important, development. And this public square is one of the features that draws people to Latte Towns. People in these places apparently would rather spend less time in the private sphere of their home and their one-acre yard and more time in the common areas.

If old-line suburbs like Wayne used to be the quintessential bourgeois suburbs, Latte Towns like Burlington and Berkeley used to be the epicenters of bohemian culture. They were once cultural opposites. But in Burlington, just as much as in Wayne, all that is changed. For the most striking thing about Latte Towns is that, though they are havens for everything that now goes by the name "alternative"—alternative music, alternative media, alternative lifestyles—they are also fantastic business centers. Towns like Napa are wine centers; Santa Monica and Soho have the cultural-industrial complex. University towns have everything from biotech to carpentry, and Burlington, too, is a thriving commercial hub. Ben & Jerry's, the most famous company in town, is not even among the 20 largest employers. People with Burlington mores now apparently feel comfortable working at IBM, which has a facility here, as do General Dynamic, GE, Bank of Vermont, and Blodgett Holdings. And business is chic in Burlington. There are four local business publications that heavily cover the town, and sometimes you can read two or three sentences in a row in each of them before some executive says something about the need for businesses to practice socially responsible investing.

The Couple's Business Guide, a featured book at the Burlington bookstores, tells about 10 couples who gave up careers in places like New York and Boston, moved up to Vermont, and started making and selling things like Positively Peach Fruit Sauce, Summer Glory Vinegar, and Putney Pasta. The case studies tend to start out with a highly educated couple disenchanted with their fast-lane urban lifestyle. They have a dream—to make the best jasmine bread in the world—so they move up to the Green Mountains and work slavishly to perfect their recipe. Then they discover how hard it is to market their product. But after five years of toil and tribulation, they have revenues of $5 million a year, and now they can rest on the veranda of their refurbished Victorian cottage with their lovely children, Dylan and Joplin, and savor the turning of the seasons.

George McGovern bought a New England bed-and-breakfast after giving up on politics, so perhaps it's inevitable that up here the man in the gray flannel suit should be replaced by the man in the weather-beaten clogs. Ben and Jerry, the ice cream mavens, represent the quintessence of Latte Town capitalism, and you can't go anywhere in Burlington without seeing an image of their two faces staring down at you, like a couple of scruffy Big Brothers.

I was sitting at an outside table at Leunig's one day, eating lunch, counting the total number of earrings my waitress had on her ears, nose, lips, and bellybutton (19, I think), and trying to read Thoreau's *Walden* (when in Rome . . .). But I kept getting distracted by an aging hippie at the next table who would not shut up about zero-based budgeting and the differences between preferred and common stock. Gray ponytailed and casual about his grooming, he was lecturing like a professor at the Harvard Business School to a young Woodstock wannabe in granny glasses and a peasant dress. She was taking notes on a yellow legal pad, and intermittently they would digress and talk about some bookkeeping practice or management technique they could adopt at their own company. And it has to be said that the aging hippie knew what he was talking about; his description of the capital markets was precise, clear, and knowledgeable.

It occurred to me as I was bouncing back between Thoreau and this conversation that *Walden* is in its own way a business book. Thoreau is constantly tallying up his expenses, and when he can turn his frugality into a profit he's not shy about boasting of his accomplishment. So maybe it's not surprising that the 1960s-era rebels who once lived on communes named Walden would, in the fullness of time, discover that business can be converted into a spiritually satisfying lifestyle. But the philosopher of Walden Pond would no doubt be a bit taken aback by how avidly the tree-hugging set has gone for the business culture.

Today's Latte Town mogul remembers that business is not about making money; it's about doing something you love. Life should be an extended hobby. Moreover, business, which was once considered soul destroying, can actually be quite enriching if you turn your profession into a craft, using natural products, like apples, and transforming them via old-fashioned artisanship into wholesome products like cider. In your packaging you can exercise high aesthetic judgment, employing cutting-edge artistic design to give your product a cosmopolitan feel. If you own a restaurant or an inn or a cafe, you can transform your business into a node of civil society, a meeting place with books and magazines and toys, where people can come to form a community. In this way business nourishes the whole person.

And the whole world. For surely the most famous feature of this kind of enlightened capitalism, which requires little description because it is so ubiquitous, is the way it links profits to progressive causes. You can save the rainforest, ease global warming, nurture Native American values, support family farms, spread world peace, and reduce income inequality, all without leaving the refrigerated aisles of the supermarket. It used to be thought that the pursuit of profit inevitably crushes values. But now many companies have determined that good values lead to greater profits—as long as there is a large educated populace willing to pay a little extra for the sake of social progress. "You can't separate your social goals from your business," says Judy Wicks, the founder of Philadelphia's leftist White Dog Cafe. Everybody makes fun of the excesses of cause capitalism—all those wheat germ toothpastes that don't kill the bacteria in your mouth, they just ask it to leave—but most educated people still favor the companies that share their values. Liberation marketing may be silly at times—there are now gardening companies that have dedicated themselves to solving the compost crisis—but it doesn't do much harm and it may do some good. Anyway, it's just another sign of how the activist ethos has been absorbed into mainstream America since the 1960s. And been altered by it, because while once people thought a true painting or a poem or a protest march could revolutionize society, now you have people such as Nike's Phil Knight who talk as if a sneaker can.

"The sensual pleasure of eating beautiful food from the garden brings with it the moral satisfaction of doing the right thing for the planet and yourself," former student radical and current upscale restaurateur Alice Waters told the *New Yorker* recently. Her outlet in Paris, she continued, is not really a business. Rather, as she wrote in its mission statement, it is "a platform, an exhibit, a classroom, a conservatory, a laboratory and a garden. It must be, in a phrase, an art installation in the form of a restaurant, expressing the sensuousness of food. . . . The restaurant must feel human, reflecting the spirit of the farm, the *terroir,* and the market, and it must express the humanity of the artisans, cooks and servers who work there."

The Countercultural Capitalists

Indeed, one of the ironies of the age is that the one realm of American life where the language of 1960s radicalism remains strong is the business world. If anything, the hippie moguls of Burlington are the mellow ones. If you want to find a place where the Age of Aquarius radicalism is in full force, you have to go higher up the corporate ladder into the realm of companies listed on the New York Stock Exchange. Thirty years after Woodstock and all the peace rallies, the people who talk most relentlessly about smashing the status quo and crushing the establishment are management gurus and corporate executives. It's the big mainstream business leaders that now scream revolution at the top of their lungs, like billionaire Abbie Hoffmans. It's Burger King that tells America, "Sometimes You Gotta Break the Rules." It's Apple Computer that lionizes "The crazy ones. The misfits. The rebels. The troublemakers." It's Lucent Technologies that adopted the slogan "Born to be wild." It's Nike that uses Beat writer William S. Burroughs and the Beatles song "Revolution" as corporate symbols. It's *Wired* magazine and its Silicon Valley advertisers who use the color schemes of 1968 Jefferson Airplane street posters.

And this tone is heard not only in the advertisements of companies that want to show how hip they are. The language of radicalism and rebellion is no less common in the business magazines or on the management channels on airplane headsets, or wherever else the ethos of American business culture is set. Home Depot's senior vice president urges his colleagues, "Think revolution, not evolution." Management gurus like Tom Peters stand in front of thousands of America's business elite and rave, "Destruction is cool!" Software companies have opened up offices in the Netherlands to help them recruit workers who want to live there to take advantage of the lax marijuana laws. Bob Dylan and Crosby, Stills and Nash now play concerts at private conferences hosted by Nomura Securities. Practically every company now portrays itself as a social movement, complete with apostate goals (smash the big competitors), a high social mission (a computer in every home), a revolutionary counterculture (Southwest Airlines calls itself "A Symbol of Freedom"). The dirtiest word in the corporate lexicon is *mainstream;* every company in America seems to be an evangelical enterprise rocking the establishment.

What's happened is simple enough. The Bobos have invaded the business world, and they have brought their countercultural mental framework with them to the old conference rooms of the bourgeoisie. It's no accident that the Bay Area, the center of the Summer of Love, is now also the home base for a disproportionate number of educated-class retailers, like the Gap, Restoration Hardware, and Williams-Sonoma. And there are also straitlaced Republicans who were never hippies but who have adopted a descendant of 1960s radicalism as a corporate philosophy. There is the hybrid culture of Silicon Valley, which mixes antiestablishment rebelliousness with Republican laissez-faire.

Especially in the business sectors dominated by information age elites—high technology, the media, advertising, design, Hollywood—business leaders have embraced an official ideology that will look very familiar to radicals and bohemians: constant change, maximum freedom, youthful enthusiasm, radical experimentation, repudiation of convention, and hunger for the new. You've got to think outside the box, the current cliché goes. You've got to be on the edge. You've got to be outside a box that's on the edge. If you're not braving the cutting edge, today's corporate leaders tell us, it's off to the ash heap of history. "Experience is out. Inexperience is in," says the founding editor of the new wave business magazine *Fast Company*. "I'm not interested in anything else but the youngest, the brightest, and the very, very talented," says Bernard Arnault, chairman of LVMH Moët Hennessy Louis Vuitton.

Today's countercultural capitalists live, or at least think they live, for new ideas, new thinking, new ways of thinking. Even the rules of language have changed. They use short sentences. Nouns become verbs. They eliminate any hint of a prose style and instead tend to talk like 15-year-old joystick junkies. Next year's cost projections? They're insanely great. The product pipeline? Way cool. How'd the IPO go? It cratered. The San Jose conference? Flipped my nuts. Serious mind rub. Real-time life experience. In their conversation and especially in their e-mail, they adopt the linguistic style of Jack Kerouac. Be spontaneous above all, the Beat poet advised. Be fast and free. Remove literary, grammatical, and syntactical formalism. Be wild and fluid so you can be pure and honest. "Something you feel will find its own form," Kerouac insisted. If Kerouac were alive today, he'd be reading to squads of enthralled vice presidents at corporate seminars in Aspen. Even dead, he is now starring in ads for Gap khakis.

I Am Not a Businessperson; I'm a Creator Who Happens to Do Business

In 1949 Leo Lowenthal wrote a much discussed essay in which he traced the evolution of profile stories in popular magazines, such as the *Saturday Evening Post.* His point was that in the early part of the century the "heroes of production" were celebrated, people who made bridges and dams and built companies. But more and more the magazines were shifting their attention to "heroes of consumption," such as movie stars and sports celebrities, who were the superstars of the leisure world. Even when politicians were profiled, he observed, the attention was on the hobbies and private personality of the subject, not his or her on-the-job accomplishments or behavior.

Today we are witnessing another redefinition of media heroism. If you look at the flattering profiles in the business magazines, you don't see men and women celebrated for being great builders or efficiency maximizers or tough-minded managers. The key is to be youthful, daring, and avant-garde, to personify change. The center of gravity of the American business culture has moved westward and youthward. Impressive formality has been replaced by open-minded daring. Corporate America has gone more casual. Microsoft executives appear on the cover of *Fortune* with beanie propeller hats on their heads. Others are photographed looking like mellowing rock stars, wearing expensive collarless linen shirts or multicolored sweaters and rag-wool socks under funky but expensive sandals. Often they'll be shown in jeans, standing proudly in the main hallway of a Rocky Mountain log mansion. You'd never find a bunch of people in blue suits, white shirts, and red ties in a software firm. These wild things will be wearing clunky boots, ripped jeans, tattered university sweatshirts, and those tiny European glasses that give you as much peripheral vision as an astigmatic worm.

In 1950s *Business Week* profiles, an executive would be shown sitting in an impressive mahogany and brass office or perhaps with his sleeves rolled up at a work site. Now the predominant visual prop is the wacky accoutrement. DreamWorks' Jeffrey Katzenberg will be shown with his Supersoaker water cannon. Others prefer Nerf guns or yo-yos or laser pens. Some will be lounging around their desk gazing at their kitsch collections. Richard Saul Wurman, an entrepreneur who stages conferences where countercultural capitalists pay big bucks to mind-meld, collects ashtrays (which, of course, are obsolete in the modern office). Others display a snowboard that is hanging from the ceiling next to an ominously broken piece of bungee cord. In Silicon Valley offices the remnants of a comic book collection may be tacked to the wall near the torn cover from a Curious George book or a photo of Gandhi. An amazing number of executives are pictured with domesticated birds like cockatoos perched on shoulders and heads, or with ugly dogs of obscure breeding panting on their laps. Marilyn Carlson Nelson, the CEO of the travel conglomerate Carlson Cos., poses with her in-line skates. Scott Cook, co-founder of Intuit, is depicted in the *Wall Street Journal* at his favorite lunch place, Taco Bell. These images up-end the old business style. Today's business leaders want to show they are playful free spirits. Members of the older business elite wanted their photos to show how much they embodied Benjamin Franklin's virtues: industriousness, thrift, reliability.

In 1963 Richard Hofstadter's *Anti-Intellectualism in American Life* described the anti-egghead prejudices of the business community. Moguls in Hofstadter's day considered intellectualism vaguely feminine and airy-fairy. Today the business leader wants to show he or she is a hero of intellection. The quintessential hero of the *Forbes* magazine profile doesn't only run an efficient business; he or she plays the flute, paints, explores, performs in a rock band with an ironic middle-aged name like Prostate Pretenders. "Sandy Lerner cofounded Cisco with her husband Len Bosack," *Forbes* writes. "Now she jousts, rides Harleys and supports animal rights and the study of British women writers. He funds weird science."

Mutual fund managers are depicted as cerebral superstars, memorizing baseball statistics, perfecting their piano technique, jetting off to bridge tournaments and philosophy symposia. Today corporate reports are often introduced with quotations from Emile Zola and Toni Morrison. Executives are busy "applying" the insights of classic thinkers to next quarter's sales strategy so they can be seen walking around with books with titles such as *Aristotle on Management* or *Shakespeare on Strategy* or *The LBO Secrets of Pliny the Younger.* Advertising executive Rosemarie Roberts tells the readers of *Fast Company* that her most influential books are *No Exit* by Jean-Paul Sartre ("Contains my basic philosophy on living: ultimately what goes around comes around") and Machiavelli's *The Prince* ("Focus, focus, focus"). They pepper their conversations with phrases like "That's a pretty interesting heuristic you've got there." Or "I don't see that surviving in the post-Gutenbergian era." Or "He's the best phenomenologist of all the vice presidents." They may snort derisively at some notion they regard as an overhyped meme. On the other hand, this will not prevent them from issuing pronouncements on the quarter hour: "Distance is dead"; "Progress has hypertrophied"; "Time has warped."

Once businessmen spoke with gravitas to project an image of calm and caution. Now they speak like sociological visionaries. Today being a CEO means that you have such lofty and daring theories and ideas that you need a team of minions chasing you around with ropes just to tie you down. And if you want to serve as consultant or guru to the corporate types, you've got to expand your mind ever bigger, to cosmic proportions. Everybody is trying to envision the Next Big Thing, and they unleash their imaginations with almost gold rush intensity.

You need a complete breakfast to keep up with the visionary thinking of today's business leaders. "We are at the very point in time when a 400-year-old age is dying and another is struggling to be born," announced Dee Ward Hock, the man responsible for the Visa card, who is now a management guru. "We're at a point of absolute, positive, supreme discontinuity," declares the consultant Watts Wacker. "So I don't study just change. I study how change is changing—the delta of the delta."

In *Fortune,* management guru Gary Hamel counters, "We live in a discontinuous world—one where digitalization, deregulation, and globalization are profoundly reshaping the industrial landscape. What we see is a dramatic proliferation of new economic life forms: virtual organizations, global consortia, net based commerce, ad infinitum. . . . We have reached the end of incrementalism in the quest to create new wealth. . . . There is an inflection point where the quest for divergence is transformed into a quest for convergence, and a new collective viewpoint emerges."

In this new era you've got to use the phrase "We're moving from an age in which . . ." a lot. After all, we are moving from a power society to a knowledge society, from a linear society to a postlinear society, from a hierarchical society to a networked society, from a skim milk society to a 2-percent-fat milk society. So everybody has to make lots of predictions. Moguls like Time Warner's Gerald Levin or Viacom's Sumner Redstone or TCI's John Malone don't mind if their predictions are proven false. The shareholders don't seem to mind! The important thing is to make predictions that are big and daring. Titans of the information age walk around comparing the size of their predictions. As long as their world historical paradigm is massive, they can dominate any room they enter. Bill Gates called his first book *The Road Ahead*. America went through a time when futurology was restricted mostly to gloomy science fiction writers. But now the mood has shifted. The future looks bright once again, and the oracles of the age are businesspeople with extravagant intellectual aspirations.

Of course, the radicalism and occasional utopianism of today's moguls are not exactly the same as the radicalism and utopianism of the student leaders of the 1960s. In some ways the business elites are just in love with the idea of radicalism. They are not as interested in specific ideas that would actually up-end the social order. An entire magazine, the *Baffler,* exists to point out the follies of this hip capitalism. Its editor, Thomas Frank, makes fun of the pseudo-transgressions of the corporate class and all their socially approved deviances. Actually, all this is another form of conservative conformity, Frank argues. But the *Baffler* is wrong to suggest it is all hypocrisy or that the capitalist bosses are merely co-opting the lovely ideals of the counterculture. In fact, it's not so sinister or so one-sided. These renegade executives are both corporate and genuinely countercultural. The two cultural rivals have embraced and co-opted each other.

The Intellectual Origins of the Cosmic Capitalists

Look at how thoroughly the standard critique of American business has been accepted by the leaders of American business. For a century writers and bohemians have been lambasting the businessman in such works as *The Jungle, Babbitt, The Great Gatsby, The Gilded Age, Death of a Salesman, Something Happened* (Joseph

Heller's business novel), and a thousand other novels, plays, movies, and TV shows (remember J. R. Ewing in *Dallas?*). In each case the businessman is anti-intellectual, antispiritual, conformist, and philistine. He is a strangled individual who has killed whatever tender or creative capacities he may once have had in order to climb the greasy pole and accumulate money. His workplace is an arid bureaucracy filled with petty schemers. To this portrayal today's business trendsetters respond, All true! Guilty as charged! They've simply gone out and tried to create a different kind of businessperson, one more in keeping with bohemian values.

In 1956 William H. Whyte wrote *The Organization Man*. Sociologists differ over how much the Organization Man existed in real life, but there is no question that the concept remains powerful in the mental framework of the educated class. Even those who have not read Whyte's book—and that includes almost everybody these days—have a picture of what the Organization Man is, and they know they don't want to be one. This Organization Man is content to be a cog in a great social machine. He feels that, alone, he is too weak to control his destiny, so he integrates himself into some large institution and surrenders to its imperatives. He believes that the organization offers him security and opportunity without any trade-offs between the two. "The young men have no cynicism about the 'system,' and very little skepticism," Whyte wrote; "they don't see it as something to be bucked, but as something to be cooperated with." Moreover, Whyte argued, they adopt a "social ethic" in which creativity and imagination are valued less than having a smooth and pleasing personality. The Organization Man was "obtrusive in no particular, excessive in no zeal."

Whyte was anticipating the sorts of arguments that would be made with greater fervor in the 1960s, particularly in the way he described the psychological effects of large organizations. The old kind of boss, Whyte said, wanted just your labor, but the new kind wanted "your soul."

Whyte's book is a brilliant broadside at the prevailing management theories of the time. He criticized companies that used personality tests to weed out those workers who might not adapt themselves to the group. He described science labs that purged quirky or difficult talents for the sake of efficiency. The companies he described sought well-socialized team players, not idiosyncratic visionaries. For example, Monsanto recruited scientists with a film that declared, "No geniuses here; just a bunch of average Americans working together." The Socony-Vacuum Oil Company distributed a booklet that read:

No Room For Virtuosos

Except in certain research assignments, few specialists in a large company ever work alone. There is little room for virtuoso performances. Business is so complex, even in its non-technical aspects, that no one man can master all of it; to do his job, therefore, he must be able to work with other people.

Whyte rejected the Organization Man's social ethos. He argued that the relationship between the individual and the organization was out of balance in American corporations. The needs of the group were overvalued and the needs of the individual were given short shrift. Whyte wasn't calling on people to drop out of organizations, merely to adjust the way they related to them. He advised the Organization Man to fight the organization, but not self-destructively. "He may tell the boss to go to hell," Whyte wrote, "but he is going to have another boss, and unlike the heroes of popular fiction, he cannot find

surcease by leaving the arena to be a husbandman."
Whyte was looking for a world in which individuals
would work within corporations, but as self-confident and
assertive individuals who would value their own needs at
least as highly as those of the organization. They would
have multiple loyalties. He was looking for organizations
that would value a person with quirky and creative genius,
not exile him because he wouldn't fit into some bureaucratic flow chart.

Technocracy

A decade later elements of Whyte's argument were
picked up by a more radical book that, in ways the author
could never have envisioned, would also have a tremendous influence on how today's capitalist conceives of business life. Theodore Roszak's *The Making of a Counter
Culture* was published in 1969, the smartest contemporary summary of the 1960s assault on the establishment.
Like Whyte, Roszak described an America dominated by
large organizations. Like Whyte, he analyzed the psychological wounds suffered by those who live and work
within these bureaucracies, which he preferred to call
technocracies. They exert a gentle tyranny on their victims, he wrote, making life comfortable and bland while
smothering individuality, creativity, and imagination. Like
Whyte, Roszak condemned the social ethic that emphasized congenial personalities and tepid social relations.

But there was a central difference between Whyte
and Roszak. Whyte was a reporter at *Fortune* magazine.
Roszak was a countercultural radical. While Whyte was
ambivalent about bourgeois values, Roszak's criticism of
the organization was much broader and deeper. He argued
that the problem with society wasn't just this or that management theory or this or that way of recruiting employees

into a company. Corporate structures were symptoms of a deeper cultural disease. For Roszak the real problem was the whole rationalistic mentality, which he called the objective consciousness.

"If we probe the technocracy in search of the particular power it holds over us," Roszak argued, "we arrive at the myth of objective consciousness. There is but one way of gaining access to reality—so the myth holds—and this is to cultivate a state of consciousness cleansed of all subjective distortion, all personal involvement. What flows from this state of consciousness qualifies as knowledge, and nothing else does. This is the bedrock on which the natural sciences have built; and under their spell all fields of knowledge strive to become scientific." Roszak is describing the counting-book mentality of the accountant, the cold scientist, the calculating businessman, the dry bureaucrat, the narrow engineer. The apotheosis of this consciousness, Roszak wrote, is the machine. The machine "is the standard by which all things are to be gauged." In the mind of the technocrat, companies, universities, and even nations are supposed to run as smoothly as a well-oiled machine.

So it's no wonder that people in organizations become cogs, machinelike. To hammer home this point, Roszak quoted the French writer Jacques Ellul:

> Technique requires predictability, and, no less, exactness of prediction. It is necessary, then, that technique prevail over the human being. For technique, this is a matter of life and death. Technique must reduce man to a technical animal, the king of the slaves of technique. Human caprice crumbles before this necessity; there can be no human autonomy in the face of technical autonomy. The individual must be fashioned by techniques . . . in order to wipe out the blots his personal determination introduces into the perfect design of the organization.

This is the constant bohemian critique. We could perceive truth and beauty if only we would stop to sense the world around us, but instead we enslave ourselves to artificial gods. We chain ourselves down with stifling social structures and inhuman ways of thinking. Bohemians had been bridling against these overrationalized ways of thinking since the days of Flaubert and his cronies in Paris. They had been seeking, as the transcendentalists did, more imaginative, mythopoetic, intuitional modes of perception. Like a century of bohemians before him, Roszak emphasized self-expression over self-control. He believed that self-expansion is the purpose of life. "What is of supreme importance," he wrote, "is that each of us should become a person, a whole integrated person in whom there is manifested a sense of the human variety genuinely experienced, a sense of having come to terms with a reality that is awesomely vast."

And Roszak's solution to the problem of technocracy was also bohemian. "The expansion of the personality is nothing that is achieved by special training, but by a naive openness to experience." He thought people living in industrial capitalist societies needed to rediscover more natural and more childlike modes of perception. "We must be prepared to trust that the expanded personality becomes more beautiful, more creative, more humane than the search for objective consciousness can make it." A more playful approach to life, he believed, could transform the reality around us: "This, so I have argued, is the primary project of our counter culture: to proclaim a new heaven and a new earth so vast, so marvelous that the inordinate claims of technical expertise must of necessity withdraw in the presence of such splendor to a subordinate and marginal status in the lives of men. To create and broadcast such a consciousness of life entails nothing less than the willingness to open ourselves to the visionary imagination in its own demanding terms."

Well, that was never going to work. If there was going to be a solution to the problems Whyte and Roszak identified with the organizational structure of American life, it wasn't going to be accomplished by the creation of a cosmic consciousness that would embarrass rationalistic thinking into submission. Roszak was being too grandiose. But that doesn't mean that he and Whyte were wrong when they criticized technocracies or the conformist and artificial social ethic they engendered. It simply means that it would take a more down-to-earth writer to provide a more practical way of rethinking organizations and social structures.

Jane Jacobs, Proto-Bobo

In fact, when Roszak was writing, the seeds of that rethinking had already been planted. In 1961 Jane Jacobs published *The Death and Life of Great American Cities*, which remains the most influential book on how Bobos view organizations and social structures.

Jane Jacobs was born in Scranton, Pennsylvania, in 1916, the daughter of a doctor and a teacher. After high school she went to work as a reporter for the *Scranton Tribune*. She lasted a year, then ventured to New York and worked in a series of jobs as a stenographer and freelance writer before landing a junior editorial position at *Architectural Forum*. In 1956 she gave a talk at Harvard expressing her skepticism about the High Modernist urban-planning philosophy that was sweeping away entire neighborhoods and replacing them with rows and rows of symmetrical apartment buildings, each surrounded by a windswept and usually deserted park. William H. Whyte invited her to turn her lecture into an article for *Fortune*, which, after some internal nervousness from the executives at Time Inc., was published as the essay "Downtown

Is for People." Jacobs then extended her argument in her book *The Death and Life of Great American Cities*. It's mostly about city planning, but Jacobs's vision transcends urban design. She creates in that book a description of the good life, a vision that has appealed to more and more people each year and that has attracted devoted followings on both the bohemian left and the bourgeois right.

At first glance, Jacobs seems pure bohemian. Here is a writer living in Greenwich Village, the bohemian Mecca. She is rising up to challenge the rationalists, the big devel opers who want to clear away neighborhoods and put up neat, orderly housing projects, parks, and high-tech expressways. She rails against monotony, sameness, and standardization. She is appalled by the rich and monumental tastes of the establishment. Meanwhile, she celebrates serendipity. Like any bohemian, she has a taste for exoticism, the African sculpture or the Romanian teahouse. She is a nonconformist, and she dresses in that downtown coffeehouse style that has since come back into fashion. In fact, her critics, the planners of the period, took her as an alienated bohemian and condemned her "bitter, coffee-house rambling."

But pause in the middle of *The Death and Life of Great American Cities* to see who the heroes of her ideal community are. Jacobs's most beautiful and influential passages describe life on her own little block of Hudson Street in Greenwich Village (pages 65–71 in the Modern Library edition). And the people who made life on that street so special were shopkeepers—Joe Cornacchia, the local deli owner, Mr. Koochagian, the tailor, Mr. Goldstein, the hardware store owner. Napoleon thought he had come up with the ultimate antibourgeois put-down when he called England a nation of shopkeepers. In bohemian literature up to that point, the small businessman had been taken as the epitome of petty-minded bourgeois values. But Jacobs does not disdain the merchants for being

grubby and materialistic. It is precisely their ordinary activities she admires: their bustle, their cleanliness, their
mundane neighborliness. One of them keeps the keys for
people in the neighborhood. Another trades local gossip.
They all keep an eye on the street. It is precisely their
bourgeois virtues that Jacobs admires.

That lovely, lyrical set piece describes the grocer, the
launderer, and the passersby as dancers in a ballet. She is
likening their movements to high art. A fruit man appears
and waves, the locksmith goes over to gossip with the
cigar store owner, kids roller-skate by, people gather
around the pizzeria. "The ballet is never at a halt," she
writes, "but the general effect is peaceful and the general
tenor even leisurely." It is hard to think of any passage of
prose that so sweetly describes the everyday world of the
ordinary street with the ordinary shops and their ordinary
rituals.

Jacobs's tone, in fact, is part of the secret to her success. It is not overcharged or histrionic, the way the voices
of contemporary writers like Jack Kerouac and later radicals like Theodore Roszak are. Neither is it pompous and
directive, the way much intellectual writing of the 1950s
is. Jacobs utterly rejects the utopianism and extremism
that were an integral part of romanticism. She rejects the
notion of the intellectual who is removed from the everyday world and lives instead in a world of ideas. As a result, she is relaxed and conversational. She is looking at
things with an eye for down-to-earth details (it may be no
accident that it was a woman who could exemplify this
way of observing reality). The urban planning of the
epoch may make Jacobs indignant, but she does not rain
thunderbolts down upon her enemies. She suggests the answer is not to theorize or to rebel, but simply to sit quietly
and be sensitive to our surroundings. The bourgeois epis-
temology often appealed to reason. The bohemian episte-
mology to imagination. Jacobs asks us to appreciate a

mode of perception that requires both sense and sensibility. It requires the practical knowledge of the shopkeeper as well as the sensitive awareness to surroundings that we might expect from a painter or novelist.

Most important, Jacobs reconciles the bourgeois love of order with the bohemian love of emancipation. A city street, she argues, looks chaotic, but it really is quite orderly. "Under the seeming disorder of the old city," she writes, "wherever the old city is working successfully, is a marvelous order for maintaining the safety of the streets and the freedom of the city. It is a complex order. Its essence is intricacy of sidewalk use, bringing with it a constant succession of eyes. This order is all composed of movement and change, and although it is life, not art, we may fancifully call it the art form of the city and liken it to the dance." This passage encapsulates the key reconciliations, freedom and safety, order and change, life and art. The good life, she implies, is composed of flux, diversity, and complexity, but underneath it all is an inner harmony.

The planners who destroyed neighborhoods did not see this because their conception of order was mechanical. The developers and Modernists like Le Corbusier saw the city as a machine—"a factory for producing traffic" in one of Le Corbusier's phrases—and so, of course, they sought to reduce it to a mechanism that would be simple and repetitive. But if you read Jacobs's description of the street, it becomes clear that she is not talking about a machine or even a place with all the connotations of rush and tension that many associate with city life. She is almost describing a forest. The shopkeepers come out onto the sidewalk almost like leaves choosing their own angle to catch the sun. The passersby come and go like animals, each performing his or her little unconscious service to the ecosystem. Jacobs is seeing the city in organic terms, not in mechanical terms. She has taken the pastoralism of Emerson and Thoreau and reconciled it with modern urban life. The city was always thought of as the ultimate renunciation of nature, but here she treats the healthy city almost as a work of nature.

In order for the ecosystem to function, it must have many different players. It must have diversity. The word *diversity,* which has become one of the key words of our age, was central in *The Death and Life of Great American Cities.* The entire second section of the book is called "The Conditions for City Diversity." It is complexity she admires, the small unplanned niches where specialized activities can thrive. These are places whose use is not determined from above but grows up from small particularized needs.

In the years since *The Death and Life of Great American Cities* was published, Jacobs's way of seeing has been vindicated again and again. The urban plans she criticized are now universally reviled. The disastrous failure of social-engineering projects across the developing world have exposed the hubris of technocrats who thought they could reshape reality. The failure of the Communist planned economies has taught us that the world is too complicated to be organized and centrally directed. We are, with Jane Jacobs, more modest about what we can know, more skeptical of planners and bureaucrats. We're more likely to trust modest individuals like Jacobs, who take the time to sit quietly and observe closely.

The Pastoral Organization

Now we can return to the workplace of today. If you look at today's management theorists or the restructuring that has been instituted by cutting-edge companies, you are immediately struck by how deeply they have been influenced first by Whyte's and Roszak's objections to the old business structures and then by Jacobs's vision of what constitutes a healthy community. Today's executives will tell you, and they will tell you again and again until you want to plug up your ears with cotton, how fervently they have rejected the old Organization Man models. "Organizations are disappearing!" Tom Peters shouts at his audiences. "At HP, people don't become cogs in some giant corporate machine," the recruiting literature from Hewlett Packard opens. "From their first day of work here, people are given important responsibilities and are encouraged to grow." Indeed, the companies that are celebrated by the management gurus are those that have stood the Organization Man on his head. Companies like DreamWorks throw out job titles because they seem too hierarchical. Others boast of cutting their management layers from seven to three, from fourteen to four. Companies today, the mantra goes, have to think biologically. They have to create lean, decentralized, informal participatory systems. They have to tear down rigid structures and let a thousand flowers bloom. The machine is no longer held up as the standard that healthy organizations should emulate. Now it's the ecosystem. It's the ever-changing organic network that serves as the model to define a healthy organization, filled with spontaneous growth and infinitely complex and dynamic interconnections.

Big companies break themselves up into flexible small teams to create what some experts call "ensemble individualism." Pitney Bowes Credit Corporation has actually designed its offices in Connecticut to resemble a small village, with cobblestone-patterned carpets, faux gas lamps, a town square–style clock, and street signs at the intersections of the hallways—Main Street crosses Center Street and so on. At AOL's building, Creative Center One, desks are arranged into neighborhoods where workers brainstorm with their neighbors for the project amidst Silly Putty sculptures and piles of caffeinated beverages. At Inhale Therapeutic Systems, chairman Robert Chess got rid of executive offices; now everybody sits in large areas called "bullpens," where they can bounce ideas off each other all day. The hearing aid firm Oticon puts everybody's desks on wheels so they can be wheeled around the vast workspace and grouped according to the ensemble arrangement of the moment. (Oticon is only one of many firms experimenting with the schools-without-walls concept that was popular with progressive educators in the 1960s.) At Procter & Gamble, elevators, which are thought to destroy give-and-take conversations, are out, while escalators, which are thought to enhance them, are in. Nickelodeon installed extra-wide stairs to encourage exchange and schmoozing. IDEO, another design company, has long rolls of butcher paper spread out over conference tables for brainstorming and doodling. All these companies and hundreds of others are trying to recreate little Jane Jacobs environments, complete with chance meetings, spontaneous exchanges, small gathering places, and the sort of constant flexibility that is really a dynamic order.

In the old organization it was the system that was king. Now, so we are told, relationships matter most. In 1967 Kenneth Keniston completed *Young Radicals,* a study of the 1960s counterculturalists in which he observed that "in manner and style, these young radicals are extremely 'personalistic,' focused on face-to-face, direct and open relationships with other people; hostile to formally structured roles and traditional bureaucratic patterns of power and authority." That's an excellent summary of the management philosophy that prevails today in corporate America. Now companies go on expensive retreats at which employees play noncompetitive games or wacky Olympics to build those relationships.

Information age companies are also trying to provoke a certain type of thinking. Gone is the old emphasis on scientific analysis and narrow specialization. Gone are

Robert McNamara–style rationalists with their sharp white shirts. Now messy desks are admired, along with the tousle-haired geniuses who sit behind them. Companies hire hyperkinetic motivators to serve as in-house Ken Keseys and inspirational Merry Pranksters. Gordon MacKenzie is an aging hippie who wears bright tie-dyed shirts and blue jeans and goes from corporation to corporation exhorting them to "orbit the giant hairball." The hairball in his lexicon is the bureaucracy, and to orbit it is to spin out into an individualized realm of creative vibrancy. MacKenzie worked for 30 years at Hallmark, ending up with the self-invented job title "creative paradox." Now he does consulting for IBM, Nabisco, and the FBI— not exactly the outfits that one associates with Byronic romanticism. Creativity is seen as the new key to productivity, having replaced the Organization Man's virtue, efficiency.

ZEFER, a Boston-based Internet consulting firm, asks job applicants to take a "Lego/Play-Doh Test" so their creative faculties can be evaluated. Kodak has "humor rooms" with games, toys, and Monty Python videos. Ben & Jerry's has a Joy Committee to liven things up. Rosenbluth International has a "thought theater" where employees can watch videos selected by the manager for culture development. Paul Birch worked as a "corporate jester" at British Airways. Meanwhile, the "learning person" at Xerox Business Services threw a "learning Woodstock" session, held in a dark room with moons and stars and planets hanging from the ceiling.

A lot of this, especially at the extremes, is silly. But at their best, today's management techniques do follow in Jane Jacobs's epistemological footsteps. They are based on the idea that the best way to learn and think is not by breaking problems down to their narrowest specializations, as a technocrat does, but on the contrary, by being sensitive to the flow and rhythms of the situation. These techniques encourage employees to see old problems in new ways, to be imaginative, to feel their way intuitively to deeper understandings of the reality that confronts them. The marketplace is not to be conceived of as a machine but as an organism filled with feedback mechanisms, interconnections, and flux.

Metis

In other words, the companies are trying to cultivate in their employees a faculty that in classical times was known as *metis*. This is an ancient Greek term that has been revived by Yale anthropologist James C. Scott. The French might call metis *savoir faire*. We might call it practical knowledge, cunning, or having a knack for something. Odysseus was the model of a person with metis because of his ability to improvise his way through unexpected situations. Scott himself defines metis as "a wide array of practical skills and acquired intelligence in responding to a constantly changing natural and human environment."

This trait cannot be taught or memorized. It can only be imparted and acquired. The philosopher Michael Oakeshott would say that you can study grammar in a classroom, but the ability to speak can only be acquired slowly through experience. Similarly, metis is acquired as a series of random acquisitions that only gradually form a whole picture. People sharing metis do not lecture; they converse. They work side by side. To acquire metis, a person must not only see but see with comprehension. He or she must observe minutely to absorb the practical consequences of things. He or she must develop a feel for the process, for the interrelationships of things. The person who acquires metis must learn by doing, not by reasoning or dreaming.

For example, an apprentice may learn the rules of cooking, but only a master chef will have the awareness to know when the rules should be applied and when they should be bent or broken. A graduate student may read a book on pedagogy, but only a metis-rich teacher will be able to guide and lead a class. Metis exists only when it is in use; often the person who has it will not be able to put his or her gifts or methods into words. It is an awareness of the flow of things, knowing which things can go together and which can never go together, which way to react when the unexpected happens. It means being able to tell what is really important and what is mere distraction. Isaiah Berlin was getting at metis when he wrote in his classic essay "The Hedgehog and the Fox": "It is not scientific knowledge, but a special sensitiveness to the contours of the circumstances in which we happen to be placed; it is a capacity for living without falling foul of some permanent condition or factor which cannot be altered, or even fully described or calculated." This sort of knowledge consists in perpetual improvisation, a sort of wise muddling through. Rejecting universal solutions, the person who prizes metis welcomes a diversity of approaches, to use that word which was so important to Jane Jacobs and all subsequent Bobos.

In this atmosphere leadership is also perceived differently. The CEO is no longer a chess grand master, an imposing, aloof figure moving pieces around the board. Now he or she is likely to be portrayed, and to portray himself or herself, as an inspirer, a motivator, or an orchestra leader. Today's CEOs boast about trying to inspire the creativity in others. With their hair-trigger sensitivity to authoritarianism or repressive authority structures, they talk about fostering collaborative relationships. The good ones do not so much dominate as lead by example, as head artist in the workshop. For example, hanging around the corporate headquarters of Restoration Hardware in Marin County for a few days, I was struck by the number of times employees praised CEO Stephen Gordon for being "loose" and "real." His associates happily recount the time Gordon led a water balloon fight and a game of Red Rover during their company retreat. Gordon's clothing is just as casual as everybody else's at the place. His office is not especially bigger or nicer than the offices of the people who work for him. The company has a liberal dog policy, so when people bring their pooches to work, they can wander into his space as freely as anybody else's. Twice a week the buyers at Restoration hold meetings to determine which new items they should carry in their stores, and in keeping with the quasi-egalitarian ethos of Bobo enterprises, everybody at the meeting gets a vote, but somehow Gordon's is decisive. The buyers happily admit that for all the creativity each of them brings to their jobs they are really just executing Gordon's vision. And so we arrive at one of the paradoxes of information age enterprises: though they flatten hierarchies and promote equality, today's CEOs tend to dominate their companies even more than those at the old corporations. In the companies Whyte described, the ethos of the organization set the tone; now it is the vision of the charismatic leader. As Xerox's John Seely Brown told *Fortune,* "The job of leadership today is not just to make money. It's to make meaning."

The Higher Selfishness

As in so many spheres of Bobo life, all that was profane has been made holy. Businesspeople talk like artists. Corporations enthuse about their social missions. Managers emphasize creativity and liberation. Phenomenally successful corporate consultants like Stephen Covey seem more like spiritual advisers than efficiency experts. Meanwhile in this through-the-looking-glass world of capitalism, the people in the marketing department talk about how much they detest marketing. The CEO says he is ambivalent about expansion. The zillionaires say they are in it for the self-expression, not the money. "The money hasn't changed a thing," Rob Glaser of RealNetworks told the *Wall Street Journal* in one interview. "The money has not changed a thing in my life," Steve Case of America Online told the *Journal* in another. "The money has not changed a thing in my life," said Jeff Bezos of Amazon.com in a third.

Workers in this spiritualized world of Bobo capitalism are not the heroes of toil. They are creators. They noodle around and experiment and dream. They seek to explore and then surpass the full limits of their capacities. And if a company begins to bore or stifle them, they're gone. It is the ultimate sign of privilege—to be able to hit the road in search of new meaning whenever that little moth of tedium flies in the door. Self-cultivation is the imperative. With the emphasis on self.

So this isn't a crass and vulgar selfishness, about narrow self-interest or mindless accumulation. This is a higher selfishness. It's about making sure you get the most out of yourself, which means putting yourself in a job that is spiritually fulfilling, socially constructive, experientially diverse, emotionally enriching, self-esteem boosting, perpetually challenging, and eternally edifying. It's about learning. It's about working for a company as cool as you are. It's about finding an organization that can meet your creative and spiritual needs. When Anne Sweeney contemplated taking over the presidency of the Disney Channel, she didn't think in résumé or financial terms. She asked herself, "Would this job make my heart sing?" and she decided yes. The PR firm Porter Novelli doesn't recruit employees with appeals to crass self-interest. Instead, it runs ads in various magazines showing a young woman in jeans sitting on a rocky beach. The copy asks, "What do *you* want?" The answer, expressed in the woman's voice, is this:

> I want to write my own ticket. High tech is a wide-open field. I'm helping to create public relations programs for companies that are on the leading edge of software development. What I'm learning is making one fabulous career. I want to hit the beach. I grew up on the West Coast. The ocean has always been my second home. Whenever I need to think things through, this is where I come. I want to keep climbing. Each year, my role gets bigger. My managers support my growth with professional development and mentoring programs. It's like being back in college. I want to go to Africa. Next year, I hope. (Incidentally, our health insurance plan is great.) I want to be my best. If there's a limit to what I'm capable of achieving, I'm not sure where it is or when I'll reach it. Never, I hope.

This is Bobo capitalism in a nutshell. College, learning, growth, travel, climbing, self-discovery. It's all there. And it's all punctuated with that little word "I," which appears in that short paragraph 15 times. The Organization Man is turned upside down. Whyte described a social ethos that put the group first. The current ethos puts "me" first.

Work thus becomes a vocation, a calling, a metier. And the weird thing is that when employees start thinking like artists and activists, they actually work harder for the company. In the 1960s most social theorists assumed that as we got richer, we would work less and less. But if work is a form of self-expression or a social mission, then you never want to stop. You are driven by a relentless urge to grow, to learn, to feel more alive. Executives who dreamed of turning themselves into refined gentlemen may have valued leisure, but executives who aspire to be artists value work. Companies learn that Bobos will knock themselves out if they think they are doing it for their spiritual selves, for their intellectual development. Lee Clow is chairman of the advertising firm TBWA Worldwide. He has established a set of work expectations that would have led to strikes decades ago. Now they are considered enlightened. "It's a rare weekend in this agency when you won't find people at work," he told the *Wall Street Journal* a few years ago. "Sometimes I'm asked what I say to people to get them to work on Saturday and Sunday. We don't say anything. But our creative people know what we expect from them. They know they'll have a chance in this big sandbox. It's designed to be a stimulating place, a fun place, an interactive place, a social place." Don't dare call it a sweatshop. It's a sandbox! This isn't business. This is play!

The Cultural Contradictions of Capitalism—Resolved!

In 1976 Daniel Bell wrote an influential book, *The Cultural Contradictions of Capitalism*. He argued that capitalism is built upon two contradictory impulses. People in a capitalist society have to be self-disciplined and a bit ascetic so they will show up to the factory on time and work hard. But they also have to be acquisitive and a little hedonistic so they will constantly want to consume more and more of the things they make. Following Max Weber, Bell thought that for a long time the Protestant Ethic had reconciled these two impulses into a single belief system. But, Bell argued, the Protestant Ethic was fading. He foresaw a world in which self-restraint had become extinct. He located two primary culprits: first, the culture of romanticism, which sought to destroy order, convention, and tradition for the sake of sensation, liberation, and self-exploration, and second, capitalism's need to continually stoke ever greater levels of consumption. Once you had massive consumer credit without shame, Bell argued, people would discover that consuming was more fun than self-restraint and begin to live more and more for the pleasures of the moment. Hedonism would increasingly trump frugality, and display would increasingly replace modesty. In Bell's future world, "the culture was no longer concerned with how to work and achieve, but with how to spend and enjoy," he wrote.

In the 1970s Bell saw antinomianism, the feeling that people should be freed from laws and restraints by virtue of personal grace, all around him. Indeed, it seemed to many that the work ethic was eroding, that the ladder of ambition was being delegitimized. Bell's thesis struck a chord. It seemed plausible to think that capitalism would unleash cultural forces that would end up destroying it.

But it hasn't happened. On the contrary, the people most influenced by the romantic cultural forces Bell described, the Berkeley-style baby boomers, have become hard-working capitalists, oriented toward the long term. The hedonism of Woodstock mythology has been domesticated and now serves as a management tool for the Fortune 500. Americans haven't even adopted European-style vacation schedules. Instead, they pull all-nighters at Microsoft and come in weekends at Ben & Jerry's. And the people who speak most devoutly about smashing order and instituting a perpetual revolution—the capitalists of the corporate world—are the ones who strive most earnestly for success. This is Modernism for the shareholders. Bell looked at America and observed a culture that emphasized antirational hedonism, and he saw an economic structure that depended on technocratic reason.

He concluded that the two forces must clash. Instead, they've blurred to create something new.

Countercultural capitalists are not restrained by the old puritanical or Protestant code. Instead, they have constructed their own ethos that creates a similar and perhaps more rigorous system of restraint. They have transformed work into a spiritual and intellectual vocation, so they approach their labor with the fervor of artists and missionaries. Their collars may not be buttoned up and their desks may not be neat, but they are, after a fashion, quite self-disciplined. Members of the educated class often regard work as an expression of their entire being, so of course they devote themselves to it with phenomenal energy. For many there is no time when they are not at work; they are always thinking.

Nor do the denizens of the Latte Town microindustries or the surfers in the countercultural workstation go in for the lavish display and hedonistic lifestyle that Bell predicted. They have created an ethos of environmentalism, healthism, and egalitarianism that makes it bad form to live in the ostentatious style that characterized the old moneyed elite. This, too, serves as a substitute for the restraint system of the much-debated Protestant Ethic. If these people believe in nothing else, they believe that you shouldn't damage your own body, which means that drinking, drugs, and carousing are out. Coffee shops replace bars as the central gathering places. As we'll explore in greater detail in later chapters, self-disciplined activities like jogging and cycling are in; by working out, these people have reduced even leisure time to a form of self-discipline.

The 1960s unleashed wild liberationist forces into American society, but that antinomianism has merged with the enterprising ethos we associate with the 1980s. This fusion has legitimized capitalism among the very people who were its most ardent critics, and it has legitimized countercultural poses amongst the business elites. Whatever its flaws, the Bobo ethos has been fantastically good for the bottom line. American businesses have thrived over the past decade and established American dominance in sector after sector. American companies are creative and efficient at the same time. Bell thought he was witnessing the end of the bourgeoisie, but at the moment it looks as if the bourgeoisie has, in fact, revived itself by absorbing (and being absorbed by) the energy of bohemianism.

4

Intellectual Life

IN 1954, Irving Howe wrote an essay for *Partisan Review* called "This Age of Conformity." His subject was the degradation of American intellectual life. "The most exciting periods of American intellectual life tend to coincide with the rise of bohemia," Howe argued. Ideas and innovations pour forth at these moments, when thinkers and artists detach themselves from bourgeois life, with its well-worn customs and conventions, and live apart in the realms of art, ideas, and spirit. But Howe sensed that the idea of bohemia was beginning to lose its force. And the culprit was money. "Some intellectuals, to be sure, have 'sold out' and we can all point to examples, probably the same examples," Howe noted. "But far more prevalent and far more insidious is that slow attrition which destroys one's ability to stand firm and alone: the temptations of an improved standard of living." Intellectuals, to use Howe's words, were no longer standing "firm and alone." They were going to work for government agencies. They were sitting on public committees, going on lecture tours, writing for mass publications, and teaching adult education classes. In sum, they were putting a foot in the worlds of commerce and politics.

What was lost in this process, Howe continued, was "the whole intellectual vocation—the idea of a life dedicated to values that cannot possibly be realized by a commercial civilization." In joining with mainstream bourgeois culture, intellectuals, Howe felt, were surrendering their total freedom. They were debasing themselves. Indeed, Howe wrote, in lamentation mode, "Writers today have no choice, often enough, but to write for magazines like the *New Yorker*—and worse, far worse." Some who did so survived with their independence intact, he concluded, but "for every short-story writer who has survived the *New Yorker* one could point to a dozen whose work became trivial and frozen after they had begun to write for it."

Well, if the Irving Howe of 1954 was upset by what was going on then, it's a good thing he's no longer around to see what is going on now. These days it doesn't even occur to us to fear for a writer's literary soul if we find her writing in the *New Yorker*. We don't feel a novelist has sold out if he gets a book on the bestseller list. We don't object much if tenured professors go off on lucrative lecture tours. Better them than yet another squad of motivational speakers. Today we have almost entirely lost the belief, which was still common in Howe's day, that intellectuals should cut themselves off from commerce and from pop-culture temptations. Just as the cultural forces of the information age have created businesspeople who identify themselves as semi-artists and semi-intellectuals, so nowadays intellectuals have come to seem more like businesspeople. We now use phrases like "the marketplace of ideas," "intellectual property," and "the attention economy" to meld the realm of the mind with the realm of the market. Intellectuals have seen their job descriptions transformed. Once so aloof, they now mingle with the rest of the educated elite, producing a new sort of intellectual for the new Bobo age.

From today's vantage point, the intellectual landscape of the 1950s really is a strange and unfamiliar place. When you go back to the writings of Lionel Trilling, Reinhold Niebuhr, Sidney Hook, William Barrett, Hannah Arendt, and the crowd that contributed to *Partisan Review,* you are struck immediately by the tone of high seriousness that prevailed. Those intellectuals went in for big "The World in All Its Aspects" essay topics that would be regarded as pompous by most writers today. Niebuhr wrote a book called *The Nature and Destiny of Man,* which certainly covers a lot of ground. They adopted prose styles that, while clear and elegant, were also portentous and loaded with authority and learning.

They were not shy on the subject of their own importance. They spent lots of time signing petitions, making statements, convening congresses, and otherwise taking "stands." Their memoirs are filled with intellectual melodrama: When Edmund Wilson published his review of so-and-so, they recount, we knew life would never be the same again, as if a book review could alter reality, as maybe in those days it could. They considered themselves, and perhaps were, shapers of history. "A single stroke of paint, backed by work and a mind that understood its potency and implications, could restore to man the freedom lost in twenty centuries of apology and devices for subjugation," wrote the painter Clyfford Still, apparently without being ridiculed. They went in big for capital letters. "These three great forces of mind and will—Art, Science and Philanthropy—have, it is clear, become enemies of Intellect," Jacques Barzun declared in 1959, launching off into characteristically grand territory. And they issued the sort of grand and often vaporous judgments that today strike us as ridiculous. Here's a statement by Bertrand Russell featured on the cover of *Dissent* in the fall of 1963, which embodies the tone of heroic denunciation that you can muster only if you have drunk deeply from the cup of your own oracular majesty:

> Kennedy and Khrushchev, Adenauer and de Gaulle, Macmillan and Gaitskell are all pursuing a common aim: the ending of human rights. You, your families, your friends and your countries are to be exterminated by the common decision of a few brutal but powerful men. To please these men, all private affections, all the public hopes, all that has been achieved in art and knowledge and thought, and all that might be achieved thereafter is to be wiped out forever.

At the heart of this style was an exalted view of the social role of the intellectual. In this view the intellectual is a person who stands apart from society, renouncing certain material advantages and instead serving as conscience for the nation. Intellectuals are descendants of Socrates, who was murdered by the polis because of his relentless search for truth. They are inspired by Emile Zola's *J'Accuse,* which confronted orthodoxy and challenged authority in the name of higher justice. They are influenced by the Russian notion of the *intelligentsia,* a secular priesthood of writers and thinkers who participated in national life by living above it in a kind of universal space of truth and disinterestedness, rendering moral judgments on the activities below. One of the most influential descriptions of the intellectual's Olympian role—as the intellectuals themselves conceived it—was written by Edward Shils in a

1958 essay, "The Intellectuals and the Powers: Some Perspectives for Comparative Analysis":

> In every society . . . there are some persons with an unusual sensitivity to the sacred, an uncommon reflectiveness about the nature of the universe, and the rules which govern their society. There is in every society a minority of persons who, more than the ordinary run of their fellow men, are inquiring, and desirous of being in frequent communion with symbols which are more general than the immediate concrete situations of everyday life, and remote in their reference from both time and space. In this minority, there is a need to externalize the quest in oral and written discourse, in poetic and plastic expression, in historical reminiscence or writing, in ritual performance and acts of worship. This interior need to penetrate beyond the screen of immediate concrete experience marks the existence of intellectuals in every society.

That's a stark social divide. On the one side is the vast majority who live in a world of "concrete situations." On the other are the few whose lives are defined by their "sensitivity to the sacred" and their "reflectiveness about the nature of the universe." But this gap was absolutely essential to the intellectuals of the day, in Europe and to a lesser extent in the United States, because it was only by staying aloof from society that they could see it clearly and honestly, or so they believed. In a later book called *The Life of the Mind*, Hannah Arendt made this point by quoting a parable ascribed to Pythagoras: "Life is like a festival; just as some come to the festival to compete, some to ply their trade, but the best people come as spectators, so in life the slavish men go hunting for fame or gain, the philosophers for truth." Only the thinker who frees himself from large organizations and worldly alliances can hope to perceive that truth, argued C. Wright Mills in *Power, Politics and People:* "The independent artist and intellectual are among the few remaining personalities equipped to resist and to fight the stereotyping and consequent death of genuinely living things."

Intellectuals in the 1950s sometimes seemed to nurture this sense of embattlement, of continually being under assault from the coarse world of commerce. They armed themselves against invasions by journalism, advertising, and the celebrity culture, fighting off the Babbitts and the philistines. "The hostility of the common man toward the intellectual is of all times and places," wrote Jacques Barzun in *The House of Intellect.* Richard Hofstadter's *Anti-Intellectualism in American Life* was a salvo in the war between mind and matter.

The biggest threat to the independent intellectual was money and its temptations. Commerce was the enemy of art. Norman Mailer got into a lot of trouble with his intellectual friends when his novel *The Naked and the Dead* became a bestseller. Its commercial success was taken as prima facie evidence that there was something wrong with it. And commercial culture didn't just attack intellect head-on with crass financial offers. It came up disguised in Trojan Horse form as middlebrow culture.

It's hard now to understand the ferocity highbrow intellectuals of the 1950s brought to bear in their assault on the middlebrow. Middlebrow culture was the sort of popular but moderately high-toned writing, art, and music that could be found in magazines like *Saturday Review* (which ran such turgid headlines as "The Future Belongs to the Educated Man" and "Art: Giver of Life and Peace") or in books recommended by the Book-of-the-Month Club or in the plays of Thornton Wilder. Middlebrows consumed high culture with an air of worthy self-congratulation, because it is good for you. Looking back on the middlebrow culture of the 1950s, it seems a little dull and pretentious but well intentioned, and certainly better than some of the proudly illiterate culture that has taken its place.

But that is not how highbrows of the 1950s saw it. They attacked it with a viciousness that takes your breath away. Virginia Woolf had decades earlier fought the same war, calling the middlebrow "sticky slime" and "a pernicious pest." Clement Greenberg called it an "insidious" force that was "devaluating the precious, infecting the healthy, corrupting the honest and stultifying the wise." Dwight Macdonald wrote the most famous attack in an essay called "Masscult and Midcult," in which he blasted the "tepid ooze" of the Museum of Modern Art and the American Civil Liberties Union and summarized middlebrow culture as "the danger . . . the enemy outside the walls . . . the swamp."

Middlebrows were not interested in joining a secular priesthood devoted to ideas. Rather, they wanted to take the realm of ideas and drag it back to earth, into the clutches of middle-class America and commercial mediocrity. They wanted to co-opt intellect and make it serve the utilitarian interests and amusements of the bourgeoisie. They wanted to read the Great Books to impress friends, to add sparkle to their conversation. The intellectuals had to crush the tentacles of commercial culture, even if it snuck up bearing reproductions of Michelangelo.

Intellectual Entrepreneurs

There is something admirable and at the same time delusionally self-confident about the intellectual self-image of this era. Who wouldn't want to live with such passionate commitment to ideas? And in truth, in those days books and ideas did seem to matter more. At the same time, the self-importance of those thinkers was often hard to take. In cutting themselves off from political insiders, intellectuals cut themselves off from the reality of what was going on. They invented conspiracies; they made bold pronouncements about the state of things that look absurdly gloomy in retrospect. In any case, today all that is as dead as the dinosaurs. Now intellectuals tend to minimize or deny the gap between themselves and everyone else, not defend it. The central feature of the information age is that it reconciles the tangible with the intangible. It has taken products of the mind and turned them into products of the marketplace. So, of course, the bifurcations that were so important to the intellectuals of the 1950s would seem archaic in this new age. Today a young college student who wants to become an intellectual looks out into the world and does not see awesome literary critics with the authority of an Edmund Wilson or a Lionel Trilling. But he or she will see dozens of academic stars, people who cross lines by succeeding in intellectual realms and also on TV, in private consulting firms or on op-ed pages, themselves a hybrid institution that didn't exist in the 1950s. The young intellectual will see such six-figure celebrities as Henry Louis Gates, the entrepreneurial Harvard professor who also hosts documentaries for PBS, writes for the *New Yorker* and *Talk,* and seems to spawn an infinite variety of conferences, encyclopedias, and other projects; Henry Kissinger, who emigrated from studies of Metternich to politics to economic consulting; Duke's Stanley Fish, who is often off on a lecture circuit road show with a conservative counterpart; E. J. Dionne, who serves as a public intellectual from the ever expanding world of think tanks; and Esther Dyson, who spins out her theories at expensive technology conferences.

In the 1970s a group of conservative intellectuals developed the theory of the New Class, which posited that a small and politically liberal intellectual class had gained disproportionate influence over American culture by controlling the commanding heights of academia, media, and culture. But with the rise of a mass educated class, it has become ever more difficult to draw the line between the world of the intelligentsia and the rest of America. The gap between intellectuals and everyone else is now a continuum. The landscape is filled with people who are quasischolarly, quasi-political, quasi-rich. Harvard academic Daniel Yergin wrote some books on the history of oil, then seized the opportunity to open a consultant's shop for energy companies (the Cambridge Energy Research Associates, with revenues over $75 million a year). Strobe Talbott turned his interest in Russian studies into a career at *Time*. He writes books on diplomatic affairs, publishes poetry, and became the deputy secretary of state. The information age economy has meant that people who have a talent for research, for analysis, for mathematics, for writing or any other realm of intellection have enormous nonacademic opportunities—in finance, in Silicon Valley, or in the multiplying realms of the commentariat: journalism, think tanks, foundations, government, and so on. The jobs off campus and beyond the little magazines often pay better. The opportunities for advancement come quicker. And the intellectual stimulation can be just as intense, the experiences more exciting. In sum, the relationship between thinking and doing has become closer.

The very meaning of the word *intellectual* has changed over the last 50 years in the way the word *gentleman* changed in the 50 before. Once *intellectual* referred to a small and select group. Then its meaning broadened and broadened to include more people. Now it has almost lost its meaning as so many different types lay claim to it.

There is no longer a small, rarefied intelligentsia living with their hangers-on in bohemian neighborhoods in New York, San Francisco, and Boston. Now there is a massive class of educated analysts and "opinion leaders" who have made the old bohemian neighborhoods unaffordable for anybody without stock options or large royalty checks. Now universities blast-fax press releases to let reporters know that their faculty members are available to comment on the controversies of the day on cable talk shows. Now writers and cultural studies professors embrace mass culture and devote conferences to Madonna or Marilyn or Manson or Marilyn Manson. In the 1950s the scene of maximum glory was to be found in the sphere of the literary critic. Today it is in the first-class section of transatlantic flights, where airborne academics hop from conference to conference, racking up frequent flyer miles and comparing notes on duty-free opportunities around the globe. Fifties intellectuals discussed *No Exit*. Contemporary intellectuals discuss no-load mutual funds.

But the crucial change is not merely that more money and greater opportunities are available for those who are good with ideas. It's the way intellectuals conceive of themselves. Columbia professor Edward Said, who is unhappy with the trend, describes the change in *Representations of the Intellectual:* "The particular threat to the intellectual today is not the academy, nor the suburbs, nor the appalling commercialism of journalism and publishing houses, but rather an attitude that I will call professionalism. By professionalism I mean thinking of your work as an intellectual as something you do for a living, between the hours of nine and five with one eye on the clock, and another cocked at what is considered to be proper, professional behavior—not rocking the boat, not straying outside accepted paradigms or limits, making yourself marketable and above all presentable."

Intellectuals have come to see their careers in capitalist terms. They seek out market niches. They compete for attention. They used to regard ideas as weapons but are now more inclined to regard their ideas as property. They strategize about marketing, about increasing book sales.

Norman Podhoretz was practically burned alive for admitting in his 1967 memoir, *Making It,* that he, like other writers, was driven by ambition. That book caused outrage in literary circles and embarrassment among Podhoretz's friends. Now ambition is no more remarkable in the idea business than it is in any other. Now Henry Louis Gates, who is chairman of Harvard's African American Studies Department, casually remarks to a reporter from *Slate* magazine, "By impulse, I'm an entrepreneur. If I weren't in the academy, I could be a CEO. Quincy Jones is my hero. I have a picture of Vernon Jordan on my wall, right over one of John Hope Franklin."

The Economy of Symbolic Exchange

The only amazing thing these days is that universities haven't opened business schools for aspiring intellectuals. The schools send marketing and finance people off into the world with full training in how to manage and rise in the business world. But intellectuals have to make their way in the job market with no official training on how to amass foundation grants, no courses on how to blurb their colleagues' books, no case studies on how to market a bestseller, no quantitative models on how to determine when a certain subject niche will become hot and how long its vogue will last. Today's intellectuals learn career strategies the way fourth graders used to learn about sex—from the bad kids in the bathrooms.

If a university were to offer a course of study on the marketplace of ideas, the writer who would be at the heart of the curriculum would be Pierre Bourdieu. Bourdieu is a French sociologist who is influential among his colleagues but almost entirely unread outside academia because of his atrocious prose style. Bourdieu's aim is to develop an economy of symbolic exchanges, to delineate the rules and patterns of the cultural and intellectual marketplace. His basic thesis is that all intellectual and cultural players enter the marketplace with certain forms of capital. They may have academic capital (the right degrees), cultural capital (knowledge of a field or art form, a feel for the proper etiquette), linguistic capital (the ability to use language), political capital (the approved positions or affiliations), or symbolic capital (a famous fellowship or award). Intellectuals spend their careers trying to augment their capital and convert one form of capital into another. One intellectual might try to convert knowledge into a lucrative job; another might convert symbolic capital into invitations to exclusive conferences at tony locales; a third might seek to use linguistic ability to destroy the reputations of colleagues so as to become famous or at least controversial.

Ultimately, Bourdieu writes, intellectuals compete to gain a monopoly over the power to consecrate. Certain people and institutions at the top of each specialty have the power to confer prestige and honor on favored individuals, subjects, and styles of discourse. Those who hold this consecration of power influence taste, favor certain methodologies, and define the boundary of their discipline. To be chief consecrator is the intellectual's dream.

Bourdieu doesn't just look at the position an intellectual may hold at a given moment; he looks at the trajectory of a career, the successive attitudes, positions, and strategies a thinker adopts while rising or competing in the marketplace. A young intellectual may enter the world armed only with personal convictions. He or she will be confronted, Bourdieu says, with a diverse "field." There will be daring radical magazines over on one side, staid establishment journals on another, dull but worthy publishing houses here, vanguard but underfunded houses over there. The intellectual will be confronted with rivalries between schools and between established figures. The complex relationships between these and other players in the field will be the tricky and shifting environment in which the intellectual will try to make his or her name. Bourdieu is quite rigorous about the interplay of these forces, drawing elaborate charts of the various fields of French intellectual life, indicating the power and prestige levels of each institution. He identifies which institutions have consecration power over which sections of the field.

Young intellectuals will have to know how to invest their capital to derive maximum "profit," and they will have to devise strategies for ascent—whom to kiss up to and whom to criticize and climb over. Bourdieu's books detail a dazzling array of strategies intellectuals use to get ahead. Bourdieu is not saying that the symbolic field can be understood strictly by economic principles. Often, he says, the "loser wins" rule applies. Those who most vociferously and publicly renounce material success win prestige and honor that can be converted into lucre. Nor does Bourdieu even claim that all of the strategies are self-conscious. He says that each intellectual possesses a "habitus," or personality and disposition, that leads him or her in certain directions and toward certain fields. Moreover, the intellectual will be influenced, often unwillingly or unknowingly, by the gravitational pull of the rivalries and controversies of the field. Jobs will open up, grants will appear, furies will rage. In some ways the field dominates and the intellectuals are blown about within it.

Bourdieu hasn't quite established himself as the Adam Smith of the symbolic economy. And it probably wouldn't be very useful for a young intellectual to read him in hopes of picking up career tips, as a sort of Machiavellian Guide for Nobel Prize Wannabes. Rather, Bourdieu is most useful because he puts into prose some of the concepts that most other intellectuals have observed but have not systematized. Intellectual life is a mixture of careerism and altruism (like most other professions). Today the Bobo intellectual reconciles the quest for knowledge with the quest for the summer house.

How to Be an Intellectual Giant

So let's take a look at how the world looks to, say, a young woman newly graduated from a fancy university who dreams of establishing herself as the Henry Kissinger of her generation. She'll emerge from college saddled with debt, but she will nonetheless find herself landing a barely paying internship at a politically safe outfit like, say, the Brookings Institution. She'll start off doing Nexis searches for some former secretary of commerce who spends his three-hour workday preparing for panel discussions on the topic "Whither NATO?" Her mood will swing from euphoria to despair. Stendhal wrote, "The first love affair of a young man entering society is generally one of ambition," and that is true for a person entering the intellectual marketplace. Her famous boss can send her on the path to fame and fortune (if he places the right call on her behalf to the editor of the *New York Times* op-ed page), or if he doesn't like her, he can block her entry into the commentariat and so compel her to begin applying to law schools. The intern will come to long for his approval, glowing when he gives it and sinking into the depths when he does not.

For the sake of her own self-respect, she will indulge in tiny afterwork rebellions. Sitting around with her friends, she will bitingly ridicule the boss she wants so badly to impress. In the warrens of every foundation, think tank, publishing house, newspaper, and magazine are young interns who can do scathing imitations of their superiors. Making fun of the boss is the careerist's form of blasphemy. The young serfs in intellectual organizations will gather around the buffet tables at book parties and conference receptions, chomping free shrimp while gossiping meanly about their secure superiors. If a bomb were to go off in one of these settings, think tank reports across America would go out filled with typos for months.

Fortunately, this initial period of torment and anxiety does not last long. If the young intellectual does make it one rung up the ladder, she will begin to experience the sense of exaggerated self-importance that will be her prime satisfaction for the rest of her life. Her first full-time job will be as a minion. This sounds lowly, but in reality it is not.

In most intellectual organizations, the hard work of researching, thinking, and writing is done by the people who are too young to get out of it. A two-tier system develops. There are paper people—the young intellectual climbers who read and write things—and there are front people—the already renowned intellectuals, government officials, magazine editors, university presidents, foundation heads, and politicians whose primary job is to appear in places, delivering the research findings, speeches, and talking points the paper people have gathered for them. The front people go to meetings, do *Nightline,* speak at fundraisers, host panel discussions, and give interviews on NPR. They get to take credit for everything. When they are not showing their faces to photographers from *U.S. News and World Report,* they are talking on the phone. Indeed, some days their job consists of coming into work, talking on the phone for three hours, going to lunch, talking on the phone for four more hours. And while they are on the phone they tell each other how much they are looking forward to the weekend, when they can get some reading done. Somehow, almost against their will, their lives have been turned inside out.

The front people get the glory and the contacts, and the paper people control the substance of what gets said.

The young intellectual at this stage of her career gets to write the scathing memos and op-eds castigating people four decades her senior for their ignorance and cowardice ("Campaign Finance Retreat: A Shameless Failure of Nerve"). She is the one who evaluates the policy ideas, companies, scripts, or tenure-track candidates that come across a front person's desk. In some ways she is at the peak of her actual power. For example, a few years ago a friend of mine ghostwrote an op-ed piece for a business executive on a bill before Congress, which was published in a national magazine. Then my friend went to work for a presidential candidate. The business executive sent the op-ed to my friend's candidate. So my friend got to write a letter in the politician's name lavishly praising the op-ed piece he had written under the business executive's name.

As penance for such gratifications, the junior paper person is forced to undergo superficial humiliations. She must hover in a cloud of consultation behind her front person as he walks down the hall (like four-year-olds, famous people seem to have a horror of going anywhere alone). In addition, front people, who don't have to carry anything, walk very fast to demonstrate their vitality. Paper people, who have to carry their own documents as well as the documents of their front, have to scurry behind in an undignified manner just to keep up. Sometimes the front will leave a room or climb into a car and pull the door shut behind him. The poor paper person will have to juggle her files and reopen the door and remind the front she exists.

Still, this buttboy stage in the career is very important because it is during this period that the young intellectual learns about the various players in the field, who is important and who is not. Thanks to the position of her famous boss, the young intellectual has access to places and people that would be closed to her if she were unaffiliated. She will be making contacts with all of the editors and other gatekeepers she will need to know if she is to forge her own career as a publicity intellectual. The difficult moment comes a few years hence, when she is, say, 28 and must break away from her front person and start to make herself a front person. If she does not perform this difficult self-weaning, she will find herself reduced to perpetual valet status. Her ability to think independently will deteriorate. She will begin to use the word *we* when asked her opinion, as in "We wrote an essay on that a few weeks ago." She will begin to confuse her own status and the status of her boss (self-aggrandizement is the opiate of the anonymous).

Subject Niche

Once she breaks free, she will have to determine her field of specialty. The purpose of a field of specialty is to give her a market niche so that when talk-show bookers, editors, or search committees are looking for someone who knows about, say, Chinese missile programs, her name will come immediately to mind. This is a difficult selection. The young intellectual must estimate future market demand—thousands of intellectuals mastered the arcane field of arms control, only to find the market reduced after the end of the Cold War. The young intellectual must also gauge market supply. If there are ten thousand young intellectuals setting out to write books about communitarianism and the theory of civil society, does she want to be another? Here she must be subtle, because in the intellectual arena sometimes it's best to follow the crowd. The more people are specializing in civil society, the more civil society conferences will be organized. More civil society arguments will be put forward and therefore there will be more demand for people to comment on or rebut them. Because each person in the field will read (slightly) more than he writes, each new entrant in this specialty increases the demand for critics and panelists. That's Say's Law. The more people are saying, the more there is to be said.

The young intellectual must also evaluate the prestige and visibility of her market niche. During the Cold War it was easy to find the prestigious intellectual specialties. You could draw a chart, and at the top corner there would be foreign policy issues that involved banks. If your specialty was East-West capital flows, you could be assured that you'd be spending a lot of time going to conferences in $300-a-night Kempinski Hotels in Budapest and Jakarta. Then, the further you got away from foreign policy and banks, the less prestigious a specialty would be. At the bottom there were fields, such as welfare and abortion, that had no banking implications whatsoever. If you went to a conference in one of these fields, you would be surrounded by people with ill-fitting sports jackets, stubby fingers, and facial hair. But the end of the Cold War has scrambled all that. Foreign policy has sunk in prestige, while domestic issues like education have risen. An expert on Latin America can now go years at a time without getting a call from a producer from *The NewsHour with Jim Lehrer*. Specialists on racial issues, on the other hand, can scarcely go a month without getting a genius grant from the MacArthur Foundation.

The young intellectual has to pick a specialty that will be in the news. She can pick the federal budget, because there has to be a budget process every year. But that is so worthy, her chances of breaking out of the PBS/NPR orbit and into the ABC/CBS/NBC orbit are slim. She could become an expert on Middle Eastern affairs, but suppose there were to be peace in the Middle East; that would be calamitous. Some young intellectuals develop a plan—how to redesign the U.N. or how to restructure the college loan system—but this is always a mistake because nobody

cares about some academic's policy idea and constant rejection tends to make intellectuals who promote programs
pushy and annoying. The opposite temptation is to become an expert in a field that is too much in the news.
Some intellectuals go out and become specialists in subjects people in the media are actually interested in, such as
teenage sexuality. But the intellectuals who do this are too
obviously publicity hungry. They tend to be the kind of
people who use the letters Ph.D. after their names on the
title pages of their books. It's better to have a specialty in a
prestigious field so you can pretend to bring respectability
to the discussion of teenage sexuality that the prime-time
newsmagazine is broadcasting.

The budding intellectual must at the same time recognize that having a specialty is just a novice's tool—like
punditry training wheels—to get her rolling. Once she becomes famous, she will no longer need a specialty to have
bookers or editors calling. They will want her for her
name. At that point she can leave her field of expertise
long behind. She can comment on anything at all. In fact,
she will be compelled to do so by the marketplace. There
is no subject she will not be asked about. And if she refuses to give an answer, on the grounds that she is not
knowledgeable enough to say, she will find that people feel
insulted. They will regard her as a pompous prude.

Demeanor

After finding a specialty, the young intellectual must
find a demeanor. It's possible to succeed in the marketplace of ideas with any set of ideas; there are fabulously
successful moderates and fabulously successful radicals.
And it's possible to succeed with any demeanor. There are
happy people who make it, as well as angry people. But
you cannot succeed if your ideas clash with your personal-

ity. You cannot be a mellow radical or an angry moderate. There is little audience for such creatures.

The main job of radicals in the Noam Chomsky or G. Gordon Liddy mode is to go around from one scruffy lecture hall to another reminding audiences that while they may be disdained or ignored by the mainstream culture, they are actually right about everything. The radical bases his career on the assumption that the world is deeply out of sorts and is in fact run by a deceitful establishment that tricks the masses into holding opinions that are incorrect. In order to prosper, the radical must be out of sorts. His audience will demand vehemence, a tinge of paranoia, omniscience (the intellectual must be able to see the truth through the establishment's web of deception), and a willingness to broadcast his brave contrarianism.

To qualify as heroic, the radical must establish his unfashionableness. He can do this by wearing brown shirts or excessively heavy boots, outfits that are unfashionable at Brooks Brothers and therefore de rigueur among radical book buyers and thought consumers. In addition, radicals have to go around finding revered figures to attack in order to demonstrate that they intend to remain deeply unfashionable despite their contracts with such magazines as *Vanity Fair*. For the same reason, comfortable academics are compelled to find ever more transgressive subjects—sadomasochism, queer studies—to research. Artists have to find ever more offensive themes. Radicals who get suddenly fashionable are immediately regarded as craven social climbers. They lose their standing with their audience, as well as most of their foundation grants and career prospects.

Moreover, the radical intellectual cannot build his career just by saying things his supporters like; he must say or do things his opponents hate. If he does no more than flatter his audience, he will achieve only modest success. If, on the other hand, he is vilified by his opponents, then his audience, his patrons and various foundation officers will rally to his side. He will become a cause, a person his audience takes into their hearts. His audience will be willing to shell out large amounts of money to buy his books or attend his lectures. They will give him standing ovations when he is introduced because the very idea of him has become sacred in their minds. (Often he will get only tepid applause after he has finished his remarks because in intellectual combat it's the combat the audience craves, not the intellectual part.)

In order to be reliably vilified, radical intellectuals and public figures must get themselves paired off with counterparts on the other extreme—Jerry Falwell and Norman Lear, gay activists and Operation Rescue. By joining these symbiotic bogeymen relationships, both sides can raise money and support off the villainy of the other. They can go out of their way to outrage their opponents—by sticking a crucifix in a jar of urine or engaging in some other prefab gesture. This earns them two weeks on the talk shows trading charges, and it stokes up the troops. Each side will claim to be more unfashionable than the other, and this war to be seen as more persecuted than your rival becomes the central preoccupation of the dispute.

While a radical intellectual must be vehement, contentious, and unhappy, moderate intellectuals must be civil, slow-talking, and placid. Moderates appeal to consumers who are basically happy with the world and therefore disturbed by commentators who generate too much heat and disharmony. Moderate audiences want to see a civil exchange of views and are impressed more by subtleties than by bold, slashing rhetorical strokes. They are attracted by genial intellectuals who say things like "I would like to associate myself with the remarks that Mr. Moyers made during his intervention." The moderate intellectual, in turn, will feel that he is so important he does not need to be interesting. So he will speak slowly and carefully, as if from a great height. Afterward he will be regarded as a thoughtful person, but nobody may remember any single thought he has uttered.

Marketing

The intellectual today does not come up with an expertise and a demeanor and then market it to the great thinking public. The production and marketing evolve simultaneously, with each process looping back and influencing the other. In her early thirties our young intellectual will still spend most of her time writing. Before she can get on TV or the lecture circuit, she must have been published enough so that her name rings a bell. As her publishing career is getting started, she will imagine that if she could write just one really notable essay in one really prestigious publication, then her career would be made. She will learn that this is untrue. On the day her first big essay is published—perhaps it is called "The Decline of Discourse" in *Harper's*—she will imagine her world has changed. But she will walk around all day, and other people will be leading their lives just as before, treating her no differently than they did yesterday. Many will have not noticed her piece—which has been the object of her fevered attention for weeks—while others who have will treat it as just another scrap in the media confetti.

Nonetheless, she must continue to get published. The *New York Times,* the *Wall Street Journal,* the *L.A. Times,* and the other newspapers and magazines receive hundreds of thousands of submissions every year, and regular appearances in such places is the way intellectuals now remind others and themselves of their existence. So within the first few hours after a news event, such as a court decision on gay marriage, our intellectual will phone the right subeditor at the right op-ed page to say that the line being taken by the shallow TV pundits is 180 degrees off the mark. Print editors like to be told this so they can be assured they have not been rendered obsolete by Geraldo Rivera. She will mention her friendship with the publisher of the newspaper (the editor will doubt the truthfulness of this tie but won't be totally sure). In making her pitch, she will assure the editor that "this piece will really move the debate." She will also describe how she can work a pop culture reference into her essay, comparing the Supreme Court to the creature in the number-one box office movie of the moment. Editors like this sort of mass-media integration, first because it gives them a way to illustrate the piece, and second because they are under the delusion that pop-culture references will propel a piece's readership into the five-digit area. Besides, this is the sort of desperate mixing of high and low that Bobo intellectuals strain to achieve in their effort to persuade people that they are not elitist or boring.

Once the editor gives a provisional go-ahead for the piece, the young intellectual will have up to four hours to write it, which doesn't exactly leave a lot of time for Edmund Wilson–like throat clearing. Nonetheless, she must conceive the piece along the lines of Chartres Cathedral. The prose style should be permanent and solid but appear light. The first two paragraphs should be like a facade— dazzling and all-encompassing. The next several paragraphs should be like a walk down the apse, always heading in a straight line toward the predictable climax but also offering glancing views of interesting side chapels. Finally, the ultimate paragraph should be like arriving at the transept, with light flooding in from all sides. Also, as journalist Michael Kinsley advises, it is best not to use semicolons, as they can be thought pretentious.

The article should also contain healthy dollops of autobiography, forcing the reader to glance down at the biographical tagline that accompanies the piece. If the article mentions some celebrity—perhaps a recently dead politician—the author will want to mention some pointless detail from her last meeting with that person or the emotions she experienced when learning of the subject's death.

To get the most attention, the essay should be wrong. Logical essays are read and understood. But an illogical or wrong essay will prompt dozens of other writers to rise and respond, thus giving the author mounds of publicity. Yale professor Paul Kennedy had a distinguished but unglamorous career under his belt when he wrote *The Rise and Fall of the Great Powers,* predicting American decline. He was wrong, and hundreds of other commentators rose to say so, thus making him famous and turning his book into a bestseller. Francis Fukuyama wrote an essay called "The End of History," which seemed wrong to people who read only the title. Thousands of essayists wrote pieces pointing out that history had not ended, and Fukuyama became a global sensation.

After the article has appeared, the young intellectual will want to let the editor of the piece know what a massive impact the article is having at the White House/the Federal Reserve/the film industry or wherever its intended target is. If she is well connected with other intellectuals, bits of praise will come in. Praise is the currency of the realm among the thinking classes. In the fifties intellectuals seemed to be forever screaming condemnations at each other, but now they endlessly praise each other. And since giving out praise doesn't cost a person anything but actually wins affection, praise is ladled out freely and praise inflation occurs. The value of each unit of flattery declines, and pretty soon intellectuals have to pass over a wheelbarrow full of praise just to pay one compliment. To accurately measure how much people actually like her work, our young intellectual will be wise to develop a praise deflation formula. If someone says he liked a piece, that means he saw it but didn't read it. If he says he loved the piece, that means he started it and made it at least halfway through but can't remember what it was about. If he calls it brilliant, that means he finished it. It is only when a reader offers the following highest form of praise that the writer knows for sure the person is being sincere: "That was an absolutely outstanding piece; I've been saying the same thing myself for years."

If our intellectual is successful, she will be offered a column. This seems like the pinnacle, but while a dozen people get riches and fame from column writing, thousands do it in wretched slavery—compelled like circus animals to be entertaining once or twice a week. The ones who succeed in that line of work have a superb knowledge of one thing: their own minds. They know what they think and they have immense confidence in their judgments. This is not as simple as it sounds, for most people don't become aware of their own opinions until someone else has put them into words. But a columnist can read an article on brain surgery for 20 minutes and then go off and give a lecture to a conference of brain surgeons on what is wrong with their profession.

For intellectuals who do not possess this gift, the next step up the ladder involves writing a book. Aside from the obvious paramount thing about a book—who the author can get to blurb it—there are three important factors the author needs to concern herself with: the publishing house, the title, and the one phrase people will remember from it. A writer's career should be traceable through her publishing houses. Her first rigorous book will be with the University of Chicago Press or some such. Her next serious book should go to W. W. Norton. Her big-think prestigious book should go to Simon & Schuster or Knopf, and at the end of her career, her blockbuster memoir—when she will finally persuade an editor to put her photo on the cover—will go to Random House. The title of her first book will begin with the phrase *"The End of . . ."* The benefit of endism is its dramatic finality; few people will remember a book called *Ideology Is Ailing.* But decades after its publication, the title *The End of Ideology* will still be referred to (even as its contents are utterly forgotten). The difficulty in writing an endist book is in finding things that haven't already ended. History, equality, racism, tragedy, and politics have all been taken, and *The Death of . . .* takes in just about everything else. *The End of Gardening* just doesn't have the ring of a bestseller.

If the endist strategy doesn't work out, the writer might go for the approach pioneered by Leon Uris in a series of bestselling novels and then taken up by Thomas Cahill in the sphere of nonfiction: ethnic brown-nosing. The way to do that is to give the book a title like *Irish People Are Wonderful: But English People Suck* and then follow it up with another book called *Jews Are Great.* An author can go decades without running out of high book-purchasing demographic groups to flatter *(Book Buyers Are Really Smart),* and where is the *New York Times Book Review* going to find a critic willing to say otherwise? A wise soul once declared that the ultimate power of the writer is that he has the choice of whom he wants to be co-opted by. In making his first book topic selections, a writer can select which audience he will spend the rest of his career flattering. However, considering the fan mail he will receive from pet lovers, a writer has to have a strong stomach before he launches off on a career with a book called *The Secret Sorrows of Cats.*

Intellectuals on book tour will need a catchphrase that talk-show interviewers can scan seconds before a segment and then use to start a conversation. For educated audiences the catchphrase might be a paradox that seems sophisticated and appeals to the Bobo's desire for the reconciliation of opposites. So a writer might say her book is an argument for sustainable development, cooperative individualism, the social market, liberation management, compassionate conservatism, practical idealism, or flexible commitment. The most successful oxymoron, *Simple Abundance,* has already been taken by Sarah Ban Breathnach in her mega-selling book of that title, and *Complicated Poverty* probably won't work.

If the author can't come up with a phrase, she will probably have to go nude unless she is already a famous TV celebrity. Going nude doesn't mean the author has to literally strip off her clothes (although it has been done by Elizabeth Wurtzel and others). Rather, just as movie stars in a career lull will sometimes pose shamelessly for *Vanity Fair* in order to get back in the buzz, authors will sometimes accept exhibitionist embarrassment for attention. They will divulge their orgasm patterns or, better yet, those of their predatory stepfathers. If they have been lucky enough to land a job in a glamorous industry such as Hollywood or Wall Street, they will divulge the embarrassing secrets of the mentors who gave them their first big break or the companies that paid them or, in a pinch, the spouses who loved them.

Conferences

Magazine writers sometimes argue that there's no sense writing a book because a magazine article can reach millions more people and costs a fraction of the effort. But book writing—aside from whatever pleasures can be derived from actually knowing something about your subject rather than just boning up on it for a few days—turns the author into panel fodder. An intellectual entering mid-career should be sitting on at least three panel discussions a month, because at the end of life the intellectual who sits on the most panels wins.

This quota is easy to fill because conferences have become ubiquitous in the information age. It is hard to imagine Andrew Carnegie and John D. Rockefeller sitting between evenly spaced bottles of mineral water and discussing "The Future of Corporate Responsibility" with Mark Twain as the celebrity moderator, but these days we are all intellectuals, and intellectuals have to panel. So even sales shows for the floor coverings industry have taken on the academic trappings of, say, the Modern Language Association (while scholarly conferences like the MLA are like sales shows). Big hotels are divided into microscopic seminar rooms. Coffee urns are arrayed on tables in the hallways, supplemented by fruit bowls and small danishes for panelists to gather around during break time. And everywhere there is the buzz of presentations on everything from the musculature of the ankle to the dinner menus in the novels of Henry James.

Whatever other purposes conferences serve—and they do build solidarity among people who think about the same things, they do offer organizations a forum in which they can flatter their donors, they do give disheveled intellectuals a chance to go to places like Orlando and San Francisco without their families—the main purpose of the conference is to serve as a status stock exchange. From the amount of attention and sycophancy a conference goer attracts, she can judge where her stock price stands in relation to the rest of the market. With a brilliant presentation and some acute hobnobbing, she can send her valuation skyrocketing, thus laying the groundwork for future job offers and other opportunities.

The first task at a conference is to be a panelist. If the midcareer intellectual isn't on a panel, she probably shouldn't be at the conference, since nonpanelists are conference lambs, and lambs soon learn that the conference lions hang out only with each other. Second, she should be the least famous person on her panel, just as in real estate it's better to buy the least expensive house in an expensive neighborhood. In the first place, it will be easier to shine among more senior intellectual celebrities. They are probably living off past cultural capital and so are likely to have done no preparation for the event. As her session gets underway, the first few minutes will be spent counting the number of people in the audience and comparing it to attendance at other panels. Then the symposiasts will listen intently to their introductions. The organizer—who usually assigns himself the moderator role in order to get some publicity compensation for his work—will inflate the brilliance of each panelist so as to reflect glory on his ability to draw big names. Listening to her puffed-up introduction will probably be the most enjoyable moment of the entire conference. This joy is marred only when the moderator goes on for too long. I was once at a conference with a long-winded moderator, and a member of the audience sketched a running bar chart comparing the length of the introductions to the length of *Berlin Alexanderplatz*.

The successful symposiast begins her remarks with preapproved jokes. At a conference of economists one should begin by telling the one about a few billion here and a few billion there and pretty soon you're talking real money, or the one about how if you laid a thousand economists end to end they still wouldn't reach a conclusion, or the one about how economists look for keys under the street lamp because that is where the light is. At least one speaker per panel should refer to Yogi Berra, and everybody in the audience must chuckle to prove how unpretentious they are. Then the speaker will have to judge how dull she can afford to be. Very eminent panelists are expected to be dull, since their words carry great weight. High government officials, university presidents, and corporate leaders are expected to speak in the Upper Institutional mode—a vocabulary so dense and vague of content as to cause people's mouths to hang open and their eyes to water. But climbing intellectuals cannot plod along like aging silverbacks. There is nothing more off-putting than a young intellectual who presumes he has won the right to be tedious without having actually achieved the requisite eminence or responsibility. Those who have not won major awards or who do not occupy powerful posts should not be using such phrases as "I would like to suggest . . ." or "My contention therefore . . ."

The average audience can remember only one point from each presentation, so the acute panelist will want hers to be large enough to generate a little butt bouncing among members of the audience. The surest way to generate such excitement is to make startling predictions about the future. But this must be done in a socially acceptable manner. Crude futurologists are considered charlatans. There are two ways to get away with it. The first is no-escape historical determinism, which means arguing that the tides of history make certain dramatic changes inevitable: the PC era is over, an age of socialist renaissance is just around the corner, the growth of evangelical Christianity will have wonderful implications for the financial services sector. The second technique is promiscuous historical parallelism. This is achieved by observing that the current moment resembles another significant date: the political climate of 1929. At that point another panelist will counter that in fact the correct comparison is to 1848, and another will impressively state that the true parallel is to the state of the Holy Roman Empire in 898.

The purpose of these chronological acrobatics is to generate questions during the discussion period. There is nothing worse for a climbing intellectual than to have to sit silently for the last half of the session as all the Q&A interventions go to other panelists. That is a sign of stock market decline. But if the panelist can put forward one theory that is sweeping and inexact, that should stir a few rebuttals. To cover her backside from people who think her notion absurd, she can emphasize that her idea is something she is merely testing, though these equivocations rarely help. The cleverer protective device is to pad out the remainder of her time by lavishly citing her fellow panelists. Three quotations from a colleague's work is what students of peacock behavior call a love display.

As the session winds down, each person in the room will crouch in a sprinter's position in order to make a quick exit to the coffee urn, where the schmoozing and the real point of the conference will take place. If you look at the newsletter from any academic or professional organization, you will observe a series of awkward black-and-white photographs that show three or four people standing in a happy semicircle clutching wine glasses or coffee cups to their bellies. These are intellectuals caught in midschmooze. They are enjoying an activity that deliciously combines work and play, which is a characteristic reconciliation of the Bobo class. The people in the picture look jovial, in part because they know their picture is being taken ("Everyone a Celebrity" is the slogan for this day and age) and in part because they are pleased to be in the presence of people as important as themselves. During the first rush of a schmooze session, if four or more conference lions gather in one place, they radiate a happy glow—so thrilled are they to be in each other's company— that they will laugh for 10 or 15 seconds at a joke nobody bothered to tell.

An intellectual who can first-name his way across a cocktail room, planting a 4.7-second seed of goodwill with each familiar friend without ever being tempted to stop and pay more sustained attention, is either an intellectual superstar or a top official at the Ford Foundation. On the other hand, an obscure person who does not bother to introduce himself when meeting someone, on the presumption that the other person must already know who he is, suffers a decline. A person who interrupts someone else's story to go off in search of more prestigious company is a jerk, but a person who interrupts his own story to talk to bigger stars is a charming force of nature. One who hands out his own essays during schmooze sessions is in danger of falling off the exchange, while another who acts as if the first amendment was invented so he could mention his old friendship with Bobby Kennedy is also in trouble.

A person who is trapped outside a conversational klatsch and cannot induce anyone in the ring to step back and let him in is in desperate straits. The people on the other side of the klatsch see his social exclusion and observe that he lacks the celebrity kilowattage to subconsciously induce his peers to step back and grant him entrance. An aspiring intellectual will find it pretty easy to gauge her stock value by who stops to pay attention to her, how long they spend, whether or not they look at her as they speak, and how many of her field's top-dog consecrators idle by to acknowledge her existence. One must read the signs while pretending not to, acting instead as if the most important thing on one's mind is the need to spear a chicken shard from the traveling waiter's tray, dip it into mustard sauce, and bring the shard to one's mouth without spilling one's drink or getting sauce on one's chin.

Television

Books and panels are fine, but in the end, those who are not on television find their lives are without meaning. The days when all you had to do to become an intellectual giant was to write a literary masterpiece, such as *War and Peace* or *Being and Nothingness,* are gone. Now it is necessary to be able to pitch your ideas to Barbara Walters and Katie Couric. As today's intellectual gets more eminent, the places where she appears should grow less and less rarefied. So a career that starts out at tiny colloquia with bearded philosophers will end up, if all goes well, on the *Tonight Show.*

To achieve this level, the intellectual will first have to attract the attention of TV producers. These bookers are caught between the demands of their vain and temperamental hosts and the crotchety male retirees who are the bulk of their viewers, so they are always looking for someone who can make their life easier. An intellectual on the rise will wake up early in the morning, formulate her sound bites, and then call up bookers on MSNBC to let them know she's available (especially in August when they are hungry for guests). If the producers are interested, they will give her a preinterview, which is a telephone audition, during which she can deliver her idea nuggets in as throaty a voice as possible. Some of the time the bookers will call back later in the day to say, "We've decided to take the show in a different direction, so we won't be needing you." That means they have found a more famous commentator to say the same thing.

Or they will book her, which means she will get to drive to Fort Lee, New Jersey, or some such place so she can appear on a cable talk show that she wouldn't watch if forced under threat of death. She will be met at the entrance and deposited in the green room, which is a tiny chamber with a TV fixed to the station and its endless denture cream commercials. The producer will linger long enough to give her two contradictory instructions: "Don't be afraid to interrupt—we like it when people mix it up." And "This is a sophisticated program. We're not the McLaughlin Group here." Then a young woman will come in and bring her to the makeup room, where the intellectual will chatter incessantly so as to demonstrate that being on TV doesn't make her nervous. When she gets back to the green room, there will be an author touring his book on Stalin's death camps, the messiah of a religious cult, and an astronomer who thinks he is going on the air to downplay the risks of an asteroid hitting the earth but who at the last minute will bow to the pressure and end up sounding alarmist. Cable networks bring in pundits in waves, like line changes during a hockey game, because the idea minstrels are the cheapest way to fill air time. The intellectual has to hope that all the guests use Q-Tips, because often the TV channels don't change earpieces between pundits.

She'll be brought into a small studio and put in a chair in front of a dented photo of the New York skyline. A cameraman who has working-class contempt for anybody who would pontificate on TV will roll his camera in front of her, and all she'll have to do over the next four minutes is pretend to have sex with the black glass square that hides its lens. After she has done this enough times, she will successfully become a caricature of herself, which is the key to television success. If she is blonde, she will become a bleached blonde. If she is a partisan, she will become ferocious. If she is thoughtful, she will develop all the verbal accoutrements of the stock professors you used to see in Marx Brothers movies. And since TV is a visual medium, she will develop an audiovisual signature: something like Tom Wolfe's white suit, Robert Novak's vest, or Anne Coulter's legs.

Irony and sarcasm do not work on television, so the intellectual's best tactic is to pretend she is having the greatest time she's ever had in her life. As the host asks the question, she will beam a brilliant smile. She will answer the question while smiling and top off her answer with another three-second smile. She'll leave everybody with a warm glow. TV is an attention medium, not a persuasion medium. On many programs people will remember that she was on but will have no recollection of what she said. So content is not always vital, but it is important that she wave her hands a lot—for visual interest—and speak in the tones of one who has just finished her third cup of coffee.

The host will have been briefed on the guests' sound bites and often will steal them. If her plan has been to say that America is suffering a loss of community unparalleled since the early industrial age, the first question from the host will be "You know, America is suffering a loss of community unparalleled since the early industrial age. Do you disagree with that?" The guest's attempt to come up with a secondary thing to say will be hampered by the out-of-body experience that many people feel during the first few seconds of a TV appearance. The brain rises out toward the ceiling and looks down on the body, which is frantically trying to think of something to say. The brain will mischievously tell the body that one "fuck" or "shit" here will lead to a career meltdown, auto-pundicide.

Nonetheless, TV does introduce the intellectual to the magic of show business. At its best it offers all the attention and buzz of intellectual activity—adrenaline, fame, influence—with none of the actual work. After a few dozen appearances on *Nightline* or *Charlie Rose,* she will be stopped at airports and recognized in restaurants, a pleasure that Lionel Trilling or Irving Howe probably never experienced.

The Convergence of the Successful

In the premeritocratic age, a person's social life was based largely on proximity. People socialized with friends from the neighborhood or church or work or the local country club. But for many members of the educated class, social life is based on achievement. Social invitations come to the job as much as the person, so the higher a person climbs up the professional ladder, the more invitations there will be to dinner parties, receptions, and other gatherings. And this despite the fact that in all of American history, there has never been a recorded case of a person who has actually become *more* charming as he became more successful.

At the top of intellectual life are semiprofessional, semisocial institutions like Renaissance weekends, Jackson Hole conferences, the TED technology confabs, and the Colorado Conference on World Affairs. They bring together people who are often total strangers. The only thing the attendees have in common is that they are all successful. These meetings serve as meritocratic Versailles, exclusive communities for the educated aristocracy, to gather and chat about their various lecture fees. Except instead of Lord So-and-So conversing with Duke Such-and-Such, at these meetings Mikhail Gorbachev will be in the corner conferring with Ted Turner, Elie Wiesel will be lecturing Richard Dreyfuss, and George Steiner will be lost in conversation with Nancy Kassebaum Baker. These institutions are run by the new consecrators of social prestige, foundation officials. Program officers are like the hostesses of the French salons, great themselves for their ability to recognize success.

If our intellectual has succeeded with essays, books, panels, conferences, and TV appearances, she will find herself invited to retreats at an Arizona rock resort. She will be asked to attend boards of directors meetings hosted by associations, universities, and corporations (which in this day and age like to have a few deep thinkers hanging about, if only for their conversation). If she is deemed clubable, there will be invitation-only conferences to discuss the next millennium. There will be Alpha clubs to join, such as the Council on Foreign Relations, the Bilderberg meetings, and the Ditchley Park conferences in Oxfordshire. There will be working groups, presidential commissions, and special research groups. Her first trip to one of these get-togethers will be like Natasha's first ball in *War and Peace.* She'll stare proudly at her name on the roster, mingling so intimately with big names of past and present.

The successful intellectual will thus be able to rise above intellectual endeavors into that social canopy where everybody gets to bathe in the golden light of each other's accomplishments. The intellectual will find herself invited to dinners that mix the financial elite, the fashion elite, the Hollywood elite, and the political elite. After a lifetime spent amidst the theory types, she will find groups who are not ashamed to be interested in pleasure, who wear clothes that actually emphasize their waists or shoulders.

The intellectual will wonder why she has neglected pleasure all her life. She will discover new joys being amidst people who are careful about their toilet, whose cheeks have that buttery complexion that is the mark of a diet of fat-free sauces. And everybody will be so charming! By now familiarity will have led her to have a jaded view of her intellectual peers. But, being fresh, the top dogs in other fields will seem dazzling and impressive. The business tycoons will seem sharp and together. The movie directors will be surprisingly engaging. The politicians will have wonderful stories.

And she will find they are pretty much like her. Intellectuals once assumed that businessmen were unlettered boobs or that movie stars were glorified cheerleaders, but with the triumph of the educated class, the young intellectual finds that she has ties to most everyone. She went to the same college as a movie star, grew up on the same Upper West Side block as a research scientist, married the cousin of a financier. She's already met many of her new companions in the green rooms of various TV networks. Moreover, she discovers that whatever different realms they have traveled, they have actually all been engaged in the same profession. They have all spent their lives building a reputation. So they have mastered much of the same cultural literacy ("Toni Morrison made an important point on *Charlie Rose* the other night . . ."). They all know how to convey the impression that they have heard of you as they shake your hand ("Oh, of course! . . . How are *you?*"). They have all mastered the fine art of false modesty ("I made a proposal about that several years ago, but no one heeded me then"). And they all can tell you the trading range of the U.S. dollar.

The intellectual will find that she can even be dazzling in such company. She'll find people who do not regard it as a joke if she quotes Tocqueville, and pretty soon she starts rotating her conversational sawhorses: one Tocqueville, one Clausewitz, one Publius, and one Santayana per dinner party. She will learn the pleasures of tasteful thinking. Pretty soon she will announce that it is time to reject the false choices of both left and right. We must all move beyond tired old categories like liberal and conservative. "Labels don't really matter anymore," she will hear herself saying. Her conversation will assume that tone of exhortatory banality that is familiar from the addresses of those who are Gravely Concerned—about public apathy, the decline of civility, the collapse of literacy.

Slowly but surely, in manners and in mind, she will be absorbed into the ethos of the Alpha class. She will find that at the top levels the educated class really has reconciled old divisions. Businessmen can mingle with intellectuals and find that their politics are not too far apart, their tastes are not too far apart, their worldviews are not too far apart.

But this merger has, paradoxically, created one new tension. This is not a great cultural gulf, such as used to exist between intellectuals and corporate types. It's more like a social annoyance. It has to do with that inescapable subject, money.

Status-Income Disequilibrium

In the 1950s, when intellectuals socialized mostly with each other, they did not feel the pain of their own middle-class income. The rich were remote. In those days an investment banker went to Andover and Princeton, while a newspaper person went to Central High and Rutgers. But now the financiers and the writers both are likely to have gone to Andover and Princeton. The student who graduated from Harvard cum laude makes $85,000 a year as a think tank fellow, while the schlump she wouldn't even talk to in gym class makes $34 million as a bond trader or TV producer. The loser who flunked out of Harvard and never showered is worth $2.4 billion in Silicon Valley. Pretty soon the successful intellectuals start to notice that while they have achieved social equality with these money types, financially they are inferior.

Imagine, for example, our worldly intellectual, now middle-aged and well established, at a dinner for the Society for the Preservation of Historic Chicago at the Drake Hotel. All night long she has been telling stories about Ted Koppel (emphasizing her recent *Nightline* appearance) and Bill Bradley (recounting their joint Aspen Institute conference in August). She's kept the bankers and lawyers and doctors at her table enthralled. They retire afterward to the hotel bar for seven-dollar martinis and are joined by a consultant from Deloitte & Touche and his wife, a partner at Winston & Strawn—a two-ampersand couple. She is just as amusing at the bar, filling the air with inside dope about the publishing industry and magazine gossip. Feeling expansive, she decides to pick up the tab for drinks, putting it on her own credit card, even though any of the others could expense it, and when the whole group stumbles outside she is so overcome by the triumph of the evening that she blurts out, "Can I give anyone a lift? Anyone going south?"

There is an awkward silence. The ampersand couple says, "Actually, we're going north, up to Winnetka." One of the doctors says he is going north too, up toward Lake Forest. Suddenly it is all ash in her mouth. She knows what the neighborhoods are like on Chicago's North Shore. The million-dollar homes stretch on for mile after mile. Some are Tudor Revival and others are Prairie School and Queen Anne, but they all are massive and immaculate. There are no weeds on the North Shore. Each house is surrounded by a huge spread of flawless lawn and masterfully landscaped grounds, with hedges so neatly sculpted they look like they're made out of green marble. Even the garages are spotless, with baby joggers hanging neatly from pegs, and the Little Tikes kiddy cars arrayed in perfect rows, the floors swept and mopped. The renovators in those neighborhoods appear inside the house every seven years like cicadas, changing the paneling in the rotunda from cherry to walnut or back again. From the time those people wake up in the morning and set foot on their preheated bathroom floor to the waning moments of the evening, when they hit the remote to turn off the gas fireplace, they are reminded that life is good, America is just, and their lives are in control.

But the intellectual has to drive down to her university neighborhood in Hyde Park. She has to zip past the menacing housing projects, and when she returns to her neighborhood at 47th Street, she finds herself waiting at a stoplight looking over at a yellow check-cashing place and a storefront operation that offers low phone rates to El Salvador. Her building, which seemed such a step up from her earlier graduate school existence, is made of old and dark brick and is low and squat. The patch of ground out front, a scraggly excuse for a lawn, is practically bare, iron bars protect the windows, and the gate is rusted and ramshackle. She walks through the chipped marble vestibule —with its faint odors—and one flight up to her apartment. In Winnetka the doctors and lawyers are greeted by a grand entrance hall, but the intellectual has only a small excuse for a foyer, which has shoes and boots lining the wall. She steps over the threshold of her apartment and finds herself confronted by a cluttered dining room table and looking into the kitchen. Suddenly she is feeling miserable. She is suffering from Status-Income Disequilibrium, a malady that afflicts people with jobs that give them high status but only moderately high income.

The tragedy of the SID sufferers' lives is that they spend their days in glory and their nights in mediocrity. At work they go off and give lectures—all eyes upon them— appear on TV and on NPR, chair meetings. If they work in the media or in publishing, they can enjoy fancy expense-account lunches. All day long phone messages pile up on their desks—calls from rich and famous people seeking favors or attention—but at night they realize the bathroom needs cleaning so they have to pull out the Ajax. At work they are aristocrats, kings of the meritocracy, schmoozing with George Plimpton. At home they wonder if they can really afford a new car.

Consider the situation of our imagined intellectual. She's earning $105,000 a year as a full professor at the University of Chicago. Her husband, whom she met while they were studying at Yale, is a program officer at a boutique foundation that takes Robert McCormick's money and uses it to promote ideas McCormick despised. He makes $75,000. In their wildest imaginings they never dreamed they'd someday pull in $180,000 a year.

Or that they'd be so poor. Their daughter turned 18 last year, and her room and board at Stanford tops $30,000 annually. Their 16-year-old son, who has such a flair for music, consumes at least that much in tuition fees, when you throw in the prep school costs, the summer music camp, and the private lessons. The nanny who is home when their 9-year-old returns from the University of Chicago Lab School each afternoon eats up another $32,000 (they pay her legally because our intellectual still dreams of an administration post). Then there are the charity costs, which are high so they don't have to feel too ashamed when they face their accountant each April (Nature Conservancy, Amnesty International, etc.). All of which leaves them about $2,500 a month for rent, food, books, laundry, and living expenses. It feels like they are utterly poor, and of course they are suffering from bracket amnesia; as soon as they reach one income bracket, they forget what life was like in the lower brackets and so can't imagine how it would be possible ever to return there.

Modern intellectuals are good at worrying about their reputations. But the person who suffers from Status-Income Disequilibrium spends a lot of time worrying about money. And it is not as if the intellectual these days fills her days with thoughts about truth and beauty or poetic evocations of spring. It is not as if she is compensated for her meager $105,000 salary with the knowledge that she can rise above the mundane pressures of the world. She has to spend her working hours marketing herself, appraising the needs of her audience, selling herself to producers, journalists, and her academic colleagues. The SID sufferer who is in publishing spends his days thinking about market niches, the same as the estate-owning executive at AT&T. He has to do just as much artificial schmoozing as the partners at Skadden, Arps or the sellers at Goldman Sachs. It's just that they are working in big money industries and the SID sufferer is working in a small money industry.

Today's intellectual is at the butt end of the upper class. She is rich enough to send her kids to the private schools and to Stanford, but many of the other parents at these places make as much in a month as her family does in a year. Eventually the kids of the SID sufferer begin to notice the income difference between their family and their classmates' families. It happens around birthday time. The other kids have birthdays at Wrigley Field (they've bought out a section) or at FAO Schwarz (they've rented out the whole store for a Sunday morning). The SID kid has his party in his living room.

When the intellectual's oldest daughter comes home for Christmas break, she'll be invited to go hang out with her Stanford classmate who lives up in Winnetka. She'll notice that when she visits the home of her friend, everything is uncluttered. The house is filled with vast expanses of table space and counter space and floor space, all of it luxuriously spare. Spareness is also the rule at work. People in that branch of the educated class have big offices with wood surfaces. And they have secretaries to route the paper flow, and their secretaries have secretaries to file things away, so there is nothing left stacked up to cover the wide-open expanse of the predator's desk. The briefcases of the financial services Bobos are wafer thin, with barely enough space to squeeze in a legal pad, because their lives are so totally in control they don't have to schlepp things from place to place. They travel luggage-free to London because, after all, they've got another wardrobe at their flat there.

The life of the SID sufferer, by contrast, is cluttered. She's got a small desk tucked upstairs in the social science building. And there are papers everywhere: manuscripts, memos, journals, magazine clippings. And at home the SID sufferer has jars and coffeemakers jamming the available counterspace, and pots hanging loosely from a rack on the wall. The SID sufferer has books all around the living room, most dating back to graduate school days (*The Marx-Engels Reader*, for example), and there are frayed copies of the *New York Review of Books* lying on the nightstand.

When an intellectual with a household income of $180,000 a year enters a room filled with moneyed types making $1.75 million a year, a few social rules will be observed. First, everyone will act as if money does not exist. Everyone, including the intellectual who can't pay her Visa bill in full, will pretend it is possible to jet off to Paris for a weekend and the only barrier is finding the time. Everyone will praise the Marais district, and it will not be mentioned that the financial analyst has an apartment in the Marais and the intellectual spends her rare vacations at one-star hotels. The intellectual will notice that the financial analysts spend a lot of time talking about their vacations, whereas all the intellectual wants to talk about is work.

When an intellectual enters a room filled with financial predators, there will be a nagging doubt in the back of her mind: do they really like me, or am I just another form of servant, one who provides amusement or publicity instead of making the beds? The sad fact is that the moneyed analysts tend not to think this way. The millionaires are plagued by the fear that while they have achieved success, they have not achieved significance. They suffer from a reverse SID—their income is higher than their status. They have Income-Status Disequilibrium (ISD). After all, they have not done much with their lives that would allow them to explore their artistic side or to achieve intellectual immortality or even to be dazzling in conversation. The millionaires notice that they have to pay for all the foundation dinners they attend while the intellectuals are thought to be important enough to get in for free. The rich are the johns of the think tank circuit.

Furthermore, the intellectuals are, in effect, paid to be interesting. They are paid to sit around all day reading things that they can then redirect into provocative prose and conversation (it's astonishing that so many do this job so badly). And the rich, meanwhile, are practically paid to be dull; they are given huge salaries to work on arcane deals that would make their dinner companions' minds go numb if they had to hear about them. Finally, the rich feel vulnerable because, despite their vast resources, they still rely on the publicity machine for their good reputations, which these professional dinner party ironists control.

Therefore, many millionaires think it would be neat to be a writer whose opinions are queried on *The News-Hour with Jim Lehrer.* Look at Mortimer Zuckerman, who owns the *New York Daily News, U.S. News and World Report,* and goodly chunks of Manhattan and Washington. He'll drive out to New Jersey to do a taping for the cable channel CNBC. It's not enough to have more money than some countries. Zuckerman wants to be a public intellectual.

The intellectuals react in diverse ways to Status-Income Disequilibrium. Some try to pass for members of the money wing of the educated class. They buy those blue shirts with white collars. They polish their shoes daily. The women in this category save up enough money to buy a Ralph Lauren or Donna Karan suit. And if they are in, say, media, publishing, or the foundation world, they use their expense account to the max. Like an asthma sufferer taking the cure at an Arizona resort, a SID sufferer can find temporary relief when traveling on business. She can stay at the Ritz-Carlton for $370 a night, with phones and televisions in every room. Hotel dry cleaning will be as nothing.

But then the business trip ends and it is back to earth. Which explains why other members of the intelligentsia go the other way and aggressively demonstrate that they still proudly adhere to their bohemian roots. You'll see them wearing Timberland boots with their suits, a signal that they are still rebelling against the money culture.

Their taste in ties and socks will tend toward the ironic; you might see one wearing a tie adorned with the logo of a local sanitation department, a garbage truck driving over a rainbow.

At home this sort of SID sufferer will luxuriate in his poverty. He will congratulate himself for the fact that he lives in an integrated neighborhood, though he couldn't afford the pearly white neighborhoods in such places as Winnetka or Grosse Pointe or Park Avenue. Most of all, he will congratulate himself on choosing a profession that doesn't offer the big financial rewards, for not devoting his life to money grubbing. He does not mention to himself that, in fact, he lacks the quantitative skills it takes to be, say, an investment banker and that he is unable to focus on things that bore him, the way lawyers can. There never was any great opportunity to go into a more lucrative field, so there was never any real moment of deliberate sacrifice.

The Death and Rise of the Intellectual

SID is painful for those who suffer from it, but in reality SID is like the coccyx. Just as the coccyx is thought to be an evolutionary remnant from when our primate ancestors had tails, SID is a remnant of the class war between the bourgeoisie and the bohemian. For centuries the bourgeois businessman and the bohemian intellectual glowered at each other from a distance and across barricades. But now their great class war has been reduced to dinner party friction. Now they mingle; they do not assassinate. Their great cultural conflict has been reduced to slight status jockeying as each tries to justify his own form of career success.

So the social role of the intellectual really has been transformed. Once the aloof member of a secular priesthood, she is now an anxious but basically comfortable member of a large class of people who are interested in ideas. Once the radical who sought to challenge the rule of mammon, she is now the worldly player, building a reputation and climbing the ladder of success. Say farewell to the self-absorbed intellectual quarrels and to all those alienated garret lifestyles; today intellectuals know their Château Margaux from their Merlot.

So what have we gained and lost? On one level it is hard not to admire the intellectual life of the fifties—Hannah Arendt and Reinhold Niebuhr, the *Partisan Review* crowd, poets and literary critics like Robert Penn Warren, sociologists like David Riesman. These were people who lived for ideas, words, and argument. They possessed minds that could soar up to rarefied heights, tossing off quotations from Hegel and Aristotle, Schiller and Goethe. This was the age before television punditry, before op-ed pieces, before jet-setting conference tours. The intellectual world seemed smaller but more intense and more vital.

And yet. And yet. There is something to be said for today's intellectual world as well, and I at least would not want to go back. Start with this question: how do we learn? Is wisdom best attained by sitting in a book-stuffed studio on Riverside Drive, reading Freud and the existentialists, engaging in intense debates with an insular crowd, most of whom live within a few square miles? Or is it gained through broader experience with the world, by putting one foot in the river of mainstream life and then by reflecting on what you found there? Is it gained by detaching oneself and judging the world from some rarefied height, or is it gained by involving oneself in the scramble and feeling the contours of reality immediately, then trying to describe what one has sensed? It's not only that modern writers have fatter wallets than the old kind. We have different epistemologies.

We are more skeptical of pure reason, of high-flown

abstractions and towering generalizations. We are more likely to follow in the footsteps of Jane Jacobs, who may not have been familiar with Heidegger, who may not have been able to match the intellectual acrobatics of the *Partisan Review* crowd, but was intimately familiar with the daily life around her. In the last chapter I described metis, the practical sort of wisdom that can be gained by doing and sensing more than by theorizing. We Bobo types prize metis more than abstract reasoning, and we are right to do so. We are right to be involved in the world, to climb and strive and experience the dumb superficialities of everyday life, just like everybody else. Our intellectuals understand the world better if they experience the same sorts of pressures that confront most people, the tensions between ambition and virtue, the distinctions between pleasant but shallow status and real accomplishment. Detaching oneself from commercial culture means cutting oneself off from the main activity of American life. That makes it much harder to grasp what is really going on. But today's intellectual, if she is honest about her own motives and compromises, can reach a more accurate sense of the state of the country and the world. Her declarations may not be as sweeping or as grand as the declarations that are made by a self-exiled intellectual who hurls thunderbolts down from the clifftops, but she will know the valley paths better, and her descriptions will be more true and her ideas more useful.

Look back again at the books of the 1950s. The years between 1955 and 1965 constitute a golden age of nonfiction. I've cited many books from that period already in this one, and I've left off some of the most influential, like Betty Friedan's *The Feminine Mystique* and Rachel Carson's *Silent Spring*. And with all due respect to people like Niebuhr and Arendt, many of the best and most influential books were written by people who would not have been considered intellectuals in that day: Jane Jacobs,

William Whyte, Betty Friedan, Rachel Carson, even Digby Baltzell. In some ways these writers and journalists had more in common with today's pundits and worldly commentators than with the intellectual mode Edward Shils defined. These people serve as better models for us today than the highbrows who self-consciously detached themselves into the realm of high culture, capital-letter Ideas, and bohemian alienation.

And they achieved one final thing. They gained an audience. The *Partisan Review* crowd was brilliant, but the journal's circulation was minuscule. Today there are more and more outlets to bring ideas to the millions, through public broadcasting, through the profusion of magazines, through the Internet. Surely writers and thinkers are right to take advantage of the new media to get ideas around, even if it means that one does have to pay more attention to the demands of different formats and learn how to smile when the TV camera flits on.

5

Pleasure

IF YOU'D like to be tortured and whipped with dignity and humiliated with respect, you really ought to check out the Internet newsletter of the Arizona Power Exchange, an S&M group headquartered in Phoenix. The organization offers a full array of services to what is now genteelly known as the leather community. For example, on a recent August 3, according to the summer newsletter, there was a discussion and humiliation session. On August 6 at 7 P.M., there was a workshop on caning. The next night the Bondage Sadomasochism Personal Growth and Support Group met with Master Lawrence, while on August 10, Carla helped lead a discussion on high heel and foot worship. A week later a visiting lecturer came to discuss "blood sports." All of these meetings were to be conducted with the sort of mature high-mindedness embodied in the organization's mission statement: "Treating the S&M, B&D and D&S experience with acceptance, caring, dignity and respect." Dignity and respect are important when you're tied up on the ground worshiping someone's boot.

The organization, which goes by the acronym APEX, has a seven-member board of directors and a long list of officers and administrators. There's a recording secretary, a treasurer, an archivist, an orientation officer, a logistics officer, and a Web page staff to design its Internet site, which is more demure than the one that might be operated by your average Rotary Club. APEX sponsors charity drives. There's a special support group for submissives who are too shy to vocalize the sort of submission they like. There's a seminar on S&M and the law. There are 12-step meetings for sadists and masochists recovering from substance abuse. Finally, there are outreach efforts to build coalitions with other bondage and domination groups nationwide.

When you read through the descriptions of the APEX workshops, you are struck by how much attention is devoted to catering these affairs. Topics like nipple piercing and nude gagging are supposed to evoke images of debauched de Sades, but in this crowd paddling and punishing are made to sound more akin to bird watching or wine tasting. You imagine a group of off-duty high school guidance counselors and other responsible flossers standing around in nothing but a leather girdle and their orthotics, discussing the merits and demerits of foreign versus domestic penile clamps. It's all so temperate and responsible. It's so bourgeois.

Sex, especially adventurous sex, used to be the great transgressive act. Dissolute aristocrats would gather their whips and manacles and repair to the palace attic. Peasants would slobber their way through lewd drunken orgies. Bohemians would throw off the fetters of respectability and explore the joys of Free Love.

But today that is obsolete. And it's not only organizations like APEX that try to gentrify norm-challenging Eros to make it responsible and edifying. There is now a thriving industry that caters to people who want to practice moral sex. There are shelves and shelves of Barnes & Noble erotica that owe more to the Iowa Writers' Workshop than to *Hustler* magazine. There are high-minded sex journals and catalogues, such as Good Vibrations, *Sex Life,* and the Xandria Collection, that advertise in the back of upscale magazines like *Harper's* and the *Atlantic Monthly.* (These high-minded sex journals are easy to distinguish because, to avoid committing the sin of lookism, they prominently feature ugly people having sex; to emphasize that sex is a life-long endeavor, they spend so much time on elderly sex you can practically hear the banging of the medical ID bracelets.) There are so many academic theoreticians writing about sexual transgressions that orgies must come to resemble an Apache dance at tourist season, done less for the joy of it than to please the squads of sociology professors who have flown in to quote Derrida.

In short, over the past few years the educated class has domesticated lust by enshrouding it in high-mindedness. The Bobos have taken sex, which for centuries has been thought to be arousing or sinful or possibly dangerous, and they have made it socially constructive.

Bobos turn out to be the parsons of the pubic region. Nearly gone are 1960s traces of Dionysian wantonness. Instead, "Play Safe" and "Play Responsibly" are the slogans that are repeated again and again in sophisticated sex literature. The practitioners talk so much about how healthy it all is that you'd think they were doing jumping jacks. To keep everything responsible and under control, weird activities are codified in rules and etiquette. Judging by the sexual encounter groups that describe their activities in newsletters, the rules at a group sex community meeting—when it is necessary to sign a legal waiver, when to wear latex gloves, when it is OK to smoke—are strictly adhered to. Theirs may not be the same as the etiquette that governed behavior in a 19th-century parlor, but in their relentless demands on self-control, they weirdly mimic those sorts of social codes.

Today's Marquis de Sades don't seem to want to create an immoral underground society. They're not trying to subvert normalcy. They're trying to join it. They want to win mainstream acceptance and so gain a respectable place in the middle-class world. "We affirm that loving more than one can be a natural expression of health, express joy and intimacy. This is a lovestyle we call responsible non-monogamy," reads the mission statement of *Loving More* magazine, the journal of polyamory. Every "affirmation group" (as they are now called) seeks a place in the land of the up-and-up: the bestiality community, the necrophiliacs, the cigar fetishists, the lovers of orthodontia, the piercists, the crush lovers (people who enjoy watching women smash things), and the macrophiliacs (people who fantasize about women who destroy buildings with their breasts).

In odd ways, these are moralistic people. Sex is now frequently seen as a way to achieve deeper moral understandings. The former monk Thomas Moore, who wrote *Care of the Soul,* followed it up with *The Soul of Sex,* just one of hundreds of the moral sex books that have been published over the past few years. Others can go to the Church of Tantra, which offers such courses as "Tantric Sex: The Spiritual Path to Ecstasy." Others use their sexual lives to advance social change. To avoid ethnocentrism, the orgies in the highbrow sex journals tend to be as diverse as the casts of kids on PBS children's shows: one Asian, one Hispanic, one African American, one Caucasian, and one Native American. I imagine that if there were a room full of people rubbing each other's excrement over each other and somebody confessed he didn't recycle, he'd be immediately expelled from the group and told never to come back. It's a weird version of propriety, but it's propriety nonetheless.

But Bobos do more than merely moralize what was once subversive. They are meritocrats through and through. So they don't just enjoy orgasms; they *achieve* orgasm. Sex in this literature is like college; it's described as a continual regimen of self-improvement and self-expansion. It's amazing how many sex workshops, seminars, institutes, and academies there are out there to cater to people who want to learn more about their bodies. What's available at the Human Awareness Institute? The Web site tells you: "Examine and shed limiting notions about love, intimacy and sexuality. Relate and communicate more effectively with others. Significantly improve your relationship with yourself. Be more loving, intimate and fully self-expressive with others. Make exciting and empowering choices in your life and relationships." Lady Chatterley's lover becomes Lady Chatterley's empowerment counselor.

These practitioners work extraordinarily hard to improve their skills and master new techniques. It's not for the Bobos to be content with the sort of normal practices of the bedroom onanist. They have to turn it into graduate school. JoAnn Loulan, the author of *Lesbian Passion: Loving Ourselves and Each Other,* offers the following exercises: "Look at your genitals every day in the mirror. . . . Draw a picture of your genitals. . . . Write a letter to your genitals. . . . Spend an hour of uninterrupted sensual time with yourself. . . . Look at yourself in the mirror for an hour. Talk with all parts of your body. . . . Spend an hour touching your genitals without the purpose of having an orgasm. . . . Masturbate for an hour." Even just reading about this curriculum is enough to give you an acute case of carpal tunnel syndrome.

Everything in the Bobo life is purposeful. The most animalistic activities are now enshrouded with guidebooks, how-to videos, and magazine articles written by people with advanced degrees. Everything gets talked about and shared. Even masturbation can be measured and evaluated by the standards of connoisseurship. And it's not only the techniques of sex that can be continually worked on and improved; it is the perceptions and knowledge that come from sex that can be deepened and refined. Sex can't be just a fun thing between the sheets. It's also got to be a profound thing between your ears. It's got to be safe, responsible, and socially constructive. Hedonism sure has changed.

The Pleasure Wars

This isn't how the sexual revolution was supposed to end up. After all, it had its roots in the romantic movement which was supposed to be a rebellion against the repressed attitudes of the bourgeoisie. Historian Peter Gay has called them the "pleasure wars," the long-running disputes that had the bohemian sensualists flouting middleclass conventions. The bohemians were the ones jeering at plodding and unerotic Charles Bovary. They were the ones championing Anaïs Nin's diaries and the shocking novels of Henry Miller. They were crusading against the censorship of sexually explicit art and literature.

The counterculture was the place where life was free, where pleasure was available. In his evocative memoir of underground life, *Down and In,* Ronald Sukenick quotes *Village Voice* columnist Howard Smith: "I came to the Village because sex was very uptight in the fifties. I wanted to fuck. I wanted women who would talk to me. I wanted women who didn't wear padded wired bras with a slip over it and a sweater. . . . At Pandora's Box I used to go to that coffee shop all the time and this waitress would lean over and say, 'Anything else I can get you?' and she wore a low-cut peasant blouse and no bra and I would almost fall out of my chair."

In the sixties the hippies ridiculed the "blue meanies," the pleasure-robbing villains in *Yellow Submarine*. Students celebrated polymorphous perversity and condemned repressive desublimation, one of Marcuse's terms that seemed to have something to do with being uptight. "The more I make revolution, the more I make love," the radicals exclaimed. In the 1960s and '70s, nudity was deemed revolutionary and rock stars really seemed radical when they sang anthems to sex, drugs, and rock and roll. They made it seem as if raucous hedonism and revolution were the same thing, as perhaps they were. And there was a romantic rationale behind all this fast living: *Le dérèglement de tous les sens*. Deregulate the senses. Great truths come from great sensations. The best live passionately and for the moment. The brave ones live free and fast and penetrate into the profound realms.

By the 1970s it seemed obvious who was going to win the pleasure wars. Swinging, or at least talk about swinging, was hip. Gay Talese's *Thy Neighbor's Wife* was written during those years, chronicling the swingers who seemed to spend large amounts of time sitting naked in groups discovering new erogenous zones. Revered novelists like John Updike and Philip Roth described acts underground pornographers wouldn't have touched two decades before. *The Joy of Sex* was a massive bestseller. New York featured at least five nudie musicals; at the beginning of their runs they were actually considered kind of cool. Erica Jong made herself famous by describing the zipless fuck. Movies in that era celebrated drug use. "A Motion Picture for the Stoned Age" is how a film called *Black and White* promoted itself. The *New York Times* ran pages of advertisements for porn movies and strip bars, so that there would be ads for *Deep Throat* right next to those for *The Sound of Music,* a sign that people no longer knew where to draw the line between decency and indecency or whether there should be a line at all.

The forces of emancipation recorded triumph after triumph. In some places children were encouraged to explore their sexuality as a means of self-discovery. A New Jersey school curriculum advised, "Grown-ups sometimes forget to tell children that touching can give people pleasure, especially when someone you love touches you. And you can give yourself pleasure, and that's okay." Old taboos were falling. Old family structures began to seem passé. Old systems of etiquette seemed positively Neanderthal. Reticence seemed like hypocrisy. Sexual freedom, at least in the realm of public discourse, was on the march.

Indeed, some social critics believe the sexual revolution continues unabated to this day. In 1995 George Gilder wrote, "Bohemian values have come to prevail over bourgeois virtue in sexual morals and family roles, arts and letters, bureaucracies and universities, popular culture and public life. As a result, culture and family life are widely in chaos, cities seethe with venereal plagues, schools and colleges fall to obscurantism and propaganda, the courts are a carnival of pettifoggery." In 1996 Robert Bork's bestseller, *Slouching Towards Gomorrah,* argued that the forces of the sixties have spread cultural rot across mainstream America. In 1999 William Bennett argued, "Our culture celebrates self-gratification, the crossing of all moral barriers, and now the breaking of all social taboos."

But if you look around upscale America, it's not all chaos and amoralism, even among the sexual avant-gardists at the Arizona Power Exchange. What they are doing is weird and may be disgusting, but it has its own set of disciplines. And when you get to the educated-class mainstream, it's hard to find signs of rampant hedonism or outright decadence. Smoking is down. Drinking is down. Divorce rates are down. Rock stars now pose more as moralistic storytellers—in the tradition of fifties folk singers—than as hedonistic rebels.

Reregulating the Senses

It's no longer accurate to say that the forces of Anything Goes are sweeping through American culture (if indeed they ever were). Instead, the picture is far more complex and confusing. In humor, for example, we have become tolerant of sexual jokes over the past 30 years but extremely intolerant of ethnic jokes. We have become far more relaxed about things like posture and proper attire but far more restrictive about anger, spitting, and smoking. We have become more tolerant about frank sexual talk in public but more censorious about lewd banter or any talk that could be interpreted as harassment. We have these high-toned sex journals in the finest bookstores, but old-fashioned Harold Robbins–style bonkbusters are déclassé. Universities tolerate tattoos and piercing that would have seemed outrageous in the early 1950s, but they crack down on fraternity drinking rituals that would have seemed unexceptional. We feel we are less strict with our children, but in fact we intervene in their lives far more than did parents in the 1950s. In *Tom Sawyer,* for example, Aunt Polly may have tried to civilize Tom with beatings and strict table etiquette, but she also allowed him hours of unsupervised time to wander and adventure. Today we don't adhere to that etiquette, but we don't allow much wandering, either. Instead, we shepherd kids from one adult-organized activity to another.

In short, moral standards don't necessarily rise and fall at once, in great onslaughts of virtue or vice. The reality is more like mixed trading in the stock market, with standards rising in one area and falling in the next, making it very hard to determine whether in the aggregate we are tightening or loosening. In 1999 Carnegie-Mellon historian Peter N. Stearns published a book called *Battleground of Desire: The Struggle for Self-Control in Modern America,* in which he traced different self-control regimes that prevailed in America during the 20th century. Stearns concluded that while we certainly practice a different control regime than, say, Victorian-era Americans, it is not immediately clear that on balance we are more permissive or licentious. Rather, our taboos and restrictions "are different, involving a distinctive set of tolerances and restrictions and in some ways, demanding greater vigilance."

The truth is that Bobos have constructed new social codes that characteristically synthesize bourgeois self-control and bohemian emancipation. Now we have a new set of standards to distinguish permissible pleasures from impermissible ones. We have new social codes to regulate the senses.

Useful Pleasures

To get a firsthand glimpse of these new codes, go down to your local park in the summertime. You'll see women jogging or running in sports bras and skin-tight spandex pants. Imagine if the Puritans could get a load of this! Women running around in their underwear in public. They'd pull out the tracts on Sodom and Gomorrah. Even a cosmopolitan historian such as Edward Gibbon would take a first glance at these women and begin speculating about the decline of empires. But look at the bra joggers more closely. It's not wanton hedonism you see on their faces. They're not exposing themselves for the sake of exhibitionism. Any erotic effect of their near nudity is counteracted by their expressions of grim determination. They are working out. They are working. They're building their muscles. They're setting goals and striving to achieve them. You never see them smile. On the contrary, some of them seem to be suffering. These near-naked young women are self-discipline personified—no pain, no gain— and the reason they are practically naked, they will tell you, is that this sort of clothing is most practical, most useful for strenuous exercise. What we see at the park is near nudity, but somehow it's nudity in the service of achievement. Dionysius, the god of abandon, has been reconciled with Prometheus, the god of work.

The Bobos take a utilitarian view of pleasure. Any sensual pleasure that can be edifying or life-enhancing is celebrated. On the other hand, any pleasure that is counterproductive or dangerous is judged harshly. So exercise is celebrated, but smoking is now considered a worse sin than at least 5 of the 10 commandments. Coffee becomes the beverage of the age because it stimulates mental acuity, while booze is out of favor because it dulls the judgment. You can go to the beach near naked in a skimpy bathing suit and that is normal, but if you neglect to put on sun block to protect against skin cancer, people are astonished. It is admirable to eat healthy, but we use the word *guilt* more often in connection with unhealthy foods— high fat, high sodium, or high calorie—than in any other context. Contemplative pleasures like taking a long bath are admired, but dangerous pleasures like speeding on a motorcycle are disdained, and driving without a seatbelt is positively immoral. Sports that are aerobic, like cross-country skiing and Rollerblading, thrive, while sports that do little to improve cardiovascular health, like pool, bowl-ing, and Ping-Pong, are low class. Even an afternoon spent playing with the kids is thought to be "a good thing" be-cause we are invariably helping the little ones improve some set of skills (watch the Bobo parents taking part in their kids' "play") or at least we are building better relationships or self-esteem ("Good job! Good for you!").

We Bobos have taken the bourgeois imperative to strive and succeed, and we have married it to the bohemian impulse to experience new sensations. The result is a set of social regulations constructed to encourage pleasures that are physically, spiritually, and intellectually useful while stigmatizing ones that are useless or harmful. In this way the Protestant Work Ethic has been replaced by the Bobo Play Ethic, which is equally demanding. Everything we do must serve the Life Mission, which is cultivation, progress, and self-improvement.

It's perfectly fitting that the two leisure-time institutions that have thrived during the Bobo age are health clubs and museums. Both places offer sensual satisfactions in uplifting settings. At health clubs you can enjoy the pleasure of an ennobling muscle burn—you get off the Stairmaster, exhausted and sweaty after 35 minutes of pure exertion, and admire your virtuous self in the floor-to-ceiling mirrors. Meanwhile, at museums you can luxuriate in a sensual cornucopia, enjoying the colors and forms of the paint and materials, while being edified by informative Acoustiguides, scholarly texts on the walls, and the wonderful bookshop downstairs. Health clubs and museums have become the chapels and cathedrals of our age, the former serving to improve the body, the latter the mind.

It's also fitting that we Bobos have taken the ultimate symbol of Dionysian release, the party, and merged it with work. A couple of years ago in the *New Yorker,* James Atlas published an essay called "The Fall of Fun," which pretty accurately captured the transformation of the literary party scene and shed light on educated-class parties as a whole.

Next to the writers, poets and essayists of earlier

decades, Atlas argued, today's creative types are a pretty tame bunch. He recalled that the literary giants he admired during his student days at Harvard drank and caroused with abandon. "My gurus were the famously hard-drinking literati of an earlier epoch: a shaky hungover Robert Lowell chain-smoking mentholated Trues at a seminar table in the Quincy House basement; a drunken Norman Mailer brandishing a bottle of whiskey and baiting the crows in Sanders Theatre; Allen Ginsberg toking up at a Signet Society dinner and chanting his poems to the hypnotic accompaniment of a harmonium. Postwar poetry was a hymn of excess."

These were artists living the bohemian way. Atlas described the booze-filled gatherings of the old literati, the smoky parties, the embarrassing scenes, the bitter feuds, and the ensuing divorces. Even the diaries of austere Edmund Wilson are filled with adultery and lewd drunkenness; Edmund found himself one day doing a threesome on a couch. Many of these people, in fact, caroused themselves to an early grave. Delmore Schwartz died at fifty-two; John Berryman killed himself at fifty-seven; Shirley Jackson died at forty-five; Robert Lowell died at sixty, relatively old for his group.

But nowadays people who drink and carouse that way are likely to be greeted with medical diagnoses—alcoholism, drug addiction, depression. Even in what used to be the bohemian quarters, as James Atlas eloquently testifies, the days of booze and brawling are over. Now parties tend to be work parties; a glass or two of white wine, a little networking with editors and agents, and then it's home to the kids. Almost nobody drinks at lunch anymore. People don't gather around kitchen tables staying up nights imbibing and talking. Everybody is healthier, more orderly, and more success oriented.

The same pattern has been acted out in other circles. Journalists used to be smoking, drinking vulgarians. Now, as the older reporters never stop reminding us, the campaign buses are filled with mild college grads sipping bottled water. Nobody gets drunk at journalist parties, and anybody who did would be regarded as a loser. Academic social life, the articles in the *Chronicle of Higher Education* tell us, is drier and tamer than it was two decades ago. Even Hollywood, which should be the epicenter of hedonism, is overrun by health consciousness, career consciousness, and (relative) moderation. More Bobos pass out business cards at parties than pass out under the table.

When it comes to alcohol consumption more generally, we are probably living through the most abstemious era since Prohibition, maybe in American history. In our age all the old terms are fading away—sours, slings, highballs, fizzes, nightcaps—despite a little self-conscious nostalgia at the cigar and martini bars. On cable I recently stumbled across an old episode of *Match Game '73*. Six celebrities were asked to complete the phrase "half-_____," and the contestant had to guess how they had filled in the blank. He guessed "half-drunk." That was a good answer because four of the six celebrities chose either "half-drunk" or "half-crocked." Today if the same *Match Game* question were asked, the most common answer might be "half-and-half."

One of the reasons the old bohemians were so wild and free was that they were rebelling against square bourgeois mores. But once the bourgeoisie assimilated the liberated culture of the 1960s, there was not much left to rebel against. Once bohemian symbols were absorbed into the mainstream, they lost some of their countercultural panache. The novels of Henry Miller seemed cool when they offended middle-class librarians, but they don't seem so daring now. Nude performance art may have been a thrilling statement once, but it lost its cachet when it became titillation for the tourist trade. When drugs were discovered by disco kids from Queens and yuppies from Wall

Street in the seventies and eighties, naturally they seemed less like mind-expanding tools and more like grubby playthings. Living for pleasure no longer makes the same rebellious cultural statement it once did.

Moreover, playtime in the earlier decades seemed more like release. People were stuck in boring jobs, so wanted a little revelry at night. Creative types felt themselves stuck in a boring society, so wanted to up-end the rules. But for Bobos work is not boring. It's challenging and interesting. So maybe it's not surprising they should make play more like work. Bobos are reconcilers, after all, so maybe it is inevitable they would strive to blur their duties with their pleasures, making the former more enjoyable and the latter more tame.

Useful Vacations

You're sitting in an outdoor cafe in the Piazza della Serenissima in one of those stone Tuscan hill towns, and you've just finished 20 minutes of rapture while touring a gemlike little basilica far off the normal tourist paths. You've pulled a few iron tables together to accommodate the urbane couples you met inside, and as you sip drinks that back home would qualify as cough syrup, you begin trading vacation stories. Somebody mentions a recent journey to the Göreme Valley of central Turkey and the glories of the caves the Hittites carved into the volcanic mud-ash, when suddenly a gentleman wearing a shirt with an enormous number of pockets leans back and interjects, "Ah, yes. But the whole Cappadocia region has just been ruined by all the tourists."

After a few minutes someone else at the table relates some fascinating bits she learned from the tour guides while on an eco tour of southern Belize. "It really hasn't been the same since electrification," the man with all the

pockets laments. You have come face to face with a travel
snob. There are a certain number of sophisticated travelers who wear their past destinations like little merit
badges. Their main joy in life comes from dropping whop-
ping hints that everywhere you are just going they went to
long ago when it still meant something. It's hard to know
where such people get the time to go all these places, unless
some evil philanthropist pays them to go around the world
making other travelers feel inferior about their cultural
repertoire. They are masters of the insufferable question.
"Didn't the atabeg of Damascus stop there in 1139?" one
of them will ask at the mention of a certain faraway oasis
before peering around the table with a hopeful expression,
as if everybody else were going to jump in to confirm that
little bit of data. They seem to spend their evenings boning
up on obscure ethnic groups: "The Mobabi tribe once
fished there, I believe, until the Contutis pushed them further upriver." And needless to say, they merge with that
other atrocious population segment, language snobs: "I
suppose you can get by with a little Chinook?" They don't
say, "I know" such-and-such a language. They'll say, "I
have a little Portuguese" or "I have a few of the romance
languages, of course," in that faux offhand manner that
makes you want to stick the person's head in a vise and
squeeze it until the eyes pop out.

Unfortunately, few people act on this noble impulse,
even though they know that when such a person appears,
the Vietnam syndrome is not far behind. This is the psy-
chosis that causes people to steer all their conversations to
a single destination: their life-altering trip to Vietnam.

The travel braggart begins slowly. Just a few sly hints
about his vast cultural capital. Then as the conversation
goes along, he gets a little more voluble. He is biding his
time, sucking you in. There will be a ray of hope when
someone else in the group starts talking about Mount
Everest. Ah, he's been Tibetted, you'll think. Surely he

can't be so smug around someone who's been to Tibet. But, of course, he was doing Tibet before *Into Thin Air.*

And then it begins. He's describing his journey up the Ho Chi Minh Trail or the rail trip from Hue on the crowded non-air-conditioned train. He starts describing all the odd glories of North Vietnam, the aroma of camphor, the flurry of bicycles. Suddenly you realize you are in a quagmire. There will be much suffering. There is no way now to withdraw from the conversation with honor.

"I never knew that feeding geese could be such a spiritual experience," he will be saying while passing around photos of himself standing with a group of locals amidst the rice paddies near My Lai (he's the one in the sunglasses). He'll be describing a former VC whose oxcart he rode on up the Red River Valley. In his stories he always depicts himself as a masterful Dr. Livingstone, but you know that when he walked into a village, the locals saw him as this big flapping wallet with dollar bills flying out. If this person were suddenly found dead with a dozen butter knives up his nose, it would be like an Agatha Christie novel; everyone would have a motive.

I suspect that what keeps us from finishing off the travel braggart is that none of us is pure. All of us in the educated class are travel snobs to some degree. It's just that while we are snobs toward the hordes of fat tourists who pile out of vast buses and into Notre Dame, he is snobbish toward us. He's just a bit higher on the ladder of sophisticated travel.

The code of utilitarian pleasure means we have to evaluate our vacation time by what we accomplished—what did we learn, what spiritual or emotional breakthroughs were achieved, what new sensations were experienced? And the only way we can award ourselves points is by seeking out the unfamiliar sights, cultivating above-average pleasures. Therefore, Bobos go to incredible lengths to distinguish themselves from passive, nonindustrious tourists who pile in and out of tour buses at the old warhorse sights. Since the tourists carry cameras, Bobo travelers are embarrassed to. Since tourists sit around the most famous squares, Bobo travelers spend enormous amounts of time at obscure ones watching non-tourist-oriented pastimes, which usually involve a bunch of old men rolling metal balls.

Since tourists try to move quickly from sight to sight, the hard-working traveler selects the slowest possible means of transportation. Bobo travelers tour the Loire Valley by barge, looking down on the packs who zip through in cars. They cruise through New Zealand by bike, dismissive of those who take the train. They paddle through Costa Rica on a raft, feeling superior to those who jet past on airplanes. If tourists seem to be flocking to one sight, Bobos will make sure they are at another. "While most tourists in Tanzania go to Serengeti National Park to see the wildlife, the Selous Game Reserve is bigger and less disturbed," writes *Natural History* magazine editor Bruce Stuts in fine cultivated-traveler mode. It doesn't even matter if the Selous Game Reserve has less to see than the Serengeti. The pleasure the Bobo traveler derives from doing the more industrious thing more than compensates.

Lewis and Clark didn't return from their trip and say, "Well, we didn't find the Northwest Passage, but we did find ourselves." But that is the spirit of Bobo travel. Our travel dollars are investments in our own human capital. We don't just want to see famous sights; we want to pierce into other cultures. We want to try on other lives.

But not just any other lives. If you observe Bobo travel patterns and travel literature, you will detect a distinct set of preferences. The Bobo, as always, is looking for stillness, for a place where people set down roots and repeat the simple rituals. In other words, Bobo travelers are generally looking to get away from their affluent, as-

cending selves into a spiritually superior world, a world
that hasn't been influenced much by the global meritocracy. Bobos tend to relish People Who Really Know How
to Live—people who make folk crafts, tell folk tales, do
folk dances, listen to folk music—the whole indigenous
people/noble savage/tranquil craftsman repertoire.

Therefore, Bobos are suckers for darkly garbed peasants, aged farmers, hardy fishermen, remote craftsmen,
weather-beaten pensioners, heavyset regional cooks—
anybody who is likely to have never possessed or heard of
frequent flier miles. So the Bobos flock to or read about
the various folk locales where such "simple" people live in
abundance—the hills of Provence, Tuscany, Greece, or the
hamlets of the Andes or Nepal. These are places where the
natives don't have credit card debts and relatively few
people wear Michael Jordan T-shirts. Lives therefore seem
connected to ancient patterns and age-old wisdom. Next
to us, these natives seem serene. They are poorer people
whose lives seem richer than our own.

The small things—an olive grove or a small chapel—
take on greater meaning to a Bobo on vacation. Ideally,
Bobo travelers want to spend a part of each day just savoring. They'll idle away at a trattoria so far removed
from the crush of events that the natives don't even feel
compelled to have an opinion about Bill Gates. They will
swoon over some creamy polenta or a tangy turtle soup
and even educate their palate with some dish that prominently features bone marrow. They will top off their coffee
cup with cream squeezed straight from the cow and enjoy
the sturdy obesity of the peasant woman in the kitchen,
the picturesque paint peeling off the walls, the smiles
of the other diners who seem to be welcoming them into
their culture.

The pace of life is so delicious in such places. But the
lease on the vacation rental only goes for two weeks, so
Bobo travelers had better do their spiritual development

quickly. Most Bobos come up with a few serendipity techniques that will allow them access to a few moments of
authentic peasant living. Hovering on the edges of local
weddings often works. Exaggerating their genealogical
connection to the place while conversing with the locals is
another winning tactic: "Actually my grandmother's second husband came from Portugal." If done correctly, these
techniques can allow the Bobo pilgrim to have 6 unforget-
table moments a morning, 2 rapturous experiences over
lunch, 1.5 profound insights in the afternoon (on average), and .667 life-altering epiphanies after each sunset.

Enriching Misery

At the tippy top of the leisure status system are those
vacations that involve endless amounts of agony and pain.
These are vacations that take you hiking on a forced
march across some glacier or trekking through arid
deserts along the path that Alexander the Great's soldiers
were induced to follow only by threat of death. Or sitting
in some bug-infested rainforest in search of environmental
awareness. Such trips are not fun, but the educated-class
trekkers are not looking for fun. They want to spend their
precious weeks off torturing themselves in ways that will
be intellectually and spiritually enhancing. So travel companies have scouted out these high-status, low-amenity
destinations around the globe. These are the sort of adventure vacations and eco tours that now thrive amongst the
educated class.

For past generations naturalism has meant a renunciation of ambition and social mobility. But Bobo naturalists bring their ambition with them. They don't just sit in
the forest; they trek up a mountain, wade through a rainforest, climb an icy rock, bike up to the Continental Divide. If there's an easy way up the mountain, they'll take

the tougher one. If there's a perfectly good train to some-place, they'll ride a bike on awful roads. They turn nature into an achievement course, a series of ordeals and obsta-cles they can conquer. They go into nature to behave un-naturally. In nature animals flee cold and seek warmth and comfort. But Bobo naturalists flee comfort and seek cold and deprivation. They do it to feel more alive and because their life is a series of aptitude tests, and so an adventure vacation becomes one too.

Corporate executives used to avoid talking about their war experiences. But today's educated executives thrill and then eventually bore you with their high-altitude conquests. A quarter of them seem either to be just back from one of those instant-glacier expeditions or to be deep in the midst of training for one. You'll be minding your own business over the salad at some dinner party when suddenly you will hear the phrases "base camp" and "white-out" wafting ominously across the table. It was all uphill for the one who is speaking, but you know the af-fair will be all downhill for you. "It wasn't just physically demanding. It was mentally demanding," the arduous va-cationer will tell his or her audience of slightly soft dinner companions, who—pathetically—aren't in the habit of going on vacations that require months of training. The tale, which will go on longer than it took Peary to reach the Pole, will be full of accounts of native guides (reposi-tories of native wisdom), discarded gear ("Things were desperate, we had to jettison the three-ounce espresso maker"), frostbitten toes (there is always some other fel-low on the trip who lost a few), and miserable days spent cooped up in tents while the wind whipped by at some un-believable speed, reducing visibility to zero. You get the impression that every spot on earth over 10,000 feet above sea level is packed with magenta-clad millionaires luxuriating in their thin-air hardships.

In the midst of such soliloquies I used to wonder why

these North Face Folks didn't just take their two-week winter vacation and go to Minnesota to join a road crew. If they wanted brutal conditions, a tough challenge, and team camaraderie, at least in Minnesota they could have filled in a few potholes and had something to show for their misery. But, of course, the trekkers aren't lugging their carabiner belts halfway across the world for public service. They want the aesthetics. They want the full in-person IMAX experience. It's not enough to suffer; one must suffer for beauty. One must put oneself through ter-rible torment—and this can come either on a cold moun-tain top or in a malarial rainforest—in order to experience the spiritually uplifting magnificence of brutal nature. One must mutilate the body for environmental transcendence.

In that sense these trips represent a fantastically ex-pensive way to renounce the flesh in order to purify the spirit. Instead of fasting or flogging yourself with chains— as past renunciation-of-the-flesh types did—you gather to-gether ten or twenty or sixty thousand dollars, fly across the world to some uninhabitable spot, and torture your-self for the sake of divine transcendence. Those monks who built forbidding monasteries on the rocky outcrop-pings of Wales must have been seeking the same sort of brutal purity, though of course they lived in their outposts for years, whereas today's trekker can experience a dial-an-ordeal in a week or two and still be back at the corpo-rate campus fresh for work on a Monday morning. But the impulse is the same. From the drug-addled hedonism of Woodstock we have arrived at the asceticism of the educated-class vacation trekker.

Serious Play

And it's not just the expedition types who exemplify this impulse. The rest of us try to affiliate ourselves with the ordeal lifestyle. We're the ones who wear those hiking boots that were constructed for climbing the Himalayas. We're the ones who go out on fall weekends in parkas that were built to withstand −40-degree temperatures. We're the ones who buy our clothing from catalogues like Lands' End, which feature pictures of hikers atop Mount Everest on the cover. I was out at the Microsoft headquarters in Redmond, Washington, recently, and everybody there was dressed for a glacier climb, with boots, rugged khaki pants, and carabiners around their belts with cell phones hanging down. It's like going into a nightclub where everybody is constantly shoving their endurance cleavage in your face.

Then I drove over to the store where these Microsofties buy this sort of gear, the 80,000-square-foot REI emporium in Seattle. It's a store that sells leisure stuff to people who spend their leisure hours strenuously, or at least would like to look like they do.

To get there, I drove my rented minivan to downtown Seattle and parked it amidst the muddied-up sport-utes in the REI garage. I walked past the postage-stamp forest the REI people have landscaped as a place for customers to test-ride their mountain bikes. After a trip up the slate-floored elevator, I was on a large front balcony with huge wooden benches. A plaque on each reassures us that the wood used for the bench was blown down in 1995; no trees were murdered in the making of this rest spot. Up above there are clocks that tell the current time atop Mount Everest and the north face of Eiger in the Swiss Alps, in case you want to make a call there.

I walked through the front door and found myself a few steps in front of the ice-ax section. Out in front of me stretched a great expanse of ordeal-oriented merchandise, aisle upon aisle of snowshoes, crampons, kayaks, tents, and parkas, a daunting profusion of equipment options. I must admit I began feeling as if I were suffering from oxy-

gen deprivation. The goal of reaching the coffee shop upstairs at the store's summit seemed an absurdity. I was like
a character in a Jon Krakauer book. Dazed by this bewil-
dering environment, I knew only that I must somehow
summon the strength to trudge on.

To my right as I entered there was a museum of outdoor gear, so I could enjoy a little edifying foreplay before
I got down to the serious shopping. At the far end of the
museum was the climbing wall, at 65 feet the largest free-
standing climbing structure in the world.

It wasn't the salespeople that made my brain spin. I
knew they'd be products of Seattle's culture of hiking
shorts macho. They bounce around the store displaying
their enormous calves, looking like escapees from the
Norwegian Olympic Team. Nor was it my fellow customers that put me in this state. I was ready for squads of
super-fit software designers with glacier glasses hanging
from Croakies around their necks (because you can never
tell when a 600-foot mountain of ice might suddenly roll
into town, sending off hazardous glare).

The thing that got to me was the load of requirements. If you are going to spend any leisure time with
members of the educated class, you have to prove you are
serious about whatever it is you are doing. "Serious" is
the highest compliment Bobos use to describe their leisure
activities. You want to be a serious skier or a serious tennis player or a serious walker or a serious cross-country
skier or even a serious skateboarder. People engaged in
any of these pastimes are constantly evaluating each other
to see who is serious and who is not. The most accomplished are so serious they never have any fun at all,
whereas if you went out onto some field or trail or court
and acted happy and goofy, you'd be regarded as someone
who is insulting the whole discipline.

Now to be a serious outdoorsperson, you have to
master the complex science of knowing how to equip

yourself, which basically requires joint degrees in chemistry and physics from MIT. For example, up beyond the ice-ax section there's a tank where customers try to test and fathom the differences between a dozen different water filters and purifiers. To traverse that spot, you have to distinguish between purifiers made from iodine resin and tri-iodine resin, glass fiber and pleated glass fiber, a ceramic microstrainer and a structured matrix microstrainer.

And it only gets worse. Every item in the store comes in a mind-boggling number of chemically engineered options that only experienced wilderness geeks could possibly understand. And from each product dangles a thick booklet so packed with high-tech jargon that it makes selecting a computer mainframe seem as simple as picking an apple off a tree. For backpacks, do you want a Sun Tooth Tech pack with 500 x 1000-denier Cordura or a Bitterroot Tech Pack with the 430-denier Hexstop trim? Do you want the semi-rigid 12-point Charlet Moser S-12 Crampon Laniers with the heel-clip in the rear or the Grivel Rambo with the rigid drop-forged points and the step-in bindings? Even something as basic as sandals comes in various high-tech versions, loaded with expedition-class straps and high-performance treads, in case you want to climb to Mount Pinatubo on your way to the Alanis Morissette concert.

I was dimly aware of some code of gear connoisseurship I should be paying attention to. For true nature techies, some things, like boots and sport utility vehicles, should be bought in forms as big as possible. Other things, like stoves and food packs, should be bought as small as possible. And other things, like tents and sleeping bags, should pack up small and open up big.

But the real reason for the REI store is upstairs on the mezzanine level, where the clothing department is. Because while not a lot of people actually go climb glaciers, there are millions and millions who want to dress as if they do. So most of the foot traffic at REI seems to be up on the mezzanine. I went up to the clothing department looking for a respite from all the high-tech mumbo jumbo of the gear section. There were indeed a few soothing racks of all-cotton shirts in muted colors. But I didn't have to walk far before I was assaulted by a blaze of cobalt blue glaring off a vast profusion of polyester. It soon became obvious that while in the seventies the polyester people were low-class disco denizens, now they are high-status strenuous nature types. Between me and the coffee shop at the far end of the mezzanine there remained a treacherous field of artificial-fiber parkas, paddle jackets, zip pants, stretch vests, anoraks, and ponchos. And each of them had ominous-sized booklets hanging down, stuffed with dissertation-level technical detail highlighting the state-of-the-artness of each item. I confess at that moment I lost the will to live. I was content just to sit down and let somebody find my lifeless body there amidst the Gore-Tex mountain bibs.

But an inner voice—which sounded like James Earl Jones's—urged me on, and pretty soon I was slogging through racks and racks of outdoor gear processed from the world's finest chemical labs: Cordura, Polartec, and all the "ex" fabrics—Royalex, spandex, Supplex, and Gore-Tex. There were $400 parkas that advertised their core vent kinetic systems and sleeves with universal radial hinges (I guess that means you can move your arms around). There were heavy-denier parka shells, power stretch tights with microfilaments, expedition-weight leggings, fleece, microfleece, and bipolar fleece (which must be for people on Prozac). My favorite was a titanium Omnitech parka with double-rip-stop nylon supplemented with ceramic particles and polyurethane-coat welded seams. I imagined myself sporting that titanium Omnitech thing and suddenly saying to myself, "Here I am in the

middle of the forest and I'm wearing the Starship Enterprise."

Finally I had to puzzle my way through the "performance underwear" section, which was a baffling maze of
Capilene and bifaced power-dry polyester, with a few
Lycra spandex briefs strengthened with MTS2 polyester.
And finally, just as I was about to turn into an underwear
Luddite screaming out for a pair of honest white briefs, I
spied the coffee shop not more than 50 yards away. I
made my way toward the side of the store that has the art
gallery, with majestic nature photos, and the lecture hall. I
made it through the bookstore and past the park ranger
station. And there, finally, was a smiling barista offering
me a warm brew and a choice from among a multicultural
panoply of sandwich wraps. I settled down amidst the
Mission furniture they have strewn up there and finally
began to realize how wholesome I was feeling.

I looked around the store and there was nothing but
healthy people, educated-class naturalists who seemed to
work out regularly, eat carefully, and party moderately.
They were evidently well informed about their outdoor-
gear options, judging by their boots, packs, and shopping
bags. Moreover, as they sat there reading Aldo Leopold's
A Sand County Almanac and such books purchased from
the adjacent bookstore, they radiated environmental concern. Here was a community of good stewards, people
who were protecting the earth and themselves. Nature
used to mean wildness, abandon, Dionysian lustfulness.
But here was a set of people who went out into nature
carefully, who didn't want to upset the delicate balance,
who studied their options, prepared and trained. If Norman Rockwell were a young man today, he'd head up to
this coffee shop to get all this wholesome goodness down
on canvas.

• • •

From the careful sadomasochists of the Arizona Power Exchange to the environmentally conscious, technologically informed nature trekkers at REI, the common threads of a Bobo pleasure principle emerge. We are not straitlaced, but we are responsible. We don't go for binges. Instead, we are driven to excel, even in our leisure time. And the final striking thing about all this discipline and self-control is that it is not based on any body of formal rules. Other groups and earlier elites may have submitted to or at least paid homage to divinely inspired moral codes: Masturbation is sinful. Drinking is a vice. But Bobos are uncomfortable with universal moral laws that purport to regulate pleasure. Bobos prefer more prosaic self-control regimes. The things that are forbidden are unhealthy or unsafe. The things that are encouraged are enriching or calorie burning. In other words, we regulate our carnal desires with health codes instead of moral codes.

Bobos don't denounce the evils of demon rum; we warn about the danger of drunk driving. We don't celebrate chastity as a godly virtue, but we do talk about safe sex and emphasize that abstinence is the safest form of safe sex. As the columnist Charles Krauthammer has pointed out, "The core of the modern sexual code is disease prevention." Similarly, the morning television shows would never have a preacher on to talk about how the devil brings sin into your life. But morning after morning they host health and fitness experts who talk about the need for rigorous exercise, self-disciplined eating, getting a full night's sleep, and leading a careful, productive life. These physical regimes are ways to encourage moral behavior through the back door. People who follow them are leading lives of disciplined self-restraint, but they are doing so in the name of their bodies instead of their souls.

Of course, many social critics would say the moral life of the educated class is impoverished if sexuality and leisure are to be evaluated primarily on health, safety, and other utilitarian grounds. If you live in a society like ours, in which people seldom object if they hear someone taking the Lord's name in vain but are outraged if they see a pregnant woman smoking, then you are living in a world that values the worldly more than the divine. You can't really know God if you ignore His laws, especially the ones that regulate the most intimate spheres of life. You may be responsible and healthy, but you will also be shallow and inconsequential.

As usual, Bobos are not blind to this criticism. They have trouble submitting to any set of formal commandments because they value autonomy too much. But they burst with spiritual aspirations and long for transcendence. They don't want to forsake pleasures that seem harmless just because some religious authority says so, but they do want to bring out the spiritual implications of everyday life. And this set of struggles—between autonomy and submission, materialism and spirituality—is the subject of the next chapter.

6

Spiritual Life

I'M SITTING on a rock in the Big Blackfoot River in western Montana. The sun is glistening off the water, and the grasses on the banks are ablaze in their fall glory. The air is crisp and silent, and I'm utterly alone but for the hawk gliding by above and the trout lurking in the water below. This is the spot where Norman Maclean set and Robert Redford filmed *A River Runs Through It,* and I'm sitting here waiting for one of those perfect moments when time stops and I feel myself achieving a mystical communion with nature.

But nothing's happening. I've been hanging around this magnificent setting for 30 minutes and I haven't had one moment of elevated consciousness. The ageless rhythms of creation are happening all around me. The crisp air whispers. The branches sway. The ducks wing by silently. If John Muir were here he'd probably be in rapture. The river would be deep in conversation with

Maclean. Aldo Leopold would be writhing around on the ground in ecstasy over the beauty of some nearby twig. But as for me, not a thing. It occurs to me that maybe it's too late in the season for transcendence.

I never noticed it before, but it always seems to be summertime when those hyperspiritual types come to Montana to explore the deeper harmonies. It's always midsummer when movies like *The Horse Whisperer* are filmed or when jaded urbanites come to Montana to have their souls restored. Now it's October and this state must be spiritually tapped out.

"Eventually all things merge into one, and a river runs through it," Maclean writes. When I read that back in my living room a few months ago, it seemed so profound. Now I can't figure out what the hell it means. The only things merging into one are my fingers into a block of frozen flesh. Frigid conditions always seem inspiring and elemental in the adventure books, but now this brisk wind just makes my extremities hurt. And instead of making me profound, this solitude is just giving me the creeps. The nature writers relish those moments when all of creation reduces down to just the elements: me, the water, the trout. But there probably isn't another human being within 10 miles of here. When I think of the calamities that could befall a person out here—a broken leg, car trouble, allergy attack—I realize there are advantages in seeking inner peace at spots close to a pay phone and an emergency rescue squad. Every twig snap begins to sound like the first hint of an onrushing grizzly. I look at my watch and realize I had better start feeling a serene oneness with God's creation pretty soon. I've got dinner reservations back in Missoula at six.

The Soul Rush

I suppose there are suckers who come in at the end of every rush. The prospectors who went to California in the late 1850s were probably too late to find large gold nuggets just lying around. And these days the Montana Soul Rush has made the competition for transcendence nuggets just as fierce. For Montana has come to occupy an exalted place in the American consciousness. It's become one of those places Where Life Is Honest and True. Back in 1948 Leslie Fiedler wrote an essay in *Partisan Review* called "The Montana Face," jibing Montanans for their romantic attachment to the simple ways of the past. But the future doesn't beckon us as bravely as it did 50 years ago, and it is precisely Montana's simplicity that now attracts us. Montana has emerged as one of the antidotes to our striving lives, as a foil to the grubby ambition of city life and the prefab mediocrity of suburban cul-de-sacs. It is the beautiful place, the forbidding place, the slow, simple place. When the producers of the Robin Williams movie *What Dreams May Come* went looking for a setting for heaven, they chose Montana.

So naturally, business moguls and Hollywood stars have come to Montana by the Lear jet load. It's not only Ted Turner, Jane Fonda, Tom Brokaw, David Letterman, Steven Seagal, and the other big names; it's the compassionate cardiologists from Chicago, the rugged realtors from Atlanta, the naturalist probate lawyers from San Jose. They've all found a place to recharge their batteries, smell the pines, and feel lonely and hard—in the summer months. Two million people voyage up to Glacier National Park alone each year and get all spiritual in the face of its grandeur. Movies like *The Horse Whisperer* serve as fables for the upper middle class: oversophisticated New

York magazine editor comes to Montana, finds simple honest man who communes with horses and helps her rediscover the important things in life. These upscalers have built a part-time, affluent Montana atop the real Montana. Their spiritualized Montana feeds off the idea of Montana and the beauty of Montana while rarely touching the lower-middle-class grind of the actual state.

The Soul Rush started when a few Montanans of a literary bent made a fateful discovery. They discovered they possessed a sense of place. Everybody lives somewhere, of course, but not all places have that spiritual aura that we call "a sense of place." Only places that are inhospitable to ambition have that. We use that phrase only to describe locales that change slowly, that are remote, that are wedded to the old ways more than the new, where opportunities for fame and riches are few. Writers used to call such places stifling backwaters. Ambitious high school students dreamt of getting out. But to members of the educated class, so burdened with opportunities and demands on their time, the changeless places are oases of contentment. People seem, at least to the bicoastal visitor's eye, to die with equanimity in such places.

"Montana's special gift is space," writes local author Glenn Law, "landscape made personal; space that reaches out to the horizon then comes back and gets under your skin. It reaches inward, wraps itself around your soul, incubates and grows." (When people try to capture "placeness" on paper, it tends to sound like a parasitic disease.) The people who actually discovered this "sense of placeness" were the regional authors. Lightly populated though Montana is, the state is packed with landscape poets. It's not only Norman Maclean, Wallace Stegner, Richard Ford, William Kittredge, and Ivan Doig, who have lived in and written about Montana. It's the thousands of less famous authors and freelance writers who are thicker on the ground than the pines. You can scarcely open a national magazine without stumbling across some Bozeman- or Missoula-based wordsmith waxing lyrical about the trees and the trout. "To trace the history of a river, or a rain-drop, as John Muir would have done," Gretel Ehrlich writes in *Montana Spaces,* one of the many Montana an-thologies that have been published of late, "is also to trace the history of the soul, the history of the mind descending and arising in the body. In both, we constantly seek and stumble on divinity, which, like the cornice feeding the lake and the spring becoming the waterfall, feeds, spills, falls and feeds over itself over and over again."

Pass the beef jerky.

And once it was clear there was a genuine regional lit-erature in Montana, naturally, teams of foundation offi-cials were going to descend on the state looking to stimulate even more Authentic Voices. You'd have the Rockefeller, Ford, and MacArthur types sending out wagon trains across the range looking for raw poets as yet unsullied by literary agents. *TriQuarterly* and other high-brow journals devoted special editions to western writing. The Montana Committee for the Humanities helped cor-ral dozens of the Authentic Voices into one massive an-thology—over a thousand pages long—called *The Last Best Place,* a tombstone-size testimony to the spirituality of these Rocky Mountain sages. It's like a great big brick of verbosity all dedicated to the supposedly silent and stoic westerner.

These days in Montana nobody can go to a riverbank without coming back with a basket full of metaphors. You see philosophic fishermen out in the water up to their waders in belles lettres, their fly rod in one hand, their journal in the other. Literary magazines with names like *Northern Lights* have popped up like wildflowers in May, along with the attendant discussion groups, folklore societies, creative-writing programs, and ceramics workshops. Suddenly the air is thick with earnest cause-mongering, and high-minded groups like the Montana Consensus Council and the Montana Land Reliance. There's scarcely a trucker on the interstate, it seems, who's not silently wrestling with his bildungsroman. The region is suddenly dotted with invading potters, independent filmmakers, and telecommuting screenwriters, and of course there are posses of realtors roaming the valleys to scoop the whole carnival of seekers into luxury log cabins and time shares.

The saloons are filled with Rocky Mountain Buddhists and sensitive cowboy sages who come down from their 20-acre spreads in the evening flashing their newly bought belt buckles, ready to drink local beers and listen to country music singers with Ph.D.s. Needless to say, there's been an increase in title rustling. Montana novelists like titles with plain elemental words like *sky, lake, mountain, snow.* So if one writer comes down from the hills to announce he's calling his novella *Bridges of Snow Falling on Mountain Cedars,* the odds are one of the other Big Sky Bellows will have already claimed that stake, and things are likely to get ugly.

I sometimes go to a guest ranch 60 miles south of Bozeman. In the eighties when you took one of the ranch's horses out for a ride, the wrangler would give you a 10-minute safety lecture on how not to get killed while horseback riding. Now, in the heat of the Soul Rush, at the same ranch they sit you down for a 70-minute lecture on the spiritual life of horses, the techniques of horse whispering, the evolutionary secrets of horse psychology, the Zen possibilities that await you on the trail. Now every wrangler has to develop a little Hermann Hesse routine, and every gas station attendant who has a dumb vacant look about him has to pretend that what he's really filled with is deep introspection.

Flexidoxy

There was a story in one of the Montana papers not long ago about Missoula's only Jewish congregation, which is presided over by Rabbi Gershon Winkler. Given the variety of Jews who have come to Missoula from places like Los Angeles and New York, Rabbi Winkler doesn't lead an Orthodox, Conservative, Reform, or Reconstructionist service. He calls his hybrid approach "Flexidoxy."

It's not a bad word to sum up the sort of spiritual pining you see in Montana, the hybrid mixture of freedom and flexibility on the one hand and the longing for rigor and orthodoxy on the other. After all, the Montana mindset has always celebrated flexibility, freedom, and independence. This is a state that until recently didn't have speed limits on its highways, so suspicious are the locals about any authority telling them how to lead their lives. And it is natural that the members of the educated class, who have their own anti-authority impulses, would come up here and find a spiritual home.

But Montana is no loosey-goosey New Age wonderland. It's not Marin County with a timberline. In the first place, the state's harsh climate discourages loose, experimental ways of living. The Montana writers may get humid when talking about the soulfulness of the trout streams, but it's the toughness and discipline of the fisherman they admire. It's the classic traditions of the sport, the endless repetitions, and obedience to the master's forms that evoke their admiration. Norman Maclean and Wallace Stegner are not 1960s or 1970s New Age vaporheads. Montanans are contemptuous of the fuzzy amateurs who come for a few moments of easy communion and then dash back to the cities when the air turns gray. Only about half the people who actually buy vacation homes up here keep them for more than a few years, after they find that the natural grandeur comes at a frigid meteorological price. Native and wannabe native Montanans define themselves against people who don't have real manure on their boots, who haven't been kicked a few times by a horse, who haven't stuck around the state long enough to be painfully lonely. This is still a state mainly of ranchers and pickup truck drivers, not Transcendental Meditation groups. Even the creative-writing instructors who come up here tend to do so because they want to live among regular, practical folk.

And there's another element of the Montana ethos that runs against I'm OK, You're OK sentimentalism. It's most apparent when Montanans start talking about their connection to the land. It's then that you begin to hear how Montana's spirituality is grounded in something tangible. When Montanans begin talking about their sense of place, you hear echoes of the blood and soil nationalism that is more common in Europe than in the States. It's a conservative, even reactionary bond. It's based on the idea that a person's connection to the landscape is deeper than rationality and choice. It is a bond that is earned through years or even generations of suffering, of blood and sweat dropped onto the ground. It's conservative because it is suspicious of change and anything that would alter the landscape or character of the beloved place. Montanans make a point of mentioning how long they have been here and how long their families have been here.

And for Montanans and the high fliers who flock to the state, the whole point of Montana is that it is not cutting edge. It is not California or New York. It is a slow place, tied down by its climate, by its remoteness, and by its traditions. Much of the Montana literature is elegiac in tone, loyal to some earlier age.

As a symbol, Montana stands for depth over breadth. It means doing the same routines year after year, not flitting from one lifestyle to another. It means settling down with a few rituals rather than endlessly sampling a smorgasbord of lifestyles. Living in such a remote place means giving up on certain opportunities—to make money or to lead diverse lives. "Ranching has no corporate ladder," Scott Hibbard writes in the anthology *Montana Spaces*. "The rancher who is owner-operator at age twenty-five will be doing essentially the same things for the same pay at age seventy-five." But Montanans seem to accept the trade-offs, believing that the additional amusements and opportunities that a bicoastal life may bring would not compensate for the permanent and profound connections that are possible in such a rooted place.

So this is why the term Flexidoxy is apt. It suggests the hybrid nature of Montana's spiritual ethic. It starts with flexibility and freedom, with the desire to throw off authority and live autonomously. But it also suggests a second and opposing impulse, an impulse toward orthodoxy, which is to say, a desire to ground spiritual life within tangible reality, ordained rules, and binding connections that are based on deeper ties than rationality and choice.

And isn't this desire to balance freedom with rootedness the essence of the educated class's spiritual quest? This is a class that came of age rebelling against the authority of the preceding elite. Starting in the 1950s, the books and movies that most influenced the educated class have railed against conformism, authoritarianism, and blind obedience. Championing freedom and equality, members of the educated class cultivated a code of expressive individualism. They succeeded in smashing old hierarchies. They cultivated an ethos that celebrates, actually demands, endless innovation, self-expansion, and personal growth. Because of the reforms initiated largely by the educated class, people have more choices. Women have more choices where to work or how to lead their lives. Different ethnic groups have more choices about where they can go to school or which clubs they can join. Freedom and choice are everywhere triumphant, right down to the gourmet whole-grain loaf you select at the farmer's market, or the kind of partner you prefer in the bedroom.

But if you look around at the educated class today, you see a recognition that freedom and choice aren't everything. Free spirituality can lead to lazy spirituality, religiosity masquerading as religion, and finally to the narcissism of the New Age movement. The toppling of old authorities has not led to a glorious new dawn but instead to an alarming loss of faith in institutions and to spiritual confusion and social breakdown. So if you look around the Bobo world, you see people trying to rebuild connections. You see it in Wayne, Pennsylvania, where upscale consumers shop for farmyard furniture that evokes traditional rituals and simple styles. You see it in Burlington, Vermont, where educated upscalers have moved in search of the connections that are possible in small towns. You see it in the vacation preferences of the educated class, the way they flock to premeritocratic enclaves where the local peasantry live stable, traditional lives. And you see it in places like Montana, where the cosmopolitan class comes looking for a place to call home.

So progressive in many of their attitudes, the Bobos are spiritual reactionaries. They spend much of their time pining for simpler ways of living, looking backward for the wisdom that people with settled lives seem to possess but which the peripatetic, opportunity-grasping Bobos seem to lack.

The question for the educated class is, can you have your cake and eat it too? Can you have freedom as well as roots? Because the members of the educated class show little evidence of renouncing freedom and personal choice. They are not returning to the world of deference and obedience. They are not about to roll back the cultural and political revolutions of the past decades, which have done so much to enhance individual freedom. They are going to

try to find new reconciliations. The challenges they face
are these: Can you still worship God even if you take it
upon yourself to decide that many of the Bible's teachings
are wrong? Can you still feel at home in your community
even if you know that you'll probably move if a better job
opportunity comes along? Can you establish ritual and
order in your life if you are driven by an inner imperative
to experiment constantly with new things? I've talked
about the mighty reconciliations the Bobos make. But
these spiritual reconciliations are the most problematic.
The Bobos are trying to build a house of obligation on a
foundation of choice.

The Limited Life

As members of the educated class have rediscovered
the virtues of small-scale local bonds and the vital role
deep connections play in a person's spiritual life, there has
been an outpouring of books and articles about community and civil society, on how to recreate the mediating
structures by which people support one another and find
their place. One of the most hardheaded of these books is
Alan Ehrenhalt's 1995 work, *The Lost City*. Ehrenhalt
went back to describe, fondly but without nostalgia, some
of the tight-knit Chicago neighborhoods of the 1950s.
These middle- and working-class places were exemplars of
the communitarian values that many people long for
today. In the St. Nick's parish neighborhood on the Southwest Side of Chicago, for example, children ran freely from
house to house, and there were always plenty of adults to
watch out for them. On summer evenings everybody hung
around outside, talking and joking with their neighbors.
Most of the shopping was done at family-owned stores,
like Bertucci's meat market. Nick Bertucci knew most of
his customers well, and they lingered in his store to trade

gossip. Many of the people in the neighborhood had job security at the local Nabisco plant; sometimes two and three generations would be working together there side by side. The vast majority of the neighborhood was Catholic, and most went to mass at St. Nick's on Sundays. Local loyalties were strong. When asked where they were from, people from the parish didn't say Chicago or even the Southwest Side. Instead, they identified individual corners: "I come from 59th and Pulaski." This was, in many ways, a wonderful neighborhood, and the people who lived there look back upon it fondly.

But as Ehrenhalt is quick to point out, there were hardships at the root of all this togetherness. Some were material. People hung out in the street on summer evenings in part because nobody had air conditioning. TV was just becoming popular, so there wasn't much easy entertainment inside anyway. Furthermore, the bungalows the families lived in were tiny, and part of the space the families did have was reserved as a genteel parlor and so was off-limits most of the time. These people didn't have a lot of privacy.

The first chapter in Ehrenhalt's book is called "The Limited Life," and it's clear that the people who lived in St. Nick's parish were restricted in more serious ways as well. The neighborhood was ethnically homogeneous, with all the insularity, parochialism, and prejudice that encourages. There were not many opportunities to get out and thrive in the mainstream American economy, in the high-flying world of State Street and Michigan Avenue. If you lacked the right manners, the right accent, or the right social connections, as most Southwest Siders did, the upper echelons of the corporate world were closed to you. In fact, the whole cosmopolitan whirl of downtown Chicago was remote for many people in the parish. It took three bus rides just to get downtown. Many families went there once a year, to look at the Christmas store windows.

There were other limits. Women had limited career

options, which was good for the local schools but probably not so good for the capable women who might have
aspired to careers other than teaching. Ehrenhalt includes
a photo taken at the school. It shows row upon perfect
row of neat students sitting at meticulously spare desks,
all of them wearing the same uniform and practically the
same expression. It evokes the world of regimented education that was to come under such comprehensive attack in
the following decade.

Furthermore, while the local men had secure jobs at
Nabisco, they were being shortchanged when it came to
salary. Their union was corrupt and cut sweetheart deals
with the company. The workers knew it, but they didn't
have too many other career options. Politics didn't afford
many choices, either. The local government was run by the
machine; local leaders swore fealty to it. Ehrenhalt features a Chicago pol named John G. Fary who spent his
whole life obediently taking orders from Richard J. Daley.
As a reward for long service, Daley sent him to Congress.
Fary told reporters, "For twenty-one years I represented
the mayor in the legislature and he was always right."
That sort of deference to authority exemplifies a mentality
that was not uncommon in the communities in the 1950s
but is alien to most places today. It is a worldview in
which obedience is a virtue, in which authority, order, and
lasting relationships are valued over freedom, creativity,
and perpetual change.

Ehrenhalt has a chapter on religious life in the parish.
St. Nick's had 1,100 seats, and on Sundays they were filled
every hour on the hour for the start of mass. This was pre-
Vatican II, so the mass was conducted in Latin. The priests
stood with their backs to the congregation, facing the
altar. Monsignor Michael J. Fennessy reminded his flock
that the devil is always active, sin and temptation are all
around; the clergy spoke more openly of Satan's active
role in the 1950s than they do today, Ehrenhalt notes.

Spiritual life was as orderly and hierarchical as economic or political life. The way to truth was one, while the paths to error were many, so it was best to stay on the straight and narrow. Christ led you to the true way; Satan tempted you off it. The sins were categorized and enumerated, as were the graces. The parish had a place in the archdiocese, and the archdiocese had its place in the larger structure of the church. The crucial spiritual questions were not the ones we in the educated class tend to ask—"What am I seeking?"—but were more oriented toward authority—"What does God command and love?" The Lord's Prayer, it should be remembered, is spoken in the first person plural—it is spoken together as a community—and its first lines remind us of God's authority and His plan: "Our Father, who art in heaven, hallowed be Thy name. Thy kingdom come, Thy will be done. On earth as it is in heaven." In short, the spiritual universe was as orderly and hierarchical as the physical universe.

And as Ehrenhalt emphasizes, this mode of Catholicism was thriving in the 1950s in Chicago. There were 2 million practicing Catholics, 400 parishes, 2,000 priests, 9,000 nuns, and roughly 300,000 parochial school students. Between 1948 and 1958 the archdiocese opened an average of six new parishes a year. And it was not just in working-class neighborhoods where this attachment to organized religion was so strong. One of the features of life in the 1950s was that higher education correlated with religious observance. People with college and advanced degrees were more likely to be regular church and synagogue goers than were their less educated peers.

The Liberated Life

But, of course, by the 1950s modernity was challenging the ethos of deference and obedience and the whole hierarchical cosmology. The writers and social critics who looked out on that world tended to believe that America had become *too* orderly, *too* passive, *too* group oriented. The general tenor of the social criticism of the 1950s—whether it was *The Organization Man* or *The Lonely Crowd*—was that a smothering spirit of deference had settled over the land. Writers of all stripes attacked conformity, passivity, and deference. William Whyte complained about the prevailing social ethic that emphasized "belongingness" and the "belief in the group as the source of creativity." David Riesman's book was widely interpreted as a critique of "Other Directed Man," of the anxious conformist who is horrified by the thought that he might offend or stick out, who repressed all "knobby or idiosyncratic qualities and vices" in order to better fit in with the group. Protestant theologian Paul Tillich saw an America populated by people who had "an intense desire for security both internal and external, the will to be accepted by the group at any price, an unwillingness to show individual traits, acceptance of a limited happiness without serious risks."

These writers drew from a distinction the philosopher John Dewey had laid down—between "customary" and "reflective" morality. Customary morality is the morality of the tribe, the group, the home, the parental rules that are never challenged. It is based on long-established rules and deference to those eternal maxims. Reflective morality is based on conscious deliberations. It starts when an individual starts thinking through the consequences of various behaviors. It's more experimental and deliberative, as each person questions old rules and draws conclusions. In the 1950s most writers hoped that Americans would mature away from customary morality toward reflective morality. This move from home and religion toward autonomy and psychology, it was assumed, was the way of progress.

So most social critics were calling for a more individualistic form of spiritual life. "We hope for non-conformists among you, for your sake, for the sake of the nation, and for the sake of humanity," Tillich preached to a college audience in 1957. In effect, the writers—whether they were sociologists, Freudians, theologians, or Beat poets—were telling the young to break loose from their communities, groups, and religious orders. Spiritual fulfillment is found when you go your own way.

Among the intellectual class, mores had changed. Writers and academics sought to instill a more individualistic ethos in their children, one that would encourage self-exploration over obedience. Children may have been taught to defer to authority on the Southwest Side, but a few miles toward the lake, in the University of Chicago neighborhood or Hyde Park, the culture was quite different. As Isaac Rosenfeld wrote in a 1957 essay in *Commentary* called "Life in Chicago," "One sure way of telling whether you are visiting an academic or non-academic household is by the behavior of the children, and the extent to which you can make yourself heard above their clatter. If it is still possible to conduct a conversation, you are in a non-academic household."

The dominant trend of social thought in those years was toward individual self-expression and away from the group loyalty and deference that were the ideals in communities like St. Nick's parish. Each person can and must find his or her own course to spiritual fulfillment, the educated-class writers were saying.

Pluralism

It didn't take long for their views to triumph. It is now better to be thought of as unconventional than conventional; it is better to be called a nonconformist than a conformist. It is cooler to be a rebel than an obedient foot soldier. Individualistic pluralism is the foundation of Bobo spiritual life.

The spiritual pluralist believes that the universe cannot be reduced to one natural order, one divine plan. Therefore, there cannot be one path to salvation. There are varieties of happiness, distinct moralities, and different ways to virtue. What's more, no one ever really arrives at a complete answer to the deepest questions or to faith. It is a voyage. We are forever incomplete, making choices, exploring, creating. We are protean.

The proper spiritual posture, therefore, is to be open-minded about new choices and paths, to be empathetic toward new opinions, temperaments, and worldviews. Jane Jacobs opens *The Death and Life of Great American Cities* with a quotation from Oliver Wendell Holmes that celebrates spiritual diversity. "The chief worth of civilization is just that it makes the means of living more complex," Holmes wrote. "Because more complex and intense intellectual efforts mean a fuller and richer life. They mean more life. Life is an end in itself, and the only question as to whether it is worth living is whether you have enough of it." This is a different set of values: diversity, complexity, exploration, self-exploration.

These values are now embraced by millions. In his book *Achieving Our Country,* the philosopher Richard Rorty puts it well. The goal of each society, he writes, is to create "a greater diversity of individuals—larger, fuller, more imaginative and daring individuals." Our efforts, Rorty continues, should be directed toward creating a country in which "the future will widen endlessly. . . . Experiments with new forms of individual and social life will interact and reinforce one another. Individual life will become unthinkably diverse and social life unthinkably free."

This is an optimistic creed. Fulfillment can be sought through perpetual self-expansion. And further, freedom can lead to order. If we give everyone maximum freedom to live their own best lives, the interplay between their efforts will mesh to form a dynamic and complicated harmony. (Remember Jane Jacobs's street.) All that is required is that people of good faith seek their own paths in an open and tolerant manner, without trying to impose their own paths on others.

Spiritual Freedom

Given the opportunity to explore their new-found spiritual freedom, the members of the educated class didn't need to be asked twice. Some of them hightailed away from the rituals and ceremonies of institutionalized religion and set off on individual spiritual quests. Jerry Rubin, whose life became a caricature of the zeitgeist shifts of his age, recalled in his memoir, *Growing (Up) at Thirty-Seven,* "In five years, from 1971 to 1975, I directly experienced est, gestalt therapy, bioenergetics, rolfing, massage, jogging, health foods, tai chi, Esalen, hypnotism, modern dance, meditation, Silva Mind Control, Arica, acupuncture, sex therapy, Reichian therapy and More House—a smorgasbord course in New Consciousness."

The New Age gurus commanded their followers to Love Thyself, and out poured great gushes of spiritual self-absorption, what different writers have called "self-approving joy," "virtuous voluptuousness," or "egoistic hedonism." Of course, not everybody went in for this stuff. America is a complicated place. But there was a moment in the 1970s and early 1980s when people still spoke unironically about the "self," when the therapeutic sensibility seemed everywhere triumphant. This was the apogee of spiritual individualism, the high water mark, at least in the educated class, of the Human Potential movement, the Free to Be You and Me mentality, the whole New Age panoply, which at heart is spirituality without obligation.

By the time Robert Bellah and his research team published *Habits of the Heart* in 1985, they found a nation,
or at least an educated class, deep into self-exploration
and no longer willing to declare obedience to received
spiritual authority. For example, Bellah and his crew interviewed a young nurse named Sheila Larson, who described her faith as "Sheilaism." She had invented her own
custom religion, with God defined as whatever fulfilled
her needs. "It's just try to love yourself and be gentle with
yourself," she said. "You know, I guess, take care of each
other."

Habits of the Heart was an important book because it
was an early sign the educated class was going to recoil
from the more extreme forms of spiritual individualism.
The authors wrote:

> We believe that much of the thinking about the
> self of educated Americans, thinking that has be-
> come almost hegemonic in our universities and
> much of our middle class, is based on inadequate so-
> cial science, impoverished philosophy, and vacuous
> theology. There are truths we do not see when we
> adopt the language of radical individualism. We find
> ourselves not independently of other people and in-
> stitutions but through them. We never get to our
> selves on our own. We discover who we are face to
> face and side by side with others in work, love, and
> learning. All of our activity goes on in relationships,
> groups, associations and communities ordered by
> institutional structures and interpreted by them.

Bellah and his colleagues were trying to point out the
sorts of problems that arise when individualistic spiritual
freedom is taken to the extreme. And these basic criticisms
have since become the conventional wisdom in Bobo circles. In the first place, maybe there is no "real self" that

somehow can be separated from all the external bonds that make up our lives. Maybe people who go deeper and deeper into the self are actually journeying into a void. Second, it is hard for the individualist to construct a pattern of rituals and obligations that give structure to life and make sense of the great transitions in life: birth, marriage, death. Furthermore, the lack of age-old rituals makes it very hard to pass your belief system on to your children. Organized religions have a set of stable ceremonies to guide and cultivate the spiritual lives of kids. Self religions do not. And so even many of the people who were at first most enthusiastic about New Age self-exploration have found themselves returning, sometimes reluctantly, to the institutionalized faiths they rejected—doing so for the sake of their kids.

But the ultimate problem with spiritual freedom is that it never ends. As Rorty points out, it widens endlessly. Freedom means always keeping your options open, so it means you never settle on truth, you never arrive, you can never rest. The accumulation of spiritual peak experiences can become like the greedy person's accumulation of money. The more you get, the more you hunger for more. The life of perpetual choice is a life of perpetual longing as you are prodded by the inextinguishable desire to try the next new thing. But maybe what the soul hungers for is ultimately not a variety of interesting and moving insights but a single universal truth. Dostoyevsky has the Grand Inquisitor say, "For the secret of man's being is not only to live but to have something to live for. Without a stable conception of the object of life, man would not consent to go on living."

Today the Inquisitor might say the Bobos are enslaved by their insatiable desire for freedom and diversity. He might warn that all the Bobos' varied experiences may dissolve into nothingness if they don't surrender to something larger than themselves. The end result of pluralism, he'd say, is an endless moving about in search of more and more lightly held ideas, none of which solves essential questions. The pluralistic ethos is fine for the search, but it makes it difficult to reach the sort of resting place that is offered by less elastic creeds, the sort of tranquillity that is promised, for example, in the book of Samuel: "Moreover, I will appoint a place for my people Israel, and I will plant them, that they may dwell in a place of their own, and move no more."

The Return of Order

The Bobos have surrendered neither their love of individual choice nor their pluralistic mindset. But there is a countercurrent, rarely so obvious as it is now. These days writers and social critics no longer quite so ardently celebrate nonconformism, the way the critics of the 1955–65 period did. They are not so optimistic that maximum personal freedom will automatically produce a dynamic but basically wholesome order. Today few writers argue that Americans are *too* group oriented or *too* orderly. They are not complaining about Organization Man or the other-directed joiners. On the contrary, today most social critics are calling for *more* community, *more* civil society, *more* social cohesion. Today writers tend to try to rein in the individualistic mindset the critics of 40 years ago were busy unleashing. Writers today, by and large, attempt to re-establish the rituals and institutional structures that were all weakened in the great rush of educated-class emancipation.

Over the past decade there has been a mountain of books and articles devoted to the subject of communitarianism, about the importance of "mediating institutions" and neighborly bonds. Hillary Clinton wrote a book called *It Takes a Village,* touting the virtues of stable small-town relations. Colin Powell launched a voluntarism crusade to get more people involved in their communities. Harvard sociologist Robert Putnam made a splash with an essay called "Bowling Alone" in which he maintained that the decline of bowling leagues was a symbol of how Americans were becoming disconnected from each other, becoming less active in the church, the PTA, and other community organizations. Can you imagine a writer in the 1960s choosing bowling leagues as a symbol of healthy community involvement? In those days bowling leagues were considered ridiculous and reactionary by members of the educated class. If they had died out in the 1960s, no intellectual would have shed a tear.

The civil society advocates and the communitarians set out to put some bounds around what they see as the radical individualism that has swept through America. Michael Joyce and William Schambra of the Bradley Foundation, which has supported many civil society efforts, write, "Americans are worried above all about the unraveling of the orderly, coherent, authoritative moral community that they were once able to build around themselves with their strong, local civil institutions." Liberals tend to emphasize that the global marketplace has undermined orderly and coherent moral communities. Conservatives tend to maintain that it is the breakdown of traditional morality. But both sides are interested in moving in the same direction, back to the bonds of local communities and small-scale authority and away from a system that allows individual choice to trump all other values.

Revival, Reconstruction, Return

One of the features of Bobo spirituality that leaps out at you is how backward-looking it is. Some groups seek spiritual fulfillment in some future utopia yet to come, but we Bobos don't look to the future for transcendence. We look to the past, to old traditions, rites, and rituals. The assumption of so much of what we do, of so many of the movies we see and books we read, is that in our efforts to climb upward, we have left something important behind. We have made ourselves so busy that we no longer know and appreciate the essential things. We have become so affluent, we have encrusted our lives with superficialities, and we have to look back and rediscover some of the simpler and more natural ways of connecting with the world. Maybe now it is time, the Bobo says, to rediscover old values, to reconnect with patient, rooted, and uncluttered realms.

This longing is evident in the way we try to construct our physical environment. Bobos surround themselves with remnants of the small, stable communities that radiate spiritual contentment. We saw the style in Chapter 2: the Shaker-inspired tables, rustic pine benches, distressed furniture, archaic farm implements, claw-footed bathtubs, prehistoric crafts, old industrial artifacts, whaling baskets, and on and on—each piece more nobly reactionary than the last. Go again inside the educated-class retail chains, Pottery Barn or Crate & Barrel. These and similar stores try to recapture some long-lost world of stability and order. Restoration Hardware, which is spreading like a home furnishings Starbucks across the nation's upscale malls, caters to its graduate-degreed clientele with old-fashioned ribbed steel flashlights (just like we used to carry in summer camp), hand-forged scissors, old-fashioned kazoos, Moon Pies, classic Boston Ranger pencil sharpeners, compartmentalized school lunch trays, and glass and steel Pyrex beakers just like the ones your doctor used to keep tongue depressors in. These are the nostalgic mementos of the communities we left behind. The small towns that were hollowed out by the shopping malls and the global marketplace. The backwaters we left behind us when we went off to college and to big-city job opportunities.

The spiritual quandary of the educated class was in fact beautifully exemplified in a video the Restoration Hardware people produced for potential investors just before they launched their IPO in 1998. The voice-over accompanying this video explains the theology behind the store: "Lurking in our collective unconscious, among images of Ike, Donna Reed and George Bailey, is the very clear sense that things were better made, that they mattered a little more." Images of the forties and fifties fill the video screen. "What happened? Slowly but surely we became a nation obsessed with production and, of course, consumption." At this point we see images of huge suburban developments and large outlet malls. "This was pretty heady and pretty good. We got so proficient at making things we had unlimited choices and an endless array of goods." The "plastics" scene from *The Graduate* comes along. "The retail environment came to reflect this mentality—more square footage, more, more, more. Then, one day, the generation used to having everything recoiled, and became the generation searching for something."

There you have it. The generation that gave itself "unlimited choices" recoiled and found that it was still "searching for something." In so many ways we seem to want to return to some lost age of (supposed) spiritual coherence and structure. We seem to sense the cost of our new-found freedom is a loss of connection to other people and true communities. We want to recreate those meaningful ligatures. And yet, more often than not, we're not willing to actually go back to the age of limits, which would mean cutting off our options.

The Great Pastiche

As a result, you now see a great spiritual pastiche. You see a mixture of autonomy and community. You see younger Bobos especially becoming active in churches and synagogues, but they are not interested in having some external authority—pope, priest, or rabbi—tell them how to lead their lives. Militant secularism is no longer on the march. Now people return to religion, but often they are not content to have just one religion; they dabble in several simultaneously. Princeton sociologist Robert Wuthnow reports on a 26-year-old disabilities counselor, the daughter of a Methodist minister, who describes herself as a "Methodist Taoist Native American Quaker Russian Orthodox Buddhist Jew."

Not everyone has spooned so many helpings from the spiritual buffet table. But even in more traditional circles, when one sees people return to religious participation, one often gets the sense that it is the participation they go for as much as the religion. The *New York Times Magazine* recently ran a special issue on religion that included the astute headline "Religion Makes a Comeback (Belief to Follow)." Francis Fukuyama nicely captured the ethos of Bobo religiosity in his 1999 book, *The Great Disruption:*

> Instead of community arising as a byproduct of rigid belief, people will return to religious belief because of their desire for community. In other words, people will return to religious tradition not necessarily because they accept the truth of revelation, but precisely because the absence of community and the transience of social ties in the secular world makes them hungry for ritual and cultural tradition. They will help the poor or their neighbors not because doctrine tells them they must, but rather because they want to serve their communities and find that faith-based organizations are the most effective ways of doing so. They will repeat ancient prayers and reenact age-old rituals not be-

cause they believe they were handed down by God, but rather because they want their children to have proper values, and because they want to enjoy the comfort of ritual and the sense of shared experience it brings. In a sense they will not be taking religion seriously on its own terms. Religion becomes a source of ritual in a society that has been stripped bare of ceremony, and thus a reasonable extension of the natural desire for social relatedness with which all human beings are born.

This is not to say that Bobo congregants are not rigorous. Often they adhere to dietary restrictions and the like with extraordinary rigor. But somehow it is rigor without submission. Whereas earlier believers felt that, paradoxically, freedom was achieved through a total submission to God's will, blind obedience of that sort is just not in the Bobo mental repertoire. Among Jews, for example, there is a growing movement of young modern Orthodox who know Hebrew, study the Torah, and observe the kosher laws. They are rigorous observers, but they also pick and choose, discarding those ancient rules that don't accord with their modern sensibilities—most any rule that restricts the role of women, for example. Furthermore, they pull back from biblical teachings whenever those teachings clash with pluralism—with any teaching that implies that Judaism is the one true faith and that other faiths are inferior or in error. This is Orthodoxy without obedience—indeed, Flexidoxy.

Organized religion, once dismissed as hopelessly archaic or as a crutch for the weak-minded, now carries with it a certain prestige. Bobos tend to feel a little surge of moral satisfaction if they can drop their church or synagogue attendance into a dinner party conversation. It shows they are not just self-absorbed narcissists but mem-

bers of a moral community. And yet the religious discourse has been changed. Now sectarian disputes, which
took up so much energy for earlier theologians, are considered a bit silly. "I'm not, of course, an expert on religion," Václav Havel writes in *Civilization* magazine, "but
it seems to me that the major faiths have much more in
common than they are willing to admit. They share a
basic point of departure—that this world and our existence are not freaks of chance but rather part of a mysterious, yet integral, act whose sources, direction and purpose
are difficult for us to perceive in their entirety. And they
share a large complex of moral imperatives that this mysterious act implies. In my view, whatever differences these
religions might have are not as important as these fundamental similarities." In other words, the religious impulse
is a flexible thing that can take many different forms in
different cultures. What's important and good is the essential religious impulse, not the particular strictures of any
one particular sect or denomination. So it doesn't hurt to
shop around, experiment with a few religions before committing yourself, or maybe even flow between different denominations, depending on your needs and preferences at
the moment. Choice reconciled with commitment.

The Grandest Reconciliation

Most people obviously think this reconciliation can
work, or at least they are going to give it a shot. And
maybe it *can* work. Robert Nisbet, whose 1953 book, *The
Quest for Community,* is the forerunner of the current interest in civil society, believed that while the best life was
to be found within community, people should not limit
themselves to one community. They should experience
many communities. "Freedom is to be found in the inter-
stices of authority; it is nourished by competition among

authorities," Nisbet wrote. In this way they could enjoy a sense of belonging, but also flexibility and freedom. Nisbet quoted the French writer Pierre-Joseph Proudhon, "Multiply your associations and be free."

But others don't believe that maximum freedom can be so easily reconciled with spiritual fulfillment. They argue that the synthesis the cooperative individualists have created is a phony synthesis. These people talk about tradition, roots, and community, but they are just paying lip service to these virtues. When push comes to shove, they always choose personal choice over other commitments. They move out of communities when a better job comes along. They abandon traditions and rules they find tiresome. They divorce when their marriages become unpleasant. They leave their company when they get bored. They fall away from their church or synagogue when it becomes dull or unrewarding. And this is self-defeating, because at the end of all this movement and freedom and self-exploration, they find they have nothing deep and lasting to hold on to.

Comparing our own lives to those he described in the tight communities of Chicago, Alan Ehrenhalt wrote that we are like the fellow who sits in front of the TV constantly zapping the remote control, that "ultimate weapon of personal choice, proceeding in the course of an hour to select and reject dozens of visual entertainments whose ability to satisfy us for more than a few minutes is crippled by our suspicion that there may be something more stimulating a couple of frequencies further on." Ehrenhalt continues:

> Too many of the things we do in our lives, large and small, have come to resemble channel surfing, marked by a numbing and seemingly endless progression from one option to the next, all without the benefit of a chart, logistical or moral,

because there are simply too many choices and no
one to help sort them out. We have nothing to insu-
late ourselves against the perpetual temptation to
try one more choice, rather than to live with what
is on the screen in front of us.

Ehrenhalt has a point. The thing we are in danger of
losing with our broad, diverse lives is a sense of belonging.
A person who limits himself or herself to one community
or one spouse is going to have deeper bonds to that community or that spouse than the person who experiments
throughout life. A person who surrenders to a single faith
is going to have a deeper commitment to that one faith
than the person who zigzags through in a state of curious
agnosticism. The monk in the monastery does not lead an
experimental life, but perhaps he is able to lead a profound one.

And so we get in Bobo life a world of many options,
but maybe not a life of do-or-die commitments, and
maybe not a life that ever offers access to the profoundest
truths, deepest emotions, or highest aspirations. Maybe in
the end the problem with this attempt to reconcile freedom with commitment, virtue with affluence, autonomy
with community is not that it leads to some catastrophic
crack-up or some picturesque slide into immorality and
decadence, but rather that it leads to too many compromises and spiritual fudges. Maybe people who try to have
endless choices end up with semi-commitments and semi-
freedoms. Maybe they end up leading a life that is moderate but flat. Their souls being colored with shades of gray,
they find nothing heroic, nothing inspiring, nothing that
brings their lives to a point. Some days I look around and
I think we have been able to achieve these reconciliations
only by making ourselves more superficial, by simply ignoring the deeper thoughts and highest ideals that would
torture us if we actually stopped to measure ourselves ac-

cording to them. Sometimes I think we are too easy on ourselves.

The irony of Bobo spiritual life is that it started out with such a bang—the moment of liberation, the throwing off of old constraints, the first delicious experiments with total freedom—but it has ended up with a quietism. The bohemians were appalled by the tepid lives of the bourgeoisie, their shallow contentment and comfortable mores. So they called upon the middle-class burghers to break free from the well-worn paths that had been laid down from time immemorial. Life should be an adventure! Yet if we are to choose our own courses, what are we to make of the people who choose other courses? Life is a diversity of incommensurate values, and every religion has a kernel of virtue, every choice fills a real human need. So the bohemian who goes charging off into a new consciousness filled with heroic dreams quickly stops short and learns to be tolerant of others. Bohemians learn not to be too zealous about their own visions, lest they offend their neighbors, and themselves. The raging bonfire of emancipation quickly turns into the cupped candle of tolerance and moderation.

Members of the educated class are suspicious of vehemence and fearful of people who communicate their views furiously or without compromise. They are suspicious of people who radiate certitude, who are intolerant of people not like themselves. Bobos pull back from fire and brimstone. They recoil from those who try to "impose" their views or their lifestyles on others. They prefer tolerance and civility instead. Bobos are epistemologically modest, believing that no one can know the full truth and so it's best to try to communicate across disagreements and find some common ground. Be moderate in your own faith because you probably don't have the complete answers, and don't try to push your faith onto others.

There is something humane about this mentality.

Bobos are pleasant to be around, which is no small thing. But, as always, there are trade-offs. Nietzsche once wrote, "Nobody will very readily regard a doctrine as true merely because it makes people happy or virtuous." After all, prophets and saints didn't believe what they believed because it made them happy. Many of them were turned into martyrs precisely because they clung to truth regardless of its earthly consequences. But Bobos are more utilitarian. Maybe that sort of surrender and heroism is beyond the reach of Bobo spirituality.

The sociologist Alan Wolfe calls the morality of the upper middle class "small scale morality." For his 1998 book, *One Nation, After All,* Wolfe interviewed 200 members of the middle and upper middle class in suburbs spread across America, a demographic sample that overlaps reasonably well with the educated class. Wolfe's group included some people who are orthodox believers and some whose faith is highly individualist, including a woman who spoke about finding her own individual God within, in the same terms as Sheila did in Robert Bellah's *Habits of the Heart* 13 years earlier. Wolfe's general finding was that upper-middle-class Americans value religion but are unwilling to allow it precedence over pluralism. "Americans take their religion seriously," Wolfe writes, "but very few of them take it so seriously that they believe that religion should be the sole, or even the most important, guide for establishing rules about how *other* people should live." The italics are Wolfe's. One hundred sixty of his respondents agreed or strongly agreed with the proposition "There is such a thing as being too religious," an apparent critique of those who use their religious creed to judge or evangelize others.

This tolerance and respect for diversity, Wolfe found, leads to a style of faith that is radically anticontentious. The people he spoke to shy away from judgmentalism of almost any sort. These upper-middle-class Americans prefer, he concluded, a morality "modest in its ambitions and quiet in its proclamations, not seeking to transform the entire world but to make a difference where it can." That means, Wolfe writes, that members of the upper middle class think of morality in personal terms. They think of establishing moral relationships with those close to them but do not worry about formal moral rules for all mankind. They offer moral advice tentatively. They have "either given up finding timeless morality or would be unwilling to bring its principles down to earth, if, by chance, they came across it." They draw moral guidance from a variety of sources, from the Bible to the movies, and improvise a flexible set of guideposts. They make moral distinctions but are quick to amend them as circumstances warrant. When faced with moral claims that inescapably conflict, they try to blur those too: "Ambivalence—call it confusion if you want—can be described as the default position for the American middle class; everything else being equal, people simply cannot make up their mind."

This is a morality, in other words, that doesn't try to perch atop the high ground of divine revelation. Nor does it attempt to scale the heights of romantic transcendence. Instead, it is content with the workable and peaceful oases on the lower ground. It follows the path of least resistance between the two hills.

Let's try to weigh the pros and cons of Bobo spirituality. It is more a temperament than a creed. Bobo moralists are not heroic, but they are responsible. They prefer the familiar to the unknown, the concrete to the abstract, the modest to the ardent, civility and moderation to conflict and turmoil. They like comforting religious rituals, but not inflexible moral codes. They like spiritual participation but are cautious of moral crusades and religious enthusiasms. They savor spiritual sentiments, so long as they are flexible, and theological discussions, so long as they are full of praise rather than blame.

They have an ability to not react; to accept what doesn't directly concern them. They tolerate a little lifestyle experimentation, so long as it is done safely and moderately. They are offended by concrete wrongs, like cruelty and racial injustice, but are relatively unmoved by lies or transgressions that don't seem to do anyone obvious harm. They prize good intentions and are willing to tolerate a lot from people whose hearts are in the right place. They aim for decency, not saintliness, prosaic goodness, not heroic grandeur, fairness, not profundity. In short, they prefer a moral style that doesn't shake things up, but that protects the status quo where it is good, and gently tries to forgive and reform the things that are not so good. This is a good morality for building a decent society, but maybe not one for people interested in things in the next world, like eternal salvation, for example.

Bobo Heaven

Given this moderate, small-scale morality, it's hard to imagine what will happen to us Bobos when the world finally comes to an end. It's hard to imagine some fiery Last Judgment, some awful moment when the God of the Educated Class separates the saved—those who bundled their newspapers for the recycling bin—from the damned, those who did not. Bobo morality is so gentle and forgiving. Dwelling as it does in the moral temperate zone, Bobo morality doesn't seem compatible with the unrelenting horror of hell. On the other hand, Bobo morality doesn't seem compatible with something as final and complete as heaven either. Maybe instead of a Last Judgment, there will just be a Last Discussion.

Or maybe, as in that Robin Williams movie *What Dreams May Come,* Montana is the closest we get to heaven. Maybe our heaven isn't some grand place far above earth and its reality. After all, we are a group who seem to get our spiritual charges from tangible things, from spiritual places and evocative objects. Maybe if we walked around with a coherent moral order built into our head, we would feel at home in the supernatural realm. But lacking that faith in that next world, we tend to experience our spiritual epiphanies while communing with the physical environment in this one. We Bobos are more likely to try to discover great truths in particulars, the wonder of a leaf or the shape of a child's ear, than in a divine vision. With our tendency to seek peace in serene places, maybe a second home on some beautiful mountainside really is as close as we can come to experiencing paradise. Maybe our heaven is grounded in a piece of realty.

Picture a saintly Bobo woman pausing on her Montana hilltop at dusk, with thoughts of her law practice or mutual funds or teaching load far away. The air is still and fragrant, and even her dogs, Caleb and George, pause to savor the silence. As the breeze comes up, she pulls her FoxFibre shirt close around her neck. Lights are coming on in the distant houses across the valley, where former urban professionals have moved to start their own specialty food companies—Uncle Dave's Pestos is just on the far ridge to the north, Sally's Sauces is over to the west, and Yesterday's Chutney is on a few hundred acres south of that. She looks out over the tangle of wildflowers on the field that was junk strewn when she and her partner bought this "ranch," and she gazes lovingly upon the old pine she hired a tree surgeon to preserve.

Someone once said the essence of American history is the conversion of Eden into money. But with a little income, effort, and the right contractors, the educated person can spend money to build Eden. For hundreds of miles around, content couples are just settling into the creaky divans of their B&Bs and cracking open books by writers who have moved to Provence, novels that are like pornog-

raphy to the overstressed. And so the Bobo decides to
head down the path toward her second home. She is careful not to compact the soil over the tree roots and remembers a wonderful phrase by Steinbeck about a gentle
person who "steps high over bugs." She passes under the
arbor she attempted to cultivate last season and the pond
she and her partner installed as a skinny-dipping space—
they're much more sensual up here, though they wouldn't
do anything that might alarm the hawks. As she approaches the house, she can hear the soundtrack of a Mer-
chant-Ivory film wafting up to greet her; the melodies echo
off the walls of the outbuildings that now serve as guest
cottages.

The biggest thing they had to do when they moved in
to this place was to triple the size of all the windows. They
wanted to meld the interior and exterior elements of the
home and so live more fully within nature. How sweet it is
to wake up in a bedroom with one wall made entirely out
of glass, allowing yourself a quiet hour to observe the sunrise (it helps if you own the surrounding 150 acres so there
will be no neighbor observing you observing the sunrise).
As she approaches the house, she slows to admire the sophisticated mosses that now grow along the walkway to
the front door. She smells the aroma of the native grasses
they planted around the house, and then she bounds
lightly onto the wraparound porch, gently patting the
aspen woodpile stacked neatly by the door. They don't
burn this wood. But they've become devotees of the woodpile aesthetic, feeling that its form and texture complete a
place such as this. As she pushes open the maple door that
was flown in from New England, she hears her partner
working away in his studio. This property has allowed
him to take up the activities he never had time for. Aside
from his new hobby as a narrator of environmental documentaries, he's playing the violin again, reading the novels
of women writers of the Asian subcontinent, and doing

community work—he's now treasurer of the local preservation society.

The living room is large but spare. The broad floor planks appear to glow and set off the redwood mantelpiece that sits amidst their massive stone fireplace. The redwood tree blew down nearly three years ago, and the stones they found a few years further back while hiking in Colorado. The furniture is rustic but comfortable. There are three of those massive curl-up chairs, each the size of a comfy Volkswagen. They're so much nicer than all those wingback chairs of her parents' generation. In the wingbacks you had to sit up straight. But in these wide shabby-chic chairs you can bend around into all sorts of relaxed positions.

The Bobo glances at the wooden ladles she has been collecting. She is taken by their slender curves, and prizes them more than any of the other objects she has harvested during her counter-connoisseur browsings. On the big wall she has displayed some old tortoiseshells and Cambodian statuettes. Her favorite statue is of the Bodhisattva, the spiritual entity who achieved enlightenment but delays entry into Nirvana in order to help others get there.

And just as she is feeling delicious tranquillity wafting over her, she notices there in the doorway to the kitchen stands the Angel of Death, the one especially delegated for the Bobos. He looks radiant in an old tweed jacket, and he must have been waiting for her for some time, for he has found one of the supersize ceramic mugs she bought at the crafts fair in Santa Fe the previous spring. The Angel of Death is full of questions about the renovations they did last year. She tells him that they decided to build the new kitchen wing using a Nordic technique called straw bale construction, which does not require the depletion of any timberland. Then they filled in the walls with rammed earth, which involves taking raw dirt and compacting it with such awesome force that it forms sturdy walls, caramel in color and radiating a woodsy aroma. The new doors were made from reclaimed wood from an old mission house in Arizona and squeak intentionally when opened. Nonapparent technology controls the heating and air conditioning and turns off the lights after everybody has left a room. The Angel of Death is enchanted by how they have tripled the original size of the ranch home and yet still preserved its original integrity. He informs her that she has just died but he doesn't plan to take her anywhere. She just gets to exist forever amidst all this glorious materiality. The only thing he requests is that she redo the floor tiles in the hall, which didn't really work out as nicely as she had hoped anyway. This final resting spot doesn't offer the bliss of salvation. But this is a sensitive, New Age eternity, and every radio frequency is filled with National Public Radio. She thanks the Angel of Death, and after a final sip of hazelnut, he fades into the distance, taking her Range Rover with him as he goes.

7

Politics and Beyond

IF YOU SIT DOWN and read through a series of books or essays with titles like "The Spirit of the Age," you'll discover that no matter when they were written, they almost always contain a sentence that says, "We are living in an age of transition." Whether it is the 1780s or the 1850s or the 1970s, people tend to feel themselves surrounded by flux. The old labels and ways of doing things seem obsolete. New modes and ideas seem as yet unformed.

We must be special. We are not living in an age of transition. We are living just after an age of transition. We are living just after the culture war that roiled American life for a generation. Between the 1960s and the 1980s the forces of bohemia and the forces of the bourgeoisie launched their final offensives. Bohemian countercultural-ists attacked the establishment, the suburbs, and later the Reagan eighties. Conservative politicians and writers attacked the sixties and blamed that decade for much that

was wrong in American life. Each force on the bohemian
left—from the student radicals to the feminist activists—
awakened a reaction in the bourgeois right, from the
Moral Majority to the Supply Siders. This last spasm in
the long conflict was a bumpy time, with protests, riots,
mass movements, and a real breakdown in social order.

But out of that climactic turmoil a new reconciliation
has been forged. A new order and a new establishment
have settled into place, which I have tried to describe. And
the members of this new and amorphous establishment
have absorbed both sides of the culture war. They have
learned from both "the sixties" and "the eighties." They
have created a new balance of bourgeois and bohemian
values. This balance has enabled us to restore some of the
social peace that was lost during the decades of destruction and transition.

The Politics of Beyondism

The politicians who succeed in this new era have
blended the bohemian 1960s and the bourgeois 1980s and
reconciled the bourgeois and bohemian value systems.
These politicians do not engage in the old culture war
rhetoric. They are not podium-pounding "conviction
politicians" of the sort that thrived during the age of
confrontation. Instead, they weave together different approaches. They triangulate. They reconcile. They know
they have to appeal to diverse groups. They seek a Third
Way beyond the old categories of left and right. They
march under reconciling banners such as compassionate
conservatism, practical idealism, sustainable development,
smart growth, prosperity with a purpose.

Whatever its other features, the Clinton/Gore administration embodied the spirit of compromise that is at the
heart of the Bobo enterprise. In the first place, the Clin-

tons were both 1960s antiwar protesters and 1980s futures traders. They came to the White House well stocked
with bohemian ideals and bourgeois ambitions. They cam-
paigned against the "tired old labels of left and right." In
1997 Bill Clinton effectively summarized his policy approach in a speech to the Democratic Leadership Council:
"We had to go area by area to abandon those old false
choices, the sterile debate about whether you would take
the liberal or conservative positions, that only succeeded
in dividing America and holding us back."

Confronted with a culture war that pitted traditional
values against liberationist values, the Clinton administration merged, blurred, and reconciled. The Clintonites
chose three key words—"Opportunity, Responsibility, and
Community"—as their perpetual campaign themes, rarely
pausing over whether there might be tensions between
them. They embraced school uniforms and other tradi-
tional-sounding gestures, as well as condoms in schools
and other liberal-sounding measures. Clinton triangulated
above the hard-edged warriors on left and right and presented a soft and comfortable synthesis. He could, he declared, balance the budget without painful budget cuts,
reform welfare without meanness, mend affirmative action but not end it, toughen the drug war while spending
more on rehabilitation, preserve public schools while
championing charter school alternatives. Battered early in
the administration with a culture war skirmish over gays
in the military, the Clintonites settled on "Don't Ask,
Don't Tell." If ever there was a slogan that captures the
Third Way efforts to find a peaceful middle ground, that
was it.

Many of Clinton's attempts to reconcile opposing
policies were unworkable. Nonetheless, the Clinton administration does leave behind an approach to politics
that is enormously influential and is consonant with the
Bobo age. This Third Way approach, neither neatly liberal

nor conservative, neither a crusading counterculturalist nor a staid bourgeois, is a perpetual balancing act. And now if you look across the industrialized world, you see Third Way triangulators perched atop government after government. A few decades ago theorists predicted that members of the New Class would be *more* ideological than previous classes, *more* likely to be moved by utopian visions and abstract concepts. In fact, when the children of the 1960s achieved power, they produced a style of governance that was centrist, muddled, and if anything, anti-ideological.

They have settled on this style of politics because this is what appeals to the affluent suburbanites and to the sorts of people who control the money, media, and culture in American society today. Today there are about nine million households with incomes over $100,000, the most vocal and active portion of the population. And this new establishment, which exerts its hegemony over both major American political parties, has moved to soften ideological edges and damp down doctrinal fervor. Bobo Democrats sometimes work for investment houses like Lazard Frères. Bobo Republicans sometimes listen to the Grateful Dead. They don't want profound culture-war-type confrontations over first principles or polarizing presidential campaigns.

Whereas the old Protestant Establishment was largely conservative Republican, the new Bobo establishment tends to be centrist and independent. In 1998 the *National Journal* studied the voting patterns of America's 261 richest towns and discovered that they are moving to the center. The Democratic vote in those communities has risen in every election over the past two decades as members of the educated class have flooded into tony places like Wayne, Pennsylvania. The Democrats won 25 percent of the rich vote in 1980 and 41 percent in 1996. In that year

Bill Clinton carried 13 of the 17 most affluent congressional districts.

The affluent suburbs send moderate Republicans or moderate Democrats to Capitol Hill. These politicians spend much of their time in Congress complaining about the radicalism of their colleagues from less affluent districts. They can't understand why their liberal and conservative brethren seem addicted to strife. The less affluent polarizers rant and rave on *Crossfire.* They are perpetually coming up with radical and loopy ideas—destroy the IRS, nationalize health care. They seem to feel best about themselves when they are alienating others. All of this is foreign to the politicians from the Range Rover and Lexus districts. Like their Bobo constituents, they are more interested in consensus than conquest, civility than strife.

Indeed, in the Bobo age disputes within parties are more striking than conflict between parties. That's because, as University of Chicago philosopher Mark Lilla has pointed out, the central disagreement today is not the sixties versus the eighties. It is between those who have fused the sixties and the eighties on one side and those who reject the fusion on the other. In the Republican Party, moderates and modern conservatives do battle with the conservatives who want to refight the 1960s. On the Democratic side, the New Democrats do battle with those who have not come to terms with the Thatcher-Reagan reforms of the 1980s.

The people of the left and right who long for radical and heroic politics are driven absolutely batty by tepid Bobo politics. They see large problems in society, and they cry out for radical change. This new centrist establishment frustrates or stifles their radical ideas, and yet they find it hard to confront this power elite head-on. The Bobo establishment seems to have no there there. It never presents a coherent opposition. It never presents its opponents with a set of consistent ideas that can be argued and refuted. Instead, it co-opts and it embraces. Whether you are liberal or conservative, Bobo politicians adopt your rhetoric and your policy suggestions while somehow sucking all the radicalism out of them. They sometimes tilt to the left and sometimes to the right. They never rise up for a fight. They just go along their merry way, blurring, reconciling, merging, and being happy. While those on left and right hunger for confrontation and change, the Bobos seem to be following the advice on their throw pillows: "Living Well Is the Best Revenge."

The Project

But this does not mean that Bobo politics lacks direction. In fact the Bobos do have a project that will shape politics in the years to come. Their political project is to correct the excesses of the two social revolutions that brought them to power.

The bohemian sixties and the bourgeois eighties were polar opposites in many ways. But they did share two fundamental values: individualism and freedom. Writers in both decades paid lip service to community action and neighborhood institutions, but the main effort was to liberate individuals. The bohemian revolt in the sixties was about cultural freedom. It was about free expression, freedom of thought, sexual freedom. It was an effort to throw off social strictures and conformist attitudes, to escape from the stultifying effects of large bureaucracies and overbearing authority figures. The bourgeois resurgence of the 1980s, on the other hand, expanded economic and political freedom. The economy was deregulated and privatized in order to unleash entrepreneurial energies. The nanny state was attacked and in some cases rolled back. Cozy corporatist arrangements were ended. Large bureaucracies were cut. Even as late as 1994, the congressional Republicans swept into power calling themselves the Leave Us Alone Coalition. They wanted to get government off people's backs in order to maximize individual freedom.

Many of the people who led the social and political movements of the sixties and the eighties naively assumed that once old restrictions were removed and individuals liberated, then better ways of living would automatically blossom. But life isn't that easy. If you start up-ending obsolete social norms, pretty soon you'll notice that valuable ones, like civility and manners, get weakened too. If you start dissolving social ties in order to unleash individual self-expression, pretty soon you'll notice that valuable community bonds are eroded as well. Efforts to weaken oppressive authority end up corroding all authority. The stature of teachers, parents, and democratic institutions gets diluted along with that of bureaucratic despots and uptight busybodies. The economic dynamism that brought such great wealth also threatened the small communities and the social stability that many people cherish. In the nineties Americans increasingly felt there needed to be a correction. If the sixties and the eighties were about expanding freedom and individualism, the Bobos are now left to cope with excessive freedom and excessive individualism.

That's why the two crucial words in the Bobo political project these days, as we began to see in the last chapter, are *community* and *control*. Across American society one sees effort after effort to restore social cohesion, reassert authority, and basically get a grip on the energies that have been unleashed over the past quarter century. So we see universities reasserting their *in loco parentis* authority, reimposing curfews as well as rules on cohabitation, drinking, unsupervised parties, fraternity hazing, and sexual conduct. Colin Powell has led an upsurge in volunteerism as millions of people donate their time supervising latchkey kids, setting up adult-organized activities, and cleaning up and thereby bringing a little order back into anarchic neighborhoods. In legislatures across the country, there have been efforts to control Internet smut, control guns, control tobacco advertising, and control, or at least label, violent television programming and video games. The country has seen a historic wave of welfare reform in which local, state, and federal agencies have imposed more rules and restrictions on welfare recipients. Cities across the nation have reimposed controls on panhandling, vagrancy, public drinking, and even littering. Community policing programs have given the police more day-to-day authority in high-crime areas.

And, of course, politicians have learned to adopt a new language. Republicans no longer talk so aggressively about getting government off our backs. "My first goal is to usher in the responsibility era," George W. Bush said in announcing his campaign for the presidency. A few months later Bush attacked "the destructive mindset: the idea that if government would only get out of way, all our problems would be solved. An approach with no higher goal, no nobler purpose than 'leave us alone.' " Meanwhile, Al Gore also sought to distance himself from some of the antiauthority impulses that had once influenced his party. "It is our lives we must master if we are to have the moral authority to guide our children," he said in announcing his candidacy. "The ultimate outcome does not rest in the hands of any President, but with all our people—taking responsibility for themselves and for each other."

Some of the most dramatic efforts to reassert authority have been in the home and in the neighborhood. Back in the 1960s a man named A. S. Neill ran a school in Britain called Summerhill, which had virtually no rules except those that were set by the children themselves. Neill's book on his Summerhill method sold well over two million copies in the United States, part of a broad movement at that time to give children maximum freedom to explore, create, and otherwise develop "naturally." Any of us who were in school in those days can point to programs and progressive reforms that were designed to enhance student freedom and so encourage greater individualism—schools without walls, open classrooms, open campuses. There were even smoking rooms in public high schools, despite the fact that underage smoking was illegal.

But these days the ethos has entirely flipped. Now leading politicians from both parties advocate the return of uniforms in public schools. Now children are monitored and supervised, enshrouded with rules and devices. Now, for example, there is unprecedented concern with children's safety, part of our fumbling efforts to protect and regulate our kids. Bicycle manufacturers have noticed a drop-off in sales as parents become less likely to allow their children to spend their days roaming their neighborhoods on bikes. Today's children spend their days awash in moral instruction to an extent unprecedented even at the height of the Victorian era: children's television shows preach incessantly on subjects ranging from recycling to racism; teachers are asked to give homilies as well as instruction, on everything from drugs to civility. After the shootings in Littleton, Colorado, in 1999, there was a tidal wave of commentary. But on one subject there was total agreement: parents need to exercise more authority over their kids. The days of Rousseauistic liberation are over.

Equally striking are the efforts, especially by the residents of upscale towns, to gain control over neighborhood growth and development. The Reaganites may have preached the virtues of laissez-faire, but that approach is decidedly out of fashion in most Bobo suburbs today. If you go into a Bobo neighborhood, you will find a powerful group of citizens promoting stricter zoning requirements, opposing new commercial development, and fighting tear-downs (when an owner tears down a house on his or her property and erects a larger one) and other "improvements." Rather than being progressive and forward-looking, upscale neighborhoods seem to be looking back, seeking to preserve their stable and orderly past or at least to create the sorts of communities that hew to the patterns of what seem to have been stable and orderly pasts. Bobos spend more time restoring lost treasures, renovating old structures, or preserving old buildings than they do creating new and experimental institutions. Every third Bobo automobile seems to have a bumper sticker on it that implores, "Save the ———." Bobos are saving old theaters, old neighborhoods, old factories and warehouses, or even historically significant diners. When they do allow new building, these mostly affluent activists will insist that the new construction adhere to the patterns of the past. They will talk about preserving local character, fighting sprawl, combating unregulated growth, and enhancing "livability" and "quality of life." Here, too, they are trying to preserve order and stability and restore community control.

Intimate Authority

The main thrust of Bobo politics is the effort to restore the bonds of *intimate* authority. Bobos are not much interested in grand efforts to assert large-scale authority. One hundred years ago Herbert Croly gave voice to the Progressive Era's desire to create a national community with a powerful national government guided by technocratic experts who would organize and rationalize American life. That was an era of consolidation, when small entities seemed to be drawn ineluctably together to form big entities—big trusts, big bureaucracies, big cities. But we no longer feel we are living in an age of consolidation;

on the contrary, deconsolidation seems to be the order of the day. So upscale Americans, like most Americans, show little desire to launch a new set of massive political enterprises, whether it is another liberal War on Poverty or a grand conservative War on Cultural Decay. They tend to distrust formal hierarchies that are imposed from above and Olympian lawgivers who would presume to govern from glorious heights. They are generally disenchanted with national politics. They tend not to see it as a glorious or capital R Romantic field of endeavor, the way so many people did earlier in the century. Utopianism of that sort is practically extinct. Instead, they are more likely to see politics as a series of humble improvisations enacted with cautious hopes and some anxiety.

Instead, they think most highly of political action that is conducted on the local level, where communication can be face to face and where debate tends to be less ideological. When confronted with thorny national problems like poverty and education, Bobos tend to favor devolution, decentralizing power to the lowest possible level. This way each person or community can discover its own pragmatic solution without having to engage in seemingly futile debates over first principles.

Intimate authority is imparted, not imposed. It is the sort of constant, gentle pressure that good parents and neighbors provide: be polite when you are introduced to someone, don't litter in the park, don't tell fibs, help people with their packages when they are burdened, comfort them when they are grieving, and reassure them when they are uncertain. Intimate authority isn't mainly about writing down formal codes and laws; it is about setting up patterns, instilling habits, and creating contexts so that people are most likely to exercise individual responsibility. It means setting up welcome wagons so that new people feel part of an interdependent community. It means volunteering at the youth center so teenagers will have a place to go and be minded. It can be as trivial as the penny jar near the cash register so that the next person will have a penny handy if it's needed. Or it can be as pervasive as residential projects along the lines of the New Urbanism movement, which are designed to make sure there are eyes on the street, people watching out for each other and subtly upholding community standards of behavior and decency.

In true reconciling fashion, intimate authority is a Third Way between excessive individualism on the one hand and imposed formal authority on the other. This is not authority as physics—one powerful body exerting pressure on a smaller body. It is authority as biology, with all the members of the ecosystem exerting a gradual and subtle pressure on the others so the whole network can thrive.

It was just this sort of constant pressure that the old bohemians found so stifling. It is why they fled small towns for the anonymity and freedom of the big city. But today most Bobos seek community and control more than liberation and release. They have become conservatives.

Blue Jean Conservatives

I don't mean that members of the educated class are overwhelmingly conservative in the sense that the Republican Party uses the term, meaning in favor of tax cuts, less intrusive government, and larger defense budgets (although certainly many Bobos support these things). Rather, the ethos that unites most Bobos is an older meaning of conservatism, a meaning that describes a temperament rather than an ideology.

Edmund Burke called the great property owners of his day the "ballast in the vessel of the commonwealth." And in many regards that is true of today's upper-middle-

class property owners. Today's Bobos seek to conserve the
world they have created, the world that reconciles the
bourgeois and the bohemian. As a result, they treasure civility and abhor partisanship, which roils the waters. They
seek to preserve the simple things that have stood the test
of time. They seek to restore gentle authority. They treasure religion so long as it is conducted in a spirit of moderation rather than zeal. They appreciate good manners and
cherish little customs and traditions. They value what
Burke called the "little platoon," the small intermediating
institutions that make up a neighborhood and town. They
seek to restore order, not foment radical change.

A 19th-century conservative, Walter Bagehot, wrote,
"It is of immense importance that there should be among
the more opulent and comfortable classes a large number
of minds trained by early discipline to this habit of restraint and sobriety." And these days it is certainly true
that Bobos have learned restraint and sobriety, albeit the
Bobo code of sobriety owes more to the American Medical Association than Victorian rigor.

Conservative in temperament, Bobos almost always
reject grand rationalistic planning, feeling that the world
is far too complicated to be altered effectively by some
person's scheme to reshape reality. Though they are an
elite based above all on education, they are not overwhelmingly impressed by the power of expertise. Instead,
they seem acutely aware of how little even the best minds
know about the world and how complicated reality is
compared to our understanding. They know, thanks to
events like the war in Vietnam, that technocratic decision
making can produce horrible results when it doesn't take
into account the variability of local contexts. They are
aware, thanks to the failure of the planned economies
of eastern Europe, that complex systems cannot be run
from the center. In other words, they are epistemologically modest, the way such conservatives as Burke and

Oakeshott would have wanted them to be. They are more interested in preserving the imperfect institutions that have already proved some usefulness than they are in taking a flyer on some as yet untested vision of the future. They have learned that revolutions usually backfire and that, when it comes to social change, steady reform is best. Many Bobos would fight like hell against being labeled conservatives, but often the ones in the hemp clogs and ponytails are the most temperamentally conservative of all. If you go to places like Berkeley and Burlington, Vermont, you see that this kind of conservatism can emerge directly out of liberalism.

The Bobo Achievement

Thanks in large part to the influence of the Bobo establishment, we are living in an era of relative social peace. The political parties, at least at the top, have drifted toward the center. For the first time since the 1950s, it is possible to say that there aren't huge ideological differences between the parties. One begins to see the old 1950s joke resurface, that presidential contests have once again become races between Tweedledum and Tweedledumber. Meanwhile, the college campuses are not aflame with angry protests. Intellectual life is diverse, but you wouldn't say that radicalism of the left or right is exactly on the march. Passions are muted. Washington is a little dull. (I know. I live there.) The past 30 years have brought wrenching social changes. A little tranquillity may be just what the country needs so that new social norms can form and harden, so that the new Bobo consensus can settle into place.

So far it seems to be working. Many of the social problems that grew at epidemic ferocity during the 1960s and 1970s have begun to ease, if unevenly. Crime rates have come down, and so have divorce rates, abortion rates, cocaine use, teenage drinking, teenage promiscuity. Meanwhile, the nation's economy, which is not unrelated to the nation's culture, has gone from strength to strength.

Bobos have reason to feel proud of the contributions they have made to their country. Wherever they have settled, they have life more enjoyable (for those who can afford it). Shops are more interesting. The food in the grocery stores and restaurants is immeasurably better and more diverse. Communities are now dotted with gathering places and meeting grounds. Homes are less formal and more comfortable. Moreover, Bobos have done wonderful things to the world of American capitalism. Bobo businesspeople have created a corporate style attuned to the information age, with its emphasis on creativity, flat hierarchies, flexibility, and open expression. It's simply impossible to argue with the unparalleled success of America's information age industries over the past decade.

On balance, intellectual life has been improved as well. Sure, some of the intellectual intensity is gone. Fewer people seem to live for ideas, the way the old *Partisan Review* crowd did. But that rarefied world was insular (in spite of the fact that its members thought they were fighting for the working class). They were cut off from daily political and social realities. Today's careerist intellectuals have a foot in the world of 401(k) plans and social mobility and so have more immediate experience with life as it is lived by most of their countrymen. This grounding means that intellectuals have fewer loony ideas than did intellectuals in the past. Few of them fall for visions of, say, Marxist utopias. Fewer idolize Che Guevara–style revolutionaries. On balance, it's better to have a reasonable and worldly intellectual class than an intense but destructive one.

Leisure has also improved. Any survey of ecological tours of the rainforest or meritocratic slumming in Tuscan peasant towns will yield a rich harvest of mockery. But the impulse to seek edifying experiences is basically an admirable one. Moreover, Bobos have achieved a reasonably decent balance between mindless sexuality and uptight Puritanism. They have domesticated many sensual activities so they can be enjoyed without posing much of a threat to the social order. That's no small achievement, either.

As we turn around and look back at the range of Bobo manners and morals, we find a bit that's risible, a bit that is too precious by half, but a lot that is wonderful. Bobos have begun to create a set of standards and mores that work in the new century. It's good to live in a Bobo world.

This New Age of Complacency

I don't want to close with a paean of praise for everything Bobo. Spiritual life is tepid and undemanding. (Indeed, it's possible to imagine a coming generation that will grow bored of our reconciliations, our pragmatic ambivalence, our tendency to lead lives half one thing and half another. They may long for a little cleansing purity, a little zeal in place of our materialism, demanding orthodoxy in place of our small-scale morality.)

Moreover, while the relative tranquillity we have achieved is not to be sneezed at, given the alternatives, it is also possible to be tranquil to a fault. In preferring politicians who are soggy synthesizers and in withdrawing from great national and ideological disputes for the sake of local and community pragmatism, we may be losing touch with the soaring ideals and high ambitions that have always separated America from other nations. I mentioned in the introduction to this book that I spent four and a half years in Europe in the early nineties. I came back

warning my friends, only half-jokingly, of the Menace of
Belgian Cultural Hegemony. I was trying to describe the
temptations that accompany affluence. We may become a
nation that enjoys the comforts of private and local life
but has lost any sense of national union and any sense of a
unique historical mission. The fear is that America will decline not because it overstretches, but because it enervates
as its leading citizens decide that the pleasures of an oversized kitchen are more satisfying than the conflicts and
challenges of patriotic service. It could have been something like this that alarmed Tocqueville as he speculated
about the future of America. "What worries me most," he
wrote in *Democracy in America,* "is the danger that, amid
all the constant trivial preoccupations of private life, ambition may lose both its force and its greatness, that
human passions may grow gentler and at the same time
baser, with the result that the progress of the body social
may become daily quieter and less aspiring."

    This is no longer a prediction for the future. Tocque-
ville's scenario has come to pass. These days most of us
don't want to get too involved in national politics because
it seems so partisan and ugly. And as a result, most Americans citizens have become detached from public life and
have come to look on everything that does not immediately touch them with an indifference that is laced with
contempt. We have allowed our political views to be corroded with an easy pseudo-cynicism that holds that all
politicians are crooks and all public endeavor is a sham.
As the public opinion polls demonstrate with utmost clarity, we have lost faith in public institutions and many private ones. We have turned a healthy skepticism about
government action into a corrosive negativism, which
makes us passive even as we stare at political practices and
policies that make us ashamed. In short, our national life
has become compressed, our public spirit corroded by

cynicism, our ability to achieve great things weakened by inaction. We are threatened with a new age of complacency, which may be just as menacing to our dreams for America as imperial overstretch or defeat in war.

The Bobo task is to rebuild some sense of a united polity, some sense of national cohesion, without crushing the individual freedoms we have won over the past generation or the bonds of intimate authority that are being restored today. That is to say, we have to consolidate the gains we have made as individuals and communities while at the same time re-energizing national politics. In that famous passage when Burke praised the "little platoons" of family and community life, he went on to make an equally important but much less often quoted observation. Local affection, he argued, "is the first link in the series by which we proceed toward a love of country and to mankind." Healthy families and healthy communities are insufficient if the nation is in decay. Healthy self-interest becomes self-absorption if it is detached from larger national and universal ideals.

That suggests a course of action that is reform at home and activism abroad. Reform of those institutions and practices that no longer make us proud: the campaign finance system, which has become a corrupting bog, the tax code, which has become complex and alienating, the welfare state, which needs to be debureaucratized. And at the same time on an international sphere, it means picking up the obligations that fall to the world's lead nation: promoting democracy and human rights everywhere and exercising American might in a way that reflects American ideals.

For Americans to become engaged once again in public life and proud of their public institutions, something else has to happen to the Bobos. They have to assume a leadership role. They are the best-educated segment of society and among the most affluent, and yet by and large they have not devoted their energies to national life. Obviously, Bobos work in government and politics, but the public arena hasn't become a focus of attention for the educated class as a whole. This has left a gaping hole in public life. Filling this hole means doing what the postwar ruling class did. It means developing a public service ethos, concluding, as people like Dean Acheson, John McCloy, George C. Marshall, and Dwight Eisenhower did, that to those who are blessed much is expected, and that public service is the highest secular service a person can perform. When we look back on the postwar ruling class, we see some mistakes and some hubris. But we also see a group of men and women who made genuine commitments to America that sometimes overrode their individual self-interest. Which of us doesn't long for an updated version of that sense of service, of that sober patriotism? And which of us doubts that the Bobos, with all their brains and good intentions, can make the same sorts of contributions if they direct their energies in the right direction?

The Bobos are a young elite, only dimly aware of themselves as an elite and unaware as yet of their capacities. This is a class of people who grew up with the word *potential* hanging around their necks, and in many ways still, their potential is more striking than their accomplishments. They have been trained, nurtured, and educated. They have been freed of some old restrictions and they have forged some new bonds. They are largely unscarred by economic depression and war. They can be silly a lot of the time. But if they raise their sights and ask the biggest questions, they have the ability to go down in history as the class that led America into another golden age.

Acknowledgments

I WROTE SEVERAL magazine articles about upscale culture before I realized they pointed to a single thesis that could be the basis for a book. I wrote about Status Income Disequilibrium, countercultural capitalists, Latte Towns, and Cell Phone Naturalists for the *Weekly Standard,* and chunks of those pieces have been adapted in these pages. I'm grateful to Bill Kristol, Fred Barnes, and John Podhoretz for encouraging me to do those pieces. This is also a good place to say how grateful I am to them for starting the *Standard* and for asking me and so many of my friends to work there. The hours we spend every week schmoozing at the office are among the great pleasures of my life.

There are other editors to thank. The section on the *New York Times* weddings pages is adapted from an essay I wrote early on for the *City Journal,* and I'm grateful to Myron Magnet for his help on that. My first foray into the realm of the affluent was done for Brian Kelly and Steve

Luxenberg of the *Washington Post* "Outlook" section. I'd also like to thank Henry Finder and Susan Morrison of the *New Yorker.* I began writing pieces on commercial culture for them relatively late in the game, when I thought I knew my subject pretty well. But their off-the-cuff insights were intimidating, since they knew so many things I didn't and had observed patterns that never occurred to me. The paragraphs on Restoration Hardware are drawn from work I did for them.

Many other people helped me along the way. First mention has to go to Erich Eichman, Dan Casse, and John Podhoretz, who read the manuscript and offered valuable advice. Michael Kinsley and Jack Shafer helped me understand the Seattle culture, and Mike even took me camping. John Baden gave me valuable suggestions about what to do and see in Montana. Irving Kristol led me to César Graña's book *Bohemian versus Bourgeois,* which helped crystallize my thinking. Tori Ritchie of *San Francisco Magazine* helped me appreciate the full cultural import of the kitchen. My agents, Glen Hartley and Lynn Chu, have been friends for over a decade; their labors on my behalf have been above and beyond the call of duty. Marion Maneker was the editor who acquired this book for Simon & Schuster; his skills are formidable. After Marion left for HarperCollins, I was honored to have Alice Mayhew take on the project. A writer couldn't hope for a more responsive editor. She seemed to ponder every word in this manuscript, and her comments improved it in ways great and small.

Finally, there is my family. My parents moved to Wayne, Pennsylvania, because Lewis Mumford said pre–World War I suburbs are the best places to live in the United States. Going to high school there, I thought the place was bourgeois and reactionary, which it was. But now it's changed and I've changed and I realize what a wonderful community it is. I'm grateful to my parents and my brother, Daniel, for our happy life there. And I'm more grateful than I can say to my wife, Jane, and our kids, Joshua, Naomi, and Aaron, for their sacrifices as I reported, researched, and squirreled away in the basement writing this book.

Index

On Paradise Drive

How We Live (And Always Have)
in the Future Tense

To Joshua, Naomi, and Aaron

Contents

The Great Dispersal

LET'S TAKE A DRIVE.

Let's start downtown in one of those urban bohemian neighborhoods, and then let's drive through the inner-ring suburbs and on to the outer suburbs and the exurbs and the small towns and beyond. Let's take a glimpse at how Americans really live at the start of the twenty-first century in their everyday, ordinary lives.

As we go, we'll find some patterns that are intriguing but probably not that important. For example, did you know that 28 percent of Americans consider themselves attractive (a figure I consider slightly high) but only 11 percent of Americans consider themselves sexy? Did you know that 39 percent of eleven- and twelve-year-olds say that Chinese food is their favorite food, while only 9 percent say American food is? Did you know that a quarter of all women have considered breast-augmentation surgery, which is kind of depressing, and so have 3 percent of all men, which is horrifying.

But we'll find other patterns that are probably more important. For one thing, we are living in the age of the great dispersal. As Witold Rybczynski has observed, the American population continues to decentralize faster than any other society in history. In 1950 only 23 percent of Americans lived in suburbia, but now most do, and today's suburbs are sprawling out faster and faster and farther and farther, so in the past few years, many exurban places have broken free from the gravitational pull of the cities and now float in a new space far beyond them.

Americans are still moving from the Northeast and the Midwest down to the South and the Southwest. But the really interesting movements are outward from cities. The people who were in move out, and the people who were out move farther out, into the suburbs of suburbia. For example, the population of metropolitan Pittsburgh declined by 8 percent over the past two decades, but as people moved away, the amount of developed land in the Pittsburgh area increased by 43 percent. The city of Atlanta saw its population grow by twenty-three thousand over the last decade, but the surrounding suburbs grew by 1.1 million.

The geography of work has been turned upside down. Jobs used to be concentrated downtown, in office buildings, stores, and urban-manufacturing zones. But 90 percent of the office space built in America in the 1990s was built in suburbia, and most of it in far-flung office parks along the interstates. The sprawling suburbs now account for more office space than the inner cities in every metro area in the country except Chicago and New York. In the Bay Area, for example, there are five times more companies headquartered in Santa Clara County than in San Francisco.

That means we have a huge mass of people who not only don't live in the cities, they don't commute to the cities, go to movies in the cities, eat in the cities, or have any significant contact with urban life. They are neither rural, nor urban, nor residents of a bedroom community. They are charting a new way of living.

These new places are huge, and hugely attractive to millions of people. The fastest-growing big counties in America—such as Douglas County, Colorado (between Denver and Colorado Springs), and Loudoun County, Virginia (near Dulles Airport)—are doubling and tripling in size every decade or so. A vast suburb such as Mesa, Arizona, now contains more people than Minneapolis, St. Louis, or Cincinnati and will soon pass Atlanta.

It's as if Zeus came down and started plopping vast towns in the middle of the farmland and the desert overnight. Boom! A master planned community! Boom! A big-box mall! Boom! A rec center, pool, and four thousand soccer fields! The food courts come first, and the people follow. How many times in human history have two-hundred-thousand- or five-hundred-thousand-person communities materialized out of practically nothing in the space of a few years? What sorts of institutions get born there, and what sorts of people emerge?

This suburban supernova subtly affects every place in America. The cities and inner-ring suburbs are affected because only certain kinds of people get left behind. Quite often the people who stay are either the very poor, because they can't afford to move; or the very rich, because they can afford to stay and live well in upscale enclaves. In the exploding exurbs, there are no centers, no recognizable borders and boundaries, and few of the conventional geographic forms—such as towns, villages, and squares—that people in older places take for granted. Up till now in human history, people have lived around some definable place—a tribal ring, an oasis, a river junction, a port, a town square. You could identify a certain personality type with a certain place. There was a New York personality, an L.A. personality. But in exurbia, each individual has his or her own polycentric nodes—the school, the church, the subdevelopment, the office park—and the relationship between those institutions is altered.

People have a different sense of place. They don't perceive where they live as a destination, merely as a dot on the flowing plane of multidirectional movement. Life is different in ways large and small. When the New Jersey Devils won the Stanley Cup championship, they had their victory parade in a parking lot, because no downtown street was home to all the people who love the team.

Virginia Tech demographer Robert Lang compares this new exurban form to the dark matter in the universe: stuff that is very hard to see or define but somehow accounts for more mass than all the planets, stars, and moons put together.

Making Sense of Our Reality

When it comes to suburbia, our imaginations are motionless. Many of us still live with the suburban stereotypes established by the first wave of critics. Yet there are no people so conformist as those who fault the supposed conformity of the suburbs. From *The Organization Man* to *Peyton Place* to *The Stepford Wives* to *American Beauty* to the vast literature on suburban sprawl, generation after generation of American writers and storytellers have paraded out the same clichés of suburban life. Suburbs are either boring and artificial, or else they are superficially boring and artificial but secretly sick and psychotic. If you were to judge by the literature of the past century, nobody is happy in suburbia.

But driving through the suburbs, one sees the most amazing things: lesbian dentists, Iranian McMansions, Korean megachurches, nuclear-free-zone subdevelopments, Orthodox shtetls with Hasidic families walking past strip malls on their way to Saturday-morning shul.

At some point in the past decade, the suburbs went quietly berserk. As if under the influence of some bizarre form of radiation, everything got huge. The cars got huge, so heads don't even spin when a mountainous Hummer comes rolling down the street. The houses got huge. The drinks at 7-Eleven got huge, as did the fry containers at McDonald's. The stores turned into massive, sprawling category-killer megaboxes with their own climatic zones. Suburbia is no longer the land of ticky-tacky boxes on a hillside where everything looks the same. It's the land of the gargantuoids.

One quickly sees that suburbia no longer hews to the stereotypes. We think of suburbs as places where families move to raise kids. But in fact, married couples with children make up only 27 percent of suburban households, according to the 2000 census. Today the suburbs contain more people living alone than families with kids. We think of the suburbs as white, but almost 60 percent of Asians, half of all Hispanics, and 40 percent of African-Americans live in the suburbs. We think of the suburbs as middle-class, but 46 percent of all people living under the poverty line reside in the suburbs.

One sees tremendous economic, technological, and social revolutions. We've already lived through one eco-nomic revolution that was largely a suburban phenome-non. According to Joel Kotkin, the author of *The New Geography,* by 1992 only a third of computer-industry employment was in cities, a figure that must have plum-meted since. There will be other office-park revolutions—in robotics, biotech, military hardware, nanotechnology, and so on. How do these bland-seeming places produce so much change, and how will they manage it? What happens when people acculturated in these sprawling suburban zones are given the power—through the biotech firms they are now starting amid the Fuddruckers—to remake human nature? What values will guide them then?

For centuries we've read novels about young people who come to the city looking for opportunity and adven-ture. For centuries we've romanticized and demonized rural and urban life, built mythologies of lonely pioneers and city gangsters. What happens to storytelling when we all realize that suburbia is not just derivative of those two places but actually dominates them? What happens when we realize that suburban culture has quietly deepened over the past few decades and become more dense and more interesting?

This simple fact is that Americans move around more than any other people on earth. In any given year, 16 per-cent of Americans move, compared with about 4 percent of the Dutch and Germans, 8 percent of the Brits, and about

3 percent of the Thais. According to the Census Bureau's Current Population Survey, only a quarter of American teenagers expect to live in their hometowns as adults, which reflects a truly radical frame of mind. Today, as always, Americans move so much and so feverishly that they change the landscape of reality more quickly than we can adjust our mental categories.

Cultural Zones

When we take this drive, we won't have to go far to see different sorts of people. Human beings are really good at finding others like themselves, so one comes across distinct cultural zones; and the people in one community sometimes know very little about the people in the community just up the road. Despite the recent popularity of aging in place, senior citizens are still moving in large numbers to a certain number of sun-drenched communities around Naples, Florida; Myrtle Beach, South Carolina; Las Vegas; and Las Cruces, New Mexico. Affluent African-Americans are moving to suburbs around cities like Atlanta, Orlando, Norfolk, and Charlotte. Highly educated white Americans are moving to developments around medium-sized cities in the Northeast and Pacific Northwest.

The late U.P.I. columnist James Chapin observed that in the information age, every place becomes more like itself. People are less likely to be tied down because their job requires them to be near certain natural resources—oil or coal deposits, fertile soil or a harbor. Today's economy relies more on human capital, which can be grouped anywhere you can put up an office building. Thus, people's relocation decisions can be based more on cultural affinity than economic necessity. People who conscientiously recycle their brown and green glass herd together in Madison, Wisconsin. They might know more about what happens in Boston or Berkeley than they do about a small Wisconsin town thirty miles up the road. Tractor-pulling people might live in, say, Waynesboro, Pennsylvania. The political joke about Pennsylvania is that it's got Pittsburgh on one end, Philadelphia on the other and Alabama in the middle. People in the more conservative parts of Pennsylvania probably have more in common with small-town folk in Tennessee and Texas than they do with their fellow Pennsylvanians near the big cities.

Far from bringing homogeneity, the age of job mobility and targeted media has brought segmentation. All sorts of perplexities emerge. Why is it that Kansas, Rhode Island, and Tennessee lead the nation in oatmeal consumption? Why is it that the number of married-with-children families declined by 16 percent in West Virginia during the 1990s but increased by 29 percent in Arizona? Why is it that hundreds of thousands of whites flee from Los Angeles and New York every decade, even as the country becomes slightly more racially integrated overall?

After the 2000 election, political analysts became obsessed by the divisions between Red America, the heartland counties that supported Bush; and Blue America, the coastal and Mississippi Valley counties that supported Gore. I came to think of it as the global-warming divide, because if the polar ice caps do melt and flood the places near water, the Democratic Party will be basically wiped out.

But there are many other ways to grapple with the new geography. The demographer William H. Frey argues that there are three Americas. First there is the new sunbelt: the fast-growing suburbs in places such as Nevada, Georgia, and Colorado. This region attracts huge population inflows (only 24 percent of the people who live in Nevada were born there, compared to 78 percent of the people who live in Pennsylvania). It has high percentages of intact two-parent families. There are only ten states that gained such families during the 1990s. Nine of them are in the new sunbelt.

Then, Frey says, there are the melting-pot states, such as California, Texas, Florida, New York, and Illinois. These states are growing because of new immigration. They are home to three-quarters of the nation's Hispanic and Asian populations.

Finally, there is the heartland, consisting of the remaining twenty-eight states, including New England, Pennsylvania, Ohio and Indiana, and the upper Midwest. This is the overwhelmingly white, slow-growing part of the country. Since young people have, by and large, been moving out of these places, aging baby boomers make up an especially large share of their populations.

Meanwhile, market researchers at firms such as Claritas and Yankelovich devise other categories for the new American divides. Claritas breaks Americans down into sixty-two psychodemographic clusters. If you are a member of the Boomtown Single cluster, you are likely to live in towns like Beaverton, Oregon, or Ann Arbor, Michigan; earn about $32,000 a year; enjoy roller-skating and Comedy Central; and drive a Toyota MR2 or a Mazda MX-6. If you are a member of the Shotguns and Pickups demographic, you probably also earn about $32,000 a year, but you live in places like Dallas, Georgia, and Hager City, Wisconsin; you enjoy chewing tobacco, tractor pulls, Diet

Rite cola, and *Family Feud*; and you drive a Dodge or Chevy pickup.

As one thinks about these and the many other categories used to explain the diversity of America, one begins to realize that whatever else has changed about Americans, we have not lost our talent for denominationalism. As early as the eighteenth century, visitors to the New World were dazzled by the explosion of religious denominations, sects, and movements. They quickly sensed that the tendency to split and multiply was made possible by space and wealth. Americans had the room and the money to move away and found new churches and new communities that they felt suited their individual needs. Since everybody was so spread out, no central authority could hope to impose uniformity. That spirit survives today, in both religious and secular ways. America is without question the most religiously diverse nation on earth. In a 1996 study, J. Gordon Melton, director of the Institute for the Study of American Religion, counted 32 Lutheran denominations, 36 Methodist, 37 Episcopal, and 241 Pentecostal—just among the Protestants. And this tendency has replicated itself in the secular spheres of life: Americans go shopping for the neighborhoods, interest groups, and lifestyles that best suit their life missions and dreams.

As we take our drive, it will become obvious you don't have to go far to see radically different sorts of people. How do all these different sorts of people regard one another? Where does each group fit into the social structure, and what sort of social structure can possibly accommodate such a flowering of types? Further: Does it make sense to say that all these individuals with varying values and tastes cohere to form one people? If so, how does being

American shape our personalities, and how will this suburban civilization, with its awesome military and economic power, seek to shape the future of the world?

I will try to do three related things in this book. First, I will describe what life is really like in today's middle- and upper-middle-class suburbs. For the most part, I won't describe what life is like for poor people or rich people (those are fascinating subjects for another day). I'm mostly after the moderately affluent strivers, the people who hover over their children, renovate their homes, climb the ladder toward success, and plan anxiously for their retirement.

Second, I will try to solve the mystery of motivation. I will try to explain why Americans move to new places so avidly and work so feverishly and cram their lives so full once they get there. I will try to explain what it is about being American that drives us so hard to relentlessly move and labor and change.

And third, I'll try to answer the question: Are we as shallow as we look? Americans do not, at first glance, look like the most profound, contemplative, or heroic people on earth. You could look around and get the impression that we are moral mediocrities, concerned only about our narrow concerns and material well-being. But toward the end of this book, I will probe to see if down beneath the surface activities of everyday life, there is a grand, complicated, and deeply American idealism that inspires not only shallow strivings but also noble ones.

In the first part of the book—Chapters 1 and 2—we will take this long-promised drive and sample some of the ways Americans live now. In the second part—Chapters 3 and 4—I will summarize two long-standing views of America. One set of observers has argued that this country, espe-

cially its suburban parts, is indeed shallow and materialistic. Another set has argued that deep inside middle Americans is a spiritual impulse that is quite impressive and
profound. People who hold this less secular view tend to be
unspecific about it, but they sense that Americans, even
suburban middle-class Americans, aren't motivated primarily by grubby bourgeois ambitions but by a set of moral
yearnings and visionary dreams that they can't explain
even to themselves.

With these two competing views in our heads, it will be
time to plunge into Chapters 5 through 8: an attempt to
describe slices of American life. It's worth repeating that
there are large parts of America that will not be covered.
But I do offer glimpses of the main activities of middle-
American existence: child rearing, learning, shopping,
working, settling, and worshipping. In this section, I'll
include some statistics to illustrate the emerging patterns of
twenty-first-century life. But I will also speak in parables,
composites, and archetypes, for the personality of a people,
as much as the personality of an individual, is a mysterious,
changing thing. One has to feel one's way into the subject,
tracing the patterns with your fingertips, developing a
responsiveness to how the constituent elements play off
one another. That's why many nations have national poets
or composers who are thought to express the soul of a people, but few nations have national statisticians or national
political scientists. One simply must tolerate imprecision of
the poetic if one is to grasp the true and powerful essence
of a place or people.

Since I am no poet, I will try to use humor to get at the
essence of the way we live, comic sociology. While this
book is motivated by love of country, it's not the ardent,

humorless teenage form of love. It's more like the love that old companions feel, in which they enjoy jibing each other for their foibles and perhaps love the foibles best of all. If at times the book seems exaggerated, caricatured, impious, or sarcastic, my only excuse is that one of the distinctive traits of Americans is that we have often tried to tell the important truths about ourselves through humor, whether in the tall tales of the nineteenth-century storytellers, the novels of Mark Twain, or the wisecracks of Will Rogers, Mr. Dooley, H. L. Mencken, or Garry Trudeau.

In the final part of the book—Chapter 9—I will present my own opinions on the central questions: What unites Americans? Are we as shallow as we look? What force impels us to behave as energetically as we do, to head out in pursuit as we do, to play such an active and controversial role in the world? And how does this force—how does being American—shape us?

CHAPTER ONE

Out for a Drive

SO LET'S GET IN the minivan. We will start downtown in an urban hipster zone; then we'll cross the city boundary and find ourselves in a progressive suburb dominated by urban exiles who consider themselves city folks at heart but moved out to suburbia because they needed more space. Then, cruising along tree-lined avenues, we'll head into the affluent inner-ring suburbs, those established old-line communities with doctors, lawyers, executives, and Brooks Brothers outlets. Then we'll stumble farther out into the semi-residential, semi-industrial zones, home of the immigrants who service all those upper-middle-class doctors, lawyers, and other professionals. Then we'll go into the heart of suburbia, the mid-ring, middle-class split-level and ranch-home suburbs, with their carports, driveway basketball hoops, and seasonal banners over the front doors.

Finally, we'll venture out into the new exurbs, with their big-box malls, their herds of SUVs, and their exit-ramp office parks.

Bike-Messenger Land

We could pick any sort of urban neighborhood to start our trek, but just for interest's sake, let's start at one of those hip bohemian neighborhoods, such as the Lower East Side of Manhattan, the U Street corridor in Washington, Clarksville in Austin, Silverlake in L.A., Little Five Points in Atlanta, Pioneer Square in Seattle, or Wicker Park in Chicago, where the free alternative weeklies are stacked in the entry vestibules of the coffeehouses, galleries, and indie film centers. As you know, the alternative weekly is the most conservative form of American journalism. You can go to just about any big city in the land and be pretty sure that the alternative weekly you find there will look exactly like the alternative weekly in the city you just left. There are the same concentrations of futon ads, enlightened-vibrator-store ads, highly attitudinal film reviewers, scathingly left-wing political opinions, borderline psychotic personals, "News of the Weird" columns, investigative exposés of evil landlords, avant-garde comic strips, and white-on-black rock venue schedules announcing dates by local bands with carefully grating names like Crank Shaft, Gutbucket, Wumpscut, and The Dismemberment Plan.

You look at the pictures of the rockers near the concert reviews, and they have the same slouchy, hands-in-the-jeans pose that Roger Daltrey and Mick Jagger adopted forty years ago, because nothing ever changes in the land of the rebels.

If you walk around the downtown neighborhoods, you're likely to find a stimulating mixture of low sexuality and high social concern. You'll see penis-shaft party cakes in a storefront right next to the holistic antiglobalization cooperative thrift store plastered with "Free Tibet" posters. You'll see vegan whole-grain enthusiasts who smoke Camels, and advertising copywriters on their way to LSAT prep. You'll see transgendered tenants-rights activists with spiky Finnish hairstyles, heading from their Far Eastern aromatherapy sessions to loft-renovation seminars.

In these downtown urban neighborhoods, many people carry big strap-over-the-shoulder satchels; although they may be architectural assistants and audio engineers, they want you to think they are really bike messengers. They congregate at African bistros where El Salvadoran servers wearing Palestinian kaffiyehs serve Virginia Woolf wannabes Slovakian beer.

Many of the people on these blocks have dreadlock envy. Their compensatory follicle statement might be the pubic divot, that little triangular patch of hair some men let grow on their chins, or the Jewfro, the bushy hairstyle that curly-haired Jewish men get when they let their locks grow out. Other people establish their alternative identity with NoLogo brand sportswear, kitschier-than-thou home furnishings, thrift-shop fashionista sundresses, conspicuously articulated po-mo social theories, or ostentatious displays of Martin Amis novels.

The point is to carefully nurture your art-school pretensions while still having a surprising amount of fun and possibly even making a big load of money. It is not easy to do this while remaining hip, because one is likely to find that a friend has gone terminally Lilith (denoting an excessive love of sappy feminist folk music) while others have taken their minimalist retro-modern interior-design concepts to unacceptable extremes, failing to realize that no matter how interesting a statement it makes, nobody wants to lounge around a living room that looks like a Formica gulag.

Downtown urban hipsters tend to have edgy alternative politics, or at least some Bennington College intellectual pretensions, and probably the New Yorker's disease— meaning that anything you might tell them, they already heard two weeks ago. You could walk up and tell them that the Messiah just came down from heaven and tapped you on the shoulder, and they would yawn and say they've been expecting that since last spring. But they are cool, and their neighborhoods are cool, and that counts for a lot.

We sort of take coolness for granted because it is so much around us. However, coolness is one of those pervasive and revolutionary constructs that America exports around the globe. Coolness is a magical state of grace, and as we take our drive through America, we will see that people congregate into communities not so much on the basis of class but on the basis of what ideal state they aspire to, and each ideal state creates its own cultural climate zone.

In the hippoisie cool zone, Charlie Parker, Thelonious Monk, Miles Davis, Lester Young, Billie Holliday, Jack Kerouac, James Dean, the Rat Pack, William Burroughs, Elvis Presley, Otis Redding, Bob Dylan, Andy Warhol, Janis Joplin, Patti Smith, and Lou Reed never go out of style. Coolness is a displayed indifference to traditional measures of success. The cool person pretends not to be striving. He or she seems to be content, ironically detached from the normal status codes, and living on a rebellious plane high above them.

In the cool zone, people go down to move up. It's cooler to be poor and damaged than wealthy and accomplished, which is why rich and beautiful supermodels stand around in bars trying to look like Sylvia Plath and the Methadone Sisters, with their post-hygiene hair, a red-rimmed, teary look around their eyes, their orange, just-escaped-from-the-mental-hospital blouses, and the sort of facial expression that suggests they're about forty-five seconds away from a spectacularly successful suicide attempt.

In the cool zone's nightclubs, you find people dressed and posed like slightly over-the-hill gay porn stars. You find that at the tippy-top of the status ladder, there are no lawyers, professors, or corporate executives but elite personal trainers, cutting-edge hairstylists, and powerful publicists: the aristocracy of the extremely shallow. Late at night in these neighborhoods, you find the Ameritrash, the club-happy, E-popping, pacifier-sucking people who live in a world of gold teeth caps, colorful scarfwear, body-conscious tailoring, ironic clip-on ties, gender-bending neo-vintage Boy George–inspired handbags, and green-apple flirtinis, which are alcoholic beverages so strong they qualify as a form of foreplay. In the cool zone, people are always hugging each other in the super-friendly European manner and talking knowledgeably about Cuban film festivals. People in the cool zone pretend to be unambitious and uninterested in the great uncool mass of middle Americans, but they are well aware of being powerful by example. Drawn by images of coolness, young people in different lands across the globe strive to throw off centuries of rigid convention in order to wear blue jeans.

Highly pierced social critics in downtown neighborhoods lament the spread of McDonald's and Disney and the threat of American cultural imperialism. But in fact, American countercultural imperialism—the spread of rock and rap attitudes, tattoos, piercing, and the youth culture—has always been at least as powerful and destabilizing a force for other cultures. It vibrates out from these urban-hipster zones, with their multicultural Caribbean *shawarma* eateries, their all-night dance clubs with big-name DJs, and their Ian Schrager hotels, which are so Zen that if you turn on the water in one of the highly hip but shallow bathroom sinks, it bounces a cascade of water all over the front of your pants, making you look like you just wet yourself because you were so awed by your own persona.

Cities, which were once industrial zones and even manufacturing centers, have become specialty regions for the production of cool. Culture-based industries that require legions of sophisticated, creative, and stimulated workers— the sort of people who like to live in cities—have grown and grown. In hip urban neighborhoods, there are few kids, and those who are there are generally quite young (when the kids hit middle school, their families magically disappear).

Surrounding these hip young urban areas are neighborhoods with plenty of kids, but they tend to be disproportionately populated with poor people and members of minority and immigrant groups. They carry their own brand of cool. In fact, they define cool, but with few exceptions, they never get to cash in on it. So they are often trapped in no- or low-income jobs, because it's very hard to go from being a high school grad to being a senior editor at *Details,* no matter how objectively with-it you are, and most of the other jobs have fled the cities or disappeared.

Cities have made a comeback of late, because the world demands cool products and ideas, but as Joel Kotkin concludes in *The New Geography,* they will not come back and be, as they once were, the main arenas of national life. "Rather than recovering their place as the geographic centers of the entire economy," Kotkin writes, "city centers are readjusting themselves to a more modest but sustainable role based on the same economic and cultural niches that have been performed by the core from the beginning of civilization"—as generation centers of art, design, publishing, entertainment, and cool.

Crunchy Suburbs

From the cool zone, we drive out of town, just across the city line, to the crunchy zone. Here one finds starter suburbs populated by people who regard themselves as countercultural urbanites, but now they have kids, so the energy that once went into sex and raving now goes into salads. They need suburban space so their kids have a place to play, but they still want enough panhandlers and check-cashing places nearby so they can feel urban and gritty.

Dotted around most cities—especially in the northern rim of the country, through Vermont, Massachusetts, Wisconsin, Oregon, and Washington—there are one or two crunchy suburbs that declared themselves nuclear-free zones during the cold war, although some would argue that the military-industrial complex was not overly inconvenienced by being unable to base ICBM launch sites in Takoma Park, Maryland. You can tell you are in a crunchy suburb by the sudden profusion of meat-free food co-ops, the boys with names like Mandela and Milo running around the all-wood playgrounds, the herbal-soapmaking cooperatives, pottery galleries, dance collectives, and middle-aged sandal wearers (people with progressive politics have this strange penchant for toe exhibitionism).

You have to remember that crunchy suburbs are the stoner versions of regular suburbs. All the status codes are reversed. So in a crunchy suburb, all the sports teams are really bad, except those involving Frisbees. The parking spaces are occupied by automobiles in need of psychotherapy because they are filled with self-hatred and wish they were Danish wood-burning stoves. The locals sit around on the weekends listening to Click and Clack, the self-amused NPR car-repair gurus who tell other crunchy-suburb people how to repair a crank shaft on their 1982 Honda Civic—the one with 285,000 miles and a Darwin fish on the bumper, next to the sticker attesting to the driver's tendency to practice random acts of kindness and senseless acts of beauty.

The true sign that you are in a crunchy suburb is when you come across an anti-lawn. Crunchy-suburb people subtly compete to prove that they have the worst lawn in the neighborhood, just to show how fervently they reject the soul-destroying standards of conventional success.

An anti-lawn looks like a regular lawn with an eating disorder. Some are bare patches of compacted brown dirt with sickly stray pieces of green matter poking out, the vegetation version of Yasser Arafat's face. Other anti-lawns burst forth with great symphonies of onion grass, vast spreads of dandelions and crabgrass, expanding waves of depressed ivies and melancholy ferns—such an impressive array of weed life uninterrupted by any trace of actual grass that you can only conclude some progressive agri-business makes a soy-based weed enhancer/grass suppressant, with special discounts for Nader voters.

When you are in these neighborhoods—maybe you've been invited over for a backyard stir-fry—you might want to ask for terrible lawn-care secrets, but you get distracted by the housepaint issue, which is another moral dilemma for crunchy-suburb residents. Painting your house exterior colonial white or production-home beige would, in these areas, be the moral equivalent of putting a National Rifle Association sign in the front yard. So crunchy-suburb residents again fall into two categories, starting with those who choose to paint their house every decade or so, but do so in such bright New Age colors—lavender, cobalt blue, fuchsia, or purple haze—that no one can possibly doubt the Buddhist bona fides of the people who live inside.

The other camp regards exterior housepaint in the same way they regard makeup, as something that was probably developed using animal testing. Centuries go by without any fresh coats, and the run-down drabness of the exteriors is highlighted only by the peace signs made out of Christmas lights that pop up around holiday time. The roofs in these homes tend to undulate in great waves and warps, because the residents either cannot afford roof repair or reject the rigid uniformity of straight lines, unchipped shingles, and the whole symmetry thing. The front porches are rusted and cracked, buried under sedimentary deposits of former lawn furniture picked up from neighborhood thrift shops (crunchy-suburb residents are not really into material things, but strangely, they still can't manage to throw anything away). The settlement in these homes is such that if you put a marble in the middle of a living room here, it would pick up so much speed as it rolled downhill that it would bore into the philosophically named housecat if she happened to be standing in its path.

The nice thing about these crunchy suburbs—aside from the fact that 96 percent of all children's book illustrators live in them—is that their residents are so relaxed. The ethos is almost excessively casual. While these folks might regard it as unusual to show up for a dinner party in anything other than black jeans and Birkenstocks, a suit and tie not made from hemp won't bend them out of shape. In other words, you may not really be part of their culture, but if you come to one of their towns, they will still welcome you. They may have little direct knowledge of anything that happens outside the nonprofit sector, but they tend to be genuinely warm toward new people. Tolerance is practically their profession. The cool zone is built on exclusion and one-upmanship, but the crunchy zone is built on inclusion and open-mindedness.

To their credit, the crunchy zones represent the last bastions of anticommercialism. The world used to be dotted with cultures that rejected the marketplace mentality. There were agrarians, old-family aristocrats, artsy bohemians, southern cavaliers, Marxists, Maoists, monks, and hoboes. But now the marketplace has co-opted or overrun each of those subcultures. Now, if you want to live an anticommercial lifestyle, or even a pseudo-anticommercial lifestyle, crunchiness is just about your only mode.

Amid the organic cauliflower stands and *Moosewood Cookbook*–inspired dinner parties, you'll find people suspicious of technological progress, efficiency, mass culture, and ever-rising affluence. The crunchies don't let their kids watch much TV, they disdain shopping malls, they prefer the small and the local and the particular and the old to the powerful and the modern. In any normal political taxonomy, they would be called conservative; though they are progressive on civil rights and social issues, they shelter the idiosyncratic, ethnic, and traditional institutions from the onrush of technology, homogenization, efficiency, and progress. But in the U.S., political orientations are defined by one's attitude to the free market, and the word "conservative" has been assigned to those who defend the free market, which of course is not a conservative institution. So crunchy towns tend to be associated with the left (though Rod Dreher of *National Review* has emerged as the champion of the Crunchy Cons—the pro-life vegetarian high-church Catholics who can their own preserves, care too much about zucchini, home-school their kids, and read Edmund Burke while wearing Swedish clogs).

Crunchy people also tend not to have a lot of money, and some of them actually don't care about it—they aren't merely *pretending* they don't care. Maybe you wouldn't want to spend your life in towns where half the men look like Allen Ginsberg, where the chief dilemma is whether to send the kids to Antioch or Hampshire College, or where Celtic folk/bluegrass songs intersperse with Phish anthems on the teahouse sound systems, but it is kind of interesting to be in a place in which the holy dollar has lost its divinity.

Professional Zones

As we drive farther, we begin to notice that the houses are getting bigger, the lawns look professionally manicured, and the driveways tend to be filled with Audis, Volvos, and

Saabs. In these upscale neighborhoods, it is apparently socially acceptable to buy a luxury car so long as it comes from a country that is hostile to U.S. foreign policy. Soon you begin to see discount but morally elevated supermarkets such as Trader Joe's. Here you can get your Spinoza Bagels (for people whose lives peaked in graduate school), fennel-flavored myrrh toothpaste from Tom's of Maine, free-range chicken broth, gluten-free challah, spelt-based throat lozenges, and bread from farms with no-tillage soil. (What, does the dirt turn itself over?)

Trader Joe's is for people who wouldn't dream of buying an avocado salad that didn't take a position on offshore drilling or a whey-based protein bar that wasn't fully committed to campaign finance reform. Someday, somebody should build a right-wing Trader Joe's, with faith-based chewing tobacco, rice pilaf grown by school-voucher-funded Mormon agricultural academies, and a meat section that's a bowl of cartridges and a sign reading "Go ahead, kill it yourself." But in the meantime, we will have to make do with the ethos of social concern that prevails at places like Trader Joe's and Whole Foods.

You get the impression that everybody associated with Trader Joe's is excessively good—that every cashier is on temporary furlough from Amnesty International, that the chipotle-pepper hummus was mixed by pluralistic Muslims committed to equal rights for women, that the Irish soda bread was baked by indigenous U2 groupies marching in Belfast for Protestant-Catholic reconciliation, and that the olive spread was prepared by idealistic Athenians who are reaching out to the Turks on the whole matter of Cyprus.

The folks at Trader Joe's also confront higher moral problems, such as snacks. Everyone knows that snack food is morally suspect, since it contributes to the obesity of the American public, but the clientele still seems to want it. So the folks behind this enterprise have managed to come up with globally concerned stomach filler that tastes virtuously like sawdust ground from unendangered wood. For kids who come home from school screaming, "Mom, I want a snack that will prevent colo-rectal cancer," there's Veggie Booty with kale, baked pea-pod chips, roasted plantains, wasabi peas, and flavor-free rice clusters. If you smuggled a bag of Doritos into Trader Joe's, some preservative alarm would go off, and the whole place would have to be fumigated and resanctified.

You usually don't have to wander far from a Trader Joe's before you find yourself in bistroville. These are inner-ring restaurant-packed suburban town centers that have performed the neat trick of being clearly suburban while still making it nearly impossible to park. In these new urbanist zones, highly affluent professionals emerge from their recently renovated lawyer foyers on Friday and Saturday nights, hoping to show off their discerning taste in olive oils. They want sidewalks, stores with overpriced French children's clothes to browse in after dinner, six-dollar-a-cone ice-cream vendors, and plenty of restaurants. They don't want suburban formula restaurants. They want places where they can offer disquisitions on the reliability of the risotto, where the predinner complimentary bread slices look like they were baked by Burgundian monks, and where they can top off their dinner with a self-righteous carrot smoothie.

The rule in these pedestrian-friendly town centers is "Fight a war, gain a restaurant." You'll find Afghan eateries, Vietnamese restaurants, Lebanese diners, Japanese sushi bars alongside dining options from Haiti, Cambodia, India, Mongolia, and Moscow. And this is not to even mention the Cosi-style casual dining spots offering shiitake mushroom panini sandwiches or the gourmet pizzerias serving artichoke, prosciutto, and brie pizzas (which can also come with a black-bean topping). When you stumble across Teriyaki Fajita Salad du Jardin, you realize it is possible to cram so many authentic indigenous cultures together that they've created something totally bogus and artificial.

Ozzie and Harriet would find it odd that their old suburban town center now has a vegan restaurant for feminist reproductive-rights activists and their support circles, but these inner-ring suburbs are sophisticated places. They are the home of the upscale urban exiles—affluent sophisticated types who disapprove of the suburbs in principle but find themselves living in one in practice. Like the crunchy suburbanites, they disapprove of the sterility of suburban life, the split-level subdivisions, the billiard rooms, and the blueberry bagels. But unlike the crunchy suburbanites, these inner-ring people just happen to have landed jobs that earn them a quarter million dollars a year, darn it, and they somehow moved into recently renovated Arts and Crafts mansions with an Olympic-sized Jacuzzi in the master-bathroom spa, the emblem of their great sellout.

The people who live in the inner-ring suburbs are hardcore meritocrats and the chief beneficiaries of the information age. This economy showers money down upon education, so the fine young achievers who went to graduate school and got jobs as litigators and mortgage-company executives can now live in towns that are close to downtown theaters and concert halls but also filled with houses big enough to support a kitchen the size of Arkansas. About

15 percent of American households now earn over $100,000 a year. There are over seven million households with a net worth over $1 million. This nation, in other words, now possesses a mass upper class, and many of these folks are congregating in the upscale archipelago of such places as Bethesda, Maryland; Greenwich, Connecticut; Tarrytown, New York; Villanova, Pennsylvania; Winnetka, Illinois; San Mateo and Santa Monica, California; Austin, Texas; Shaker Heights, Ohio; and the Research Triangle Park of North Carolina. In the mornings, there are so many blue *New York Times* delivery bags in the driveways of these towns, they are visible from space.

Back when the old WASP elite dominated these places, they were rock-ribbed Republican. But the new educated elite has brought new values and new voting patterns. In 1998 *National Journal* studied the voting patterns of the richest 261 towns in America and discovered that the Democratic share of the vote had risen in each of the previous five elections. In 2000 the Democrats went over the top. A Democratic presidential candidate carried the area around the Main Line, outside of Philadelphia, for the first time in history. And the first Democrat ever won the area around New Trier High School, north of Chicago. Once Republican strongholds, the inner-ring suburbs have become Democratic zones, thanks to the influx of the educated and affluent cultural elite, with their graduate degrees, high incomes, and liberal social values.

These places have their good and bad features. On the downside, they are strangely insular. Though the people here are in most ways well informed, and often can name the foreign minister of France, they tend to live in neighborhoods where everybody has a college degree (only about a quarter of adult Americans do), and they often don't know much about the rest of the country. They might not know who Tim LaHaye and Jerry Jenkins are, even though these men are among the nation's best-selling authors, with over fifty million books sold. They often don't know what makes a Pentecostal a Pentecostal, even though Pentecostalism is the most successful social movement of the twentieth century, starting in Los Angeles with no members a hundred years ago and growing so fast there are now roughly four hundred million Pentecostals worldwide. They can't name five NASCAR drivers, though stock-car races are the best-attended sporting events in the country. They can't tell a military officer's rank by looking at his insignia. They may not know what soy beans look like growing in the field. Sometimes they can't even tell you what happens in Branson, Missouri, though, as sort of the country music Vegas, it is one of the top tourist destinations in the country. On the other hand, they are really good at building attractive and interesting places to live. This is, after all, the red-hot center of the achievement ethos, and while few people in these neighborhoods have fought in wars, many have endured extensive home renovations.

So if you are in an inner-ring suburb, you are likely to be amid people who have developed views on beveled granite, and no inner-ring dinner party has gone all the way to dessert without a serious conversational phase on the merits and demerits of Corian countertops. People here talk about their relationships with architects the way they used to talk about their priests, rabbis, and ministers. Bathroom tile is their cocaine; instead of blowing their life savings on narcotic white powder, they blow it on the handcrafted Italian wall covering they saw at Waterworks.

The sumptuary codes in these neighborhoods are always shifting. Highly educated folk don't want to look materialistic and vulgar, but on the other hand, it would be nice to have an in-house theater with a fourteen-foot high-definition projection screen to better appreciate the interviews on *Charlie Rose*. Eventually these advanced-degree moguls cave in and buy the toys they really want: the heated bathroom floors to protect their bare feet, the power showers with nozzles every six inches, the mudrooms the size of your first apartment, the sixteen-foot refrigerators with the through-the-door goat cheese and guacamole delivery systems, the cathedral ceilings in the master bedroom that seem to be compensation for not quite getting to church. Later, when they show off to you, they do so in an apologetic manner, as if some other family member forced them to make the purchase.

Inner-ring people work so arduously at perfecting their homes because they dream of building a haven where they can relax, lay aside all that striving, and just cocoon. They have deep simplicity longings, visions of having enough money and space so they can finally rest. Yet you know they are wired for hard work, because they feel compelled to put offices in every room in the house. Mom has an office in the kitchen, Dad has an office off the bedroom, the kids have computer centers near the family room, and it's only a matter of time before builders start installing high-speed Internet access in bathrooms. That dream of perfect serenity and domestic bliss will just have to be transferred to the vacation home.

Inner-ring people tend to have omnivorous musical tastes. They're interested in zydeco and that Louisiana dance music they heard on *Fresh Air,* even if they do tend to drift back to Melissa Etheridge and Lyle Lovett. They prefer independent bookstores, and they bend down and read the recommendations in the staff-picks section. That's how they stumbled across Anita Diamant, Paul Auster, and Wally Lamb before they got really popular.

If they are not perpetually renovating their properties, inner-ring people are off on allegedly educational vacations improving their minds. When Christopher Columbus returned from the New World, he didn't go to Queen Isabella and say, "Well, I didn't find a trade route to India, but I did find myself." That, however, is exactly what highly educated inner-ring people are looking for in a vacation. They go on personal-growth Greek cruises sponsored by alumni associations, during which university classics professors lecture on the Peloponnesian wars while the former econ majors try to commit adultery with the lifeguards.

As you sit with them intimately in their reading alcove (not the one in the master bedroom suite; rather, the one beside the office, near the nanny suite) they tell you about the weeklong painting seminar they took with Comtesse Anne de Liedekerke in Belgium, the cooking seminar in Siena, the tiger-watching adventure in India, or the vineyard touring week in Bordeaux. When they put all this hard-won knowledge to work by using the word "geometric" in reference to a cabernet, you want to applaud their commitment to lifelong learning, but you are distracted because your butt is shaking as a result of the eighteen-inch woofer their architect cleverly embedded in the built-in divan you are resting upon.

When people in their twenties are surveyed on where they want to live, more of them answer inner-ring suburbs than any other place. It's easy to see why. These places combine the sophistication of the city with the child-friendly greenery of the suburb. The people here are well educated, lively, and tolerant (unless you want to, say, build a school in their neighborhood, in which case they turn into NIMBY-fired savages ripping the flesh from your bones with their bare hands).

Immigrant Enclaves

As you drive out from the inner-ring suburbs, you find yourself on these eight-lane commercial pikes with strip malls up and down either side, a Taco Bell every four hundred yards, and so many turn signals and left-hand turn lanes that crossing the street is nearly impossible because you never know where the cars are coming from. These avenues are just about the ugliest spots on the face of the earth. You're stuck at one red light after another, with views of fast-food drive-through lanes, grungy convenience stores, storage-center warehouse facades, and more fluorescent-lit nail salons than the mind can comprehend. The strip malls have names like Pike Center or Town Plaza, because no one even bothered to think up a distinctive title. Every half mile or so, in between the car lots, cell-phone stores, and discount mattress outlets, there will be a lone five-story office building that has all the aesthetic charm of a sixty-foot water heater. Turn onto a side road, and you may find yourself in one of those suburban light-industry districts where, after a few years, everything comes to look like the inside of an auto garage. Most upscale suburbanites come to these neighborhoods only when they are selecting new floor surfaces for their renovated kitchen, since most of the companies in this zone distribute things most people never have to think about: truck hitches, flexible packing foam, and cut-rate sprinkler equipment.

But if you look closely, you begin to see something else: big restaurant signs with names like China Star Buffet, small Oriental groceries offering cellophane noodles, live tilapia fish, and premade bibim bap salad. Then you see Indian grocery stores with videocassettes from Delhi, boxes of crackers from Bombay, and imported spices in big brown barrels. You notice the taiga Japanese bookstore, newspaper boxes offering the *Korean Central Daily,* Pakistani cyber cafés, Bosnian banks, and a Shiseido cosmetics outlet offering "movie-star brown" hair coloring for Asians. Perhaps there is a Vietnamese diner featuring bunh mih xui mai, which is "sloppy joe" in Vietnamese.

These stores often have advertising posters taped to the front door—for DynaSky calling cards to Peru, or a Christian prayer meeting hosted by Shim-San Jung and his worship team. We have crossed over into the land of the invisible. In stark contrast to the nearby inner-ring suburbs, no mass-market lifestyle magazines are geared to the people who work in these suburban distribution zones. TV shows are never set here. The big daily newspapers don't do features on the trends that sweep through the strip malls and the industrial areas. These places just have their own customs and patterns that grew up largely unnoticed by the general culture. At a scraggly playing field on Saturday mornings, there will be a crowd of Africans playing soccer, then on Sunday it will be all Hispanics. Somehow it just got established that one day was for Africans and the other day was for Hispanics, and you never see them playing each other. Then you go over to the basketball courts, and maybe the Pakistanis have ripped down all the rims so they can play cricket without any interference from the basketball players.

These places are growing. One out of every nine people living in America was born in a foreign country—roughly 32.5 million people, according to the last census—which means there are now more foreign-born Americans than ever before in the country's history. Traditionally, immigrants settled first in cities. But that's no longer true. Today they are more likely to go straight to midsize towns and underutilized suburban gaps. The 2000 census revealed that minorities were responsible for the majority of suburban population gains made in the 1990s, so now you'll see little Taiwanese girls in the figure-skating clinics, Ukrainian boys learning to pitch, and when I opened the Loudoun County paper one day and came across the National Scholar Award winners, these were some of the names that were listed: Kawai Cheung, Anastasia Cisneros Fraust, Dantam Do, Hugo Dubovoy, and Maryanthe Malliaris.

Over the past decade, immigrants from Asia have flooded into the Hickory and Charlotte areas in North Carolina; Lincoln, Nebraska; and the Grand Rapids area in Michigan. There are huge numbers of Asian immigrants in New Jersey's Middlesex and Somerset counties. The San Gabriel Valley in California is the largest center of Chinese immigrants in the country.

Meanwhile, Hispanics have moved in large numbers to places like Fresno and Bakersfield in California, as well as Orlando and Las Vegas. It is still true that 50 percent of the counties in the nation are over 85 percent white (if you take a brush and sweep it from Maine down through western New York, Pennsylvania, and Ohio, across the Midwest through Wisconsin, Iowa, and into the Dakotas and Montana, you are—excepting the big cities—basically covering Caucasianville), but the southern and western parts of the country are quite diverse, and there are immigration pockets everywhere: Arabs in Michigan, Iranians in Orange County, and so on.

In the older northeastern and midwestern areas, the immigration residential patterns are distinct. There are certain immigrant zones and certain native zones. Old cities like Detroit and Hartford are clearly segregated. But in the new suburbs, and in the booming towns of the South and West, different groups merge. Neighborhoods in these parts of the country are less likely to have reputations or fixed points on the status system. Families are more likely to shop for homes strictly on the basis of price. So in places like Arlington or Garland, Texas; Stockton, California; Albany, New York; Saint George or Fort Lauderdale, Florida, whites, native minorities, and immigrants tend to live and work side by side.

These immigrant-heavy places defy generalization. Most of the new arrivals are just scraping by, scrounging for day labor at the contractor pickup points, lacking health insurance, crammed into split levels four to a room. Others are doing well, running a barbershop with twenty Vietnamese and Filipino coworkers and then driving home each day in a Lexus SUV. If you tour the open houses in a McMansion neighborhood of, say, Great Falls, Virginia, or Orange County, California, you will be stunned by how many of the luxury homes belong to immigrants who own businesses in these light-industrial zones. They have faded pictures of Mom and Dad in China on the grand piano, and Islamic prayer rugs from Lebanon in the basement. These peoples' attitudes about their millions are roughly the same as Pamela Anderson's attitude about her breasts: They worked damn hard to get them, and now that they've got them they are sure as hell going to show them off.

These immigrant zones are among the most baffling places in the country. Market-research firms have to scramble to help companies make sense of them. They've discovered that Hispanics spend a far greater percentage of their income on footwear and clothing for children under two, and a far lower percentage on stationery and tobacco products than the average American consumer. Whites spend much more on entertainment and much less on clothing for teenage boys. Blacks spend more on poultry and telephones and less on furniture and books. Whites are the most likely of all racial groups to visit a home-furnishing store but the least likely to visit an electronics store. These aggregates don't get you very far. You've got new groups of people in new sorts of places, so of course everyone is creating temporary ways of living.

But you can see that some powerful transforming energy is being let loose. And we can be fairly sure that the traditional immigrant entrepreneurialism will give birth to new companies and new fortunes. (Interestingly, five of the nine immigrant groups most likely to produce millionaires come from the Middle East, according to a study done by Thomas J. Stanley, the author of *The Millionaire Mind*.) We know that thanks to the current immigration wave, the U.S. population will surge over the next few decades; we can project, thanks to Bill Frey, that in 2050 the median age in the U.S. will be 35, while the median age in Europe will be 52; and we can be reasonably sure that the new immigrants will climb into middle-class life, using and changing established institutions as they go.

Suburban Core

We have now driven deep into the heart of suburbia. Here there are split-level communities, cul-de-sacs, soccerplexes, regional shopping malls with ever more grand titles (plaza, galleria, court), edge cities (which have city skylines but no actual city life), and all the other stereotypical appurtenances of Homo suburbianus. When you get out here in the postwar suburbs that are now around a half century old, you can see why they've discombobulated so many social critics. All the other places we've been on our drive would be familiar to our ancestors. The city neighborhoods and inner-ring areas are organized according to the patterns and models of past great cities and towns. The immigrant clusters hearken to homelands across the globe. But the split-level/rancher suburb is an entirely self-contained civilization. These places were designed to be utopias set apart from the crowding and congestion and customs of the old places, from the problems of the past and the flow of human history. They are immune to time, geography, life, and death.

Even today, suburban streets are never just streets—they are terraces, courts, drives, and circles. You drive by home after tidy home, each on its well-tended quarter or eighth or sixteenth acre, and you see the same icons of suburban life development after development: Big Wheels, swing sets, adjustable-height basketball hoops, garden-hose storage rolls, pink and purple girls' bikes with sparkly handlebar tassels, stay-at-home dogs barking behind the bay-shaped picture windows, allegedly squirrel-proof bird feeders, vinyl siding, rusting tool sheds, RE/MAX for-sale signs posted by the mailboxes, holiday-theme banners over the doorways, faux gaslight lanterns staked in the front yard.

Thanks to their owners' relentless commitment to home maintenance, even the older houses do not bear the mark of time. Generations have come and gone, individuals have lived and died, and yet these neighborhoods still carry the whiff of Eisenhower America. The Oldsmobiles may have been replaced by PT Cruisers. Chuck Berry is out and Eminem is in. The brick ramblers now have second-story additions, but the lawns look the same. The shrubs still get pruned, the gutters get cleaned, the cars get washed in the driveways, the weeds get killed, the driveways get patched and repaved, the decks get waterproofed and coated, and the garage doors go up and down and up and down.

The same rituals are observed, and all those things that once seemed hopelessly outré—cheerleaders, proms, country clubs, backyard barbecues, and stay-at-home moms—still thrive, in some ways more than ever. The trick-or-treaters are still greeted with oohs and ahs, the mischief-night eggings get reenacted, the storm windows come out and the screens go in season after season, year after year, and decade after decade.

No wonder artists are offended. Individuals don't seem to matter here. These places do not appear grand and glorious, like a canyon or mountain or a teeming metropolis, and yet they are humbling because they are so impervious to you and me. We might rail against this cul-de-sac culture, we may hate it and curse it. But it will remain this way through all the passage of time, committed to the same values: tidiness, tranquility, domesticity, safety, predictability. These hard-core suburbs will stay what they have always been: bourgeois values in real estate form. This ethos is awesomely powerful. The postwar suburbs allow families earning around $51,000 a year—about the median income in the U.S. today—to establish a sense of respectability, financial security, and comfort. This split-level civilization would not have remained so coherent for so long if it didn't solve certain human problems and appeal to the aspirations of many sorts of people who have moved to precisely these locales.

If you want to understand these places, you have to start with golf. You won't get suburbia right—in fact, you won't get America right—if you underestimate the powerful cultural influence of golf. Sometimes middle America seems shaped more by golf than by war or literature or philosophy.

I'm not talking about the game of golf, the actual act of walking through eighteen holes and striking a little white ball. For most people, the game is too expensive and time-consuming. I'm talking about the golf ideal, the golf vision of perfection, the golf concept of chivalry, valor, and success. At least in its American incarnation, golf leads to a definition of what life should be like in its highest and most pleasant state.

In the ideal world as defined by golf, everything is immaculate. The fairways are weedless stretches of soft perfection. The greens are rolling ponds of manicured order. The sand traps are raked smooth. The homes along the fairways look scrubbed and affluent. Even the people are neat; everybody is dressed casually but nicely.

But golf is more than just an environment. It suggests its own state of spiritual grace, a Zenlike definition of fully realized human happiness. In the realm of golf, that state of grace is called par. And par is the established suburb's version of nirvana.

When a golfer is playing at par, his swing is sweet and his manner is confident. He has slipped away from the tensions that usually bedevil him on the course, and he has achieved a state of harmony. He is still competitive, driven, and success-oriented, yet he feels an inner calm. He has defeated his primary foe—anxiety—and operates in a mystical groove. Everything seems simple, manageable. In this victorious state, it seems almost normal that he is wearing a pastel yellow sweater and comfortable-looking green slacks.

Like Tiger Woods, Arnold Palmer, Jack Nicklaus, and Lee Trevino, each in his own way, the chivalric golfer has mastered the fine art of false modesty. Golfers never puff themselves up, as boxers do. They fill the air with half-humorous declarations of their own shortcomings. The chivalric golfer, when playing at par, has a narrow emotional range. He does not lose his temper and throw his clubs in the pond; neither does he dance on the green. He may punch the air once or twice in an approved and highly Protestant manner. After the round, he may allow that he felt good out there. But every comment will be three notches more modulated than it needs to be.

The chivalric golfer is able to look calmly at the problem in front of him and focus his concentration on it. He is backed, as all American life is, by a great body of management theory, personal advice, and self-help takeaways. The golf life is filled with clinics, advice columns, and personal coaching. The golfer is also equipped with state-of-the-art technology. Everything he owns is made from titanium; the club he swings on the long tee has a head roughly the size of an oil drum and the technical pedigree of an Exocet missile.

Yet out there on the course, he alone is the master of his fate. He spends a good part of his time looking at things. First he looks at the fairway, then he looks at the ball. Then he looks at the green. He is manifestly good at looking at things. His face is calm yet focused. He makes subtle calculations in that engineering-like brain of his. He consults with his caddy in the ego-massaging manner of a far-seeing CEO at a board meeting. He has that slacks-and-pastels thing going. Then he decides and strides manfully up to the ball, exuding purpose. He strikes the ball, and the ballet begins all over again.

Much of traditional suburban America aspires to golf's paradisiacal vision. The modern suburb enshrines the pursuit of par. It is not a social order oriented around creativity, novelty, and excitement. The suburban knight strives to have his life together, to achieve mastery over the great dragons: tension, hurry, anxiety, and disorder. The suburban knight tries to create a world and a lifestyle in which he or she can achieve that magic state of productive harmony and peace.

When you've got your life together, you can glide through your days without unpleasant distractions or tawdry failures. Your DVD collection is organized, and so is your walk-in closet. Your car is clean and vacuumed, your frequently dialed numbers are programmed into your cordless phone, your telephone plan is suited to your needs, and your various gizmos interact without conflict. Your spouse is athletic, your kids are bright, your job is rewarding, your promotions are inevitable, everywhere you need to be comes with its own accessible parking. You look great in casual slacks.

You can thus spend your days in perfect equanimity. You radiate confidence and calm. Compared to you, Dick Cheney is bipolar. You may not be the most intellectual or philosophical person on the planet, but you are honest and straightforward, friendly and good-hearted. As you drive home, you observe that the lawns in your neighborhood are carefully tended, so as to best maintain the flow of par. Your neighbors all know that one cannot allow too much time to pass between mowings, and one cannot mow when the grass is wet, lest it lead to clumpings and unevenness. One cannot cut the grass too short, lest one stress the lawn. One cannot leave one's garbage can out at the end of one's driveway long after the garbage has been collected, lest one disturb the par of the streetscape.

All of these things are done in the name of good order, so essential to the creation of par. Perhaps in your area, the members of the community association serve as defenders of the par. They might be the ones who guard against disharmonious housepaint hues and overly assertive flag-poles. In other areas, sheer social pressure might direct everybody in the common pursuit of par. Bitter sarcasm is frowned upon, for it represents a crease in the emotional surface of the neighborhood. Brightly colored annuals in the window boxes are praised, for they enhance cheeriness. Loafers are approved of, for they send off relaxation vibes. Kids in the cul-de-sac are jointly monitored, for kids are at once the suburbs' whole point, yet the focus of so many anxious thoughts, that they are a potential chasm in the flow of par.

This common pursuit of the together life leads to the conformity that the social critics have always complained about. On the other hand, the pursuit of tranquility is also a moral and spiritual pursuit. It is an effort to live on a plane where things are straightforward and good, where people can march erect and upward, where friends can be relaxed and familiar, where families can be happy and cooperative, where individuals can be self-confident and wholesome, where children can grow up active and healthy, where spouses are sincere and honest, where everyone is cooperative, hardworking, devout, and happy.

That's not entirely terrible, is it?

The Exurbs

Now we are out in the outer suburbs, the great sprawling expanse of subdevelopments, glass-cube office parks, big-box malls, and townhome communities. This new form of human habitation spreads out into the desert or the countryside, or it snakes between valleys, or it creeps up along highways and in between rail lines. This kind of development seems less like a product of human will than an organism. And you can't really tell where one town ends and the other begins, except when, as Tom Wolfe observed, you begin to see a new round of 7-Elevens, CVS's, Sheetzes, and Burger Kings.

We don't even have words to describe these places. Over the past few decades, dozens of scholars have studied places like Arapahoe County, Colorado; Gwinnett County, Georgia; Ocean County, New Jersey; Chester County, Pennsylvania; Anoka County, Minnesota; and Placer County,

California. They've coined terms to capture the polymorphous living arrangements found in these fast growing regions: edgeless city, major diversified center, multicentered net, ruraburbia, boomburg, spread city, technoburb, suburban growth corridor, sprinkler cities. None of these names has caught on, in part because scholars are bad at coming up with catchy phrases, but in part because these new places are hard to define.

You can't even sensibly draw a map because you don't know where to center it. Demographer Robert Lang tried to draw a map of a zone north of Fort Lauderdale, Florida. He located all the roads and office parks and arbitrarily drew the borders. If he'd slid his map north, south, east, or west, some roads and buildings would have disappeared, and others would have appeared. But there would have been no noticeable change in density, no new and definable feature, just another few miles of suburban continuum.

And yet people flock here. Seventy-three million Americans moved across state lines in the 1990s, and these places—across Florida, north of Atlanta, shooting out beyond Las Vegas, Phoenix, Denver, and so on—drew them in. You fly over the desert in the Southwest or above some urban fringe, and you notice that the developers build the sewers, roads, and cul-de-sacs before they put up the houses, so naked cul-de-sacs to nowhere spread out beneath you. One day I stood and watched a crew carve a golf course out of the desert near Henderson, Nevada, one of the fastest-growing cities in America. A year later, and fifty thousand people are living where there was nothing.

People move to these centerless places in search of the things people have always sought in a home: extra counter space in the kitchen, abundant storage space in the basement, and plenty of closets. Those are the three most important amenities to home buyers, according to market research. More grandly if more ironically, people move because they want order. They want to be able to control their lives. They've just had a divorce with their old suburb because it no longer gave them what they craved. They've had it with the forty-five-minute one-way commute in northern California. They're tired of wrestling with the $400,000 mortgage in Connecticut. They don't like the houses crowded with immigrants that are appearing in their New Jersey neighborhoods. They want to get away from parents who smoke and slap their kids, away from families where people watch daytime talk shows about transvestite betrayals or "My Daughter Is a Slut," away from broken homes, away from gangs of Goths and drug-gies, and away from families who don't value education, achievement, and success.

The outer-ring suburbs have very few poor people, and relatively few rich people. While many of the successful people in inner-ring suburbs are professionals—doctors, lawyers, professors, and journalists—many of the people in outer-ring suburbs are managers in marketing, sales, exe-cution, and planning. The professionals don't think of themselves primarily as capitalists; as competitive, revenue-maximizing machines oriented toward the bottom line. Managers are much more likely to measure their success this way. The subtle distinction leads to a whole shift in attitudes, opinions, and political preferences. Managers are more likely to be competitive, sports-oriented, and, as political analysts Ruy Teixeira and John Judis have noticed, Republican. Professionals are more likely to be verbally skilled, university-oriented, and Democratic.

Sometimes people move to the exurbs to get away from the upscale snobs moving into the inner-ring neighborhood where they grew up. I recently ran into a woman in Loudoun County, Virginia, where AOL is located, who said she had spent most of her life in Bethesda, Maryland, today an affluent inner-ring suburb next to Washington. "I hate it there now," she said with venom in her voice. As we spoke, it became clear that she hated the gentrification, the new movie theater that shows only foreign films, the explosion of French, Turkish, and new-wave restaurants, the streets full of German cars with Princeton and Martha's Vineyard stickers on the back windows, the doctors and lawyers and journalists with their educated-class one-upsmanship.

She sensed they looked down on her, and she was probably right. So she did what Americans always do when something bothers them. She moved on. The philosopher George Santayana once observed that Americans don't solve problems, they leave them behind. If there's an idea they don't like, they don't bother refuting it, they simply talk about something else, and the original idea dies from inattention. If a situation bothers them, they leave it in the past.

The exurban people aren't going to stay and fight the war against the inner-ring traffic, the rising mortgages, the influx of new sorts of rich and poor. They're not going to mount a political campaign or wage a culture war. It's not worth the trouble. They can bolt and start again in places where everything is new and fresh. The highways are so clean and freshly paved you can eat off them. The elementary schools have spick-and-span playgrounds, unscuffed walls, and all the latest features such as observatories, computer labs, and batting cages.

The roads in many of these places are huge. They have names like Innovation Boulevard and Entrepreneur Avenue. They've been built for the population levels that will exist in two decades, so today you can cruise down flawless six-lane thoroughfares in trafficless nirvana, and if you get a cell-phone call, you can pull over to the right lane and take the call because there is no one behind you.

People who move out here are infused with a sense of what you might call conservative utopianism. On the one hand, those who move to the exurbs have made a startling leap into the unknown. They have, in great numbers and with great speed, moved from their old homes in California, Illinois, Wisconsin, New York, and elsewhere to these places that didn't exist ten years ago. The places have no past, no precedent, no settled conventions. The residents have no families or connections here. There are no ethnic enclaves to settle into, and no friends. Sometimes people move here without even a job.

When they make the decision to move, they are picturing for themselves what their new lives will be like. They are imagining waterskiing buddies and Little League teams. They are imagining happy high school graduations, even though that high school may still be nothing but a steel frame. They are imagining outings with friends at home-style Italian restaurants that don't exist yet, outings to Science Olympiads with unformed teams, road trips to spring training with friends they haven't met, who are now sitting in their old suburb and haven't contemplated moving here. But they will.

And while they are making a radical change in their lives, they are really pursuing a conservative vision. It is no accident that people in the exurbs, while instinctively apolitical and often cynical about the political process, are, when they vote, overwhelmingly Republican. These places are sometimes seventy-thirty Republican, and if you look at every state where Republicans scored an upset senatorial victory in 2002—Georgia, Colorado, and Minnesota, to name a few—they did so with huge gains from the fast-growing exurbs.

The exurbs are built to embody a modern version of the suburban ideal. Demographic studies show that they look like 1950s suburban America—intact two-parent families, 2.3 kids, low crime, and relatively low divorce rates. You sometimes get the impression that these people have fled their crowded and stratified old suburbs because they really want to live in an updated Mayberry with BlackBerries.

There is nobody here who is socially far above or below you (at least until the country clubs get built and the tennis rankings come out). Unlike in the cities or the inner-ring 'burbs, there is relatively little social competition. You can go through your entire life—at home, at the office, in church—wearing comfortable, conservative nonthreatening casual wear that emphazises khaki, navy blue, and other unobtrusive colors. Postmen get hernias lugging all the Lands' End catalogs.

This is, after all, where those cheery people who broadcast on the morning drive-time radio shows live. The exurbs are the new epicenters of competitive cheerleading and other sports that you can do while smiling. Theology is too troubling a topic for general conversation, and politics is not that interesting, so the new neighbors converse happily about how much better the traffic is here than wherever they used to live. People talk a lot about sports, the kids' ice-hockey league, NBA salary levels, college football, or the local over-sixty softball league—the one in which everybody wears a knee brace and it takes about six minutes for a good hitter to beat out a double. Since nobody can understand what their neighbors actually do—she does something with cell phones, he's involved in some sort of marketing—residents are likely to be known by their leisure-time interests: He's the one who spends his life e-mailing practice schedules to the soccer parents, she organizes the drill team, she's scuba woman and perpetually off in the Caribbean underwater, he's Carnival Cruise man, longing to tell you how many restaurants there were on his last vacation boat.

When these exurban communities started exploding in the early 1990s, people wanted to live around golf courses, because that was part of the suburban ethos they grew up with. During that decade, the number of golf communities nearly doubled to 2,386, according to the National Golf Foundation, even though the number of golfers scarcely budged. But by the year 2000, there had been an interesting shift in values, according to surveys done for the building industry. Prospective home buyers were less likely to demand country clubs in their new neighborhoods. Instead, they wanted walking paths, coffee shops, Kinko's, clubhouses, parks, and natural undeveloped land. In other words, they wanted community.

They come here, remember, with visions of friendships and happy barbecues. They want everything new but also a sense of place. They also want community; and, confronted with a Bowling Alone world, they have shifted their priorities. So they have been ideal customers for the new but burgeoning theming industry. Themists are people who can take something bland and give it a personality and a sense of place. They are hired by builders and retailers to make sure people have a more intense experience when they visit a store, a restaurant, a mall, or a residential development.

The most influential exurb communities are Kentlands or King Farm in Maryland; Ladera Ranch in Orange County; Belle Creek in Colorado; Celebration, Florida; and the Parks of Austin Ranch in Texas. These are attractive new urbanist communities with front porches on almost every house, and people are so community-oriented and friendly that as you walk down the sidewalks, they're going to make damn sure they say "Howdy!" These are places that have village greens, wooded playgrounds, community centers with neighborhood spas, protected-view corridors, Transit Tot day-care centers next to light-rail commuter stations, faux antique tower clocks in recently constructed town squares. There are more pagodas and koi ponds in these places than in all of Asia.

The new-urbanist ethos started in socially conscious communities like Portland, Oregon, but it has spread nationwide. It's made life better and more community-oriented. A man can wake up on a Sunday morning and take his family to the seeker-sensitive nondenominational Willow Creek–style megachurch, which has a 3,800-seat multimedia worship auditorium that was completed the month before. If he's in the mood, the man can watch the service via video in the outdoor café by the parking lot, or if he's feeling traditional, he can watch the video in the faux-Gothic basement stone chapel. After services, which he can watch on the projection-TV screens hanging from either side of the stage, with hymn lyrics projected helpfully below, he can take his wife and kids out to the lifestyle center ten minutes up the road. That's the Italian piazza streetscape that a shopping-mall developer plopped down in the middle of nowhere. You park on the fringe, near the retro-design eighteen-screen movie theater, and walk down Main Street, which has a Barnes & Noble, a Crate and Barrel, a Galyan's, an artisanal bread store, a few Cosis or a Starbucks, a Restoration Hardware, and of course a brew pub. The stores all have awnings, different brick-and-stucco storefronts, and maybe a few loftlike mixed-residential apartments up above, to give them the streetscape feel that Jane Jacobs, an urban theorist, described. There's a cell-phone transmission tower designed to look like a campanile, and the street has been artfully curved so there are no long view lines of the surrounding parking lots, thereby allowing the pedestrians to feel comfortably enclosed.

The man and his family can eat outside at one of the Europeanized panini grills, under wicker shade umbrellas, and the servers will fill their iced-tea glasses every thirty seconds or so. They can watch the trolley go by, wait for a concert by the Dixielanders, the senior-citizen jazz band, or be entertained by one of the street jugglers hired by the development firm to give the place the vibrant street life that is required if the builder has any hope of winning national development awards.

Later, the man and his family can go over to the town rink, which has ice skating in the winter and mini golf in the summer; or browse through the pomegranates at the farmer's market, featuring real live Mennonite agriculturists.

Then the family can split off to take care of the Sunday-afternoon chores. Mom takes the girl off to her stick-handling clinic at the ice rink before heading off to run her errands, and Dad takes the boy to baseball practice before going off to buy that new barbecue grill they need.

The Grill-Buying Guy

I don't know if you've ever seen the expression of a man who is about to buy a first-class barbecue grill. He walks into Home Depot or Lowe's or one of the other mega-hardware complexes, and his eyes are glistening with a far-away visionary zeal, like one of those old prophets gazing into the promised land. His lips are parted and twitching slightly.

Inside the megastore, the man adopts the stride American men fall into when in the presence of large amounts of lumber. He heads over to the barbecue grills, just past the racks of affordable house-plan books, in the yard-machinery section. They are arrayed magnificently next to the vehicles that used to be known as riding mowers but are now known as lawn tractors, because to call them riding mowers doesn't fully convey the steroidized M1 tank power of the things. The man approaches the barbecue grills with a trancelike expression suggesting that he has cast aside all the pains and imperfections of this world and is approaching the gateway to a higher dimension. In front of him is a scattering of massive steel-coated reactors with names like Broilmaster P3, Thermidor, and the Weber Genesis, because in America it seems perfectly normal to name a backyard barbecue grill after a book of the Bible.

The items in this cooking arsenal flaunt enough metal to survive a direct nuclear assault. Patio Man goes from machine to machine comparing their various features—the cast-iron/porcelain-coated cooking surfaces, the 328,000-Btu heat-generating capacities, the 2,000-degree tolerance linings, multiple warming racks, lava-rock containment dishes, or built-in electrical meat thermometers. Certain profound questions flow through his mind. Is a 542-cubic-inch grilling surface enough, considering he might someday get the urge to roast a bison? Can he handle the TEC Sterling II grill, which can hit temperatures of 1,600 degrees, thereby causing his dinner to spontaneously combust? Though the matte-steel overcoat resists scratching, doesn't he want a polished steel surface so he can glance down and admire his reflection while performing the suburban manliness rituals such as brushing tangy teriyaki sauce on meat slabs with his right hand while clutching a beer can in an NFL foam insulator in his left?

Pretty soon a large salesperson in an orange vest—looking like an SUV in human form—comes up to him and says, "Howyadoin'," which is "May I help you?" in Home Depot talk. Patio Man, who has so much lust in his heart, it is all he can do to keep from climbing up on one of these machines and whooping rodeo-style with joy, still manages to respond appropriately. He grunts inarticulately and nods toward the machines. Careful not to make eye contact at any point, the two manly suburban men have a brief exchange of pseudo-scientific grill argot that neither of them understands, and pretty soon Patio Man comes to the reasoned conclusion that it would make sense to pay a little extra for a grill with V-shaped metal baffles, ceramic rods, and a side-mounted smoker box.

But none of this talk matters. The guy will end up buying the grill with the best cup holders. All major purchases of consumer durable goods these days ultimately come down to which model has the most impressive cup holders.

Having selected his joy machine, Patio Man heads for the cash register, Visa card trembling in his hand. All up and down the line are tough ex-football-playing guys who are used to working outdoors. They hang pagers and cell phones from their belts (in case a power line goes down somewhere) and wear NASCAR sunglasses, mullet haircuts, and faded T-shirts that they have ripped the sleeves off of to keep their arm muscles exposed and their armpit hair fully ventilated. Here and there are a few innately Office Depot guys who are trying to blend in with their more manly Home Depot brethren, and not ask Home Depot inappropriate questions, such as "Does this tool belt make my butt look fat?"

At the checkout, Patio Man is told that some minion will forklift the grill over to the loading dock around back. He is once again glad that he's driving that Yukon XL so he can approach the loading-dock guys as a co-equal in the manly fraternity of Those Who Haul Things.

As he signs the credit-card slip, with its massive total price, his confidence suddenly collapses, but it is revived as wonderful grill fantasies dance in his imagination:

There he is atop the uppermost tier of his multilevel backyard dining and recreational area. This is the kind of deck Louis XIV would have had if Sun Gods had had decks. In his mind's eye, Patio Man can see himself coolly flipping the garlic-and-pepper T-bones on the front acreage of his new grill while carefully testing the citrus-tarragon trout filets simmering fragrantly on the rear. On the lawn below, his kids Haley and Cody frolic on the weedless community lawn that is mowed twice weekly courtesy of the people who run Monument Crowne Preserve, his townhome community.

Haley, the fourteen-year-old daughter, is a Travel-Team Girl who spends her weekends playing midfield against similarly ponytailed, strongly calved soccer marvels such as herself. Cody, ten, is a Buzz-Cut Boy whose naturally blond hair has been cut to lawnlike stubble, and the little that's left is highlighted an almost phosphorescent white. Cody's wardrobe is entirely derivative of fashions he has seen watching the X Games. Patio Man can see the kids playing with child-safe lawn darts alongside a gaggle of their cul-de-sac friends, a happy gathering of Haleys and Codys and Corys and Britneys. It's a brightly colored scene—Abercrombie & Fitch pink spaghetti-strap tops on the girls and ankle-length canvas shorts and laceless Nikes on the boys. Patio Man notes somewhat uncomfortably that in America today the average square yardage of boyswear grows and grows, while the square inches in the girls' outfits shrinks and shrinks. The boys carry so much fabric they look like skateboarding Bedouins, and the girls look like preppy prostitutes.

Nonetheless, Patio Man envisions a Saturday-evening party—his adult softball-team buddies lounging on his immaculate deck furniture, watching him with a certain moist envy as he mans the grill. They are moderately fit, sockless men in Docksiders, chinos, and Tommy Bahama muted Hawaiian shirts. Their wives, trim Jennifer Aniston lookalikes, wear capris and sleeveless tops, which look great on them owing to their countless hours on the weight machines at Spa Lady. These men and women may not be Greatest Generation heroes, or earthshaking inventors such as Thomas Edison, but if Thomas Edison had had a

human-resources department, and that department organized annual enrichment and motivational conferences for
midlevel management, then these people would be the marketing executives for the back-office support consultants to
the meeting-planning firms that hook up the HR executives
with the conference facilities.

They are wonderful people. Patio Man can envision his
own wife, Cindy, the Realtor Mom, circulating among
them serving drinks, telling parent-teacher-conference stories and generally stirring up the hospitality; he, Patio Man,
masterfully wields his extra-wide fish spatula while absorbing the aroma of imported hickory chips—again, to the
silent admiration of all. The sun is shining. The people are
friendly. The men are no more than twenty-five pounds
overweight, which is the socially acceptable male-paunch
level in upwardly mobile America, and the children are
well adjusted. This vision of domestic bliss is what Patio
Man has been shooting for all his life.

Patio Man has completed his purchase, another triumph in a lifetime of conquest shopping. As he steps into
the parking lot, he is momentarily blinded by sun bouncing
off the hardtop. He is no longer in that comfy lifestyle center where he and his family took their lunch. Now he is
confronted by the mighty landscape of a modern big-box
mall, one of the power centers where exurban people do
the bulk of their shopping.

Megastores surround him on all sides like trains of
mighty pachyderms. Off to his right there's a Wal-Mart, a
Sports Authority, and an Old Navy large enough to qualify
for membership in the United Nations. Way off on the horizon, barely visible because of the curvature of the earth, is a
Sneaker Warehouse. Just off the highway beyond, is a row

of heavily themed suburban chain restaurants, which, if they all merged, would be known as Chili's Olive Garden Hard Rock Outback Cantina—a melange of peppy servers, superfluous ceiling fans, free bread with olive oil, taco-salad entrées, and enough sun-dried-tomato concoctions to satisfy the population of Tuscany for generations.

This parking lot is so big you could set off a nuclear device in the center and nobody would notice in the stores on either end. In fact, in the modern American suburbs, there's often not just one big-box mall, there are archipelagos of them. You can stand on the edge of one and look down into a valley and see three more—huge area-code stretches of parking area surrounded by massive shopping warehouses that might be painted in racing stripes to break up the monotony of their windowless exteriors. If one superstore is at one mall, then its competitor is probably down the way. There's a PETsMART just down from a PETCO, a Borders near a Barnes & Noble, a Linens 'n Things within sight of a Bed Bath & Beyond, a Target staring at a Kmart staring at a Wal-Mart, a Best Buy cheek by jowl with a Circuit City.

Patio Man doesn't know it yet, but cutting diagonally across the empty acreage in the very lot he is standing in, bopping from megastore to megastore, is his very own beloved wife, Realtor Mom. She's cruising across the terrain in her minivan, but it's no ordinary minivan. If crack dealers drove minivans, this is the kind they'd drive. It's a black-on-black top-of-the-line Dodge Grand Caravan ES, with phat spoilers, muscle grillework, road-hugging foglights, and ten Infinity speakers that she controls with little buttons on the back of her steering wheel because reaching over to the knobs is too much effort.

Her eyes narrow as she heads for the Sam's Club mega-store. She sees an empty parking spot just next to ones set aside for pregnant women and the handicapped, not over twenty yards from the front door. As she zooms in, she notices competition coming from the northeast. There's a rule in the suburbs: The bigger the car, the thinner the woman. And sure enough, here comes a size-six Jazzercise wife in a Lincoln Navigator, trying to get her spot. But the Navigator woman has made two horrible mistakes. First, she's challenged a minivan driver who is in no mood to appear even more tame and domesticated. And second, she doesn't seem to realize that in America it is acceptable to cut off any driver in a vehicle that costs a third more than yours. That's called democracy. So Realtor Mom roars her massive kid-hauling Caravan and swerves into the spot just ahead of the Navigator. If the Navigator woman wants to park this close to the store, she'll have to put on her turn signal and wait behind that family piling into the Odyssey, the one that will take till sundown to strap everybody in and read a few chapters of *Ulysses* before they pull out.

Realtor Mom is halfway through her shopping expedition. She's already trekked through the Wal-Mart Super-center to pick up a CD head cleaner and a can of Dust-Off. America clearly entered a new phase in its history when Wal-Marts started supersizing; it was as if somebody took a blue whale and decided that what it really needed was to be quite a bit bigger.

Though Realtor Mom likes Wal-Mart, it's the price club that really gets her heart racing, because price clubs are Wal-Mart on acid. Here you can get laundry detergent in 41-pound tubs, 30-pound bags of frozen Tater Tots, frozen waffles in 60-serving boxes, and packages of 1,500

Q-tips, which is 3,000 actual swabs since there's cotton on both ends. These stores have been constructed according to the modern American principle that no flaw in design and quality is so grave that it can't be compensated for by mind-boggling quantity. The aisles here are wider than most country lanes. The frozen-food section looks like a university-sized cryogenics lab, and the cutlery section could pass as a medieval armory. The shelves are packed from the linoleum floor clear up to the thirty-foot fluorescent-lighted ceilings with economy-sized consumer goods on massive wooden pallets. Sometimes you look up and consider what would happen if there were an earthquake right now, and you think, Great, I'm going to be crushed to death under a hillside of falling juice boxes.

The first time Realtor Mom went into one of the places and got a load of the size of the household goods, she naturally wanted to see what kind of person would come here shopping for condoms. But what's truly amazing is that wherever you go in a price club, everybody in every aisle is having the same conversation, which is about how much they are saving by buying in bulk. Sometimes you overhear "If you use a lot, it really does pay" or "They never go bad, so you can keep them forever" or "It's nice to have fifteen thousand Popsicles, since someday we plan on having kids anyway . . ." All the people in all the aisles feel such profound satisfaction over their good deals that they pile the stuff into their shopping carts—which are practically the size of eighteen-wheelers, with safety airbags for the driver—so that by the time they head toward the checkout, they look like the supply lines for the Allied invasion of Normandy.

But they feel they've accomplished something. In pur-

chasing Post-it notes by the million, they have put something over on the gods of the marketplace. They have one-
upped the poor nonclub members who have betrayed their
families by failing to get the best deal. They are the savvy
marketplace swashbucklers who have achieved such
impressive price-tag victories that they will return home in
glory to recount tales of their triumphs to tables of rapt
dinner guests. Bragging about what a good deal you got is
one of the many great art forms that my people, the Jews,
have introduced to American culture.

This trip, Realtor Mom is saving a bundle on frozen
sausage-and-pepperoni Pizza Pockets. She's making a
killing on tennis balls and vermouth-flavored martini
onions. She has triumphantly advanced in the realm of
casual merlot and inflatable water-wing acquisition. She
has stocked up on so many fat-free, salt-free, lactose-free,
and cholesterol-free items that the boxes she's carrying
might as well be empty.

She, too, heads back to her vehicle with a sense that she
has shopped victoriously. In this complicated and time-
stressed world, she has demonstrated, at least for an
instant, her mastery of everyday life. She has achieved par.

As it transpires, she finishes her rounds just as Patio
Man is pulling out of the mall with his backyard wonder-
grill tucked snugly into the back of his Yukon. She recog-
nizes his DADSTOY vanity license plate (she has the
MOMSCAB companion plate), and she honks brightly to get
his attention. Pretty soon they've both got their cell phones
with the walkie-talkie features out four inches in front of
their noses, and they chat affectionately about their
tremendous purchases.

They drive home together. They turn left on Executive

Avenue and head past the Chez Maison apartment complex and the Falcon Preserve gated-home community
toward their own townhome cluster.

The town fathers in their suburb have tried halfheart-
edly to control sprawl. As Patio Man and his wife cruise
over a hilltop and look down on the expanse of suburb
below, they can see, stretched across the landscape, little
puffs here and there of brown smoke. That's bulldozers
kicking up dirt while building new townhomes, office
parks, shopping malls, firehouses, schools, AmeriSuites
guest hotels, and golf courses. As a result of the ambiva-
lently antigrowth zoning regulations, the homes aren't
spread out with quarter-acre yards, as in the older, more
established suburbs; they're clustered into pseudo-urbanist
pods. As you scan the horizon, you'll see a densely packed
pod of town houses, then a half-mile stretch of investor
grass (fields that will someday contain thirty-five- thou-
sand-square-foot Fresh Mex restaurants but are now being
kept fallow by investors until the prices come up), then
another pod of slightly more expensive but equally dense-
packed detached homes.

Realtor Mom and Patio Man's little convoy is impressive—8,000 pounds of metal carrying 290 pounds of
human being. They finally bear right into their community—their street has been given the imperious but baffling
name Trajan's Column Terrace—and they pull into their
double-wide driveway in front of the two-car garage and
next to the adjustable-height Plexiglas backboard.

Their home is a mini-McMansion gable-gable house.
That is to say, it's a 3,200-square-foot middle-class home
built to look like a 7,000-square-foot starter palace for the
nouveaux riches. On the front elevation is a big gable on

top, and right in front of it, for visual relief, a little gable juts forward so it looks like a baby gable leaning against a mommy gable.

These homes have all the same features of the authentic McMansions (as history flows on, McMansions have come to seem authentic), but everything is significantly smaller. There are the same vaulted atriums behind the front doors that never get used and the same open-kitchen/two-story great rooms with soaring Palladian windows. But in the middle-class knockoffs, the rooms are so small—especially upstairs—that the bedrooms and master-bath suites wouldn't fit inside one of the walk-in closets of a real McMansion.

As the happy couple emerges from the vehicles, it is clear that they are both visibly flushed and aroused. With the juices still flowing from their consumer conquests, it's all they can do to keep from humping away like a pair of randy stallions right there on the front lawn under the shade of the seasonal holiday banner hanging above the front door. But that would violate the community association's public copulation guidelines. So, with the kids away at their various practices, and not due to get carpooled home for another hour, the two erotically charged exurbanites mischievously bound up to the master suite and experience even higher stages of bliss on the Sealy Posturpedic mattress, on the stainproof Lycron carpeting, and finally and climactically, atop the Ethan Allen Utopia-line settee.

This today is one version of the American Dream: wild, three-location suburban sex in close proximity to one's own oversized motor vehicles and a brand-new top-of-the-line barbecue grill. In the course of our drive through middle- and upper-middle-class suburbia, we've seen other contemporary versions of the dream. But still, in all our segmented diversity, there are certain traits that Americans tend to share, traits that join the many flavors of suburban culture and distinguish us from people in other lands. We'll get a glimpse of some in the next chapter.

CHAPTER TWO

Thyroid Nation

WE'VE LEFT OUT LARGE swaths of America in the course of our drive. We've scarcely peered into urban America, and we haven't even ventured into rural America. If we had continued our drive outward from the exurbs, we would have crossed the meat loaf line, that invisible divide in the landscape across which restaurants are far less likely to have sun-dried tomato concoctions and far more likely to have gravy.

If we'd gone out there, we would have come across more American-made cars and different sorts of bumper stickers: "Friends Don't Let Friends Drive Fords" and "Warning: In Case of Rapture, This Vehicle Will Be Unmanned." We would have found an entirely different attitude toward money. A lot of people don't have much, even though they don't exactly look poor. Rural America has suffered some appalling economic blows over the past few decades—falling commodity prices, the decimation of small manufacturing plants, farm after farm going bankrupt. While many young people move away, those who remain decide that money is not their god. There is intense social pressure not to put on airs. In many rural precincts, if you had some money and tried to drive a Mercedes, you'd be asking for trouble. If you hired a cook for a dinner party, people would wonder who died and made you queen.

If we'd continued to rural America, we would have entered a giant deflation machine. Gas is somehow fifty cents cheaper a gallon, parking tickets are three dollars, and there are racks and racks of blouses at the Dollar General for $9.99. There are no Saks Fifth Avenues, Neiman Marcuses, or Tiffanys in these rural regions, just Kohl's and Value City, and it's nice to be in a place where you can afford nearly everything for sale (when you're in a city or an inner-ring suburb, you are constantly afflicted with high-end products ridiculously out of your price range).

In many small towns, you can set yourself a goal: Try to spend twenty dollars a person on dinner. You can order the most expensive thing on the menu—steak au jus, seafood delight, "slippery beef" pot pie, whatever—and you probably won't be able to do it. You can ask the locals to direct you to the nicest restaurant in town; they'll send you to a Red Lobster or an Applebees. You'll spy a restaurant that seems from the outside to have some pretensions—maybe a "Les Desserts" glass cooler for the key lime pie and tapioca pudding. But you'll check out the entrée prices and realize that you didn't crack that twenty-dollar barrier.

This truly is a segmented country. In rural America, they love QVC, Danny Gans, and the Pro Bowlers Tour; high schools close the first day of hunting season. In the inner-ring suburbs, they love Tavis Smiley, David Brancaccio, and socially conscious investing; and the farmers' markets empty out for gun-control marches. In rural America, churches are everywhere; in suburban America, Thai restaurants are everywhere. In rural America, it's unwise to schedule events on Wednesday night, because that is the night for prayer meetings. In inner-ring suburbs, you can schedule events any night, but you probably don't want to go up against *Sex in the City.*

Forty percent of Americans consider themselves evangelical Christians, according to the Barna Research Group. In cities and inner-ring suburbs, you don't hear much God talk (people are quiet about it), while in the exurbs, they are loud and proud. America is segmented politically, too. In 2000, Al Gore won among big-city voters by over three to one, while George Bush won among rural and exurban voters by nearly as big a margin. Ethnically, we remain split. SUNY demographer John Logan analyzed the 2000 census data and found that racial segregation by neighborhood is stubbornly persistent. Despite increasing numbers of middle-class African-Americans, people congregate in ethnic enclaves. We all loudly declare our commitment to diversity, but in real life, we make strenuous efforts to find and fit in with people who make us feel comfortable.

More menacingly, social and economic stratification seems to intensify every year. The sociologist Seymour Martin Lipset once observed that two great themes run through American history—the desire for achievement and the desire for equality. These days you might look around and get the impression that we have embraced the ideology of achievement and forsaken equality. The highly educated make more and more money, while the less educated struggle harder and harder. I recently heard a McKinsey consultant give a presentation to senior executives on how to retain star employees. You have to pay them far more than regular employees, he advised. Then he added, "Sometimes companies in the Midwest resist a little before they do this." You could hear an entire cultural code cracking under the weight of that aside.

Business consolidation widens the inequality. The banking system used to be decentralized. Small towns had their own banks, with their own executives and boards of directors. Hence, each small town had its own executive class. But now banks have consolidated, as have so many other businesses. The executives are congregated at the corporate headquarters in affluent areas, the loan decisions are made by formula, and small towns no longer have much of a local upper class.

The American education system has become a vast inequality machine as well. The National Assessment of Educational Progress shows that the gap between the best and worst fourth-grade readers is widening as the good schools extend their lead on the lagging ones. Go to an affluent inner-ring suburb—such as Lower Merion, Pennsylvania; Bethesda, Maryland; or Palo Alto, California—and you will find that graduating seniors at the local public high schools have average SAT scores over 1200 combined. The average student in these upper-middle-class public schools is in the top 10 percent nationwide. But in a rural high school or an inner-city school, the average SAT score might be around 800 or 900.

High-achieving parents are marrying each other and breeding kids who are high-achievement squared, who will in turn make a lot of money and breed their own kids who are high-achievement cubed. Studies show that as the meritocracy purifies, Americans are even more likely to socialize with and marry people at education levels similar to their own. It begins to look like an inherited educational caste system, except that it's somewhat voluntary. A survey done for *American Demographics* magazine revealed that 34 percent of female high school grads said they would prefer to marry someone with only a high school degree, while only 4 percent would like to even date someone with a doctorate. They wouldn't feel comfortable spanning that vast cultural divide.

The Social Structure in the Age of Sprawl

Some people look across this segmented landscape and see signs of an incipient class war. The rich are getting richer, and the wages of the middle class are stagnating, or worse. Surely, people say, there will be some sort of explosion or reaction sooner or later. Others look across the landscape and see a slow-boiling culture war. In the conservative heartland, people are religiously observant, traditionalist, and moralistic. Along the liberal coasts, people are secular, liberation-minded, and relativist.

But people who predict class or culture wars misunderstand the social structure in an age of sprawl. Because of its vast space and money, America is not a hierarchical place. It doesn't have the sort of easily understood social structure that allows people to locate where they are on a bottom-to-top pecking order. America doesn't divide neatly into two or three massive social classes.

Perhaps there was once such a pecking order, with the Vanderbilts and the Rockefellers on top, along with a few blue-blood families, the old-line firms, and the rest of the Protestant elites. Perhaps there was once a single economic power structure, along with a dominant set of mainstream and hegemonic cultural understandings and standards of behavior. Perhaps there was once a definable and coherent political establishment that lived in Georgetown or Manhattan and silently ran things.

But in the era of great dispersal, everything spreads out. With all these vast, growing suburbs, there is even more geographic space. If you don't like the neighbors moving into town, you get out. With the panoply of channels, specialty magazines, and Internet sites, there is social space. With the explosion of alternative-lifestyle enclaves, there is cultural space. If the southern Baptists don't really sympathize with your decision to be a Wiccan, then you find your own Wiccan cluster. With the spread of fund-raising channels, there is political space. Power in Washington is no longer wielded by a few master powerbrokers in Georgetown. There are now thousands of interest groups and donors spread around the country, and it is up to each aspiring politician to cobble together a coalition.

In other words, living in an abundant society that's rich in financial and technological possibilities, you don't have to fight over scarce land and cultural space. You can move on and build your own milieu. Everything that was once hierarchical turns cellular.

As you look across the landscape of America—from hip bohemia to ethnic enclaves such as South Boston, through the diverse suburbs into exurbia and the farthest farm towns—you don't see a lot of conflict. You see a big high school cafeteria with all these different tables. The jocks sit here, the geeks sit there, the drama people sit over there, and the druggies sit somewhere else. All the different cliques know the others exist, and there are some tensions. But they go to different parties, have slightly different cultures, talk about different things, and see different realities. Although individuals may live in two or three overlapping cliques, the cliques don't know much about one another, and they all regard the others as vaguely pathetic.

In America, too, people find their own social circles, usually with invisible buffer zones. You may have moved to suburban Des Moines, but then you find a quilting club, and there are quilting meetings, national quilting conventions, and quilting celebrities such as Ike Winner, the Quilting Cowboy, and Marianne Fons and Liz Porter, hosts of the PBS show *For the Love of Quilting*. You've found your community, and as in every clique, it has its own status system, its own causes, its own validation systems, and its own exaggerated sense of its role in society.

There is no one single elite in America. Hence, there is no definable establishment to be oppressed by and to rebel against. Everybody can be an aristocrat within his own Olympus. You can be an X Games celebrity and appear on ESPN2, or an atonal jazz demigod and be celebrated in obscure music magazines. You can be a short-story master and travel the nation from writers' conference to writers' conference, celebrated for your creativity, haircut, and style. Perhaps you are an NRA enthusiast, an ardent Zionist, a Rush Limbaugh dittohead, a surfer, a neo-Confederate, or an antiglobalization activist. Your clique will communicate its code of honor, its own set of jokes and privileges. It will offer you a field of accomplishments and a system of recognition. You can look down from the heights of your own achievement at all those poor saps who are less accomplished in the field of, say, antique-car refurbishing, Civil War reenacting, or Islamic learning. And you can feel quietly satisfied about your own self-worth.

"Know thyself," the Greek philosopher advised. But of course this is nonsense. In the world of self-reinforcing clique communities, the people who are truly happy live by the maxim "Overrate thyself." They live in a community that reinforces their values every day. The anthropology professor can stride through life knowing she was unanimously elected chairwoman of her crunchy suburb's sustainable-growth study seminar. She wears the locally approved status symbols: the Tibet-motif dangly earrings, the Andrea Dworkin–inspired hairstyle, the peasant blouse, and the public-broadcasting tote bag. She is, furthermore, the best outdoorswoman in the Georgia O'Keeffe Hiking Club, and her paper on twentieth-century Hopi protest graffiti was much admired at last year's Multidisciplinary OutGroup Research Conference. No wonder she feels so righteous in her beliefs.

Meanwhile, sitting in the next seat of the coach section on some Southwest Airlines flight, there might be a midlevel executive from a postwar suburb who's similarly rich in self-esteem. But he lives in a different clique, so he is validated and reinforced according to entirely different criteria and by entirely different institutions.

Unlike the anthropologist, he has never once wanted to free Mumia. He doesn't even know who Mumia is. But he has been named Payroll Person of the Year by the West Coast Regional Payroll Professionals Association. He is interested in college football and tassels. His loafers have tassels. His golf bags have tassels. If he could put tassels around the Oklahoma football vanity license plate on his Cadillac Escalade, his life would be complete.

These people sit on the plane, hip to hip, and they would be feeling mutually superior if they gave each other a moment's thought. One of the great observations about this country is that here, everybody can kick everybody else's ass. The crunchies who hike look down on the hunters who squat in the forest downing beers, and the hunters look down on the hikers who perch on logs smoking dope. The fundamentalists look down on the Jewish Buddhist Taoist liberals who think redwoods are a religious shrine, and the Jewish Buddhist Taoist liberals look down on the fundamentalists who think natural-history museums are filled with evolutionist propaganda.

As you may have noticed, 90 percent of Americans have way too much self-esteem (while the remainder has none at all). Nobody in this decentralized, fluid social structure knows who is mainstream and who is alternative, who is elite and who is populist. Professors at Harvard think the corporate elites run society, while the corporate elites think the cultural elites at Harvard run society. Liberals think their views are courageously unfashionable, and conservatives believe they are bravely dissenting from the mainstream media.

Most people see themselves living on an island of intelligence in a sea of idiocy. They feel their own lives are going pretty well, even if society as a whole is going down the toilet. They believe their children's schools are good, even if the nation's schools in general are terrible. Their own congressperson is okay, even if most of the others should be thrown out of office. Their own values are fine, even if civilization itself is on the verge of collapse. We all live in Lake Wobegon because we are all above average. We are all okay; it's the vast ocean of morons who are mucking things up.

Ours is not a social structure conducive to revolution, domestic warfare, and conflict. The United States is not on the verge of an incipient civil war or a social explosion. If you wanted to march against the ruling elite, where exactly would you do it? The problems we're more likely to observe during our drive through suburbia are withdrawal, segmentation, and disunion. Seduced by the splendor of our glorious great rooms and the insular comfort of our validation groups, we're more likely to take advantage of all the space and ignore everybody else, become detached from public life, and even more ignorant of the other cliques and communities all around. Then what happens to this common enterprise we call America? And will our tendency to disperse ruin this wonderful union we call America?

Full Throttle

When you step back and think about it, this tendency is not breaking up America; it *is* America. It was in 1782 that an astute visitor to these shores, the Marquis de Chastellux, observed, "In a nation which is in a perpetual state of growth, everything favors this general tendency; everything divides and multiplies." That's been true ever since.

We may not all be chasing the same thing, but we are all chasing something. What defines us as a people is our pursuit, our movement, and our tendency to head out. Today's movement to ever more distant suburbs is merely the current iteration of the core American trait.

In 1910 a man named Henry Van Dyke wrote a book called *The Spirit of America,* which begins with the sentence "The Spirit of America is best known in Europe by one of its qualities—energy." That is what you see across this country. Wherever we are heading, we are getting there at great speed and with great energy. It's not the steering wheel that distinguishes us, it's the throttle. The mystery of America is the mystery of motivation. Where does all the energy come from?

It was the energy to move that brought many people here in the first place. During the twentieth century, the population of France increased by 52 percent, the population of Germany increased by 46 percent, and the population of the United Kingdom by 42 percent, but the population of the United States increased by 270 percent. About 120 million Americans, 46 percent of the country, moved between 1995 and 2000. The number of local moves has actually decreased with increased home-ownership rates. But the number of long-distance moves has remained constant.

When we are not striving to move outward, we are striving to move up. Americans are the hardest-working people on the face of the earth. We work more hours per year than even the Japanese. The average American works

350 hours a year—nearly ten weeks—longer than the average European.

Furthermore, this work is not compulsory. For the first time in history, people at the top of the income ladder work longer hours than people at the bottom. Over the past twenty years, the proportion of American managers and professionals who work over fifty hours a week has increased by a third. If you present people with this statement: "I make a point of doing the best work I can even if it interferes with the rest of my life," 60 percent of Americans say it applies to them, compared to only 38 percent of Germans, who are not pikers when it comes to hard work.

We switch jobs frequently. The average job tenure in the U.S. is 6.9 years, compared to 10.4 years in France, 10.8 years in Germany, and 11.3 years in Japan.

If we are not rushing to work, we are rushing to church or softball or tutoring. The American tendency to switch religions—sometimes several times over the course of a lifetime—is probably unprecedented in world history. Nearly a fifth of adult Americans have converted at some point in their lives, according to the 2001 Religious Identification Survey. Although the exact numbers are under heavy dispute, Americans attend religious services at rates well above those of all comparable nations. Fifty-eight percent of Americans say their belief in God is very important to their lives, compared to only 12 percent of the French and 19 percent of the British, according to a UNESCO survey. About 86 percent of Americans believe in heaven, twice the German percentage. Our tendency to donate time to community service and voluntary associations such as Big Brother programs is also unmatched. Global surveys reveal that about 80 percent of Americans belong to some sort of voluntary association, compared with only 36 percent of, say, Italians and Japanese. About one-third of Americans do unpaid work for religious organizations, compared to 5 percent of the French and 6 percent of the British.

Nearly three-quarters of Americans make charitable contributions, with those toward the lower end of the income scale donating a higher percentage of their income than any other group. We have tailored our tax system to reinforce this national trait. Americans donate more money per capita than any other people, about $1,100 per year on average, with evangelical Christians giving about $3,600 a year per adult. No other nation has such a private non-profit sector.

The fabric of our everyday lives is frenetic. We are the nation of the take-out coffee cup. In most other countries, people drink their coffee out of porcelain cups. According to a GfK Ad Hoc Research Worldwide study, 57 percent of Americans eat out in a given week, compared to 12 percent of the French and 10 percent of the Germans. We eat out because we don't have time to cook, and the restaurant of choice is often someplace cheap, casual, and fast. When Europeans, for example, eat out, it tends to be at someplace slow, expensive, and fine. Only 8 percent of Americans say they typically spend thirty dollars or more when they eat out. Half of all Dutch people do.

We have constructed our society so that we have a relatively open field in all directions, so our energies can take us to both good and bad extremes. We have high marriage rates and very high divorce rates. High incomes but also high spending, and hence low savings. We are productive but also wasteful. We are quick to embrace innovations such as credit cards and e-commerce, but also quick to jump at get-rich-quick manias and dot-com bubbles. We have high job-creation rates but also high layoff rates. We have income mobility but also high violent-crime rates and high incarceration rates. We spend more money per school pupil than any other nation, have the highest high school and college graduation rates, and offer some of the best universities in the world but also some of the worst elementary and secondary schools. We devote a higher percentage of GDP to health care than any other people, and have the best hospitals, but more than 40 million of us are uninsured. We are incredibly rich, but our distribution of income is strikingly unequal, and the American welfare state is much smaller than that of comparable nations. Because Americans are relatively allergic to restrictions, regulations, and restraint on their mobility, our government is smaller. The American government collects about a third of the national GDP in taxes, compared to 52 percent in Sweden and 40 percent in Belgium and France, and these gaps are increasing. Only 38 percent of Americans say that government should work to reduce income inequality, compared to 80 percent of Italians and 70 percent of Austrians.

As Seymour Martin Lipset observes in his book *American Exceptionalism,* "America continues to be qualitatively different. To reiterate, exceptionalism does not mean better. This country is an outlier." I suspect that every nation, like every person, is unique and exceptional. Our exceptionalism takes the form of energy and mobility and dreams of ascent. As Lipset documents, we are the most individualistic, the most rights-oriented, the most optimistic, and the most committed to personal liberty. Of course, many people in America are risk-averse, and go to their secure bureaucratic jobs until they can retire and live out the rest of their days safely and happily. But on balance, and compared to people in other cultures, we don't want barriers in the way of our ambitions and desires, and we seem more willing to tolerate the risks, insecurity, and inequality that come as freedom's downside.

Whether in the city or the inner-ring suburb or the outer-ring exurb or beyond, we are witnessing different effusions of the same impulse to move out and up.

Rhino of the Earth

The energy and mobility of average Americans translates into many things. It translates first into money. All those thrusting, aspiring people in the downtown lofts, the suburban town centers, the immigrant zones, the exurban office parks, and the rural factories have made this country outlandishly affluent. With under 5 percent of the world's population, the U.S. accounts for about 31 percent of the world's economic activity. American gross domestic product per worker is about 30 percent greater than that of Germany or Japan.

The affluence of the upper class isn't the amazing thing. It's the affluence of the middle class. Americans spend $40 billion on lawn care each year, more than the total tax revenues of the federal government in India. The average American family spends $2,000 a year on food in restaurants. According to Cotton Incorporated's magazine, *Lifestyle Monitor,* American women between the ages of sixteen and seventy have, on average, seven pairs of jeans in their wardrobes. Nearly three-quarters of the new cars on the road have cruise control and power door locks.

American homes are by far the largest in the world. According to data compiled by the UN and the U.S. Department of Energy, the typical American occupies a house with 718 square feet per person. Australia comes in second, with 544 square feet per person. In Canada, the average person has 442 square feet; in crowded nations such as Holland, the average person has 256 feet, and in Japan, the average person has only 170 square feet.

Ours is a country with six hundred certified pet chiropractors. The average household headed by someone with a college degree has an income of about $72,000 a year. If you live in that household, you are richer than 95 percent of the people on the planet. You are probably richer than 99.99 percent of the people who have ever lived. In comparative terms, you are stinking rich.

This affluence translates into power. Americans in their townhome communities and subdivisions didn't seek to dominate the world. Many of them have rarely been abroad and are comfortably oblivious to much of what goes on at other latitudes and longitudes. But through their incredible hard work, their entrepreneurial zeal and creative energy, they have propelled the United States upward to occupy an unprecedented position in world affairs.

Thanks to the unexplained and unquenchable energy of all those different lifestyle seekers, the United States dominates the globe. Three-quarters of recent years' Nobel laureates in economics and the sciences live and work in the United States. The U.S. is responsible for 40 percent of the world's spending on technological research and development. American movies account for about 83 percent of world box-office revenues. American drug companies bring more new drugs to market than all the other drug companies in all the other nations combined. American venture-capital firms dwarf the venture-capital firms in all other nations of the globe. The U.S. military spends more on defense than the next fifteen nations combined. As the Yale historian Paul Kennedy recently noted, never before in human history has one nation been so dominant in the world; never before has one nation's economic and military might so eclipsed that of its closest rivals and allies.

If there were a rhino in the middle of your room, you wouldn't be reading this book, you'd be staring at the rhino. The United States is the rhino of the world. And when you get down to it, all that might is based on the work, the creativity, and the mysterious inner drive of the Patio Men and Realtor Moms, the inner-ring litigators and the bohemian software geeks. We are living in the age of the American Empire, and America is a suburban nation, so we are living in the age of the First Suburban Empire. And what the heck is that?

The paradox of suburbia is that people move there to pursue their private dreams. They want to live in a nice house with a nice yard and have a nice career and nice kids who go to nice schools. Yet because of their energy and productivity, they have propelled the United States into its rhino position.

Suddenly, people from other parts of the world are reacting to us and confronting us and demanding our attention. Whether it is Osama bin Laden or Saddam Hussein or the antiglobalization protesters or politicians in places as diverse as France, Israel, North Korea, and China, everybody is trying to do something to the United States, trying to flatter it, attack it, humiliate, it, mold it, or improve it. All sorts of world problems end up landing in the American lap, whether it is crises in the Middle East, AIDS in Africa, or weapons of mass destruction anywhere. The middle class suburbanites chased private happiness, but their country has an inescapably public role. The people who live in the most powerful nation on earth don't really control their own agendas. They find themselves under attack for reasons they haven't thought much about. They have to act on the world stage, which is a place that doesn't interest most of them.

Our Nation, Our Selves

In normal circumstances we don't really think about it: how being American shapes our personalities and who we are and the path our lives take. But in extraordinary circumstances, we become acutely aware of what it means to be a member of a nation and a people. Thousands of Americans were killed on September 11, 2001, simply because they were American or worked in America. In the months and years since, we have become more aware of our nationality, of other peoples' perceptions of America, and the distinct and problematic role that America plays in the world.

The British writer George Orwell began to think about the significance of nationality during the early years of World War II. He was living in London, and at night German planes would try to destroy his city. He wrote an essay called "The Lion and the Unicorn," which began, "As I write, highly civilized human beings are flying overhead trying to kill me." He knew that those highly civilized German human beings were trying to kill him not because of who he was personally, but because he was English, and he began to wonder what that meant. "Till recently it was thought proper to pretend that all human beings are very much alike," Orwell wrote, "but in fact anyone able to use his eyes knows that the average of human behavior differs enormously from country to country. Things that could happen in one country could not happen in another."

What is this identity, Englishness? Orwell wondered. What can the England of the mid-nineteenth century have in common with the England of the mid-twentieth? But, he continued, "What have you in common with the child of five whose photograph your mother keeps on the mantelpiece? Nothing, except that you happen to be the same person."

Your nation, Orwell went on, "is your civilization. It is you." It changes. "But like anything else it can change only in certain directions, which up to a point can be foreseen. That is not to say that the future is fixed, merely that certain alternatives are possible and others are not. A seed may or may not grow, but at any rate a turnip seed never grows into a parsnip." It is important, he concluded, to know what England is before guessing what part England can play in the world.

In some ways, each of us is like nobody else. In some ways, each of us is like everybody else on earth. And in some other ways, each of us is like our countrymen. We have inherited and been molded by some shared mentality. Our personalities, in ways we appreciate or not, approve of or not, have been shaped by America. We are not detachable creatures who have been formed in absentia from the culture in which we were raised. Across the polymorphous perversity of our landscape, and even across the transformations of our history, there are some assumptions and attitudes that bind us together.

Despite all the changes, what Alexis de Tocqueville wrote about this country in the 1830s remains eerily applicable today. And it's not only Tocqueville's descriptions that still seem to fit, it's those of Crèvecoeur, who lived here in the eighteenth century; of James Bryce, who came here in the late nineteenth, and of many others. When we drive through suburbia and out to the exurbs, we are seeing much that is unprecedented, but the new aspects are the most recent embodiments of centuries-old ideas, impulses, and aspirations.

As we observe people in their townhomes, home theaters, and luxury pickup trucks, with their donut holes, their Dippin' Dots ("The ice cream of the future"), their baggy jeans and laceless sneakers, we do begin to wonder: What drives Americans to cram their hours and minutes with activity, to spend and move and disperse? What impels Americans to spread so quickly, to buzz so feverishly, and to spread vibrations out across the globe? What is the source of all this energy?

Observers, foreign and domestic, have tried to answer these questions. Some have interpreted our tendency to move and work and disperse as part of a noble and utopian effort to realize certain ideals—freedom, happiness, and spiritual fulfillment. Others have argued that our energy is merely part of some manic drive to avoid the deep and profound issues of life, to skate along the surface of existence and wallow in material luxury and incessant gain. In Chapter 4, we'll take a look at those who believe we are driven by a spiritual wind. But first let us probe into the depths of superficiality and consider the case made by those who consider Americans the spoiled blond bimbos of the earth.

CHAPTER THREE

Americans: Bimbos of the World

IF GOD IS OMNIPOTENT, omniscient, and good, why does He allow morons to succeed? One notices this phenomenon constantly; the most empty-headed, asinine individuals float helium-like ever higher into the firmament of success, from plum post to plum post, without ever demonstrating extraordinary talent, original intelligence, or even a noteworthy grasp of the matters at hand. Often they have pleasant faces and a certain animal magnetism, and their ascent seems to be accelerated by the fact that they are not burdened by the weight of an interesting personality. They've somehow acquired the reputation as One Who Is Chosen, so when leadership jobs open up and selection committees meet, they are called.

Their unbearable lightness is pleasing to the selectors, who either want somebody safe and manipulable or are themselves members in the community of the eminently vapid. So the zero-gravity hero ascends one more level in his merit-free rise to greatness, where he will be in a position to promote other empty eminentoes, who will promote still more hollow leaders, so that gradually, day by day, they will all find themselves in a golden circle of high-cheekboned innocuousness—girded on left and right by a band of pleasing, unoriginal, stress-free, talentless paragons radiating benign self-satisfaction upon one another without end. Amen.

This phenomenon represents a gaping flaw in the structure of the universe. It is a cosmic screw-up in the Divine Plan. How in this universe can it be that those who have a critical sensibility roughly equivalent to a golden retriever's, and who are so manifestly spiritually inferior to oneself, nonetheless manage to rise and rise? What's galling is not the undeserving success of this person, nor that he drives around in a Porsche Boxster, nor that he lives with his coldly gracious wife and her buttery-chunks hair and their blandly perfect and effortlessly slender children on an immaculately manicured horse farm with a helipad. No, the material trappings of success are not what gall. Maybe you wouldn't want such niceties even if you could afford them.

The infuriating thing is that he is not even aware of his shortcomings. Vapidity is the one character flaw that comes with its own missile defense system. The vapid person by definition does not possess the mental wherewithal to be aware of his own vapidity. This person has a blessed imperviousness, a milk-and-honey obliviousness to the meagerness of his actual merit. It hasn't occurred to him that he is not the richest, the fullest, the deepest emblem of human accomplishment and worthiness. His conscience, like everything else about him, is clean.

Nine times out of ten, the universe is structured in such a way that he is never forced to come face-to-face with his true self. He is born to grace, grows up in the land of charm, is nurtured in the fraternity of self-confidence, floats up through the career of plush paneling, fund-raising networks, and golf resorts, rests in the paradise of garrulous companionship, and retires at long last to Aspen, where he finally dies of happiness. The reckoning never comes! The moment of truth is avoided. Moreover, he is untouchable by the likes of you. You could scream tirades at him, write long essays denouncing his hollowness, construct mathematical formulae proving his mediocrity. He would whiz by in his golf cart to play out the back nine, and you'd be left spluttering into the void. Look at his résumé! Look at his impressive shoulders, graying temples, slender nose, and perfectly trimmed nails. And then look at you in your scuffed shoes, spluttering.

You stand there praying: If he would stop his cart just once, and turn to acknowledge, "Yes, I am shallow! I am undeserving!" then you would gladly grant him his Boxster and his buttery-chunks wife and his effortlessly slender children and the weedless horse farm, and you would be at peace with the world. But it will never happen. This paragon of success is the Lord of Self-esteem—the unapproachable, the all-powerful, the one who will not be brought low.

The inescapable fact is that the universe is divided between Blondes and Brunettes. This is not a matter of the color of one's hair. This is a cosmic trait. The Cosmic Blonde floats through life on a beam of sunshine, from success to success. The Cosmic Brunette obsesses and reflects, frets and fumes, turns inward, and clings to the view that the examined life is the only life worth living, despite all the evidence to the contrary. The Cosmic Brunette writes and reads books, worries, condemns and evaluates, judges, discerns and doubts. The Cosmic Blonde water-skis.

Go into any town, and you can see the Blondes and Brunettes engaged in their rival spheres. This is, I emphasize, not a matter of physical traits; many people who are born with fair hair are actually Brunettes of the soul, and vice versa. Nor is it a matter of intelligence. Some people with the highest IQs also possess a sunny imperviousness, an innate sense that life is to be enjoyed and that anything complicating fun and ascent can be safely ignored on the highway to Telluride. And some of the world's dumbest people have Brunette personalities—hence the appeal of sensitively suffering pop singers. You see them in any town, rich or poor, suburb or city. The Cosmic Blondes slip from health club to country club with their power-of-positive-thinking expressions, their BlackBerries clipped efficiently on their fat-free hips, their laser-surgeried eyes carefully tinted to match the leather interior of their Lincoln Navigators, which are so big they look like the Louisiana Superdome on wheels, guzzle so much gas that Saudi princes line the driveway gaping and applauding, and are so overbearing that they are scarcely out of the dealership before they've got little Hondas and Toyotas embedded in their grillework. The Brunettes, on the other hand, putter around in their low-slung Japanese sedans with a clutter of books and magazines on the backseat and bird-watching equipment in the trunk, deriving their usual passive-aggressive pleasure from their talent for looking down on people who are their economic and political superiors.

Bimbo to the World

This phenomenon is relevant today, because for many people around the world, the United States is the Cosmic Blonde of nations. People around the world concede that American culture has a certain appeal. They don't deny that the United States is an awesomely powerful nation, or that Americans are economically successful. How could they?

What people around the world do deny is that the U.S. is the most profound of nations, or that we are the most intelligent and reflective of peoples, or that we have mastered the art of truly savoring the important things in life. America's image is to the world what southern California's image is to the rest of America. When many foreign observers look at America, they see the culture of Coca-Cola, McDonald's, Disney, boob jobs, Bart Simpson, and boy bands. They see a country that invented Prozac and Viagra, paper party hats, pinball machines, commercial jingles, expensive orthodontia, and competitive cheerleading. They see a slightly trashy consumer culture that has perfected parade floats, corporate-sponsorship deals, low-slung jeans, and Cinnamon Frosted Cocoa Puffs; a culture that finds its highest means of self-expression through bumper stickers ("Rehab Is for Quitters") or the kind of message T-shirts motorcyclists wear ("If You Can Read This, the Bitch Fell Off"). In short, people see the Universal Blonde of nations.

The anti-Americanism that flared up around the time of the 2003 war with Iraq didn't emerge out of nothing, and the rage was not fueled merely by a disagreement about policy. Anti-Americanism, as political theorist James W. Caeser has noted, is based on the belief that there is something deeply arrogant at the core of American life that threatens the rest of the world.

It's amazing how early America was stereotyped as a money-grubbing, empty-headed, shallow-souled, energetic, but incredibly vulgar land. François la Rochefoucauld-Liancourt, who traveled to the United States in the 1790s, declared, "The desire for riches is their ruling passion." In 1805, a British visitor, Richard Parkinson, observed, "All men there make [money] their pursuit." "Gain! Gain! Gain! Gain! Gain!" is how the English philosopher Morris Birkbeck summarized the American spirit a few years later. Around 1850 the disillusioned Russian writer Michail Pogodin lamented, "America, on which our contemporaries have pinned their hopes for a time, has meanwhile clearly revealed the vices of her illegitimate birth. She is not a state, but rather a trading company."

The judgment was reinforced by succeeding waves of foreign observers. Charles Dickens described a country of uncouth vulgarians chasing, as he put it, "the almighty dollar." Oswald Spengler worried that Germany would devolve into "soulless America," with its worship of "technical skill, money and an eye for facts." Matthew Arnold likewise fretted that global forces would Americanize England: "They will rule [Britain] by their energy but they will deteriorate it by their low ideas and want of culture."

By the start of the twentieth century, people around the world had concerns that America's brand of crass materialism would spread. In 1901 the British journalist William Stead published a book called *The Americanization of the World*. In 1904 the German Paul Dehns wrote an influential essay with the same title. "What is Americanization?" he asked. "Americanization in its widest sense, including the societal and political, means the uninterrupted, exclusive, and relentless striving after gain, riches and influence."

Many of these observers came to regard America as the money-mad Moloch of the earth, the corrupter of morals and vulgarizer of culture. Benjamin Franklin was viewed as the quintessential prosperous, smug American, the ultimate man on the make, Homo americanus. Gifted at piling up a fortune, and armed with a shrewd if perpetually self-interested intelligence, he was also seen as self-satisfied, unreflective, and complacent. "The *summum bonum* of his ethic," Max Weber famously declared, was "the earning of more and more money." D. H. Lawrence was even more vituperative. Sure, Franklin could produce, experiment, man the cash register of life, and maybe shave a few pennies from the ledger. "But man has a soul," Lawrence protested. "The wholeness of man is his soul, not merely that nice little comfortable bit which Benjamin marks out. . . . And now I, at least, know why I can't stand Benjamin. He tries to take away my wholeness and my dark forest, my freedom. For how can any man be free without an illimitable background? And Benjamin tries to shove me into a barbed wire paddock and make me grow potatoes."

These days, opposition to our alleged Cosmic Blondeness comes in two forms—the virulent and the merely nervous. Virulent anti-Americans see us as the blonde slut of the universe, seducing the young and subverting traditional values. These people sometimes teach at madrassas or join terror organizations. Some seek to expose our essential hollowness and weakness with a devastating act; they seek to contrast their heroic and self-sacrificing deeds with the materialistic mediocrity of American commercialism. "The Americans love Pepsi-Cola, we love death," an Al Qaeda leader observed after the attacks on the World Trade Center and the Pentagon. Others proselytize from radical group platforms or in universities and opinion journals. They feel spiritually superior to Americans but are economically, politically, and socially outranked. They conclude that the world is diseased, that it rewards the wrong values. They have no real strategy to bring the U.S. low, just their rage, their burning sense of unjust inferiority, their envy mixed with snobbery. As Avishai Margalit and Ian Buruma remarked in *The New York Review of Books,* "With some on the left, hatred of the U.S. is all that remains of their leftism; anti-Americanism is part of their identity." Jean-François Revel put it more broadly (no doubt too broadly): "If you remove anti-Americanism, nothing remains of French political thought today, either on the Left or on the Right."

The people in the merely nervous school distrust America because they see it as representing a particularly immature, aggressive, and imbalanced strain of democratic capitalism. Suspicious of our fevered energy, disliking our hormonal popular culture, discomfited by our gun ethos, our advertising harlotry, and our military might, they regard Americans as muscle-brained blond cowboys roughriding over the globe. They look on in horror as Americans charge off on John Wayne–style crusades: We dim boobies have no idea what sort of instability we are about to cause. We will go marching off as we always do, naively confident of ourselves, yet unaware of the situation's complexities.

In Graham Greene's novel *The Quiet American,* the

protagonist, Alden Pyle, is a well-intentioned, earnest man-child who dreams of inspiring democracy but stirs up chaos and destruction. "I never knew a man who had better motives for all the trouble he caused," one of the characters remarks about him.

With Friends Like These

That's the case for the prosecution. What about our friends? America does have its defenders. Most people in most countries in most times have been favorably disposed toward the United States. And these friends do rise up in our defense. They get on their feet, clear their throats, and speak, and we wait eagerly for their rebuttals. We wait for the soul-stirring encomiums to our greatness, gratitude for our gifts to the world, admiration for our democracy, freedom, generosity, and success.

What comes tumbling from their lips? Concessions. Yes, they allow, Americans are gum-chewing, synthetic, and childish. But look at how vibrant they are. Sure, they're naive and oblivious to history, but look how optimistic they are. Sure, their children are spoiled, their women too masculine, their sexual attitudes prudish, their friendliness phony, their foods fatty and fast, but look how amusing, crazy, and fun they can be. Yes, Americans have business contacts instead of deep friendships. Yes, they practice savage capitalism, have meager and callous welfare systems, and execute their minorities. Yes, they are incapable of contemplation and true enjoyment and live in the grip of puritanical religious fanaticism. Yes, they lack depth of character, and most of them lack any appreciation of the fine arts. Yes, they are terrified of real intellectual debate, and yes, they crudely try to impose their will on the world. But look at their delightful energy, their liberating freedom, their colorful personalities, their technological virtuosity, their military might, and they did bail us out during two world wars.

This is the defense. These are our character witnesses!

It's been this way all through history. The visitors who are most in love with America will feel compelled to slip in—amid all the adoring praise for our glorious future and our wonderful liberty—a little shiv of equivocation about our shallow souls. Alexis de Tocqueville, the most brilliant and unavoidable writer on this subject, noticed the hectic pace of life in the United States. A Frenchman, he wrote, felt connection to his land, his village, and his ancestors, and thus respected the long "woof of time," while an American had no such set of connections across the centuries. "Democratic man," he wrote, meaning Americans, "does not know how to orient his life. Material goods are the sole fixed point, the sole incontestable value amidst the uncertainty of all things." Therefore, Tocqueville continued, the longing and striving for wealth and possession come to dominate life in America, and to flatten character:

> Each of them, living apart, is as a stranger to the fate of the rest; his children and his private friends constitute to him the whole of mankind. As for the rest of his fellow citizens, he is close to them but he does not see them; he touches them, but he does not feel them. . . .

If your object is not to create heroic virtues but rather tranquil habits, if you would rather contemplate vices than crimes and prefer few transgressions at the cost of few splendid deeds, if in place of a brilliant society you are content to live in one that is prosperous, and finally, if in your view the main object of government is not to achieve the greatest strength or glory for the nation as a whole but to provide for every individual therein the utmost well-being, then it is good to make conditions equal and establish a democratic government.

To some, this sounds remarkably like the comfortable but unheroic world of the American suburb.

Many of the foreign visitors who have admired and defended America have also feared its insidious pleasantness. During the Cold War, the Italian writer Luigi Barzini wrote a string of books with titles like *Oh, America!* and *Americans Are Alone in the World,* rhapsodizing about America and all things American, from our politics to our magazines. But at low moments, even he wondered about these "poor people who don't know what to do with themselves, who have everything money can buy and industry, science and advertising can provide—new machines, new diets, new medicines, new religions, wonderful movies, the best climate in the world—and [you] wonder whether they would be more or less miserable dead."

The contemporary British military historian John Keegan, as true a friend of America as can be imagined, can't fathom why Americans are so totally incapable of relaxing, pausing for reflection, or even dawdling leisurely over a meal. In his book *Fields of Battle,* he describes the scene at the Princeton University faculty club, where he'd go during his visiting professorship in hopes of relaxing with some colleagues over a lunchtime gin and tonic. Instead, "descending to the restaurant floor, I would spend an hour mesmerized by the sight of distinguished academics transfixed by their lonely reading, raising their heads only to take savage canine bites at enormous indigestible sandwiches clutched in a free hand. Strange zoo-like feelings possessed me, as if I were present at the feeding time of a species of superintelligent primates hitherto unknown to science."

This isn't exactly what you want to hear from your advocates. It isn't the patriotic banner you want to march under when you go to defend your nation: "God Bless America! Energetic Vulgarity Is Our Cause! Affluent Mediocrity Is Our Way!"

It's always the same: We are vital but spiritually stunted. The American historian Henry Steele Commager studied the vast foreign literature on America and found that most people who came here liked what they saw. He summarized the bundle of traits that show up again and again in descriptions—first and foremost, observers see America as the land of equality, as the land of the future. It's the land of opportunity, the land of industry and hard work, the land of plenty. But there is the inevitable parade of flip sides. In *America in Perspective,* Commager noted that just as foreign visitors tend to identify the same positive traits in America, they also repeat the same criticisms decade after decade, generation after generation:

> The passion for equality, it was charged, made for mediocrity, for a general leveling down of distinc-

tion and of talent. The concern for material well-being produced a materialistic civilization, one in which the arts flourished only by indulgence, as it were. The passion for work, or for mere activity, left little time for the amenities of life, and Americans were rude. An easygoing tolerance played into the hands of the vulgar and corrupt, permitted the invasion of privacy, the exaltation of the mediocre, the violation of law and order. An excessive nervous vitality made for instability and rootlessness, gave an air of impermanence to almost everything that Americans undertook.

In other words, our foreign friends don't exactly deny our Cosmic Blondeness; they just savor the silver lining, our eager openness to everything, our capacity for mindless fun. They come from time-scarred, serious civilizations where sophisticated people spend their time keeping up with the Kafkas. And they're enchanted by us, the convertible nation, ripping off our tube tops, yipping like banshees as we cruise down the freeway from cineplex to surf shop. How charming! How wild! How seductive the Americans are, with all their careless money and ingenuous vitality!

"There is no pessimism in America regarding human nature and social organization," the French existentialist Jean-Paul Sartre sniffed. The United States, Georges Clemenceau wittily observed, is the only nation in history that "has gone directly from barbarism to degradation without the usual interval of civilization."

Indeed, it is French intellectuals who have mastered the art of the pro-American insult. A great French writer, say, arrives in the United States and is greeted by a throng of our leading thinkers. Dinners are arranged at sophisticated townhouses, local academics are assembled, subtle sauces prepared. But the French writer will have none of it. "Please," he insists, "take me to your Elvis impersonators." The French writer, you see, is on safari for puerile paradoxes. He wants to explore the meaning of vapidity, the exquisite sadness of glitter, and the penetrating tranquility of violence. He wants to head straight for the hyper-reality, for Vegas, for Orlando.

The quintessential French love letter to the U.S. is Jean Baudrillard's 1986 book, *America*. It is of course a brilliant book. That is to say, the subject of the book is Baudrillard's brilliance. There are scenes of Baudrillard being brilliant in Utah, being brilliant in Los Angeles, being brilliant in New York. America has only a minor supporting role. "Americans believe in facts, but not in facticity," he writes. Aah! Brilliant! A Puerile Paradox! One pictures him posing like a great Gallic hunter next to this bon mot he has bagged on the American desert. It is a marvelous stuffed insight, a trophy mot he can hang on his wall at home.

One imagines him thumbing a ride through Nevada. A trucker picks Baudrillard up, and he begins unfurling some of the observations he will put into his book. "Here in the most conformist society the dimensions are immoral. It is this immorality that makes distance light and the journey infinite, that cleanses the muscles of their tiredness," Baudrillard intones as the trucker barrels the big rig down the asphalt. Baudrillard is pleased with the string of words, but the truck driver is looking sideways at him, trying to figure out what this French guy is talking about. Baudrillard continues his soliloquy. His self-regard radiates out in waves, putting a strain on the air-conditioning system. He is inhabiting a higher realm, the realm of the seer of supple things. He pictures himself repeating these ironic profundities on French TV, holding the microphone up to his mouth like a seductive cigarette, with one of those "God Is Dead but My Hair Is Perfect" looks that French intellectuals have mastered in the presence of febrile undergraduates.

Baudrillard drones on to the trucker: "The pigmentation of the dark races is like a natural make-up that is set off by the artificial kind to produce a beauty which is not sexual, but sublime and animal." The truck driver glances about for a baseball bat. But Baudrillard, lost in the glory of his oracular brilliance, goes on: ". . . extreme heat, the orgasmic form of bodily deterritorialization. The acceleration of molecules in the heat contributes to a barely perceptible evaporation of meaning. . . ." In another second, the trucker has gunned it to 85 mph, and with a flick of the opposite door handle and a shove, the soliloquizing semiotician has been pushed onto the highway, where he has been transformed into a rolling, bouncing postmodernist ball, thrilled in his last brilliant thought to have been the object of such a daring countertextual act, a purity of will, a jejune comment on the transgression of meaning.

The Inner Sociologist, the Self-Lacerator of the Soul

But Americans never actually react that way. How one reacts to the international critique depends on where you sit on the Blonde/Brunette divide. The Cosmic Blondes are amazed. Amazed! That anyone could not see the true nature of our own splendid American selves! Amazed that anyone could misinterpret our warmth, generosity, idealism, and nobility! Their reactions come in phases. America is at some level the Sally Field of nations—"You like me! You really really like me!"—and so the Cosmic Blondes wonder what the hell the problem is with our marketing department. We do a lousy job of communication, they say. If we could only polish our brand, tell our story, craft our message. If the truth were ever allowed out, if it were presented just right, then all the world would see us and love us, and history would end in a chorus of exultation.

Then, when that reaction gets stale, there is the other classic Cosmic Blonde reaction—that these hostile judgments about us are unpleasant, and since they are unpleasant, they must be unimportant. The Blondes grunt at the peculiarity of the sour losers who dislike us so. They figure vaguely that these people must have some problem or something, and retreat behind their milk-and-honey obliviousness to go on with the great sunshine beam of their lives.

The Cosmic Brunettes in America do not act this way. These, recall, are the people who write, read, and reflect (you are quite probably one yourself, as am I). The Brunettes look at the foreign critique of American society and think, Why do they hate us? Once you ask that question, you can always find something wrong with America with which to answer it. The Brunettes wheel out the inner sociologist, the deep dark self-lacerator of the soul, and they come to the measured judgment that the foreigners have a point. They are not completely right, for the Cosmic Brunette never finds anybody else's opinion 100 percent perfect. But with caveats, with equivocations, with amendments and cavils, it must be conceded that the basic posture of our observers has some merit.

Indeed, America's Cosmic Brunettes have been saying many of the same things themselves. American culture is essentially the history of Cosmic Brunette reactions to the crude driving energy of mainstream Blonde success. The transcendentalists, the Bohemians, the Marxists, the beatniks, the hippies, the academics, the indie-film screenwriters, the literati, the MacArthur genius-grant culturati, the religious activists, and the conservative think-tankers have all taken their turn on the national stage, rebelling against the Blondeness of America's bitch goddess success. The Cosmic Brunettes sit in coffeehouses, make movies, consume novels, hold conferences, and nibble European sorbets while contemplating the soul-crushing self-satisfaction that is middle-American life.

Sometimes it appears as if the Brunette mind of America went off in one direction and the Blonde body went off in another. The body is all about getting and gaining, climbing and making, blind optimism, catchpenny opportunism. The mind stands aside, vaguely repelled by what it sees as narrow selfishness, smug complacency, and synthetic culture. It's as if there's an unbridgeable chasm, and you have to choose which side you're on. On the one side there is money, acquisitiveness, success, and SUVs. On the other side there is spirit, imagination, creativity, and tenure.

Just as Europeans were quick to see America as a vulgar, money-mad land, many American writers and artists have been quick to decide that the way middle Americans live is an insult to the noble ideals that our country is supposed to represent. "The cursed hunger of riches," Cotton Mather thundered in 1706, "will make man break through all the laws of God." His kinsman, Eleazer Mather, looked at Boston life and called for "less trading, buying, selling but more praying, more watching over hearts, more close walking, less plenty and less inequity." He concluded, "Outward prosperity is a worm at the root of godliness, so that religion dies when the world thrives." The Shakers also rejected abundance and ever increasing prosperity. Their vision of the simple, honest life remains attractive to millions of Americans who buy the simple yet tasteful armoires, television stands, and dining room sets inspired by their creed.

Thomas Jefferson argued that America must renounce manufacturing and remain a land of independent yeoman farmers in order to retain its virtue. He feared America would become a nation of "gamblers" and "jugglers" doing "tricks with pieces of paper." Around the time of the American revolution, the founders—students of classical history—had imbibed a depressing view of the life cycle of great nations. Simplicity leads to strength and power. Strength and power lead to wealth and luxury. Wealth and luxury lead to corruption and decline. "Human nature, in no form of it, could ever bear prosperity," John Adams wrote in a letter to Jefferson.

Americans feared their own material success and the corruptions it might breed. The country was identified from the first as blessed with plenty and hungry for more. Yet its moral leaders have always regarded wealth and success as a potential poison that shrivels the soul and eventually devours itself. And so has arisen the tension that propels American culture: America hungers for success, and manifestly is a success, and at the same time suspects that worldly success will be its undoing.

By the early nineteenth century, the southern cavaliers

saw themselves as a moral antidote to the acquisitive commercialists of Yankee industrialism. Western pioneers were also depicted, mainly by easterners, as straight-talking adventurers who would serve as remedy for the crowded and moneyed corruptions of the coastal cities.

Henry David Thoreau emerged as the most important dissident against the American longing for success. In *Walden*, he posited that the way Americans live is a mistake. "The mass of men lead lives of quiet desperation," he argued, in one of the most famous lines in American literature. "They are employed, as it says in an old book, laying up treasures which moth and rust will corrupt and thieves break through and steal. It is a fool's life." The goods and luxuries that Americans toil so hard to acquire don't make them happier. "Most of the luxuries, and many of the so-called comforts of life, are not only not indispensable, but positive hindrances to the elevation of mankind. With respect to luxuries and comforts the wisest have ever lived a more simple and meager life than the poor."

In 1863, in the midst of the Civil War, Thoreau published an essay in *The Atlantic Monthly* called "Life Without Principle," in which he protested the workaholism of American life. "This world is a place of business. What infinite bustle! I am awaked almost every night by the panting of the locomotive. It interrupts my dreams. There is no Sabbath. It would be glorious to see mankind at leisure for once. It is nothing but work, work, work." If you spend a day alone in the woods, you are called a loafer, Thoreau lamented. And yet "The ways by which you may get money almost without exception lead downward." The people who hustle in the mainstream of American life, he continued, are shallow, mosquito-like creatures. Their conversation is inconsequential, their concerns are trivial, their politics are inhuman.

Americans have always read and admired Thoreau, and the millions who have never read him are influenced by his ideas and nod when they hear echoes in sermons, in movies, and at dinner-party conversations, or when they read them in the pages of simplicity magazines. But reformation never comes. America still continues to hustle and prosper. The money piles in, and the homes and the cars and the media centers grow finer and more luxurious. The American producer and consumer is an anxious but unstoppable whirlwind.

The result is that idealists, the Cosmic Brunettes, tend to withdraw and feel themselves alienated from mainstream American life. Thoreau's companions purified themselves of the materialism and ambition of the world. They either retreated literally, as he did (very briefly) into the forest; opted for a life shorn of luxuries and frantic getting and spending; or they ascended intellectually, as Ralph Waldo Emerson did at one point in his life, onto the Olympus of high ideals and moral abstractions. "It is a sign of the times," Emerson observed, that "many intellectual and religious persons withdrew" from "the market and the caucus"—capitalism and politics—to find something "worthy to do." They looked at life as it was actually lived, with corrupt politicians, growing and greedy businesses, and vulgar mass culture, and they were prone to fits of despair. "Ah my country!" Emerson wailed in one dark mood. "In thee is the reasonable hope of mankind not fulfilled. . . . When I see how false our life is . . . all heroism seems our dream and our insight a delusion."

If optimism was compulsory in Blonde America, then

short-term pessimism became nearly compulsory in Brunette America. The founding fathers' "really great and noble dream had become a good deal like a stampede of hogs to the trough," Henry Adams lamented.

Henry James had a character say in his short story "The Madonna of the Future": "An American, to excel, has just ten times as much to learn as a European. We lack the deeper sense; we have neither taste, nor tact, nor force. How should we have them? Our crude and garish climate, our silent past, our deafening present, the constant pressure about us of unlovely circumstances are as void of all that nourishes and prompts and inspires the artist as my sad heart is void of bitterness in saying so!"

No wonder the foreign critique hit home. If you go back over the past half century of novel writing and social criticism—during the time when American success was most obvious—you find that the anxieties of success have produced a long Chorus of Bemoaning. America goes through a wave of declinism about every seven to ten years. As I look over my bookshelves at the books, essays, and novels of the last fifty years, I could build, if I had sufficient balancing ability, a pile of books that would loom high over my head, a mountain of cultural pessimism attesting to the hollowness of contemporary life.

To keep the pile manageable, I wouldn't include any books written before, say, 1950, leaving off such classics as *Babbitt* and *The Man in the Gray Flannel Suit*. I'd choose David Riesman's *The Lonely Crowd,* with its portrait of the other-directed man who subordinates his own inner nature so he can conform to the habits of his neighbors. Then there'd be Richard Hofstadter's *Anti-Intellectualism in American Life,* and William Whyte's *The Organization*

Man, which describes the modern American as a bureau-cratized cog in the corporate machine. Just for variety's sake, I might throw in *The Catcher in the Rye,* on the sensitive person's inability to make connections in contemporary society; a video of *Rebel Without a Cause,* on the stifling banality of middle-class parents; a copy of *Death of a Salesman,* on the emptiness of the American version of success.

From the 1960s, there'd be the Port Huron Statement, the founding document of the New Left and a manifesto against the stifling technocratic banality of the modern order; and Theodore Roszak's *The Making of a Counter Culture.* Of course, I'd have to include Eldridge Cleaver's *Soul on Ice,* which puts an Afrocentric spin on the frigidity of mainstream American life. At one point Cleaver paints a vivid picture of white people dancing: "They gyrated and whirled and flailed their little dead asses like petrified zombies trying to regain life's warmth, and to spark a bit of life into their dead limbs, cold asses, stony hearts and those stiff mechanical, inert joints."

Now the pile is up to my waist, and here we begin to see an interesting change. Up to this point, the general theme has been that Americans' shallow materialism turns them into bland conformists. But from here on up, the general theme will be that Americans' shallow materialism turns them into self-absorbed individualists. The first book in this new mode is Daniel Bell's *The Cultural Contradictions of Capitalism,* which decried "the tedium of the unrestrained self." Then comes Christopher Lasch's *The Culture of Narcissism:* "Self-absorption defines the moral climate of contemporary society." I'm just up to the mid-1970s, and already the pile is around my neck, and I'm afraid it might burst through the ceiling, so I leave out all the 1970s New Age efforts to escape arid, rationalized American life into higher realms of est, Zen, Eastern mysticism, crystals, and spiritual grace.

In 1985, Robert Bellah et al. published *Habits of the Heart,* which portrayed the disintegration of communities as people retreated from the meaninglessness of their jobs and public lives into the lonely comfort of their homes. By the 1980s, conservatives as well as liberals were likely to decry the banality of American culture. In *The Closing of the American Mind,* published in 1987, Allan Bloom argued that students live in a world of "easygoing nihilism." Floating in a warm bath of relativism, fearing conflict, picking up one value one day and an opposite value the next, they are comfortably untroubled by their lack of firm beliefs and guiding principles. "I fear that spiritual entropy or an evaporation of the soul's boiling blood is taking place."

By the time we get to the 1990s, the pile is over my head. I'm peering up at books such as Francis Fukuyama's *The End of History and the Last Man,* which warns of the arrival of the Last Man, the lukewarm child of comfort, afraid of conflict, obsessed by health and safety, untroubled by any disturbing passions, content in his world of money, mildness, and easy pleasures. I see Robert Putnam's *Bowling Alone,* which documents the decline of community and healthy human bonds throughout American society. Nonetheless, I grab a stepladder and stack on top Al Gore's *Earth in the Balance,* to represent the environmentalists' concern that in our cold, arrogant effort to pile up more belongings, we are losing touch with nature and our truest selves. I'd include Robert Bork's gloomy bestseller *Slouching Towards Gomorrah,* on the decline of just about everything, and Michael J. Sandel's *Democracy's Discontent,* which explores the concern that "the moral fabric of community is unraveling around us"; also nearly everything ever written by Gore Vidal, Susan Sontag, Kevin Phillips, Noam Chomsky, Juliet Schor, Michael Lind, Jonathan Kozol, Lewis Lapham, Michael Moore, Pat Robertson, Jerry Falwell, E. L. Doctorow, Thomas Pynchon, and the Unabomber.

I also throw a video of *American Beauty* onto the pile, to represent all the thousands of movies and millions of TV episodes detailing either the mediocrity of American suburban life or the sickness festering beneath its bland and hypocritical surface. Naturally, I include the vast literature on suburban sprawl, which protests the ugly, monotonous, soul-destroying landscape of modern suburban life.

By this time the pile is so high, I've been through so many gloomy and depressing books, that I'll probably want to go in the kitchen and suck the gas pipe.

Many of these books are brilliant, some of the best that have been published in our lifetime. And they do not all say the same thing; you could discern several categories. There is the left-wing gloom from writers who think that American-style capitalism has ravaged our souls. There is the conservative version, which says bourgeois mediocrity has undermined classical virtues and distracted us from religious truths, thus turning us into comfort-loving Last Men or godless, decadent hedonists. Then there is the conservative pessimism that purports to be a defense of American culture while showing little faith in it. Writers of this school—dissident conservative academics, mostly—argue that the noble American traits have been corrupted by intellectual currents coming out of France, Germany, and the universities, as if the American soul were such a delicate flower that it could be dissolved by the acid influence of Herbert Marcuse.

Finally, there are the freelance pessimists who believe that whatever condition made America great—the family farm, the Greatest Generation, the Depression mentality— has vanished or been forsaken in the land of shopping malls and theme parks.

If you scan these documents all at once, or even if, like a normal person, you absorb them over the course of a lifetime, you find that their depictions congeal into the same sorry scene. America, especially suburban America, is depicted as a comfortable but somewhat vacuous realm of unreality: consumerist, wasteful, complacent, materialistic, and self-absorbed. Sprawling, shopping, Disneyfied Americans have cut themselves off from the sources of enchantment, the things that really matter. They have become too concerned with small and vulgar pleasures, pointless one-upsmanship, and easy values. They have become at once too permissive and too narrow, too self-indulgent and too timid. Their lives are distracted by a buzz of trivial images, by relentless hurry instead of genuine contemplation, information rather than wisdom, and a profusion of superficial choices. Modern Americans rarely sink to the level of depravity—they are too tepid for that—but they don't achieve the highest virtues or the most demanding excellences; nor do they experience the grandest passions or the sublimest expressions of nature's grandeur. As W. E. B. Du Bois put it long ago, "Our machines make things and compel us to sell them. We are rich in food and clothes and starved in culture. . . . All delicate feeling sinks beneath floods of mediocrity."

CHAPTER FOUR

The Spiritual Wind

BUT WHAT IF THAT'S all wrong? What if Thoreau was wrong to think that the ordinary life most Americans choose is a mistake? What if Spengler was wrong to think that Americans are soulless creatures driven by their desire for the almighty dollar? What if even Tocqueville's fear that Americans are disoriented by their materialism, and driven to lonely lives of self-regard and muffled ambitions, was unfounded? What if Lasch was wrong about narcissism, Whyte was wrong about conformity, Bloom was wrong about nihilism, Bork was wrong about hedonism, and the radical Islamicists were wrong about decadence? What if all these writers, and the hundreds more who write along these lines, have failed to observe some crucial trait beneath the crass surface of American life that redeems and corrects for the obvious flaws?

After all, most of these criticisms come enshrouded in predictions of American decline. The pessimists have long predicted that a cultural catastrophe would crash upon this nation and fracture it; or that some other nation—the Soviet Union, United Europe, Japan—was on the verge of overtaking the sagging U.S. as the globe's top dog. But America has an amazing ability to not decline. American standards of living surpassed those in Europe around 1740. For about 260 years, in other words, America has been rich and allegedly money-mad and materialistic. Yet Edward Gibbon would have nothing to write about here, because economic, military, or even social decline hasn't come. On the contrary, despite the supposed sickness of the American soul and the vulgarization of American culture, there have been clear signs of regeneration over the past decades: Crime has dropped, illegitimacy has dropped, and teenage pregnancy has declined, as have teenage suicide rates, divorce rates, and poverty rates.

Americans have shown a remarkable tendency to remain undecadent. Look, for example, at how we spend our money. The Consumer Expenditure Survey reveals that during the 1990s—the wondrous fizzy decade of splendiferous stock-market returns and walloping prosperity—Americans spent less on just about every item in the Hugh Hefner/Larry Flynt/*Maxim* magazine/*Robb Report* repertoire. Americans in 2000 spent less than they did ten years before on steaks, martinis, cigars, jewelry, watches, furniture, toys, and sound equipment. They increased their spending on education, housing, transportation, and computers. Americans spent 10 percent less on food in general but 15 percent more on fresh vegetables. They spent 14 percent less on clothing, the largest decline in any category, though they did spend 12 percent more on shoes. They spent less on entertainment, as baby boomers went less frequently to rock concerts, and chose to go, less expensively, to the movies.

Overall, this is not the picture of a nation of superficiality and self-indulgence. American beaches still aren't Rio-style thong expos; nor are they Southern European nudist zones, where seventy-year-old women who grew up with corsets and propriety suddenly get the urge in advanced retirement to throw off the vestments of civilization and let their vein patterns hang out in the breeze. Despite leadership from the top, we haven't learned to relax about adultery, and serious sex surveys do not depict a culture of serious kinkiness and sensuality. Picture a typical American man going on the Internet looking for some pornography. In a few minutes, he can't help himself, he's clicked over to LendingTree.com, and he's checking out the latest mortgage rates.

Obviously, huge problems remain, but if you go back and read the leading social scientists of the past few decades, you are struck by the fact that they were invariably too pessimistic, too stuffed with gloomy predictions and forebodings of catastrophe, the vast majority of which never came true. America is a country that goes every year to the doctor and every year is told that it has contracted some fatal disease—whether it is conformity, narcissism, godlessness, or civic disengagement—and a year later, the patient comes back with cheeks still red and muscles still powerful. The diagnosis is just as grim, and the patient is just as healthy.

It brings to mind a question: If middle America is so stupid, vulgar, self-absorbed, and materialistic, which it often is, then how can America itself be so great?

The Counter Tradition

Quietly, alongside the torrent of writing about the crassness of American life, there is another, less crowded intellectual tradition. This line is advanced by writers who believe that the materialist baubles—the sport utes and the clip-on nails—are surface products of a deeper spiritual striving. They argue that America is an exceptional nation infused with unique purpose and spirit.

In one of his later and generally neglected essays, "The Fortune of the Republic," Emerson put it most succinctly: "They [who] complain of the flatness of American life have no perception of its destiny. They are not Americans." They don't see that America is "a garden of plenty . . . a magazine of power. . . . Here is man in the garden of Eden; here, the Genesis and the Exodus." And here, Emerson continued, would come the final Revelation.

Walt Whitman, who was not blind to his nation's many faults, also perceived that America's "extreme business energy," its "almost maniacal appetite for wealth," was just part of its "vast revolutionary" drive. "My theory includes riches, the getting of riches, and the amplest products," Whitman wrote in his essay "Democratic Vistas." "Upon them, as upon substrata, I raise the edifice [of revolution] . . . the new and orbic traits waiting to be launched for in the firmament that is, and is to be, America."

For writers in this tradition, material striving blends with spiritual aspiration. The race for riches is just a manifestation of a deeper metaphysical striving that's in the midst of realizing its glorious destiny. American life, by this account, is amphibious. It is crass but also visionary, practical but also fantastic. America is the most moralistic nation on earth and also the most materialistic. As the historian Sacvan Bercovitch put it in his book *The American Jeremiad,* "A crucial distinction was *not* made in this country"—the distinction between the sacred and the profane.

Other writers have hinted at the same phenomenon. An American, according to George Santayana, is "an idealist working on matter." Santayana spent much of his life in the U.S. but never felt at home here and returned to Europe in his later years. But his book *Character and Opinion in the United States* remains one of the most intelligent inspections of the American spirit. Santayana believed it was a complete mistake to think that Americans are driven by a love of money. If Americans truly cared about material things, they would hoard and protect them. But they are loose and careless with their stuff, eager to move on to the next new thing: "The American talks about money, because that is the symbol and measure he has at hand for success, intelligence and power; but as to money itself he makes, loses, spends, and gives it away with a very light heart." Instead, there is some deeper impulsion: "To be an American is of itself almost a moral condition, an education and a career."

Later, Luigi Barzini, in his essay "The Baffling Americans," made this argument at slightly greater length:

What few imitators have understood is that the secret of the United States' tremendous success was in reality not merely technology, know-how, the work ethic, the urge to succeed or plain greed. It

was a spiritual wind that drove the Americans irre-
sistibly ahead from the beginning. What was
behind their compulsion to improve man's lot was
an all-pervading sense of duty, the submission to a
God-given imperative, to a God-given code of personal behavior, the willing acceptance of all the
necessary sacrifices, including death in battle. Few
foreigners understand this, even today. The United
States appears to them merely as the triumph of
soulless materialism.

These writers are on to something, but they are always
maddeningly vague. They almost never explain in an over-
arching or specific way what they mean when they say
Americans are driven by a "spiritual wind," or that being
American is a "moral condition." Their observations come
in fragments, aphorisms, and stray notes. They sense a spiritual force motivating Americans. They feel that somehow
the materialism is infused with moralism, but they seem
unwilling to investigate or nail down its features and
effects.

That's probably because most of us are trained to think
and write about society as a collection of social conditions,
economic forces, or—at the most abstract—political and
philosophical ideas. We are not quite comfortable crossing
over to the religious and the transcendental. After all,
sophisticated people in the past few centuries have tended
to assume that the world is becoming more secular as it
becomes richer and better educated. The most influential
thinkers have sought to explain behavior largely by "hard"
and "scientific" secular terms. Writers from Adam Smith
and Karl Marx to Sigmund Freud have worked up sophis-

ticated and brilliant social-science models to describe why people behave the way they do, and these tools have tremendous explanatory power.

Yet there is something else out there, some religious or mythical or metaphysical yearning that refuses to die, and that shapes everyday life in ways that cannot be predicted easily by journalists, social scientists, or even philosophers. Writers in this second tradition of writing about America— and I am thinking about Barzini, Santayana, and above all, Whitman—sense the religious impulses that infuse American society, but they don't quite lay it out for us.

The Idealistic Nation

In the old days, preachers did it better. America, historians remind us, was born in a seedbed of religion. There is a vast and ever growing literature on Puritan belief, on the sermons of Edwards and Mather and so on. I suspect so many writers are drawn to this subject because in the seventeenth, eighteenth, and even the nineteenth centuries, Americans were articulate about their guiding religious and transcendental beliefs. We are still shaped by such beliefs, we just don't know how to talk about them as well.

When you read early American sermons, you find much that is alien now, but it is also possible to infer—and historians such as Sacvan Bercovitch seem to have spent their careers doing precisely this—which metaphysical passions still influence us. For example, seventeenth- and eighteenth-century ministers were explicit in their belief that America was the redeemer nation. As the historian Perry Miller put it, the Puritans felt that God had assigned them to run an errand into the wilderness and thus create a new society and a new church that would fulfill His plan for the human race.

America, in the minds of these preachers, was a new Jerusalem, the setting for the final salvation, and the settlers themselves were a new chosen people who, in rejecting the corruptions of the Old World, would help create a second paradise in the New World. America, in other words, had a sacred mission, in their eyes, to fulfill the biblical prophecies. "There are many arguments to persuade us that our Glorious Lord will have an Holy City in America; a City, the street whereof shall be pure gold," Cotton Mather preached in his 1709 sermon "God's City: America." By the time of the revolution, the theme had been secularized. John Adams declared: "I always consider the settlement of America with reverence and wonder, as the opening of a grand scene and design in providence, for the illumination of the ignorant and the emancipation of the slavish part of mankind all over the earth."

In the eyes of these early Americans, the United States was not merely a nation, it was an eschatology. It was a vision of human fulfillment. This sense that America had a divinely ordained mission did not diminish with the years. "Our whole history appears like a last effort of the Divine Providence in behalf of the human race," Emerson wrote. In 1865, Edward Beecher observed, "Men in all walks of life believed that the sovereign Holy Spirit has endowed the nation with resources sufficient to convert and civilize the globe, to purge human society of all its evils, and to usher in Christ's reign on earth."

Or, as Herman Melville famously summarized the creed in his novel *White-Jacket*:

The future is endowed with such a life, that it lives to us even in anticipation . . . the Future is the Bible of the Free. . . . We Americans are the peculiar chosen people—the Israel of our time. . . . God has predestined, mankind expects, great things from our race; and great things we feel in our souls. . . . We are the pioneers of the world; the advance-guard, sent on through the wilderness of untried things, to break a new path in the New World that is ours. . . . Long enough have we been skeptics with regard to ourselves, and doubted whether, indeed, the political Messiah had come. But he has come in us.

Today few believe that Americans are God's new chosen people. But Americans are different enough from other peoples to consider themselves an exceptional nation, with an exceptional mission in the world. Whether they know it or not, they have inherited a certain style of idealism, a faith, and a fulfilling and chiliastic creed.

It is often declared that America is not only a plot of land but also an idea and a cause. As the political theorist Martin Diamond has observed, words like "Americanization," "Americanism," and "un-American" have no counterparts in any other language. Nobody says that a country or culture is being Italianized or Japanized or Chinese-ized, yet the Americanization of the world has been a topic of debate for a century. This doesn't mean just that there are McDonald's and Tom Cruise movies sweeping the landscape; it means some distinctive creed, mentality, and way of life is felt to be overrunning earlier patterns and cultures.

As Leon Samson, a radical socialist, put it in his 1933 book *Toward a United Front*:

When we examine the meaning of Americanism, we discover that Americanism is to the American not a tradition or a territory, not what France is to a Frenchman or England to an Englishman, but a doctrine—what socialism is to a socialist. Like socialism, Americanism is looked upon . . . as a highly attenuated, conceptualized, platonic, impersonal attraction toward a system of ideas, a solemn assent to a handful of final notions—democracy, liberty, opportunity, to all of which the American adheres rationalistically much as a socialist adheres to his socialism—because it does him good, because it gives him work, because, so he thinks, it guarantees him happiness. Americanism has thus served as a substitute for socialism. Every concept in socialism has its substitutive counter-concept in Americanism, and that is why the socialist argument falls so fruitlessly on the American ear. . . . The American does not want to listen to socialism, since he thinks he already has it."

Or, as Sacvan Bercovitch argues in *Rites of Assent*:

Only "America," of all national designations, took on the combined force of eschatology and chauvinism. Many forms of nationalism have laid claim to a world-redeeming promise; many Christian sects have sought, in open or secret heresy, to find the sacred in the profane; many European Protestants have linked the soul's journey and the way to wealth. But only the "American Way," of all modern symbologies, has managed to circumvent the contradictions inherent in these approaches. Of all symbols of identity, only "American" has succeeded in uniting nationality and universality, civic and spiritual selfhood, sacred and secular history, the country's past and paradise to be, in a single transcendent ideal.

The Exceptionalists

Few writers explore this line of argument today. It's deeply unfashionable to talk about a distinct national character. But even if Americans are not united by a creed, they are united by the fact that they are creedal. While they have many different ways of defining a proposition that the nation should stand for, they share a mentality that assumes the nation should stand for something—something working toward perfection. What Americans share, in other words, is an inherited sense that history has a story line; and that each of us, individually and as a citizen of the nation, plays a role in bringing the story to its happy ending.

This mentality leads to a few behavioral traits. For example, historians point out that a tremendous strain of anxiety runs through U.S. history, the nagging and sometimes panicked sense that we are failing to live up to our ideals and mission, that if we Americans fail, then that will be the most terrible failure in human history.

This anxiety propels Americans to strive and reform perpetually. It helps account for the periodic awakenings and moralistic crusades that recur throughout American history—the Great Awakenings, the abolitionist movement, the temperance movement, the civil rights, antiabortion, even anti-smoking movements. America is not only the nation where you can get a super-size tub of french fries to go with your thirty-two-ounce double cheeseburger, it is also just about the only nation where people blow up abortion clinics. Whether it is fatty food or moral crusades, nothing here ever stops at its logical conclusion; some crusading fervor propels things a few steps beyond.

Historians have often noted a strain of perfectionism running through American life. As Richard Hofstadter once wryly remarked, "The United States was the only country in the world that began with perfection and aspired to progress." This trait has its roots as a religious and, more specifically, Protestant perfectionism, the striving to be finished Christians. "Nothing short of the general renewal of society ought to satisfy any soldiers of Christ," declared the nineteenth-century Methodist author William Arthur. But it soon pervades society in a generalized sense that one must perpetually strive to eliminate the tensions inherent in a world caught between promise and fulfillment.

So Americans developed an elaborate faith in education and a zeal for political causes that promise to purify the nation and the world. They are gripped sometimes by a zeal for purgative wars that will cleanse the world of some evil. Most of all, they have a zeal for permanent self-improvement, an impulse to move constantly toward the realization of one's perfect self.

When he arrived on these shores, Luigi Barzini was immediately struck, as others have been, by this strange compulsion "to tirelessly tinker, improve everything and everybody, never leave anything alone." He was amazed by the incredible profusion of self-help manuals in every bookstore, in every pharmacy, on every magazine rack:

One could learn for a few dollars how to speak masterfully in public, be irresistible, dominate a meeting, mesmerize superiors or opponents, make friends, sell everything to everybody, and in the end, with the first million in the bank, spot prodigious investment opportunities, investments that multiplied themselves like amoebas. . . . People hopefully bought these books by the millions, as true believers buy sacred relics or bottles of miraculous holy water.

In *Character and Opinion in the United States,* George Santayana argued that Americans go through life with two worlds in their heads. In one part of their brain, they see the real world; but in the neighboring part, they see the perfect imagined world, assumed to be close by and realizable. These two worlds sometimes get confused and intermingle. Americans' "moral world always contains undiscovered or thinly peopled continents open to those who are more attached to what might or should be than to what already is. Americans are eminently prophets; they apply morals to public affairs; they are impatient and enthusiastic."

An American is thus imbued with a distinctive orientation: future-mindedness. "His enthusiasm for the future is profound; he can conceive of no more decisive way of recommending an opinion or a practice than to say that it is what everybody is coming to adopt. This expectation of what he approves, or approval of what he expects, makes up his optimism." He continues:

At the same time, the American is imaginative; for where life is intense, imagination is intense also.

Were he not imaginative he would not live so much in the future. But his imagination is practical and the future it forecasts is immediate; it works with the clearest and least ambiguous terms known to his experience, in terms of number, measure, contrivance, economy and speed. He is an idealist working on matter. . . . All his life he jumps into the train after it has started and jumps out before it has stopped.

The Mystery of Motivation

Over the past two chapters, I've sketched two broad ways of describing life in the United States. One sees middle-American life as essentially mediocre, materialistic, driven by worldly longing. The second sees a life that is primarily metaphysical and imaginative, in which everyday Americans are driven to realize grand and utopian ideals *through* material things. These two views are different answers to the mystery of motivation. Everybody agrees that Americans are driven by some impulsion to be energetic, hardworking, and radioactive. They disagree about the nature of that impulsion. Those who suspect America see it, with the German philosopher Martin Heidegger, as "the most dangerous form of boundlessness, because it appears in a middle-class way of life mixed with Christianity, and all this in an atmosphere that lacks completely any sense of history." Others see the impulsion as a noble and salvific force pushing history toward a glorious material and spiritual fulfillment.

I would like to think that the second way of looking at

America is the true way. I would like to think that an ideal-ist flame does burn in every American split level, that every-day American life is shaped by grand metaphysical visions, a holy sense of mission, and a commitment to redeem the failures of the present by committing oneself to a glorious future. I would like to believe that we are all driven by some spiritual impulsion of which we are perhaps not even aware. This condition of mind is simply the water in which we swim. This worldview is so ingrained in our culture that it isn't even necessary to pass it down consciously from parent to child.

But it's hard to be sure that normal American life truly is that heroic. W. H. Auden once wrote that "The Com-muter can't forget / The Pioneer." Possibly every commuter, or at least some commuters, really are pioneers pushing into the wilderness of the future, driven by a radical hope-fulness, a green light shimmering across the water that redeems, Gatsby-style, all the shallow fleshiness of life. Maybe America is in fact enflamed and ennobled not by a creation myth but by a fruition myth, a noble vision worth striving for.

But maybe a commuter is just a commuter. Maybe he or she is just the person you see through the rearview mirror in the car behind you at the red light—spilling coffee, applying her lipstick, picking his nose. Maybe all that stuff about utopian visions and missionary causes was just made up by some of our more poetically minded writers and romanti-cists. Or maybe what was a grand mentality has been grad-ually buried under layers of trivial concerns. Maybe the forces of affluence or selfishness or modernity or triviality have smothered what were once admirable ideals. Maybe middle-class American life *is* shallow and uninspiring.

Let's look into the matter. Let's move away from the writing about America and get back to looking at life as it is actually lived in America. Let's take a few dips into the stream of normal American behavior, looking for signs of materialistic crassness but also imaginative hope. Maybe even among the barbecue grills and the big-box malls, we'll find some reflections of that redeeming fire or signs of that spiritual wind.

It's not necessary to be too solemn during our little excursions into American life. Sometimes a little satire is in order. In any case, here we go.

CHAPTER FIVE

Growing

I'M TRYING TO PERSUADE my kids to go into the soon-to-be-lucrative field of playdate law. I'm convinced that in a few years, parents are going to be suing each other because their child received insufficiently nutritious afternoon snacks while visiting playmates' homes.

The way I see it, the role of the playdate lawyer will begin long before the actual playdate. First the attorney will offer advice on which of, say, a second-grader's classmates would be a good fit for a developmentally appropriate and cognitively enhancing play session—which classmate has sufficient conflict-resolution skills and toy-sharing capacities and the sort of at-home recreation resources necessary to provide an experientially diverse afternoon. Then the attorney will work with the other party to make the playdate overture and explore whether the two children have any free afternoons in common, or whether their soccer league/ballet/SAT prep/recorder lesson/hockey practice/therapist schedules make *any* playdate impossible.

Assuming the two children have a free afternoon within the next four-year period, the playdate lawyer will begin negotiating the predate agreements, which are parent-to-parent contracts setting down clear guidelines on all of the normal playdate issues: GameBoy preferences, mean-older-sibling control measures, food-allergy concerns, pet anxieties, and early-pickup contingency plans in case one of the parties decides in the middle that this playdate simply isn't enriching enough.

Within the larger field of playdate law, I suspect a sub-specialty will emerge around the VSIs (video-screen issues). Attorneys in this niche will negotiate separate predate protocols on whether there should be a Nintendo ban or Nickelodeon consumption limits during the playdate, and whether computer games should be prohibited, and if so, whether that includes the ones that teach phonics and typing skills. Some parents will prefer to sign a Document of Joint Understanding forbidding the viewing of all Disney videos, while others will deem it acceptable for the children to spend time watching videos from the *Little Mermaid/Lion King* era but none after *Pocahontas*.

Finally, the playdate lawyer will accompany the parent on the predate inspection, ensuring the host family adheres to the conventional safety norms. In other words, making sure that they have childproof devices over every outlet, cabinet handle, and stove control; that they have motion sensors within fifteen feet of any stairway; that the corners of any hard surface have been rounded to prevent gouging;

that all construction paper in the house is made from specially treated flame-retardant fibers; that the lawn has been aerated to make it soft in case of falls; and that all LEGOs are water-soluble to guard against choking.

Once the county inspector has verified that the home is a peanut-free zone, and that the air contains none of the ambient food-additive particulates that have been found to induce hyperactivity and ADHD in laboratory rats, the attorney will do a final walk-through and certify that the playdate is officially arranged. The parents then exchange pager numbers and medical records, and the kids are all set to have a fantastic time—unless either party offers to pick up the other family's child from school, in which case a whole other range of transportation security measures must be dealt with.

The way I see it, the issues inherent in playdate law are sufficiently complex, and the parents' stake in their child's development is sufficiently overwrought, that before long the Ubermoms will be litigating against each other in droves. I suspect parents of all sorts will be tempted to go to court to resolve playdate conflicts, but the Ubermoms will be especially likely because of their superior parenting skills.

Ubermoms

Ubermoms are women who graduated Phi Beta Kappa in economics and engineering, earned MBAs with honors, and rose to the level of senior vice president for corporate strategy at Fortune 500 companies before giving up the job to raise a family, thus channeling their enormous drive, massive intelligence, and $950,000 worth of education on the nurturing of their junior achievers.

You see the Ubermoms at the board and parent-association meetings of most high-achieving elementary schools. You can spot them easily, because they generally weigh less than their children. They may have given birth to their youngest one, say, twelve hours before, but they still have washboard abs and buttocks firmer than foot-balls. That's because even at the moment of conception, which occurs during highly aerobic multiorgasmic inter-course, the prospective alpha mother is doing special breast exercises to prevent sagging. While her love partner is con-tentedly dozing by her side in postconnubial bliss, as his sperm is breaching the membrane of her incredibly fit and fertile egg, she is staring at the ceiling calculating which year her child will be ready to enter nursery school and when she can run for chairperson of the school auction.

During pregnancy, Ubermom—assuming she decides not to enter that year's Tour de France—is generally found in tranquil yoga positions, performing special pregnant-woman weight-lifting exercises, and devoting the energies she formerly spent on career advancement to walkathons that raise awareness of life-threatening and other diseases. During the second trimester, she'll be marching, biking, jogging, and running for lupus, leukemia, MS, heart dis-ease, breast cancer, and the flu. When a friend gets the flu, Ubermom puts on her lycra and goes around the block raising money. Her lapels are ablaze with so many pink, green, black, yellow, and red awareness ribbons she looks like the UN headquarters when she stands still.

She also spends her prebirth months altering society's conceptions of female beauty, studying medical textbooks on amniotic fluids, reading thoughtful articles by trained psychologists in magazines such as *Child* and *Parenting* ("Could Your Praise Be Hurting Your Child?" "How Safe Is Your Drinking Water?"), calculating how many children to have (three is the new two, one parent informed me recently), coming up with prebirth colic-prevention strategies and selecting pretentiously nonpretentious names she thinks will look good on preschool cubbies. (If she has a girl, she's thinking of naming her Campbell, Griffin, McKenzie, or one of the other clan names from *Braveheart*. If it's a boy, she's vacillating among Max, Sam, Caleb, and a few other names that she associates with stylishly retro 1930s ethnic deli owners.) In 1951, 25 percent of American babies had one of the ten most popular names—John, Mary, Mike, and so on. But by 1999, when significant numbers of Ubermoms and Uberdads had identified baby naming as one more realm of individuation and self-expression, only 12 percent of American babies were given one of the ten most popular names.

Ubermom babies generally weigh more than Saint Bernards. The mothers have been ingesting so many vitamin-enriched soy-based dietary supplements during pregnancy, and their baby's resulting growth has been so phenomenal, that the little creatures enter the world looking like toothless defensive linemen.

In the delivery room, the Ubermoms generally cut the umbilical cord themselves (assuming they're not busy adjusting the video lighting) and then, focusing their attention on the delivery doctor, utter the words that mark the highest stage of Ubermomism: "So, is her Apgar score above average?"

As you know, Americans live to be tested. From the

first gulp of breath, the little American boy or girl has his or her aptitude prodded, poked, measured, evaluated, and compared. This basic system of comparing, grading, and evaluating does not cease so long as the heart continues its pitter-patter. The baby who begins life with the Apgar score continues through years of grades, elementary school accountability tests, SAT exams, workplace-aptitude measures, and retirement-plan evaluations unto death. The American is conceived amid a flurry of quality-control evaluations ("Was it good for you, honey?"), lives in an atmosphere of progress reports, and dies amid a carefully calibrated burst of obituaries, funeral evaluations, and testimonials. If God were an American, the Last Judgment would be a multiple-choice questionnaire with one of those bubble answer forms you fill out with a number-two pencil, and American babies would be scoring 680 or 720 minimum because of their superior test-taking skills.

Ubermom is not yet done with her delivery-room gasping and heaving, and already she's got one of those *What To Expect* . . . books in her hands. She's reading the chapter "What to Expect After Three and a Half Minutes," which tells her that at this point in its development, her child should be able to mewl, may be able to wheeze, and might possibly be able to puke, and when she sees her little one vomiting up a storm, she looks around at the assembled medical professionals, expecting them to announce that this baby is the best they've ever seen and that she is to be moved immediately over to the special gifted-and-talented ward for Ivy-bound infants and their mothers. I've long contemplated writing a book called "What to DEMAND When You're Expecting: Pregnancy for Fascists," but that probably won't sell, because new parents are in a temporary soft, fuzzy stage.

The first day of her baby's life is an exciting one for Ubermom, because it is also her first session with the lactation consultant. Since 1995 the number of consultants in the U.S. accredited by the International Board of Lactation Consultant Examiners has more than doubled, so there are now at least eight thousand lactation experts advising American mothers on how to breast-feed. As the activists at La Leche League, a pro-breast-feeding advocacy group, put it, "Breast milk is liquid gold, and it's yours to give." So the Ubermoms take the time for thorough nipple and areola preparation. They know what positions will produce superior latching between their baby's gums and their breast. They know what it feels like when their baby has achieved an effective seal, the leak-free suction environment that will make for steady milk flow. And they know all this not only because they take the time to master the proper skill set, but because their culture has produced hundreds of thousands of experts, advisers, child psychologists, social scientists, and medical researchers to analyze every aspect of child rearing and embalm the whole nurturing process with advice, findings, warnings, books, and gear.

The furnishing of a newborn's room these days is roughly comparable to the construction of an orbiting scientific laboratory. Space must be found for all the requisite air-filtering mechanisms, odor-free diaper-disposal systems, stereos for the *Mozart for Babies* CDs that will be playing constantly to enhance the little one's early-life brain functions. Hanging over the baby's crib will be a black-and-white graphic mobile to enhance spatial-recognition skills. The patterns on this mobile should complement the patterns on the flash cards that modern parents flash before babies at mealtime and during car trips in the hope of generating a few extra IQ points.

American women are having their first children later and later. The rate of first births for women in their thirties and forties has quadrupled over the past thirty years, while rates for women who have their first child in their twenties have dropped by a third. People in their early twenties are still too stupid and horny to get overwrought about raising their kids. But the Ubermoms in their late thirties and early forties are smart enough to know how to shape their children into being perfect, without being overbearing about it, like some of those other parents one could name.

So in the first few weeks of life, Ubermom will measure her child's walking reflexes, begin the baby-massage regimen her personal coach recommended, and get the little tot his or her first aerobics instructor. I once saw what looked like an Ubermom roundup on one of the lawns in New York's Central Park. There was an outer ring of Hispanic nannies standing next to empty strollers. In the inner ring was a circle of white mothers sitting on blankets with their babies; and in the center was a fitness counselor showing mothers how to move their babies' arms around for maximum firmness and flexibility.

By the time her child is in the pre-preschool years, Ubermom is boosting her junior achiever's prephonics-acquisition skills. She's patiently counting Cheerios at the breakfast table to accelerate number recognition, she's working with her baby on the extra-large pudgy-fingers computer keyboard lest the infant fall behind in alphabet mastery, and she's reading multicultural animal tales so her child grows up prejudice-free.

All of this will allow Ubermom to hold her head up in the most ruthless jungle of all, the nursery school parents' social. In this Hobbesian state of nature, competing Ubermoms drop broad hints about their child's budding musical abilities; the stay-at-home moms give parenting pointers to the working moms, who are quietly contemplating homicide; and the overweight moms huddle in the corner feeling like they are the walrus display at the zoo. One uber-Ubermom, who, after months of careful positioning, has gotten herself named class parent, is busy voicing her concerns over the school's fire-drill policy, while two other Ubermoms face off at the punch bowl. Ubermom A secretly reflects that while her three-year-old can sing the entire alphabet song, identify six of the ten first numerals, and was clearly the most promising student in the parent-toddler poetry workshop, Ubermom B's little boy spends all day on the ground staring at toy-truck wheels. Meanwhile, Ubermom B is thinking that while her little guy is so mature he leads the class in tearless drop-offs, every time Ubermom A tries to kiss her daughter good-bye, the girl sobs hysterically and clings to her mother's legs as if she's being abandoned to the Khmer Rouge.

Great Expectations

Dorothy Parker once said that American children aren't raised, they are incited. They are given food, shelter, and applause. It is true that since time immemorial, observers of the United States have commented on how indulgent and deferential Americans are toward their children.

That's because, as we tirelessly tell one another, our

children are our future. "Every child begins the world again," Henry David Thoreau declared. A newborn's life seems (and much of the time is) radically open, with potentialities limitless and vast. With our loose social structures and geographic dispersion, the future of an American child is unknowable. It's impossible to know if the child will keep his or her parents' religion (possibly not), live in the same state (probably not), follow in his parents' career footsteps (almost certainly not). The greatest successes or the saddest failures seem possible.

As the anthropologist Margaret Mead observed, American children are expected to lead lives *unlike* their parents'. In many families, it is expected—and in some immigrant families, it is demanded—that children shall exceed their parents. Each generation understands that it shall surpass the last, and each generation has a duty to see that the next one can do the same. And so from age three, American kids grow up with a question ringing in their ears: What do you want to be when you grow up? Not what do you want to do, but what do you want to *be*. What divine future existence dances in your brain, what field of glory? While the answers may change over a kid's childhood—from astronaut to shortstop to rap star to veterinarian—subtle frowns of disapproval greet anything that is not lofty. Somewhere around nursery school age, kids are infused by their parents, teachers, and caregivers—by the whole adult establishment—with the ideology of potentiality. So many roads beckon. Life is plastic; one makes out of it what one wills. There is nothing you cannot do if you set your mind to it. Indeed, life is a quest, a climb to realize your fullest potential, and develop your capacities through perpetual improvement.

The Sloan Study of Youth and Social Development recently found that 80 percent of high school seniors expect to work in a professional job, 71 percent expect to become millionaires, and 40 percent expect to be millionaires by the time they are fifty. These are expectations of an insanely high level, and they are radically higher than the expectations similar students had four decades ago.

American children, raised in an atmosphere of hope, are also raised with the inevitable flip side of hope, anxiety. If you return to the U.S. after a long time abroad, you are immediately struck by how fraught American culture is on the whole subject of childhood. Stories of kidnapping fill the local news. Child-abuse scandals are prosecuted and misprosecuted with almost Salem-witch-trial fervor. Drugs, cigarettes, and Internet porn are seen as evil specters at the door and outside the windows, seeping through any crack into the sanctity of the home. Brain chemistry is destiny, so you'd better stimulate those synapses by the time the neurons either form or perish at age three. Newsmagazines are filled with ominous stories on Dangerous Day Care and Driveway Dangers. Child-rearing magazines are filled with perfectionist instruction on the most minute matters; *Parenting* magazine recently ran an article called "Nose Blowing 101," on how to hold a tissue under your child's mucus.

The names of activist groups such as the Children's Defense Fund and Focus on the Family suggest wartime preparedness. Libraries are filled with book upon book, report upon report, with such titles as *Stolen Childhood* and *The Threatened Child*. The most influential education report of our lifetimes was called "A Nation at Risk." It's not just that the schools are mediocre; the whole nation is at risk.

The most devastating evidence of American parent-hood's overwrought nature is that most of the child-care books—which are written by experts who spend their entire lives thinking about child rearing—don't tell parents to concentrate more on child rearing. The experts—and there are more than ten thousand parenting books on Amazon.com—feel compelled to tell parents to relax. The entire literature of parental instruction can practically be summed up in the phrase "Don't worry. This happens to everyone."

Somehow this advice only sends parents deeper into the carpe-diem dilemma. On the one hand, childhood is supposed to be a happy, innocent time. It is the one time in life, the precious, never-to-return moment, when a person should be free to have fun, to not feel the insistent pressures of work, obligation, and responsibility. Yet there is an equal and opposite voice: Irresponsibility now will lead to failure and doom later on. If little Sarah doesn't develop the right work habits, what sort of life will she have? The future is lurking just ahead, making its demands. Parents are perpetually bouncing on the horns of the dilemma, making little guilty jokes about the amount of therapy their kids will someday need to correct for vague errors made in the character-molding years.

In 1844, Ralph Waldo Emerson wrote in his journal, "I wish to have rural strength and religion for my children, and I wish city facility and polish. I find with chagrin that I cannot have both." Today many parents wish spontaneity, eccentricity, and imagination for their kids, and also industriousness, self-discipline, and success. They long to inculcate their children with both sets of values, but they look up one day and notice that the values of achievement always take precedence. Preparation for success trumps spontaneity and eccentricity.

It's no wonder so many parents drive around in vehicles that look like tanks. It's no wonder that the inside of the average minivan looks like a battlefield that's hosted marauding armies wielding cracker crumbs, juice boxes, and candy wrappers. The whole country is on a war footing when it comes to raising kids.

The Most Supervised Generation

Roughly two-thirds of women with kids under three are in the workforce, compared to roughly one-third twenty years ago. At the same time, children—at least those in two-parent families—spend more time with their parents than they did before.

The University of Michigan's Institute for Social Research runs the most exhaustive and reliable studies on how parents and children spend their day. Today, the institute reports, the average child spends 31 hours a week with his or her mother, up from about 25 hours a week in 1980. The average child spends 23 hours a week with his or her father, up from 19 hours a week. This does not mean that families are able to dawdle together over the dinner table. But it does mean that parents have gone to extraordinary lengths not to let jobs get in the way of child rearing. They have added work time, but on average, they have not stolen those hours from child-rearing time. The time has come out of housework, relaxation, and adult friendships.

Middle-class families often become factories for producing happy and successful children. Parents become co-CEOs in the manufacture of junior achievers. They measure themselves by what sort of life preparation they are providing for their kids. They orient their vacations for maximum childhood pleasure. They sacrifice golf, socializing, reading, even their sex lives. And when a friend has a newborn, they give the following advice: "From now on, you won't have time to do the things you used to enjoy doing, but don't worry, you'll find a whole new set of things you'll enjoy more."

The University of Michigan time diaries reveal that over the past twenty years, there has been a quiet revolution in the way kids are raised in America. The amount of time spent in unsupervised play has declined dramatically, while the amount of time spent in adult-supervised skill-enhancing activities has gone up. Between 1981 and 1997, the amount of time children between the ages of three and twelve spent playing by themselves indoors declined by almost a fifth. The amount of time spent watching TV declined by 23 percent. The amount of time studying increased by a fifth. The amount of time doing organized sports increased by 27 percent.

Drive around your neighborhood. Remember all those parks that used to have open fields and undeveloped forests? They've been carved up into neatly trimmed soccer and baseball fields, crowded with parents in folding chairs who are watching their kids perform. In 1981 U.S. Youth Soccer had 811,000 registered players. By 1998 it had nearly 3 million.

This is the probably the most supervised generation in human history. Never before has such a high proportion of our young people been enrolled in school. Now 91 percent of five-to-fifteen-year-olds are in school, compared to 83 percent in 1950. Now there are fewer than thirteen students per teacher in school, compared to more than twenty-six students per teacher then, if you take the average of all the many different types of school districts.

School is tougher. During the 1960s and 1970s, schools assigned less and less homework, so that by 1981 the average six-to-eight-year-old was doing fifty-two minutes of homework a week. By 1997 the amount of homework assigned to the average child of the same age had doubled to over two hours a week. Meanwhile, the school day, which had shortened during the 1960s and 1970s, has steadily lengthened, as has the school year. Requirements have stiffened. Before 1983 the average school district required one year of math and one year of science for high school graduation. Now the average high school calls for two years of each.

The culture of schools has tightened, too. In the 1970s, rebelling against the rigid desks-in-a-row pedagogy of the 1950s, schools experimented with open campuses and schools without walls. The language of education has changed, and the emphasis is on testing, accountability, and order. Especially order. Zero tolerance is a mantra. Increasingly, and in surprising numbers, kids whose behavior subverts efficient learning are medicated so that they and their classmates can keep pace. The United States produces and uses about 90 percent of the world's Ritalin and its generic equivalents, and the number of students on the drug shoots upward every year—especially in the middle- and upper-middle-class suburbs. As Neil Howe and William Strauss observe in their book, *Millennials Rising*: "Ironically, where young boomers once turned to drugs to prompt impulses and think outside the box, today they turn to drugs to suppress their kids' impulses and keep their behavior inside the box."

In short, the childhood of unsupervised loitering, wandering, and exploring has been replaced by the childhood of adult-supervised improvement. Bike riding around town has given way to oboe lessons and SAT prep. Time spent hanging out on the corner is now spent in the backseat of the van, going from after-school tutoring to community service. More people are competing harder for those precious college-admissions slots and highly skilled job openings, and as a result, Americans are engaged in a massive cross-generational conspiracy to produce success. The urge to launch our children into marvelous futures of ascent and happiness makes Ubermoms of us all.

The System

There exists in this country a massive organic apparatus for the production of children, a mighty Achievatron. Nobody planned it. There is no central control deck. But all the anxious parents, child psychologists, teachers, tutors, coaches, counselors, therapists, family-centered activist groups, and social critics organically cohere into an omnipresent network of encouragement, improvement, advice, talent maximization, and capacity fulfillment. This system is frightening, when you step back and grasp its awesome power, its ability to mold little ones for frictionless ascent and smooth their eccentricities to maximize social aerodynamics. Worse than being run through the assembly line is not being run through it. The main tragedy of the country—and it is a genuine

tragedy—is that millions of kids never make it onto the conveyor belt. They are left behind.

But in many middle-class homes, kids perform so many
self-enhancement tasks that they suffer from what toy
manufacturers call "age compression." The toys, such as
Barbies or Hot Wheels, that used to appeal to eight-year-
olds now appeal to four-year-olds. The eight-year-olds have
moved on to laptops. Parental conversation consists largely
of quoting their children's brilliant aperçus to each other.
The refrigerator door becomes a shrine to children's
prowess. I look into my garage these days, and I see a vast
landscape of protective gear. My daughter, who is nine, is
already a four-helmet kid. She has a bike-riding helmet, a
horseback-riding helmet, a batting helmet, and an ice-
hockey helmet. These helmets serve as testimony to a certain sort of active, scheduled, yet massively protected
childhood.

Never underestimate the Achievatron's power to transform daily life. Go to a hockey rink at six A.M., and there
will be kids lugging body-bag-sized equipment valises from
the SUVs into the rink. By six-twenty they'll be doing belly
flops across the blue line while a young woman in an
Amherst Women's Hockey sweatshirt glides by at twice the
speed of sound, offering pointers. Then the games start,
and you've got these miniature humans, in hockey leagues
with names like Squirt and Mite, zooming around at 30
mph, executing passes like the Toronto Maple Leafs.

Go up to any semirural Sheraton on a summer weekend, and parked outside will be pickup trucks with little
trailers hitched on the back and travel-baseball-team logos
painted on the outside: the Bethesda–Chevy Chase Heat,
the Florida Lightning, the San Diego Stars. (Communities

tend to name their teams after weather systems or astronomical features, since it's no longer politically acceptable to use ethnic groups.) The hotel pool area will be teeming with kids who have baseball tans—brown on their necks and faces and pale on their foreheads, where their caps protect them from the sun. On one side of the pool will be groups of middle-aged women with "Baseball Mom" T-shirts; on the other side, the dads will be gathered in serious consultation over the scouting notes on their eleven-year-olds' next opponents.

The entire weekend economy of small-town America seems to depend on prepubescent sports tournaments with boxing-bout names—Beast of the East, Clash of the Champions, Fling in the Spring—to which teams travel hundreds or even thousands of miles to play. The teams arrive in great convoys, with exclamation-laden cheers and admonitions ("Go Jordan! #6! Goin' to the 'ships!") painted on the rear windows of the SUVs. Parents exist mainly to drive their kids places and carry their kids' gear, haul out hitting tees, practice nets, professional-quality baseballs by the bucket, and banners with résumé-like championship results to hang over the dugout. The kids have sports bags that would make major leaguers blush, different gloves for different positions, and two-hundred-dollar big-barrel bats with names like the Power Elite—because even radical writers like C. Wright Mills get their book titles co-opted by the competitive sports industry.

These kids practice three nights a week. They play 80 to 140 games a year. In the winter, they work out in gyms and get special tips from former minor leaguers turned eighty-dollar-an-hour youth baseball instructors offering specialized wisdom on the right elbow angle to adopt as you begin your trigger motion, or on the proper slide step to come to the plate with when there are runners on base.

When did it become normal that by age ten, kid athletes should be specializing in one sport year-round? But few parents pull their kids out of competitive sports, because they see—it is impossible not to see—that their kids love it. Studies from the Institute for Social Research (yes, there have been studies on this, too) show that most kids enroll in these activities because one of their friends was doing it, so they asked their parents if they could do it also. The kids initiate the activity, not the adults. Moreover, the kids love the team, the camaraderie, the fun of playing and practicing and achieving and learning. They are happy creatures in the land of achievement.

The Achievatron is easy to ridicule but not easy to reject. Hardly a dinner party goes by without somebody noting how kids' sports are out of control. But what's really happening is that the spirit of improvement has taken over sports, just as it has taken over every sphere of life. How can one reject getting the most out of your abilities on the sports field when one accepts that regimen in everything else? While everyone can point to examples, there are few parents who are maniacally overpressuring their kids. The kids are still kids. They love goofing around with one another and forget the losses five minutes after they have occurred (with the parents, it takes about an hour). The coaches, far from being martinets or drill sergeants, are mostly remarkably generous human beings.

In fact, sports coaches have become the leading moral instructors in America today. They are the only ones who dare to tell kids to tuck in their shirts, say please and thank you, and be respectable. They are the ones who get kids who have trouble cleaning their rooms to polish their shoes and clean their equipment. They are the ones who confront kids at a moment of humiliating failure—a goal between the legs, an interception—and give them specific advice on how to handle adversity. They're the ones who talk unabashedly about character, sportsmanship, old-fashioned politeness. The best coaches insist on a code of chivalry that has somehow survived untarnished in an age of scoffing and irony. They still demand deference to authority, loyalty, and individual subordination to the team in ways that nobody else does outside of the military. Most coaches preach a code of effort, hard work, and discipline so straightforward that it seems archaic when it comes out of the mouth of anybody else in American society.

As for the parents, most are decent and only want their kids to learn and have a good time, and they freely make asses of themselves as their way of contributing to the upbeat spirit that is obligatory at all youth sporting events.

Say a normal Little Leaguer comes up to bat and finds himself facing one of these man-childs so common these days—a six-foot-tall eleven-year-old with shoulders roughly the width of Manhattan who throws the ball at 70 mph and looks like he began shaving at age four. As the batter approaches the batter's box, all the team parents will begin incanting his name, "Hey, Danny, Danny, Danny!" and the coach, utilizing the baseball savvy that elevated him to this position of authority, will offer advice such as "Okay, Danny, be a hitter up there," as if the kid were going up there to be a snow shoveler if he hadn't been offered that proper wisdom. Then the man-child will throw a four-seam fastball on the inside corner that Danny can barely see, let alone swing at. At this point, kids, who are realists, will say to themselves, "I can't hit this. I guess I'll be striking out this time." But the parents, who have given themselves the responsibility of offering encouraging inanities no matter what the situation, will scream out things like "Okay. Now you've seen it. Now you've got the timing down" or "No problem. You can do this!" So the man-child throws an even faster pitch on the outside corner at the knees, and the batter, too stunned to swing, is trying to remember where he left his bag of sunflower seeds on the bench. The parents have switched to a new line of insanely upbeat propaganda: "That wasn't your pitch anyway" or "Little line drive here. Don't try to kill it. Just meet the ball." Danny's parents are deep in prayer, silently offering to trade God five years of their lives if only Danny could jack one into left-center field, and the coaches and the other savvy baseball parents are barraging the kid with advice: "Square your feet up . . . keep your head down . . . hands straight to the ball . . . move back in the box."

The kid hears none of this, because while he is at bat, he is deep in his own zone of concentration, and the parents and coaches vaguely know this, but they have to keep shouting, because how else are they going to disguise their own irrelevance? So the man-child throws a ball two feet over Danny's head, and Danny, who has decided to begin his swing fifteen seconds before the ball is released on the freak hope that he might catch up with it, swings lamely and misses, and it's strike three and all the parents, who all display a capacity to ignore reality and lie like dogs such as would impress even a political consultant, greet him as he walks back to the dugout with a chorus of spin: "Good at-bat, Danny . . . you were right on it . . . you'll get him next time . . ." The coach gives him an encouraging tap on the top of the helmet, and pretty soon Danny is cheerfully ensconced on the bench with his sunflower seeds while the next batter goes up for his whiffing, and the parents, like a Greek chorus overdosing on Prozac, repeat their reality-free cries of support.

The Theology of Achievement

The achievement ethos is built on an idealistic premise: There is, at the core of each human being, a wonderful destiny waiting to be realized. It is not just the talented few who have great potentialities lurking within. Each person has a noble destiny that can be realized, given the right output of effort, direction, and support. Each person was born with promise, and each has a God-given right to a chance to achieve the fullest of his or her capacities.

Not all societies give such prominence to this belief. In some civilizations, people are more inclined to seek the harmony that comes with total submission to God's will. Others are built on the love for the nurturing presence of loved ones and community. It is better to stay home with one's kin than to venture forth in search of achievement and success. But American civilization encourages us to strive to realize our best self. Our identity, we often assume, is formed not by where we are born or who our ancestors are. Our identity is defined by what we do and accomplish. Each of us has a gift to offer the world. Just as Marx wrote that "Milton produced *Paradise Lost* as the silkworm produces silk, as the activation of his own nature," so each of us has some contribution, if only we can find it, to offer our fellows.

Each personality is perpetually in the process of unfolding, of fulfilling itself through energy and exploration. Life becomes a journey. We don't know what our individual destinations look like, much less the destinations of our sons and daughters. But it is through our efforts to forge ahead that we discover who we are, what direction we are trying to travel, what gift we might have to share. As the theologian Jürgen Moltmann put it when describing the Christian eschatology in *Theology of Hope*, "Man has no subsistence in himself, but is always on the way towards something and realizes himself in the light of some expected future whole."

There is an exalted noble dream of democratic greatness buried at the core of our achievement ethos. There is an optimistic faith in the basic goodness of every individual, and it will show itself when the obstacles to achievement are removed, when people are given a chance to bloom. As so many foreign visitors have noticed, we are a people with an unbounded faith in the true inner self, in our own essential goodness.

As anybody who looks at meritocratic life knows, this creed is not easy on its disciples. There is no rest. Expectations don't sleep. There's a little voice saying, "Not there yet." Parents expect colossal things from their children, and from an early age kids feel the burden of those goals. They measure their progress by their prowess. Whatever you are doing, you should never be merely as good tomorrow as you are today. If you are a bird-watcher, you achieve a life list. If you are a punk musician, you become a better punk musician. If you are a swing dancer, your moves perpetually improve. Capacities are there to be cultivated, heading toward some never achieved perfection.

We tell ourselves and our children that the purpose of life is not merely to achieve worldly success—money, fame, prestige. Then we assign them a curriculum of self-improvement that makes mere worldly success look as easy as kindergarten. For example, Anna Quindlen, the novelist and *Newsweek* columnist, recently gave a commencement address at Villanova University that offered the students the sort of advice we are always giving the young and each other: "Get a life," she said, "A real life, not a manic pursuit of the next promotion, the bigger paycheck, the larger house."

She assigned a few tasks:

> Get a life in which you notice the smell of salt water. . . . Get a life in which you are not alone. Find people you love and who love you. And remember that life is not leisure, it is work. . . . Get a life in which you are generous. Look around at the azaleas. . . . Work in a soup kitchen. Be a big brother or sister. . . . Consider the lilies of the field. Look at the fuzz on a baby's ear. . . . Just keep your eyes and ears open. Here you could learn in the classroom. There the classroom is everywhere.

That's good advice. But consider how arduous it is. "It is so easy to exist instead of live," Quindlen said. You can rest assured that her listeners won't renounce their career goals. Nor did she say they should. She was invited to address the crowd precisely because she herself has had such a phenomenally successful career. The destitute are rarely asked to give commencement addresses. Yet she is asking us to pile goodness on top of plenty, patience on top of hustle, tranquility on top of aspiration. When does Anna Quindlen expect us to sleep?

This is the culture of upwardly mobile childhood. And when you look at the frantic strivings of today's young meritocrats, what you are seeing is the latest and maybe most fevered version of a long line of American strivings. It was the early settlers who established the code that life is a pilgrimage toward perfection. Jonathan Edwards told his flock never to be content with their virtues, never to feel satisfied. "The endeavor to make progress" in developing one's character, he declared, "ought not to be attended to as a thing by the bye, but all Christians should make a business of it. They should look upon it as their daily business."

Benjamin Franklin more or less invented the mode of childhood we see around us today. He was the original enterprising boy. "It was about this time," he wrote somewhat ironically of his childhood ambitions, "that I conceived the bold and arduous project of arriving at moral perfection." Franklin made a little scorecard of the thirteen virtues such as industry ("Lose no time. Be always employed at something useful") and temperance ("Eat not to dullness. Drink not to elevation"). Then he gave himself daily performance reviews, marking his scorecard when he found himself guilty of imperfection.

One of the first outstanding American sociologists, Lester Ward, described "this all-pervading spirit of improvement" that marks American life. The constellation of American stock characters is dotted with young people on the make: the Horatio Algers, the Sammy Glicks, the ambitious immigrant kids, the gangsters trying to rise from obscurity to success, the politicians ascending from log cabin to White House. There is no real resting spot. "It is provided in the essence of things," Walt Whitman acknowledged, "that from any fruition of success, no matter what, shall come forth something to make a greater struggle necessary."

Take one of these young meritocratic kids raised on *Mozart for Babies,* tutored at age six, coached at age eight, honed and molded and improved and enlightened every day of his life, and imagine telling him at some point in middle adulthood that the ascent is over. All his dreams have been realized. There is no more need to exert himself. Do you think he'd be happy? Of course not. Inertia would reduce him to the gravest misery. He is bred to want more and better and deeper, to ceaselessly reform and improve himself. He has become, for better and worse, an American.

CHAPTER SIX

Learning

AS YOU KNOW, the college-admissions process is the confirmation or bar mitzvah of American life, the central initiation rite when a boy becomes a man, or when a girl becomes a woman.

It is no easy ritual. Many students begin contemplating their college application around age twelve (roughly twelve years and nine months after their parents have begun worrying about it). By age fourteen, they are thoroughly immersed in the cult of the fat envelope. They are laboriously prepping for standardized tests, honing application essays—inspiring stories of personal growth and transformation downloaded from the Internet—all while girding themselves for the moment of ultimate judgment.

High school years, which once upon a time were devoted to cruising, malt shops, and necking, are increas-

ingly spent being corresponding secretary of this and treasurer of that. All around the country, one's peers and college-admissions competitors are taking AP courses,
winning trophies at Social Studies Olympiads, leading
debate teams, managing their a cappella group's international tour, getting accepted into honor societies, and performing hours upon hours of résumé-enhancing, legally
mandated, yet seemingly altruistic community service. "I
don't know where these kids find lepers," George Washington University president Stephen Trachtenberg has
observed, "but they find them and they read to them."

To get into top schools, students need to get straight
A's, or close. That means they must embrace the rigors of
the GPA mentality. They must learn not to develop a consuming passion for one subject, lest it distract them from
getting perfect marks across the board. They must carefully
and prudentially budget their mental energies. They must
learn the tricks of good studenting (without necessarily
developing a deep interest in the classes' actual content) so
that they can, to paraphrase Joseph Epstein, take whatever
their teachers throw out at them and return it back in their
warm little mouths.

In his memoir *My Early Life,* Winston Churchill wrote
that "where my reason, imagination or interest were not
engaged, I would not or could not learn." But that's not the
case with today's successful students, for they can learn—
or at least get good grades—in all circumstances. They
must become masters of the subtle suck-up, exhibiting
sycophantic skills just this side of nauseating, without ever
quite going over the line. They must apply themselves to
their homework, their career-building summer jobs, and
their after-school activities without ever letting their raging

hormones suck them into the fits of distracting passion and madness that Mother Nature intended for these adolescent years.

By the time they apply to college, the best of them have, to judge by their applications, founded a few companies, cured at least three formerly fatal diseases, mastered a half-dozen languages, and monitored human-rights abuses in Tibet while tutoring the locals on conflict-resolution skills and environmental awareness. Their résumés are so impressive, and the competitive standard they set is so high, that no American adult could get into the college he or she attended as a youth.

Then, having put their pubescent résumé in good order, they face the ultimate choice: What institution's window sticker will their parents be able to affix to the back of their car? It is with electron-microscope subtlety that they measure and compare the quality and prestige levels of different universities. Which school has higher status, Brown or Columbia? Which school will be more fulfilling, Claremont or Occidental? During the course of your life, when people ask you where you went to school, which institution will come tripping more impressively off the tongue, Tulane or Vanderbilt? Which schools, in the vast academic pecking order, will you select as your "reach" schools, and which will be "safeties"? The society dames in Edith Wharton novels comprehend amazingly subtle social gradations, but nothing like the ones that separate America's institutions of higher learning. The ranking of these schools is at once so important, yet so fundamentally bogus, that it takes teams of university-trained status professionals at *U.S. News & World Report* to quantify the differences between Penn State and the University of Michigan.

Say a student survives this ordeal. Say he, or more likely she (since women earn a quarter more bachelor's degrees and a third more master's degrees than men), crosses the endless mountain chains of the application process, endures the long, isolating winters of study, activity, and SAT prep, and arrives at the promised land of college admissions—and is accepted! The fat envelope arrives! And the next fall she loads up the U-Haul for one of America's prestigious campuses, a university with an endowment that tops the GDP of 140 of the world's 200-odd nations. The trek is over. The land of milk and honey has been attained. The student is finally on her own, free from pressuring parents and overbearing guidance counselors. She can now let Dionysus out for a romp, kick back, and enjoy the mad magic of youth—never mind what the future may hold.

Does she? No, she kicks it up a notch. From the achievement-oriented movers and doers they were as teenagers, today's high-achieving Americans turn, once on campus, into the Junior Workaholics of America. The Achievatron, remember, rewards energy as much as intelligence. The ones who thrive are the ones who can keep going from one activity to another, from music to science to sports to community service to the library and so on without rest. Once that pattern of exertion has been established, it is not even possible, in the full bloom of youth, to slow down. The habits are ingrained. The internal reactor is humming along, pumping out gigawatts. The Holy Bee, the patron saint of busyness, must be served.

If you go to college campuses, especially competitive college campuses, you may run into the student who is heading off at six A.M. to crew practice, then a quick bite at the coffee shop, then class, the library, resident-adviser duty, science lab, class, tutoring, Bible study, work, choral practice, career-recruiting seminar, year-abroad information meeting, discussion group, and so on until midnight, when it is time to hit the e-mail. She will brag to her friends about how little sleep she gets, or about how much work she has ahead of her, or about how she never has a moment to get back to her room during the day, because there is simply too much going on.

I went to lunch a little while ago with a young man in a student dining room that by one-ten had nearly emptied out as students hustled back to the library and their classes. I mentioned that when I went to college in the late 1970s and early 1980s, we often spent two or three hours around the table, shooting the breeze and arguing about things. He admitted that there was little discussion about intellectual matters outside of class. "Most students don't like that that's the case," he said, "but it is the case." So he and a bunch of his friends formed a discussion group that meets regularly with a faculty guest to discuss serious subjects. If they can get it scheduled into their Palm Pilots, they can get it done.

One finds students applying time-quadrant techniques to maximize their mental efficiency. They read *The 7 Habits of Highly Effective Teens*. In 1985, 16 percent of freshmen told researchers at UCLA that they frequently felt stressed at school. By 1999, 30 percent of the respondents reported feeling "frequently overwhelmed by all I have to do." And many of them like it that way. They aren't living this frenetically because they're compelled to. It's not the sticks that drive them on, it's the carrots. Opportunity lures them, the glorious future. There's so much neat stuff to do.

American universities are diverse and enriching places, packed with learning, experiences, and opportunities. American young people are nearly twice as likely to attend college as young people in Western Europe, and American universities spend, on average, about twice as much money per student as their French, German, or British counterparts. Like gluttons in the candy store, students want to take advantage of it all, enjoy it all, experience it all, launch themselves into adulthood. Four-fifths of college students, according to a Jobtrack.com study, believe it will take them ten years or less to achieve their career goals.

With so many options and so little time, students must develop a strategizing, professional mind-set in order to allocate their energies efficiently. Interests must be judged and ranked. Which courses will help professionally? Which will be fun but won't require much work? What readings will really be on the test? Which activities can be jettisoned under stress, because while they might be interesting, they don't contribute to the process of personal-growth maximization? In the land of time pressure, one has to strive for personal fuel efficiency.

Students may be fuzzy about what destination awaits them, but they know they are heading for something. College is one step on the continual stairway to paradise, and they're aware that they must get to the next step (corporate job, law school, medical school, whatever). This professional mind-set gets more pronounced at community colleges and the less prestigious four-year schools, where getting a good job is more likely to be the main point of the exercise. In 1969, according to UCLA's annual survey of freshmen, developing a meaningful philosophy of life was listed by 76 percent of students as a key collegiate goal. By

1993 only 47 percent of students felt it necessary to say that. Meanwhile, 76 percent of students said that becoming "very well-off financially" ranks as a very important reason to go to college. At many community colleges, there are no frills, no Gothic architecture, no lineage, no arboretums, no ancient faculty rituals. There are just low brick buildings, linoleum floors, and aspiring students struggling with work, bills, and kids. They are hungry for skills, success, and advancement.

Today's college students, by and large, are not trying to buck the system; they're trying to climb it. Hence, they are not a disputatious group. One often hears on campus a distinct verbal tic: If someone is about to dissent with someone in a group, he or she will apologize beforehand, couching the disagreement in the most civil, nonconfrontational terms available. On the whole, professors love and admire their students, but they are a little disturbed by how noncontentious they are, how willing they are to jump through whatever hoop is placed in front of them for the sake of pleasing teachers, mentors, or the achievement system itself. These students are, in general, exceedingly deferential to authority. Very few will challenge or contradict a professor, any more than an employee would be likely to challenge or contradict the boss.

At Princeton I saw a recruiting poster from Goldman Sachs in the student center. Under a photograph of a group of wholesome-looking young people relaxing after a game of lunchtime basketball, the text read "Wanted: Strategists, Quick Thinkers, Team Players, Achievers." Nearby was a recruiting poster from the consulting firm KPMG, showing a pair of incredibly hip-looking middle-aged people staring warmly into the camera. The text read, "Now that you've made your parents proud, join KPMG and give them something to smile about." A few decades ago, recruiting posters wouldn't have appealed to a student's desire to make her parents happy.

The Unalienated

When you read about America's universities in the media, you might get the impression that the top colleges are left-wing hothouses filled with multicultural radicalism and fevered anti-American passions. That's not quite right. It's true that most professors are liberals, and in its wisdom, American society has decided to warehouse its radicals on university campuses—in departments that serve as nunneries for the perpetually alienated. But most students do not live in an overly politicized world.

There is, one must always remember, a large cultural gap between the students and the faculty. Remarkably few students—alarmingly few, actually—seriously contemplate a career in academia. They think of becoming high school teachers or reporters or even soldiers, but if you ask them what life is like in academia, they talk about the pedantic specialization of academic research, the jargon and impenetrable prose, the professor's cloistered remove from the real world and the low salaries.

The faculty at most schools is significantly to the left of the students. The students know this and accept it as part of the inevitable structure of the universe. They know who the radical professors are and regard their radicalism as an endearing blemish, the way a professor's absent-mindedness would have been regarded in an earlier generation. The

weird thing is that while most students don't share the radical ideologies, they do find them convenient.

Truth is indeterminate, the (once) cutting-edge literary
critics argued. Texts can be deconstructed in an infinitude
of ways, and words are signifiers open to a diversity of
meanings. Every point of view deserves respect. The
enlightened person should be open to everything—opinions, lifestyles, and ideologies—and closed to nothing. One
should never judge The Other harshly, but should respect
minority or multicultural alternatives. These notions may
have been promulgated by people who thought of themselves as radicals—they were French deconstructionists,
tenured revolutionaries, or transgressive countercultural
provocateurs.

But they are ideas perfectly suited to the ethos of the
achievement-oriented capitalist. After all, why should the
achiever want to make enemies or waste time in angry conflict? Why should the time maximizer struggle to find that
thing called Absolute Truth when it is more efficient to settle for perception? Why should one get involved in the
problematic rigor of judging? Easygoing tolerance is energy-
efficient. The world of floating signifiers and upended
cultural hierarchies, in which nothing has any fixed attachment to a universal truth, and in which it is as valid to write
a paper interpreting denim as Dante, is a world of maximum fluidity and flexibility: just the sort of world the
opportunity-seeking meritocrat wants to live in. In other
words, the radical ideas that were first espoused in fits of
protest and anger—ideas that were meant to tear down
reactionary hierarchies and question the foundations of
truth—now seem like convenient intellectual habits for people of mild disposition and strategizing minds.

The current generation of college students doesn't see itself as a lost generation or a radical generation or a beatnik generation or even a Reaganite generation. They have relatively little generational consciousness. That's because this generation is, for the most part, not fighting to emancipate itself from the past. The most sophisticated people in the preceding generations were formed by their struggle to break free from something. The most sophisticated people in this one aren't. Many of them are ambivalent about the extreme meritocratic system they grew up in, but they do not see an alternative. For those growing into adulthood during most of the twentieth century, the backdrop of life was a loss of faith in coherent systems of thought and morality. Educated people knew they were supposed to rebel against authority, reject old certainties, liberate themselves from hidebound customs and prejudices. Artists rebelled against the stodgy mores of the bourgeoisie. Radicals rebelled against the commercial and capitalist order. Feminists rebelled against the patriarchal family. And in the latter half of the twentieth century, a youth culture emerged that distilled these themes. Every rock anthem, every fashion statement, every protest gesture, every novel about rebellious youth—starting with *The Catcher in the Rye* and *On the Road*—carried the same cultural message: It's better to be a nonconformist than a conformist, a creative individualist than a member of a group, a rebel than a traditionalist, a daring adventurer than a careerist striver.

Though they might retain the youth-culture patina, today's college students don't live in that age of rebellion and alienation. Nothing in their environment suggests that the world is fundamentally ill-constructed or that life is made meaningful only by revolt. They have not witnessed senseless bloodbaths or seen any World War I– or Vietnam-type evidence that the ruling establishment is fundamentally incompetent, murderous, or corrupt.

During most of the twentieth century, the basic ways of living were called into question, but those fundamental debates are over, at least for most of today's college students. Democracy and dictatorship are no longer engaged in an epic struggle. Islamic extremists may challenge Western modes, but the mullahs have few allies in your average college dorm. Pluralistic democracy is the beneficent and seemingly natural order. The globalization protesters notwithstanding, no fundamental argument pits capitalism against socialism; capitalism is so triumphant, we barely contemplate an alternative. Radicals no longer assault the American family and the American home. Even theological conflicts have settled down. It's somewhat fashionable to be religious so long as one is not militantly so.

When I have taught on campus, I have amazed students with readings from eras when the frame of debate was not nearly so narrow as it is today, when people talked about radically restructuring the way average folks live. The students are interested in such visions, but they are surprisingly unromantic about the manifestos that used to come from communists, agrarians, or socialist utopians and other outsiders. "We saw what happens to those big ideas," these twenty-first-century students say. "They fail and they lead to disaster." It's better to be modest, realistic, and small-scale, they continue. That makes them wise, perhaps, but not confrontational. So authority does not seem threatening to them. They are less likely than previous generations to feel they must rebel against their parents. Responding to a 1997 Gallup survey, 96 percent of teenagers said they got along with their parents, and 82 percent described their home life as "wonderful" or "good." I'm not sure families are quite that healthy, but the results show what young people want things to be. Roughly three out of four teens said they shared their parents' general values. When asked by Roper Starch Worldwide in 1998 to rank the major problems facing America today, students aged twelve to nineteen named as their top five concerns: selfishness, people who don't respect law and the authorities, wrongdoing by politicians, lack of parental discipline, and courts that care too much about criminals' rights. It is impossible to imagine teenagers of a few decades ago calling for stricter parental discipline and more respect for authority. In 1974, for example, a majority of teenagers told pollsters that they could not "comfortably approach their parents with personal matters of concern." Forty percent believed they would be "better off not living with their parents."

The current college students live in a world that is more open to different lifestyles and callings, more fluid and flexible. According to a survey commissioned by the Independent Women's Forum, 87 percent of college students believe it is wrong to "judge anyone's sexual conduct but my own." They grew up in a world in which the racial and gender barriers were lower, and the mental categories of past generations have been washed away. For them, it's natural that an Ivy League administrator has a poster of the Beatles album *Revolver* framed on her office wall. It's natural that hippies work at ad agencies and found organic ice-cream companies, and that management consultants quote Bob Dylan atop their final reports.

They don't have the same awareness of mental barriers

between establishment and rebels, between respectable striving society and antistriving subversives. For them, all the categories are mushed together, so they can go work at Bank of America and support Greenpeace, trade overseas and sympathize with the antiglobalization protesters. All is fluid and free. They've learned that this open-ended world is one good for development. What those twentieth-century radicals were really trying to tear down, it now appears, were the structures that would inhibit the flowering of one's best self. Now it matters somewhat less if you are a man or a woman; you can achieve. Now it matters somewhat less if you are straight or gay; you can achieve. You can achieve, you can achieve, you can achieve.

If opportunities to succeed are more open, the competition has grown more fierce as a result.

Fuckbuddies

This competitive environment changes college life in all sorts of unexpected ways. Even the biological necessities get squeezed out. There is a fair bit of partying on campus, and a lot of drinking, but many students have found they have no time for dating and/or serious relationships. They are more likely to go out in groups—the group has replaced the couple as the primary social unit—and then they hook up for occasional sex. I've been amazed by the number of young women who come up to me after an event on campus to say, "I don't have time for a relationship, so of course I hook up." They say this in the tone one might use to describe commuting routes, the same tone they use when toting up lists of their hookup partners in late-night e-mails. At some schools you hear about buddy sex or fuckbuddies, the friends you go to for the occasional roll in the hay. At Princeton I ran across students who said they have friendships, and then they have friendships with privileges—meaning sex.

A study conducted by Peggy Giordano and Monica Longmore of Bowling Green found that 55 percent of eleventh-graders had had sex with a casual acquaintance. College students talk about prudential sex—the kind you have for leisure without any of that romantic Sturm und Drang, as a normal part of life (though many of them are lying).

Some bizarre rituals grow out of this new social scene. First, there no longer is a big-man-on-campus social structure. In the age of dispersal, remember, everything hierarchical turns cellular. So at most schools, there is no clear pecking order, with one clique of beautiful or rich or popular students on top and everybody else scattered in less prestigious social circles down below. I've been amazed by how few college students even know what the acronym "BMOC" stands for.

Instead, there is a profusion of groups defined by interest, dorm, or activity. Most students are casual members of several groups, to which they display different parts of themselves. A young man may reveal his inner doubts among the Fellowship of Christian Athletes and show his outer bravura on the track. Different groups don't even listen to the same type of music. A 1950s study by the University of Chicago sociologist James Coleman revealed that teenage musical tastes were similar, with half saying that rock and roll was their favorite kind of music. Now those musical tastes have been segmented into rock, classic rock, rap, alternative, hip-hop, folk dance, rave, house, and a hundred other genres, and each clique has its own constellation of preferences.

Second, there is the weird return of chauvinist-piggism, as if in the age of prudential climbing, it suddenly became acceptable to play—in a suitably self-conscious manner—at being an *Animal House* frat boy. Highly educated college men read *Maxim, FHM,* or one of the other laddie magazines. Unlike *Playboy* or *Penthouse,* which had intellectual pretensions, these magazines are pure in their pursuit of horniness. Women in their pages are reduced to cleavage. Men exist solely at that crossroads where celebrity babes in lingerie meet power tools, plasma TVs, and serial-killer computer games. The articles, which tend to be within the "How to Score at Funerals" genre, are short but didactic shallowness primers. (In the world of *Maxim,* size matters in every aspect of human existence except attention span.)

This behavior is socially acceptable on campus, despite a generation of feminist consciousness raising, because it is all conducted in a mood of knowing irony (or at least faux irony), and because the new mores call on all of us to be liberated sexual beings together. We men can leer at your breasts, and you women can leer at our buns. We can be Bob Gucciones equally, and we'll call it gender equity.

Finally, ambiguity hangs over nearly every social bond. After the hookup, the sex partners enter what one of my students called the "Now that we've seen each other naked, we have to at least talk to each other" phase. There are infinite types of hookups—with friends, near-strangers, potential love interests—and infinite gradations of sexual activity. Afterward, the man and the woman will go back to their other buddies and wonder, What kind of hookup was it? What did it mean? Was it for fun? Was it serious? Or was it just another in the long string of wants and activities that fill a college student's day? In the midst of a political-science paper, another of my students, a woman, nicely captured how personal relationships blend into the smorgasbord of life-enhancing campus interests and activities, at least at one elite university:

> Most Yale women, for example, except for the premeds, aren't clamoring for equal rights or the chance to be called on in class anymore. They want a long wool coat for the winter, a Macintosh laptop computer with an MP3 player, a course load that doesn't include books by dead white men exclusively, a gay man for advice and a straight man for every other weekend or so, one good pair of Manolo Blahniks sometime in the future, to maintain a woman's right to choose, something to finally be done (for Christ's sake) for the women being circumcised in Africa and suffocated under burqas in the Middle East, a cigarette or a shot or a joint when the company is right, a husband at some point though no point soon, a good education, a GPA above 3.5, and a network of connections for when she graduates.

This is the point at which we fogies are supposed to lament the decline in courtship, the total absence of the romantic ideal, which says that there must exist one person in the world with whom each of us can unite at all levels, and that one should save oneself for that person and not sully intimacies in such a casual way. Indeed, I was out drinking late one night with a group of students at a small Midwestern liberal arts college, and the woman to my left, from Michigan, mentioned that she would never have a serious relationship with someone she wouldn't consider marrying. "That sounds traditional," I said to her.

"I didn't say I wouldn't fuck anyone I wouldn't consider marrying," she responded.

One young man at our table from an Indiana farm town heard the exchange, and for the next few minutes I could see him brooding. Finally, he exploded with a short tirade on how the women on his campus had destroyed romance by making it so transactional. He didn't quite call the three women on my left sluts, but he was heading in that direction.

As he spoke, I could feel them shaking with rage, making little growls of protest but politely not interrupting him. I knew they were only waiting to let rip. Eventually, they let him have it. They didn't deny his version of reality, that sex is sometimes transactional. Their main point was that guys have been acting this way all along, so why shouldn't they?

As we left the bar, the young man walked me part of the way to my hotel and commented that the Michigan girl who'd made the comment was really cute. He thought he might give her a call.

Now, the first thing to be said about this state of affairs is that every survey of youth sexual activity over the past several years reveals that young people are having less sex than their predecessors were ten and twenty years ago. Young women may talk more baldly about sex, but it is simply not true that they are more promiscuous or casual about it. Their conversational style is a reflection of the amazing self-confidence of the women on these campuses. The single most striking, if hard to define, difference between college campuses today and college campuses twenty years ago is in the nature and character of the female students. They are not self-confident just socially. They are self-confident academically, athletically, organizationally, and in every other way.

In general, the women carry themselves with an appearance of ease that must have been matched by only that of the old WASP bluebloods when schools were oriented around their desires. Twenty years ago, if memory serves, it was mostly we men who performed the role of seminar baboons—speaking up and showing off with knowledge, just as today it is mostly men who fill the op-ed pages with ideas and pontifications.

In my discussions with student groups, there were always several women who projected authority with a grace that was unusual two decades ago. These women—who were born around 1983—appeared uninhibited by any notion that either they shouldn't assert themselves for fear of appearing unfeminine, or that they should overexert themselves to prove their feminist bona fides. Those considerations appeared irrelevant. Of course, people in every group suffer from the normal insecurities, but in general, and at least on the surface, young women today carry themselves with a wonderfully straightforward assurance.

The changing character of women was bound to change the courtship rituals. One night over dinner at a northern college, a student from the South mentioned that at her local state university, where some of her friends go, they still have date nights on Friday. The men ask the women out, and they go as couples. The other students at the dinner table were amazed. The only time many young people have ever gone out on a formal date was their high school senior prom. You might as well have told them that in some parts of the country, there are knights on horseback jousting with lances.

One of the young men at the dinner table piped up and said that his generation happened to come along during a time of transition. A generation ago, there was one set of courtship rituals. Twenty years from now, he continued, there will be another. But now there are no set rules. There is ambiguity.

A literature professor told me that he had come to notice a strange pattern among his students. Many of the nineteenth-century novels he teaches, he said, end with the heroine leaving her family and friends and going off to marry her one true love. Recently, he continued, he had found his students rebelling against that choice. To them, it didn't make sense to sacrifice your relationship with your friends to build a marriage. To them, the friendship relationship was higher, more intimate, and more satisfying than the sexual or even the romantic relationship. Friendships are forever, whereas just look at romance . . . that breaks apart. As one male student put it, in a phrase I heard a few times, "Bros before hos." (The female counter to that phrase is "Chicks before dicks.")

It should be said that these students are idealizing friendships. Every longitudinal study of young people shows that Americans between sixteen and twenty-two build and abandon intimate friendships with astounding speed. The friends of freshman year are probably not the same friends of junior year. And yet it is that ideal—the happy, flexible clique with an undertone of sexual tension (just like on *Friends*) that beckons as the preferred social bond. This is an amazing inversion of decades-old, if not centuries-old, social norms.

The literature professor went on to say that his students think they're making life more efficient for themselves by having these loose, informal bonds. After all, the girl doesn't have to sit by the phone waiting to be asked out. There is no nervousness about when to start going steady. There are fewer traumatic breakup scenes. But on the other hand, the professor noted, nobody really knows where they stand. Relationships are abandoned without any formal end, sometimes without a fight or even a word. I heard about a few in which the guy thought he was going out with the girl, but the girl had an entirely different understanding. The ambiguity allowed each to interpret their friendship (or love affair) in contradictory ways, with trouble looming down the road. The professor concluded that on balance, the fluidity and ambiguity of the students' social lives led to greater misery.

I've bounced his observations off many students, and some think he is overstating the situation. Many students are involved in long-term relationships. But fewer, I believe, than two decades ago. And it's undeniable that students bring a prudential frame of mind to their romantic activities. College is a busy time. It's better, many of them reason, to put off serious relationships until such time as one's career is established and there's time to invest in love. Several mentioned that the best time to think seriously about it is at the ten-year reunion, after you're established on your career track and have the financial resources to start a family.

In fact, these students are merely following the advice of their parents, the same people who would be quick to condemn them for taking the magic out of love. How many parents do you know—liberal or conservative, atheist or evangelical—who would enjoy seeing their child devoting the bulk of his or her collegiate energies to a boyfriend or girlfriend, rather than to the vast array of activities and learning opportunities available at these phenomenally expensive schools? Very few. Parents who are ambitious for their kids imbue them with a calculating, strategizing mind-set. It's not surprising that they have carried this over, to some extent, into the arena of romance and sex.

Character

The students in America's colleges are bright, lively, funny, and generous. Their behavior is in many ways exemplary, especially compared to past generations. They are not the pains in the ass to their parents that many of their parents were to theirs.

Their commitment to community service is one of the marvels of the age. Their volunteer work may have started out as a way to impress admissions officers, but their interest in it has transcended shallow careerism. You go to schools and find that 20, even 30 percent of the students spend some meaningful time each week helping the less fortunate.

Today's college students are remarkably eager to try new things, to thrust themselves into unlikely situations, to travel the world in search of new activities. At the more elite universities, every other student you meet has just come back from some service adventure in remotest China or Brazil. During my conversations with them, I would sometimes realize with a start that they were two decades younger than I. With their worldliness, their sophisticated senses of humor, and their ability to at least fake knowledge of a wide variety of fields, they socialize just like any group of forty-somethings. Most of all, they have a passion for personal growth that is amazing. They want to make money and become successful, but they also want to become good people, inside and out, if only they had some clear idea of how that is achieved; if only they had a vocabulary that would enable them to talk about their moral desires.

And that is the part that gnaws. It is not that they have bad character or no character. I haven't yet seen a machine that allows us to peer into a generation's souls and measure whether they are deep or not. We are right to be skeptical about generalizations on the moral health of America's youth. But we can observe their public lives and the way they conduct themselves in social situations. It is not too hard to see that at the very least, talk about character has been crowded out amid all the rush, bustle, and achievement.

On the whole, college students are articulate on every subject save morality. When you talk to them about character, you notice that they are hesitant to say anything definitive, as if any firm statement about which lifestyle choice is conducive to firm character development might break the code of civility. When you ask if their school builds character, they inevitably start talking about legislation. They mention their school's honor codes, the sexual-harassment rules, or the antidrinking policies. This may be character in the negative sense—efforts to prevent students from doing bad things. But it doesn't get at what an earlier generation meant when they used the phrase "noble character."

Although today's colleges impose all sorts of rules to reduce safety risks and encourage achievement, they see passing along knowledge, not building character, as their primary task. If you ask professors whether they seek to instill character, they often look at you blankly. They are on campus to instill calculus, or nineteenth-century history, or whatever their academic specialty happens to be. "We've taken the decision that these are adults and this is not our job," Princeton professor Jeffrey Herbst once told me in an interview. "We're very conservative about how we steer. They steer themselves," said that school's dean of undergraduate students, Kathleen Deignan. "I don't know if we build character or remind them that they should be developing it," ruefully added the then dean of admissions, Fred Hargadon.

To put it at its baldest, the Achievatron micromanages the tiniest issues in young people's lives. Their SAT prep, their recycling habits, their brain chemistry, their drinking-and-driving tendencies. But when it comes to instilling character, the most difficult task of them all, suddenly it's "You're on your own, kiddo." The laissez-faire ethic reigns.

We assume that each person has to solve these questions alone (though few other societies in history have made this assumption). We assume that if adults try to offer moral instruction, it will backfire, because young people will reject our sermonizing (though truth be told, they more often seem to hunger for precisely this kind of big-question guidance). We assume that such questions have no correct answer that can be taught.

Or maybe the simple truth is that adult institutions no

longer try to talk about character and virtue because they simply wouldn't know what to say. It is interesting, by way of comparison, to go back a century or so ago, before the code of the meritocrat had fully established its hegemony over education and life. The most striking contrast between the college atmosphere of those days and these is that collegians then were relatively unconcerned with grades and academic achievements, but they lived in a web of moral instruction.

Americans are famously devoted to education. New England had its first college when the Massachusetts Bay colony was all of six years old. By 1910, the United States had nearly 1,000 colleges enrolling over 300,000 students (at a time when France had 16 colleges enrolling 40,000 students). The elite universities of that day aimed to take privileged men (or, at some institutions, women) and toughen them up, teach them a sense of discipline, right thinking, and social obligation. In short, universities aimed to instill in the students a sense of honor and chivalry.

Universities were intentionally short on the creature comforts. Rooms and living arrangements were Spartan— which must have been a rude shock for the boys who grew up in aristocratic mansions (unless they'd had a taste of such conditions at Spartan prep schools). Students passed through harrowing extracurricular challenges and ordeals. At Princeton, the freshman and sophomore class would stage annual snowball fights. In actuality, they threw rocks at each other, and in the university archives are photographs of students after the contests. Their eyes are swollen shut, their lips are broken open, they have contusions across their cheeks, and there are signs of broken noses and broken jaws on many faces.

These schools tried to instill courage. "Teaching men

manhood" was the phrase in use at Harvard. Speaking for the age, Charles William Elliot, the president of Harvard, declared that "effeminacy and luxury are even worse evils than brutality." Sports, he went on, could transform a "stooping, weak and sickly youth into a well-formed robust one." Football games were so bloody, and so frequently produced fatal injuries, that President Theodore Roosevelt—who was not averse to machismo—tried to instill some restraint.

John Hibben was the president of Princeton in the teens and 1920s, in many ways a conventional elite-university president of his time. His sermons to the student body would not have seemed unusual to anyone then. But they sound odd to us because of his explicit formula for character building. He rarely gave a student address without mentioning the devil. Like many others on campus, Hibben spoke of the cataclysmic battle that takes place in every human soul. There is good and evil in each of us. We are half angel and half beast. And it is necessary to build the strength of the noble side of our character so that when the ultimate test comes, the muscles and the resources will be there to fight off temptation.

Here is an excerpt from Hibben's address to the Princeton graduating students of 1913, the generation that would soon be going off to war:

> You, enlightened, self-sufficient, self-governed, endowed with gifts above your fellows, the world expects you to produce as well as to consume, to add to and not to subtract from its store of good, to build up and not to tear down, to ennoble and not degrade. It commands you to take your place

and to fight in the name of honor and of chivalry, against the powers of organized evil and of commercialized vice, against poverty, disease, and death which follow fast in the wake of sin and ignorance, against all the unnumerable forces which are working to destroy the image of God in man, and unleash the passions of the beast. There comes to you from many quarters, from many voices, the call of your own kind. It is the human cry of spirits in bondage, of souls in despair, of lives debased and doomed. It is the call of man to his brother . . . such is your vocation: follow the voice that calls you in the name of God and of man. The time is short, the opportunity is great; therefore crowd the hours with the best that it is in you.

No doubt many of the young men in the audience that day were stuck-up country-house toffs for whom this kind of talk merely delayed a trip in their roadsters to a New York nightclub. But many of those students would go off to the trenches in France, and students from that social class died in that world war, as in the next one, in disproportionate numbers. Furthermore, many of the students raised on similar exhortations—including Teddy Roosevelt and John Reed at Harvard, Allen Dulles and Adlai Stevenson at Princeton—seem to have absorbed the idea that life is a noble mission and a perpetual battle against sin, that the choices we make have consequences not just in getting a job or a law-school admission but in a war between lightness and dark.

Today the days of the blue bloods are gone, and nobody wants them to return. We live in a much fairer society—one in which education is spread more broadly, so that the numbers of students at Ohio State and the University of Texas dwarf the numbers in the Ivy League schools. Still, the Hibbenses of the old aristocracy did take the system they were born into and articulate a public moral language, the language of chivalry and noblesse oblige. They did create activities and institutions designed to instill character.

Today's schools, unless they are religious schools, do not transmit a concrete and articulated moral system—a set of precepts instructing men and women on how to live, how to see their duties, how to call upon their highest efforts. Today's schools rarely even analyze the specific sorts of virtues this achieving culture requires, and the peculiar sorts of vices it rewards. The best members of the WASP aristocracy knew that privilege corrodes virtue in certain ways. They worked up a moral language to fight that. We have only the dimmest idea of how the achievement ethos corrodes virtue in certain other ways. And we have not begun to come up with a way to counter it.

The Obstacle Course

The achievement machine encourages some virtues. The young people who thrive in it are industrious, energetic, bright, flexible, responsible, tolerant, broad-minded, nice, compassionate, considerate, and lively.

These practices and virtues are not to be sneezed at. Moreover, the ethos presents a distinct set of challenges. Today's young people live mostly amid peace and prosperity, it is true, but has there ever been a generation compelled to accomplish so much—to establish an identity, succeed in school, cope with technological change, maneuver through the world of group dating and fluid sexual orientations, and make daily decisions about everything from multiple careers to cell-phone plans, all the while coping with a blinding diversity of friends, neighbors, and social patterns?

Meritocrats acquire accumulating personalities. They accumulate not only knowledge and skills, money and things, but also ideas, experiences, beliefs, and precious moments. But—and here's the key question—how do you organize your accumulations so that life does not become just one damn merit badge after another, a series of résumé notches without a point?

The life built around self-fulfillment and capacity maximization is one of flexibility, change, improvement, and ascent. But where in that life is there room for character, which is stolid, heavy, immovable, and inconvenient? Throughout each day society reinforces the message "You must be an arrowshot moving ever upward into the stratosphere toward your best self." At rare moments in life, commencements and other high-minded occasions, society also adds, "You must also be an oak planted stubbornly into the bedrock of moral truth." How do you become an oak that is also an arrow? How do you do that in the cracks of your eighteen-hour day? College students search earnestly for the wise old head that will answer that question. They hunger for the solution. But that is the one subject on which the authorities are strangely silent.

True Ambition

When America's young strivers do seek out moral instruction, they're confronted with people who offer them impossibilities. On the one hand, there are moralists, mostly but not entirely on the left, who tell them to renounce commercialism, materialism, and vulgar endeavoring. Live simply. Be content. Slow down, make boysenberry preserves, and read romantic poetry. These are modern progressive stoics. Then there are those, mostly but not entirely on the right, who tell young people to become Augustinians. Develop a consciousness of the permanent nature of humanity and of original sin. Be aware and confront the tragic nature of existence. Commit yourself to the fixed truth of natural law, and submit to the traditions of orthodox faith.

Both these moral traditions are noble. The only problem is that they are both so antithetical to the optimistic, climbing, burbling nature of American life as to be almost irrelevant. The hopeful young products of the achievement machine are not, in the full bloom of youth, going to renounce success, striving, and material things. They may buy some country furniture as a token homage to their well-intentioned desire to live simply and reject material things, but they will use the farmer's table as a computer stand, and they'll be back surfing the Net.

The hopeful American dreamers, who have their heads filled with visions of their own future glories, are never going to develop the tragic view of life that is supposedly the prerequisite for the probing and profound soul. They are not going to cultivate moral depths by contemplating the permanence of sin. They may go to a church, even a conservative one, but their faith will be optimistic and sunny, filled with good news, not a battle against depravity. They will have imbibed the centuries-old American assumption, born out of abundance and experience, that everybody, except maybe Hitler, is well intentioned in his heart; everybody wants to do what is right.

It is unrealistic to think that American dreamers are going to embrace moral philosophies that are incompatible with American life as it is actually lived. If there are to be character-building philosophies, and a moral vocabulary suited to real-life American students, they will have to grow out of the ascent-assuming nature of real life.

We can make the climb meaningful by lengthening the horizon of ambition, by reminding our students and ourselves that the goal is not the big house, the happy retirement, or even the noble reputation—though those things are fine—but knowing that each ascent is connected to a larger historical mission, and that mission will be realized only across generations and by institutions that transcend an individual lifetime.

The chief temptation these students face is not evil, it is nearsightedness. Parents, teachers, and coaches hone them for the future but not the distant future. As a result, students know there are hoops to jump through: school, tests, graduation. But the terrain beyond is fuzzy. They are rarely asked to apply their imagination to the far-off horizon—to envision some glorious errand for themselves, then to think backward from that goal.

During my time on campuses, I have met many students who accepted the system's definition of success. The system encouraged them to get into college, and they did that. The system said that Stanford, Duke, Northwestern, and a handful of other schools were the definition of success. So they achieved that. Then the system encouraged them to get into law, medical, or business school, so they were headed for that. I've met students who took the

LSATs, the MCATs, and the business-school admissions tests, figuring they'd see what sort of test they did best in, then head for that line of work.

I meet students who have a secret passion for philosophy but major in economics under the mistaken impression that economics represents a higher step up the meritocratic ladder. I meet students who apply for the special competitive majors and programs not because they have any interest in the curriculum, but because if something is hard to get into, then it must be good, so it is a prize they must grasp. I meet students who feel compelled to do summer internships at investment banks and consulting groups because the system encourages that kind of ascent-oriented summer job. These students know that all spring, people will be asking them how they're going to spend their summer. They don't want to answer, "Lifeguarding," because that will make them sound like losers in the climb up the ziggurat of success. They are engaged in objectless striving, working furiously at one level, so they can be admitted into the next and more exclusive arena of striving.

If I were a magazine entrepreneur, I would start a magazine called "CareerPaths." Each issue would describe how various successful people got where they are. Many bright college students don't have a clue about the incredible variety of career paths. They don't have the vaguest notion as to how real people move from post to post. Some students believe they are facing a sharp fork in the road. They can either sell their souls for money and work eighty hours a week at an investment bank, or they can live in spiritually satisfied poverty as an urban nursery school teacher. In reality, of course, the choices between wallet and soul are rarely that stark. Other students operate under the assumption that there are only six professions in the world: doctors, lawyers, corporate executives, and so on. They haven't been introduced to the massive array of unusual jobs that exist; as a result, they fall into the familiar ruts. In a weird way, the meritocratic system is both too professional and not career-oriented enough. It encourages a professional mind-set in areas where serendipity and curiosity should rule, but it does not give students, even the brilliant ones at top schools, an accurate picture of the real world of work. And if these students are myopic about career prospects, you can imagine how unprepared they are to imagine what a human life should amount to in its totality.

If you go to college alumni offices, especially at smaller schools, you will sometimes find the alumni books. At the fifth- or tenth- or twenty-fifth-year markers, alums are asked to write one-paragraph summaries of how they have spent their time since graduation. These entries make for sobering reading. Some people—the ones we would all regard as successful—who have made partner or president have written paragraphs so mind-numbingly boring that they make your mouth hang open and your eyes dry up. They know their paragraphs are boring, and they apologize for it in the text, but there is nothing they can do about it. Within the lines of their little essays, one finds this retroactive question: What imaginary future did I hope to achieve beyond jumping through the next hoop placed in front of me?

Nobody expects twenty-year-olds to have life figured out. But the Achievatron rarely forces students to step back and contemplate the long term. It rarely forces students to think in terms of how a complete life should be lived. When they get together and talk about their futures, it is always in that semiknowing tone that they are involved in a game, and they have to figure out the rules to get to the next level.

And if you do push students in this way, it is startling how modest they tend to be, especially if they sense that someone other than they might someday read their mission statement and laugh at them. "I will start a business," one may declare, or "I will retire at age fifty and sail the world." What would be wrong with imagining something truly big? "I have a mission to help create a world in which all nations are democratic"; or "I have a mission to help create a world in which there is no cancer"; or "I have a mission to help create a world in which there is no starvation"; or "I have a mission to devote my life to God's word." These are all callings to which one could valuably surrender oneself. They all demand impossibilities and in this way are fit objects of hope. Each is an incorruptible dream that would redeem the normal material efforts that inevitably occupy many of our everyday hours. None can be achieved within a single lifetime, so each connects its bearer with the flow of history and the lives of those yet to be born.

Yet envisioning such a mission—thinking creatively about what you should devote your life to, exploring the range of missions that are out there, measuring which mission is highest, and which is best suited to your talents—is an ambitious and unrealistic activity virtually ignored by the vast achievement machine. They are too grand and pretentious and unprofessional. The paradox of modern American life, especially in regard to the young, is that while it seems driven by ambition, its citizens are not ambitious enough.

CHAPTER SEVEN

Shopping

LET US NOW MOVE from the ordeals of youth to a few pastimes of adulthood. The quest for perfection doesn't stop when we hit the age of majority. In fact, it never stops.

We adults look around, for example, and observe that while brain surgeons and Nobel laureates probably have their good points, surely glossy-magazine editors are the most impressive people in America. Every month, in the front of their magazines, many of them have to write those six-hundred-word columns with titles like "From the Editor's Desk" or "Welcome" that are supposed to establish rapport with readers. There's usually a signature on the bottom of the page to make it seem personalized, and a photo of the editor herself looking sensational yet casual.

Since nobody wants to read a lifestyle magazine edited by a shlump, the editor has to use the text to establish that she is perfect yet not stuck-up about it. She drops little hints about how she pays infinite attention to all the things we're too disorganized to master; she spends her morning sorting truffles at farmers' markets, her lunch hour hand-painting scenery so her gifted children can perform back-yard puppet shows in French and Italian, and her evenings jetting off to obscure ski resorts in Iran that use ponies instead of ski lifts. Yet while she is creating the impression of flawless accomplishment in all facets of the art of living, she also has to show that she is fetchingly modest and neighborly. She's just like us. She gets annoyed by the foibles of life—say, over-air-conditioned villas in Andalu-sia—just as we do. And if she bumped into us in the super-market, she'd really, really like us, and she'd want to share intimacies over extremely well-selected coffee.

Donna Warner, editor of *Metropolitan Home*, men-tioned in one editor's letter that she'd been searching for a pocketbook for months. But her problem, darn it, was that she was too discerning. "My problem is that I know exactly what I want (and I do mean *exactly*)." And before you can say Ritz-Carlton, she has us jet-setting around the world in search of the right shoulder strap. "I pursued my purse in Paris and went on a satchel search in San Fran-cisco. Naturally, I've been all over Manhattan at length."

Naturally!

"Every time I get on a plane my heart races," writes Dana Cowin of *Food & Wine* in the tone of obligatory enthusiasm that is essential to this genre. "No, it's not fear of flying—it's the anticipation of adventure. When I toured Burgundy on a bicycle trip organized by Butterfield & Robinson, I spent my days pedaling along vineyard roads and my nights learning about wine from local vintners. In

San Francisco, I walked every inch of the Italian enclave of North Beach, in search of divine espresso and homemade focaccia." Amazing. We have done the same thing while touring our local strip malls on a trip organized by the $14.95 Airport Service Van Company.

Jane Pratt, the editor of *Jane,* looks cryogenically youthful in her funky but fun editor's picture. "Kate White, who's the editor of *Cosmo* and one of the genuinely nicest people, had heard that I'd just gotten engaged and ran up to congratulate me after the Tommy Hilfiger show this morning," Jane gushes. But that doesn't mean she's uptight about the coming event. "The wedding day is still not something I'm just living for. Actually, last night I suggested putting it off for another year and Andrew said, 'Whatever you want, honey.' See, isn't he the greatest?"

You'd think spending month after month, year after year, churning out page after page on lip-gloss trends, armoire placement, or powerboat design would get you down, but these editors have, to use their favorite word, *passion*. They spend their lives in perpetual bouts of rapture and delight, finding new product lines they just have to show us. "We have a passion for our families, for our pets; we love to be surrounded by wonderful things to look at and listen to, or we live in anticipation of the next great meal. We love our homes and the way our homes look," writes Dominique Browning of *House & Garden,* speaking for all of us who join her in the magic circle of subscribers.

And these editors get to share it all with us. The other theme of these letters is that the issue you hold in your hand contains unimagined riches—glorious prose, fascinating features, original and useful ideas—and that the editors happen to be so fortunate (read, brilliant) as to have it all come together under their direction. Few other professions require such regular self-puffery. But these glossmasters pull it off—and with such falsely modest charm—because it's not about them. It's not about the advertisements. It's not about the products. It's not even about the self. It's about something much wider and more profound. "Fitness is about living a balanced life, one with physical, mental, emotional and spiritual growth and change," writes Barbara Harris, the editor of *Shape* magazine.

It's about the highest aspirations, the noblest causes. Dominique Browning, who is the Goethe of this field, enlisted us one month in her crusade against bad pruning. "I detest the amputated limbs, branches lopped off abruptly at midsection. . . . Such practices leave stumps that aim heavenward and yet are hopelessly thwarted in their yearning. . . . I can almost hear the torment and accusation in those stumps—testimony to the cruel cancellation of life." We are marching in solidarity with the great-souled editor.

Similarly, Michael Molenda, editor of *Guitar Player* magazine, laments the decline of culture: "Sound bites and media 'Cliffs Notes' are the opiate of the short-attention-span masses. We don't read. We don't question. We don't honor—or even have much knowledge—of the past. We're living in the 'whatever' years, where avoiding responsibility is a national pastime." Food for thought for amp enthusiasts.

By the time you get to Martha Stewart's magazines, you're almost impressed that whatever little disagreement she might have had with the Securities and Exchange Commission, she hasn't bought in to the falsely-modest etiquette. She doesn't even pretend to be just like us. In

Martha Stewart Living, she prints a monthly calendar mapping out her schedule over the coming days: March 27—take down and clean storm windows; March 28—appear on *The Early Show* on CBS; March 29—accept the Iphigene Ochs Sulzberger Award at the Waldorf-Astoria; March 30—prune raspberry canes. You're lucky the woman lets you buy her magazine.

And that's really the purpose of America's magazines: to help you get better, deeper, in fact, perfect. If you don't feel you are leading the perfect life, all you have to do is go over to the nearest magazine stand, and you're confronted by a buzzing hive of self-improvement. At every angle and for every taste, there are magazines to tell you how to make one little niche of your life better. In the health section, there are more "Buns of Steel in 20 Minutes a Day" cover stories than can be imagined. The magazine *Malt Advocate* fills you in on the merits and demerits of oak bourbon casts. *Murder Dog,* the magazine on rap artistry, contains stray hints on how to keep your pants up while the waistband is floating magically around your thighs. *Robb Report* has advice on how you can improve the atmosphere of your wet bar by selecting just the right whale-foreskin bar stool. For lovers of small cylindrical carnivores, there's a publication called *Ferrets USA,* which discourses on the pros and cons of four-story ferret bungalows, the charms of ferret-motif personal checks, and the virtues of Totally Ferret snack treats. This journal offers its readers, who apparently have high saccharine tolerances, examples of adorable ferret names, such as Popcorn, Poochins, and Cutems.

You look around the magazine racks, and there is no aspect of human existence that doesn't have some periodical offering advice on how it can be made better. You wouldn't be surprised to come across *ToughGums: The Magazine for Frequent Flossers* or *Inhale! The Bellysucking Monthly for the Embarrassingly Overweight* or *Pluckings: The Magazine of Tweezer Enthusiasts*. If you page through these magazines, you find that the devotees of each obsession are contemptuous of people who haven't taken the time to master their pathetically small sphere of expertise. Foodies can read *Chile Pepper* magazine, in which the editors seem to disdain pepper poseurs who can't tell the difference between a habanero and a cayenne. The adventure magazines are contemptuous of overequipped nature pseuds who couldn't even tell you if their parka is made from microfibril with left-hand-coiled strands or not. I recently read a bitter attack in *Field and Stream* on "torque dorks," idiots who haven't taken the time to perfect their torque-wrench techniques and so go through life with improperly mounted tires on their boat trailers.

But no matter how accomplished you are in your own little niche world, you can never rest. Each month brings a new issue with new trends, new products, and new info. Suppose you are a reader of a shelter magazine called *Victorian Home*. That probably means you were voted Least Likely to Show Cleavage in high school. Aside from that, it should mean that you don't have to keep up with the trends. Your whole design motif is based on reclaiming something from the past. But it doesn't work that way, because with every issue, subscribers learn that as we go through the twenty-first-century, there will be new and better ways to live more Victorian. You can be more Victorian than the Victorians.

The readers want it. Somewhere in the furnace of their bellies, there is a little voice telling them to be better Victorian decorators, better ferret equippers, better outdoor-adventure trekkers. There is some impulse to autopyg-malianism—the urge to transform oneself from the humdrum drone you used to be into the perfect God of the Rugged Adrenaline (if you read the adventure magazines) or the Goddess of Popularity (if you read *Cosmo*). We are so surrounded by the gospel of self-improvement that we might forget how overpowering it is. But all around us, from every magazine on the rack, there is the same cry: Go Ahead, Get Better, Go Ahead, Get Better. Work harder. Learn more. Catch the trends. Buy the latest gadgets. Build the right environment. Master the right activities. Inside you is the Ideal You waiting to be born. Life can be perfect.

It doesn't come easy. Glossy magazines have found they can't draw readers with long feature stories alone. They need curricula. They need "Fifty Ways to Drive Him Wild in Bed." They need "How to Fertilize Your Garden with Shredded Credit Card Come-ons." They need "The Six Things You Need to Know Before You Attempt a Do-It-Yourself Nose Job."

Nothing is left unimproved. *O,* the magazine dedicated to the first letter of Oprah Winfrey's name, recently had a feature called "Walk Like a Goddess." Most O readers, even those without historically significant first initials, know how to walk—but good is never good enough. "A goddess is both graceful and grounded," the magazine informs us. How to achieve that? "Hold your head so that your chin is horizontal to the floor. . . . Fully extend your front leg with each step. . . . To lengthen the neck and spine, imagine your head is floating above your shoul-ders. . . . Rotate [your] thumbs forward to open up [your] shoulders." It all works. Get up now, start rolling your thumbs and floating your head. Pretty soon your shoulders will open like 7–Eleven, your chin will be horizontal as a patient etherized upon a table, your spine stretched out like toffee on a spool. With one exercise, you will have taken a small but fully extended step for humanity and a giant leap toward fulfilling your life mission of releasing your inner goddess.

Here we begin to see the feature that we observe so often in American life—the ability to slather endless amounts of missionary zeal on apparently trivial subjects and thereby transform them into harbingers of some larger transcendence. The glossy magazines don't exactly tackle the big subjects. Passing on those articles that must come over the transom on the Problem of Evil and the Nature and Destiny of Man, the editors of, say, *Pen World* nonetheless devote such religious fervor on the subject of stylus design that you almost get the impression something sacred is going on here. "Fasten Your Seatbelts—New Spring Pen Introductions Soar!" was the cover line on a recent issue.

Similarly, the contributors to *Fly Rod &Reel* don't get cynical because, instead of writing the great American novel, they have to spend their lives pouring out four-thousand-word essays on this year's fishing-gear innovations. On the contrary, they are genuine reel enthusiasts who seem to start butt-bouncing in their chairs when the new shipments arrive with the latest Super Speed Shaft spool, which provides total freespool, Magforce magnetic control, a take-down sideplate feature, and hard-anodized construction to resist saltwater corrosion. There's an emotion here, accoutremania, that resembles love; getting the right gear seems like a path to par, the suburban version of Zen harmony and inner peace.

For many people, the pathway to perfection is achieved through connoisseurship of extremely narrow product lines. Most of us have hobbies and interests that are completely ridiculous to many of the people around us (including and especially our loved ones). Yet our mastery of some little sphere of life, our expertise in a tiny corner of human existence, is important, part of our life's journey and part of our identity.

For example, I have a watch that only tells time. But on the racks, one finds several magazines serving the watch-nut population, for people whose self-worth depends largely on their wrists. These publications are printed on paper so rich and glossy that it might be made from butter-scotch. Each issue features a few new watches that transcend mere watchdom to become manifestations of the horologically sublime. *American Time* recently ran a cover story about Patek Philippe's Star Caliber 2000, which has 1,118 moving parts, a nocturnal sky chart, a perpetual calendar, and a chime system that exactly replicates the tone and rhythm of the bells of Big Ben at Westminster Palace. Only twenty of those watches were made, and they were to be sold in five sets of four, priced at $7.5 million per set.

In the watch magazines, there are ads for Italian display cabinets that will "exercise" the watches you never get around to wearing. There are features reassuring readers that people who have a life, such as Jay Leno, also care a lot about watches. There are profiles of watchmakers, who of course are not just engineers in a factory somewhere. They are portrayed as Watch Whisperers—profound, thoughtful men and women with European names and bad teeth who channel the ancient watch mysteries into the wristwear you see on these pages. Finally, there are instruction articles reminding you that every month brings new and better watches, new challenges for the watch aspirant, new trends to master and excellences to achieve, for why on earth would you want a grade-5 titanium case that is only 90 percent titanium, when you could have a grade-1 case (99 percent titanium) and live confident in the knowledge that if your arm is ever run over by a Boeing 747, your timepiece at least would emerge unscathed.

Sacramental Longing

Many people have commented on the luxification of American life. It's not enough to have a twenty-two-foot powerboat; a forty-six-foot inboard cruiser with sleeping cabins and bathrooms is better. The explanation for the trend is the one Thorstein Veblen sketched out in *The Theory of the Leisure Class:* People want to show off. But consider a boat nut, a person who subscribes to boating magazines, cares about boats, and gets a glow of self-validation from the knowledge that he has achieved boating excellence. Of course, such a person is going to spend his decades realizing his ever higher boating capacities. He can't buy the same boat he bought last time. He has to move up, move forward, progress to higher levels of deck superbness. This is the central fact of perpetual improvement. No hobby or passion can ever stop at its logical conclusion. It has to reach some level of otherworldly excellence that is at once completely ridiculous and somehow transcendent.

Freud thought he could get to the essence of people by analyzing their sleeping dreams. But individuals reveal more about themselves in their waking dreams. It is in the things they want, in the way they envision their blissful tomorrows, and, in particular, in the things they use to realize their perfect selves that individuals distinguish and reveal themselves. What people are doing as they page through these magazines is this: They are enjoying the longing. They are constructing fantasies of what their lives might be like, using the goods and images they see in these magazines. They are not there yet, and in truth they may never get there, but they get pleasure from bathing in the possibility of what might be, of sloshing about in the golden waters of some future happiness. They achieve a transubstantiation of goods, using products and gear to create a magical realm in which all is harmony, happiness, and contentment, in which they can finally relax, in which their best and most admirable self will emerge at last.

As a few of our most perceptive writers have noted, there is some sacred intent entwined in all the material yearning that characterizes middle- and upper-middle-class American life. In a review of a biography of John Updike, the writer Jay Tolson points out that Updike is a great American novelist precisely because he is able to capture the mystical element contained in consumer longing:

> What makes Updike a particularly shrewd analyst of civilization, particularly as it is played out on the North American continent . . . is that he perceives—really sees, with that remarkable Dutch painter's eye of his—the sacramental residue, in both the scientific and acquisitive habits of our culture. He portrays it, among other ways, in the desperate affairs and couplings of his characters, in their desire for ultimacy through the possession of

others, and in the elaborate savorings of that possession. He depicts it, too, in the fine regard his
characters have for things—their appreciation of
the subtle distinctions between, for instance, a
Toyota Camry and a Toyota Corolla.

This mystical transubstantiation takes place in the venues
of everyday life—at the magazine stand or on the train or
in the doctor's office. Paging through ads is not a lofty or
highly charged experience. Yet in these ordinary moments
of life, the imagination is going about its business: measuring different futures, cooking up semiconscious fantasies,
stoking the fires of anticipation, longing for different
goods, homes, and lives, savoring the pleasures of fantasy.

The key aspect to understand is that the imagination
never rests. As cognitive scientists are discovering, the
imagination is not some rarefied gift that artists use to
paint pictures. It's the brain at work every second of every
day, blending one set of perceptions with others.

When we pick up a cup of coffee, we experience many
sensations: the smell, the color, the feel of the cup in our
hand, the weight. These perceptions register in different
parts of the brain. Somehow the brain blends them
together. We have no idea how. This is imagination in its
most rudimentary form: blending disparate sensations. At
higher levels, the imagination blends what is with what
could be. Without our permission, and without our ability
to control it, our imagination takes physical sensations—
me looking at a perfect kitchen in a glossy magazine—and
it blends a fantasy landscape, me with my perfect family in
the perfect kitchen and the dishes are clean and the meal
was relaxed yet perfect.

Imagination is slippery. It lives halfway in the world of physical reality and half in the realm of what isn't, what could be or never could be. In the realm of the imagination, it is very hard to draw a sensible distinction between the material and the nonmaterial. When we confront a new house, or a new car, or a new blouse, we see the physical object, but our imagination is racing ahead, concocting future pleasures and possibilities.

Each of us has little templates in our minds, cognitive scientists have found, influenced by culture, genetics, and individual will, so certain products or goods set off those light shows in the imagination, while other products leave us cold. You may be aroused by the aroma of a certain wine or perhaps the sight of a certain powerboat, depending on your background and tastes. But when a product or an image in a magazine hits the right ignition button, it is like July Fourth in the brain. The imagination goes wild. The longing begins.

Fantasy Snacks

These glossy magazines are nutrition for the imagination. It's common to say that they're like pornography. *Food & Wine* is pornography for food. *AutoWeek* is pornography for cars. *Condé Nast Traveler* is pornography for beaches, and *House Beautiful* is pornography for Italian-made truffle shavers. *Playboy* and *Penthouse* have the same kind of lavish photo spreads, the same glistening perfections, the same fantasies and lusts, just for different things.

For millions of people, the ridiculously perfect images—

the worlds in which every breast is round and firm, every house is immaculate, every vacation destination is uncrowded, and every thigh is firm—are the images that arouse the imagination most powerfully. Why else would so many men spend billions of dollars a year looking at pictures of women who are nothing like real women, let alone the women they are likely to sleep with? Why else would so many people subscribe to *Architectural Digest* and pore over flawless interiors that no human beings could actually live in and that few could ever afford? Why is it that the magazines that sell best off the racks are the ones with bright photos of smiling celebrities on the cover—stunning movie stars, rock stars, royalty, and athletes who are far better-looking than the people we know, far richer than anybody around us, and are depicted living in a social stratosphere far removed from the realm most of us inhabit?

In short, why do we torture ourselves with things we don't have and aren't likely to get? Why do we eagerly seek out images of lives we are unlikely to lead?

It is precisely because fantasy, imagination, and dreaming play a far more significant role in our psychological makeup than we are accustomed to acknowledging. We are influenced, far more than most of us admit, by some longing for completion, some impulse to heaven. The magazine images are not really about hedonism, about enjoying some pleasure that fits into our life here and now. They're not even mainly about conspicuous consumption, finding the right item that will help us show off and look richer and more sophisticated than our friends and neighbors. These magazines are about aspiration.

What they offer is the possibility of a magical conversion process. By mastering the skills described in the magazines, cultivating the tastes, building the sorts of environment, wearing the right fashions, adopting this or that diet, I will be able to transform my present caterpillar self into the shimmering butterfly that is the future me. The magazines show us the avenue to this infinity, and they fill in, in concrete detail, the substance of our vague longings for contentment.

As Jackson Lears writes in his history of the advertising industry, *Fables of Abundance,* "Gradually I began to realize that modern advertising could be seen less as an agent of materialism than as one of the cultural forces working to disconnect human beings from the material world." Lears argues that advertisements focus private fantasy. They detail a vision of the good life. They validate a way of being in the world. They are, he emphasizes, a way of reanimating material existence. They create playgrounds in the mind. They are one of the places adults can play, can enter into the realm of enchantment, anticipation, and ecstasy.

Lears is not entirely sanguine on the subject of ads. Dubious at best about capitalism and the marketplace, he is disturbed that they implicitly construct an image of "a striving self in a world of fascinating but forgettable goods." Imagination is not only more important than we tend to admit, it is more double-edged. It tricks us into doing things that we probably shouldn't do, into wanting things that we probably don't need. It is never content with the here and now. It is often the enemy, not the friend, of sober contemplation and quiet reflection. It's no accident that it is often the most imaginative people who lead the most disorganized lives.

Stairways to Paradise

Some people see advertisers as devious manipulators who manufacture wants and create dissatisfactions. That's not quite right. The people who look at advertisements *want* to want. They are not passive victims in these fantasies.

Turn the pages of any magazine, and what is there on offer but a yearning for ultimacy? Every magazine has its own vision of heaven and its own way to get there. For example, *Architectural Digest* offers a heaven for those whose ideal of perfection revolves around recently renovated horse farms decorated in tastefully muted color palettes. In the paradise of this magazine, the homes are inevitably rustic yet elegant. The rooms are intimate while generously proportioned (stretching as they do through several zip codes). Clients and interior designers work in perfect accord, much as the lion lies down with the lamb, delighting in the Italian carved giltwood half-urns for the master bedroom, exulting in the early-American quilts that set off the Japanese lanterns on the George II mahogany side tables, expiring with satisfaction in the perfectly shaded bed of lavender that lines the hillside adjacent to the vineyard.

In the promised land revealed in *Architectural Digest,* everything is immaculate. The Han Dynasty sideboards are unscuffed, the Flemish throw pillows don't bear so much as a crease. The homes look like they are lived in by people who vacuum the inside of their toasters and floss their Oriental carpets to stand all the little hairs up straight. In fact, in this heaven, there are no people. The rooms are almost always shown deserted. The sheets on the beds look virginal, and while the dining rooms are sometimes shown already set, with soup poured in the china, it is clear that no actual human could ever be permitted to exhale amid such pristine perfection. It's as if the houses are so wonderful, the owners and their design professionals spontaneously combusted with joy while taking a final savoring gaze at the Bauhaus motifs in the pigeonierre.

There is another set of magazines for people whose idea of heaven is a little more populated and close at hand. These are the women's lifestyle magazines, such as *Real Simple, Ladies' Home Journal,* and the alphabetically challenged *O.* These are magazines for women who have learned the hard way that they will have to provide for themselves all the things they once thought they were going to get from men: steady support, soft reassurance, patient pleasure, creative inspiration, open-hearted emotion. Still, they can dream.

In these magazines, claw-foot bathtubs are always placed lusciously in the center of vaulted-ceilinged bath-spas. Though the children can be heard working on their college applications in the family room, and the faint aromas wafting from below suggest that the husband is whipping up his special pasta primavera while doing his pec-flexing exercises in the kitchen, the wife is left alone to luxuriate in her neutrally colored bathtub, sloshing about lazily with her exfoliating sea sponge, and savoring the lemongrass aromas of her decaffeinated Persian tub tea.

The heaven of these magazines is an unharried sanctuary. Children bid for their mother's attention only when they are adorable. Oversize comfy sweaters and tube socks are considered the height of sexiness. Maya Angelou lives next door and drops by to offer marmalade, warmth, and validation. Every husband is James Taylor, and his main longing is for nights of soft cuddling. In this realm, women delight themselves by creating whimsical yo-yo designs, which they share during the legendary birthday parties they organize for their kids. Evenings are spent in pajamas eating popcorn while watching old movies and giggling with extremely unsulky teenage daughters. Not only are the husbands James Taylors, they also leave love notes on the pillows, read Barbara Kingsolver novels in the Jacuzzi, and make perfect snow angels come wintertime.

There are, of course, other heavens envisioned in the panoply of American niche magazines. For example, if you decide at some point in your life to become an outlaw biker, there are publications like *Easyriders* to help you become the best outlaw biker you can possibly be. In the biker heaven revealed on page after page, all the men and women have kick-ass, crotch-quaking hogs—perhaps with six-inch 44-magnum risers, an Andrews B grind cam, a set of Wiseco .030-over pistons, Axtell cylinders, and an S&S carb all packed into a Big Twin Chrome Horse frame. In this heaven, all the righteous bikers live up to the highest codes of outlaw connoisseurship, which essentially consists of taking everything approved of by readers of *The New York Review of Books* and doing the opposite.

Biker badasses roar through this promised land with their flaming-skull tattoos, their Dixie bandannas, their ZZ Top hair-explosion beards, their POW/MIA flags, and their "I Do Drunk Chicks" T-shirts stretched across their fuck-you bellies. In biker heaven, all the men are masters of witty repartee—"Show us your tits!" All the women chug beer from the pitcher and dream of becoming strippers. Anybody who would wear pastels is in hell.

Biker heaven is a garrulous place. The magazines are

filled with photos of delirious masses of black leather-clad biker dudes gathered at rallies. It's like the blessed union of the conspicuously nonhygienic. There are pictures of people smokin' and cruisin' and flashin' and chuggin' and mud-wrestlin' and huggin' and practically fornicatin', and everybody looks absolutely ecstatic to be joined in the brotherhood of the bike.

Stogie Utopia

Finally, and impressively, cigar lovers have their own paradise dreams. Their magazine, *Cigar Aficionado,* is a huge caramel slab of a magazine, and each month it features a celebrity on the cover with a humongous phallic symbol in his or her mouth.

Like all niche consumer magazines, *Cigar Aficionado* is built upon a series of pointless discriminations. There can't be just one or two cigar shapes; there have to be four hundred. Some of the cigars reviewed in the magazine are thick and rounded and look like nuclear submarines, others are fat and bulbous and look like the Hindenburg, others are menacing, like a railroad spike. Some scientist should do a study to see if cigar owners experience a phenomenon similar to what happens to dog owners: Do their penises come to resemble the rods they stick in their mouths?

Of course, the magazine also provides all manner of self-improvement advice for people who aspire to a cigar-centered lifestyle. Some of the articles seem superfluous— "Swearing Is Fun"—but many must be useful: shopping routes in Havana; fine points in the art of cigar rolling; price trends in the cigar auction markets (where prices can top $1,400 per cigar); how to use knives, piercers, and single- and double-blade guillotines to cut your stogie.

The perfect *Cigar Aficionado* reader pulls his Lamborghini up to his oceanfront home, which has one of those humongous built-in aquariums that look so good in casinos and your better class of Chinese restaurants. His cell phone is smaller than his fingernail and doubles as a sex toy for one-night stands. His exquisitely cut Anderson & Sheppard suit whispers as he walks, and his custom-made John Lobb Ltd. shoes are so soft they barely leave an imprint in his shag carpets. As he sips his four-hundred-year-old port and slips one of his platinum-edition James Bond DVDs into the stadium-sized high-definition diamond-vision media center, he contemplates whether it is really worth it to travel to Russia just so he can break the sound barrier in a rented MiG, or whether his time would be better spent at the Dean Martin fantasy camp for frustrated crooners.

The remarkable thing about *Cigar Aficionado* is that it allows readers to demonstrate how effectively they, too, have lived up to the magazine's beau ideal of perfect living. In the back of most issues is a section in which readers send in photographs of themselves and their friends enjoying cigars, and the magazine publishes them page upon page. Now, it should be said that all photograph albums are partly propaganda efforts. None of our lives are one-tenth as happy and successful as the ones depicted in our albums. We enlarge the good and edit out the bad or unflattering. We do it because we want to trick our future selves—and our neighbors, if we can get them to look—into believing that compared to the drab gray lives of other people, our own existence has been an endless string of multiple-climax fulfillments. We like to live imaginatively in the ideal of the past as well as the future.

But the photo albums in the back of *Cigar Aficionado,* even measured against the normal distortions of the genre, are quite remarkable. The cigar is never the point. These are trophy photos meant to display some awesome level of personal achievement or magnetism, pictures of already achieved heaven. The shots generally were taken during some moment of testosterone-rich wonderfulness. There will be a bunch of guys in extra-extra-large golf shirts with tobacco logs sticking out of their grinning teeth on the eighteenth green at Pebble Beach. There will be a bunch of guys with tobacco logs sticking out of their grinning teeth on some Vegas pool deck. There will be a bunch of women at a bachelorette party, who, upon seeing themselves in this magazine, will realize that no matter how virtuous a woman may be in real life, it is impossible to look chaste in a cocktail dress with an eight-inch rod sticking out from between your lips.

Many of the people who submit shots look like normal, unobjectionable, and marginally tasteful human beings. But the best photographs do not come from the dignified Winston Churchill wing of the cigar-loving community. They come from the "You da' man!" Joey Buttafuoco wing of the cigar-loving community. So some of the shots of cavorting males imply their own captions: "A Big Night at Hooters" or "When We Wear These Shades, We Think We Look Like the Blues Brothers" or "Five Seconds After This Picture Was Taken, We All Started Air-Guitaring."

The photographs tend to fall into three genres. There is first the Men and Their Toys genre. There will be a shot of a guy with a big cigar in his mouth, posing in front of a gleaming Lincoln Navigator with vanity CIGR LOVR license plates, looking so proud of himself you'd think he'd just given birth to the thing. The best shot I ever saw in this genre featured a cigar smoker crouching in front of his Corvette, with his three-car garage and two rider mowers visible in the background—a masterpiece of compressing all of one's penis-augmentation devices into one small photograph.

Then there is the Expense Account Living genre, of people gathered in luxury boxes at college football games, at resort hotels for sales conferences, and best of all, at casino cigar bars. These latter shots, presumably taken at Sylvester Stallone film festivals, tend to picture men whose fashion sense is a delightful blend of George Hamilton and the Russian mafia. They appear uninhibited by their planetarium-sized bellies. They are outfitted with the full array of male hand jewelry—pinkie rings, bracelets, and multiple-warhead Rolexes—bravely willing to risk getting their gold chains painfully entangled in their chest-hair toupees.

Finally, there is the I'm As Obnoxious As I Want to Be genre. In the normal life cycle of the working male, there are many moments when one must be obsequious. But there comes a butterfly moment around middle age when it is no longer necessary to be deferential to bosses, solicitous toward clients, on eggshells with teenage children. During this stage, a man can let his inner Wart Hog out for a romp.

Men who have not yet achieved this level of freedom tend to venerate their Wart Hog–liberated peers. The extremely arrogant fifty-five-year-old male has always been a venerated figure in our culture—Howard Cosell, Bobby Knight, Bill O'Reilly, etc.; men so free that they can tell the whole world to go to hell.

The extremely grand Robusto is to the obnoxious middle-aged male what the sword was to the chivalrous knight—his shaft, his weapon, his symbol of honor. The photographs these men submit are often to smugness what paintings by Rubens are to chubbiness. They don't care if you think menopausal men should have outgrown their fascination with assault rifles. They don't care if you think it's inappropriate for sixty-year-old men to hang around with cosmetically enhanced women who wear gold lamé E-Z Off party dresses. These men pose with their chests puffed, their hair ambitiously combed over, surrounded by bevies of women who look like they have double-platinum frequent-buyer cards from Wonderbra, and whose own handling of their own cigars can only be described as extremely fellatian.

It is impossible to imagine a British magazine running a feature like this, or a French magazine or a Lebanese magazine or a Chinese magazine. (Actually, the French invented the guillotine because they hoped to get rid of people like this.) If you glimpse the photographs quickly, they do seem to confirm the stereotype of modern Americans as crass vulgarians. But if you study the impulse behind these shots with a kinder eye—which admittedly takes Gandhian forbearance—you do see the quintessential American impulse: to depict some perfect world in which money, friendship, comfort, pleasure, and success all roll into one to create perfect bliss. These cigar aficionados have merely created images of their personal paradise and captured them in photographic form. As we see again and again in suburban life, this paradise drive, this longing to realize blissful tomorrows, can take both the highest and lowest forms, involve the most noble and the most crass qualities, sometimes in the same person or in the same hour.

Like their somewhat more reflective peers, these cigar aficionados have constructed images of what their world is like when all the work, all the self-improvement comes to fruition. Even here, in its most elemental form, the impulse to utopia is recognizable. We fancy ourselves a practical, hardheaded people. But the fact is, utopian fervor animates American life. We don't only dream of these paradises. Deep down, we expect to achieve them, and we know they are there in the future, calling to us. We are oriented toward the ideal the way a moth is oriented toward light.

Anticipatory Hedonism

If you study people as they shop, you quickly perceive that the economists' model of human behavior—in which rational actors calculate costs and benefits—doesn't explain the crucial choices. (Why do some people fall in love with Jaguars but not Corvettes?) Nor does Thorstein Veblen's model, in which consumers are involved in a status race to keep up with the Joneses. (Do you really think that's how you select your purchases? And if you don't, what makes you think everyone else is more shallow and status-crazed than you are? Furthermore, in a decentralizing world, which Joneses are you supposed to keep up with, anyway?)

The key to consumption is not calculation or emulation, it's aspiration. Shopping, at least for non-necessities, is a form of daydreaming. People wander through stores browsing for dream kindling. They are looking for things that inspire them to tell fantasy tales about themselves. That apple corer at Crate and Barrel can help you make those pies you've always savored; you can imagine the aromas and the smiles when you bring them out for dessert. That drill from Sears can help you build a utility closet; you can imagine the organized garage and the satisfaction of having everything in its place. That necklace is just what your wife would love; you can imagine the joy she will feel when you give it to her.

Often the pleasure that shoppers get from anticipating an object is greater than the pleasure they get from owning it. Once an item ceases to fire their imagination—when it no longer inspires a story about some brighter future—then they lose interest in it, and their imagination goes off in search of new and exciting things to dream about and buy. (Kids can go through this process with dispiriting speed, as anybody can tell you on a Christmas afternoon.)

People might browse through things they cannot possibly afford, simply because the pleasure they get from daydreaming in a luxury showroom compensates for the frustration of not being able to buy anything. The shoppers may play a distinctly modern game: They know that Gatorade won't make them jocks, that Nike sneakers won't make them jump like Mike. At the same time, they enjoy the fantasies and are happy to play along.

Sometimes shopping sets off a dream or a sensation that is actually revealing and true. In Virginia Woolf's short story "The New Dress," a woman tries on a dress:

> Suffused with light, she sprang into existence. Rid of cares and wrinkles, what she had dreamed of herself was there—a beautiful woman. Just for a second . . .

> there looked at her, framed in the scrolloping
> mahogany, a gray-white, mysteriously smiling,
> charming girl, the core of herself, the soul of herself;
> and it was not true vanity only, not only self-love
> that made her think it good, tender and true.

Woolf beautifully captured the way the woman's vision has both the quality of hallucination—it exists for a moment, the woman's cares and wrinkles vanish—but also the quality of truth, because in this moment, the woman sees her truest and best self, which does exist deep down.

People tend to buy things that set off light shows in their imaginations, which fit into the daydreams. For many people, shopping is its own joy, a way of envisioning a better life to come.

In his book *The Romantic Ethic and the Spirit of Modern Consumerism*, Colin Campbell calls this desiring/consuming/daydreaming state "modern autonomous imaginative hedonism." He is describing the hedonism of the not there yet. This is an imaginative hedonism rather than a sensual hedonism: When a person is deciding what to buy, she is not experiencing the good by merely fantasizing about what the experience of the good will be like. This is not an aristocratic Marie Antoinette–style hedonism practiced by people who already have access to everything. Rather, it's a middle-class Walter Mitty hedonism practiced by people—regardless of their current economic situation—who hope to fulfill their ideals someday.

Nor is it entirely benign. Campbell says that shoppers suffer from a "pleasurable discomfort"—pleasurable because they enjoy living in their daydreams, discomforting because shoppers are aware that they remain, in real life, unfulfilled. Still, shoppers are bathed in hope. The products they confront might be trivial baubles or shams, but shoppers get caught up in the romance and spend optimistically if not always wisely. Campbell argues that shopping is not the opposite of working. Shopping is not about instant gratification while work is about deferred gratification. Both activities are part of the same process of pursuing satisfaction.

The magazine stand, the department store, and the mall are all arenas for fantasy. The more upscale you go, the more imaginatively evocative the stores become. Cartier is less utilitarian than Dollar General. Lamborghini is more fantasy-oriented than Ford. People with money flock toward things that don't only serve a purpose but stir the heart. They are drawn by their imagination to move and improve and chase their fantasy visions of their own private heaven. The cash register is a gateway to paradise.

CHAPTER EIGHT

Working

WHEN I WAS A TEENAGER, I stumbled across a small paperback autobiography by Ray Kroc, called *Grinding It Out,* in which he recounted his first visit to the little McDonald's hamburger stand in Illinois. Amazed by the quality of the food and service, he told Dick McDonald, one of the owners, that they should expand the company. But McDonald was content with his life and wasn't interested in growth. "His approach was utterly foreign to my thinking," Kroc wrote, so he decided to expand McDonald's himself. He soon realized that the key to the restaurant's success was not the hamburgers, it was the fries. "The french fry would become almost sacrosanct to me, its preparation a ritual to be followed religiously."

Naturally, I was impressed by this statement of faith. If, at twelve or thirteen, I had been blessed with the same sort of entrepreneurial fervor that fired Kroc, I would have had a life-transforming moment. I would have had myself grow up to be about six-five, with a monumental head of hair and enormous teeth, and I would have become a motivational speaker. My message would be: "Find Your Fry! Follow Your Fry!" If I had done this, books like *Who Moved My Cheese?* and *What Color Is Your Parachute?*, currently in their third or fourth centuries on the bestseller lists, would be mere footnotes in publishing history. I'd be the one with the line of motivational videos, my own adrenaline-pumping Caribbean-cruise seminars, and a string of $2 million a throw pep rallies for midlevel corporate dreamers in minor-league hockey arenas.

"Find Your Fry! Follow Your Fry!" would suggest the key to success in this world is having the ability to focus an entire lifetime's worth of zealotry onto one small thing, product line, or concept. Religious people spread their zealotry around on a vast theology. Political zealots spread theirs across a huge vision of society. But Ray Kroc's fanaticism lasered down on that one thing, the fry. For him, the fry was the alpha and the omega, the burning center under his magnifying-glass-concentrated beam of energy and ambition.

So you must Find Your Fry! (In motivational speaking, you cannot be stingy with upper-case letters and exclamation points.) You must find the insight or product wrinkle that will become your own personal key to paradise. Once you encounter that life-altering moment when you and your Fry! become one, every waking hour is devoted to your Fry! Every thought, when you are twenty and when you are sixty, is devoted to the ultimate realization of your Fry! And you come to believe that your Fry!, if you can only perfect it, will change the world. If you can make the perfect Fry!, then peoples will unite, enmities will fade, history will come to a glorious completion, and you, not coincidentally, will become enormously rich and successful. You will not only be revered and emulated, you will join the other Fry! followers in the stratosphere of success. The secret to American economic success is that we have millions of people in this country capable of devoting intensity to infinitesimally narrow product niches.

This is the country, after all, where it wasn't good enough to have liquid highlighters. Somebody dreamed up the exciting possibility of nonliquid highlighters. This is a country that offers consumers an infinite variety of change sorters (none of which work) and more designer-water options than the mind can comprehend. In America we have space-saving pop-up dish racks, prewaxed home dusters, turkey- and bacon-flavored dog biscuits, and self-propelled vacuums. If you open up the SkyMall catalog from the airplane seat pocket during your next flight, you can browse for wristwatch-style motion-sickness sensors, illuminated-shaft safety umbrellas, rechargeable candles, the extra-slim Martin backpack guitar, automatic rotating blackjack card dealers, built-in compass cuff links, and antibacterial toothbrush purifiers. Behind each of these ingenious and highly unnecessary items there is some inventor, some tinkerer, some junior Thomas Edison dreaming of his patent-protected millions, and of his contribution to humanity. And for every product and innovation there is a larger army of sales reps hawking it, production managers building it, senior executives managing it, and IT professionals organizing data about it.

"Would anyone but an American," a nineteenth-century

visitor asked, "have ever invented a milking machine? or a machine to beat eggs? or machines to black boots, scour knives, pare apples, and do a hundred things that all other peoples have done with their ten fingers from time immemorial?" Maybe, maybe not. But it is true that in this land of two hundred iced-tea flavors and four hundred shower-head designs that people get ahead by finding their Fry!

And it is not only gadgets. It is management procedures, consulting schemes, best practices notions, Six Sigma philosophies. Sales conferences across the land are filled with slightly deranged enthusiasts earnestly pushing their own conceptual breakthrough that will build teams, enhance customer loyalty, revolutionize corporate governance, ensure profitability, unify mankind, assure eternal peace and global understanding, and trim flabby thighs all in thirty days! At a business conference for food executives in Miami, I saw the world's fourth best yo-yoer give a motivational talk. The yo-yo was this man's Fry! He did amazing tricks and told the executives that they should approach their work with a sense of play. Yes! They wrote it down. A sense of play! Maybe one of them was having a Fry! moment.

You can see the Fry! followers every day in the magazines, or in the course of your daily life. They are obsessed, they are passionate, they are driven, and they are totally nuts. They could even be accused of being slightly narrow. "People ask me, 'What do you do? Golf? Tennis?' I say, 'I do ice, I just do ice,'" the ice merchant James Stuart told *The New Yorker*. Here are some samples from a single day's edition of *The Wall Street Journal*:

When Helen Greiner was eleven, she went to see *Star Wars,* and saw R2D2 and thought, Robots! She devoted her life to small robots. She went off to MIT, interned at NASA's Jet Propulsion Lab, and now she runs iRobot Corp., which is going to build little robots. Within ten years, she insists, every U.S. home with a computer will have a robot, too. "If we don't take robotics to the next level," she told the *Journal* reporter, "we'll have a lot of explaining to do to our grandchildren."

Charles Lieber dedicates himself to growing nanowires only a few atoms thick, which will conduct electricity. "It's really an amazing time. . . . My students are working day and night, and . . . I've never worked so hard in my life," he exclaims.

Mary-Dell Chilton is working on a technique to place new genes at specific spots on plant chromosomes. "I am in the lab day, night, Sundays, and holidays," says the woman who has been labeled the Queen of Agrobacterium.

Some people spend their lives flitting from occupation to occupation, imagining that if they could only find the product or dream that would ignite their passion, then all fulfillment would be theirs. But of course it's not the product that supplies the fulfillment but the obsession with excellence in whatever niche you stumble into. Many of these Fry! followers didn't grow up thinking they would devote their professional lives to the cause of idiot-proofing electric can openers. Many of them didn't dream of becoming water choreographers for casino fountains, or of imposing account-sharing and cross-selling information systems across a range of autonomous business units at a major corporation. But then they found themselves in a job, and after a while they were absorbed. Gradually, they came to feel they had found their place in the cosmos. Or perhaps it happened all at once. Perhaps there was that magic day when they read in a magazine some little datum—say, that in 1961, 90 percent of American children were potty-trained by age two and a half; by 1997, only 22 percent were, and it hit them: Pull-Ups diapers! Millions of parents will need pull-up diapers for their unpotty-trained three-year-olds. A Fry! was born.

Confronted with some specialized task that seems at first glance to be a certain formula for brain death, many people find a challenge, a hope, and an opportunity to transform their lives.

The Quiet Zealots

It is not brains that are most closely correlated with business success, it is persistence and intensity. Thomas J. Stanley surveyed hundreds of millionaires for his book, *The Millionaire Mind,* and according to his research, millionaires are not exactly Einsteins. The average millionaire in the U.S. had a collegiate GPA of about 2.92, a B– average. The average SAT score for the millionaires is 1190, good but not nearly good enough to get you into an Ivy League college—and that average was pulled up by the doctors and lawyers in the group, who had much higher scores than the entrepreneurs.

What matters is energy, discipline, and focus—the components of Fry! fanaticism. Stanley noticed that many millionaires have undergone a shaming experience. Somebody told them they were too stupid or too disorganized to succeed. They resolved to prove the asshole wrong.

The odd thing is that these obsessed people often look bland and uninteresting from the outside. If you wandered around some suburban American workplace, some typical cubicle farm, you'd never guess what sort of fervor burns inside certain individuals as they stand around trying to remember which is their favorite flavor packet for the company coffee machine.

I don't know if the human mind can truly grasp the tediousness of pod after pod of the highway-side office parks where many Americans now pursue their passions. I don't know if the brain, which functions on electrical impulses, after all, can measure the sheer existential nothingness of an office-park lobby in the middle of the afternoon: the empty or comatosely manned security desk; the whisper of labor-unintensive lobby vegetation, which is a grouping of sturdy houseplants and the sort of small, not very attractive trees that kill poetry on the lips. If you try to read the building directory, you fall asleep. It's a list of vacuous company names of either the three-initial-abstraction type (DRG Technologies, MLF Solutions) or the compound-word/spare-capital-letter type (SignWave, MedTech, MerchanDesign).

The buildings themselves are five-to-eight-floor layer cakes of tinted glass and composite stone. They have takeout cafés near the atrium, FedEx drop-off boxes just beside the main driveway, huddles of smokers near the outdoor fountains, airport shuttles cruising by throughout the day, and rows and rows of open parking.

You join a bunch of the cubicle-farm people in, say, a retail company upstairs in one of the conference rooms, which has views that would be considered glorious by entrance-ramp connoisseurs. If it is a working lunch, perhaps they have Southeast Asia–inspired sandwich wraps and potato chips that nobody eats because their crunch is so embarrassingly loud. The men look like the sort of daring fashionistas who, when they come home from a two-piece-suit shopping spree at Today's Man, their wives look up from the paper and call out, "What shade of gray did you buy this time?" The women do not mind that neither their company ID badges nor their navy blue work suits were identified as the height of fashion during fall shows in Milan this year.

These cubicle-farm folk spend their pre-meeting chatter time complaining about coworkers, or which personnel moves were listed in the latest issue of *POP,* the trade journal for people in the point-of-purchase industry. Yet deep inside one or two of them is this obsession, this Fry! fantasy. Perhaps one of the people at this table dreams of revolutionizing supermarket razor displays and has exactly the concept to do it. Perhaps another is contemplating breaking off to start a company that markets the little concrete bumps that prevent you from pulling too far into your parking space at the mall. Perhaps one of them has figured out how to build cardboard display signage that is hollow inside, and thus 30 percent cheaper to produce. Maybe others spend their days thinking about how to reduce glare on cash-register display screens so that older employees can read them better; or perhaps they obsess over how to speed up the receipt printer so the checkout lines can move a tiny bit faster.

These are the drivers of the American economy. The press concentrates its attention on the remarkable figures, the dot-com geniuses, the zillionaire investment bankers, or the paradigm-shifting, over-the-horizon-peering, outside-the-box-thinking corporate rebels who let their wacky but brilliant employees scooter down the company hallways while squirting each other with Super Soaker water cannons. But the real engines of American capitalism are the people you see in the most unremarkable locales—sitting around in the bland office parks or checking in to the suite hotels.

In the late 1990s, business writer Jim Collins and his research team went out to find the companies that beat the market year after year, decade after decade. He found that the real growth leaders were the sort of dowdy companies that worry about the speed of cash-register-receipt printers and send their budget-conscious middle managers on the road to Residence Inns: Walgreens, Kroger, Wells Fargo, Circuit City, and Pitney Bowes. These companies outper-formed the overall stock market during the 1980s and 1990s by anywhere from 400 percent to 1,800 percent. They are led by quiet executives in flavorless work envi-ronments, and the book Collins wrote about them, *Good to Great*, became a huge bestseller and was devoured by a million similar executives who, on the outside, don't look any spicier.

How do they build great companies? According to Collins, they didn't capitalize on any technological revolu-tion. They are not in fast-growing industries—Walgreens builds drugstores, Kroger is a supermarket chain. They were not aggressive in mergers and acquisitions. They did not have innovative compensation schemes (in fact, their executives earned slightly less than their competitors). They did not spend more time than their competitors on strategic planning. They did not hire superstar CEOs from outside. Instead, Collins argues, they found one small thing, or a few things, they could do better than anyone else in the world, and they did that thing over and over, and they got better and better at it. They found their Fry!

One of the advantages these companies had was that they did not suffer from what Collins calls the liability of charisma. The corporate culture at these places encouraged simplicity and humility. In these places, it would have been socially unacceptable for an executive to portray himself as a flamboyant genius, a countercultural maverick, or an intellectual pioneer. The social standards encouraged self-effacing behavior, modesty, and reserve. "Throughout our research," Collins continues, "we were struck by the continual use of words like disciplined, rigorous, dogged, determined, diligent, precise, fastidious, systematic, methodical, workmanlike, demanding, consistent, focused, accountable, and responsible."

Many of these companies had been trudging along fine for several decades, but there came a point when their stock began to take off, when they moved from good to great, in Collins's terminology. Oddly, though, none of the employees knew at the time that they were involved in some dramatic transformation. They had no name for the new phase their company was going through. There was no key innovation, launch event, strategic decision, or breakthrough that correlated with the takeoff in performance. Each company had spent the prior few years attracting and promoting excellent employees, and the accumulation of small improvements built up over time and eventually cohered into rapidly accelerating growth, sustained decade after decade.

These companies are staffed by quiet zealots. One employee at Wells Fargo described its former CEO, Carl Reichardt, this way: "If Carl were an Olympic diver, he would not do a five-flip twisting thing. He would do the best swan dive in the world, and do it perfectly over and over again."

In the past few years, dozens of books have reinforced Collins's basic message. *Leading Quietly* hit the *New York Times* bestseller list. *Searching for a Corporate Savior: The Irrational Quest for Charismatic CEOs,* by Harvard professor Rakesh Khurana, argued a similar line. *Execution* hit the top of the *Wall Street Journal* bestseller list, with its message of executing and finishing your strategies rather than simply thinking outside the box and developing a revolutionary mind-set.

The world of American business is not really one of swashbuckling executives who learn the leadership secrets of Attila the Hun. In reality, it is a world of outwardly genial but inwardly intense Fry! followers. Many of them are so interested in doing their job well that they don't have the time to be flamboyant or interesting. Their self-expression often comes out in their work, not in their lifestyle. Many of them love making money and have amazingly little competence for spending it. Seventy percent of the millionaires Thomas Stanley surveyed for his books *The Millionaire Mind* and *The Millionaire Next Door* have their shoes resoled and repaired rather than replaced, and the average millionaire spends about $140 on a pair of shoes. After Visa and MasterCard, the most common credit cards in the millionaire's wallets are charge cards for Sears and JCPenney. Ford is the most popular automaker among the group. In the 1996 study, Stanley reported that the typical millionaire paid $399 for his most expensive suit and $24,800 for his or her most recent car or truck, which is only $3,000 more than the average American spent.

If you filmed a TV show accurately depicting the lifestyles of these rich and not famous, it would be hopeless. These people have incredibly low divorce rates. They still clip supermarket coupons, if only to demonstrate the value of thrift to their children. They are far less likely to gamble than other Americans. They shop at price clubs. They spend a significant amount of time with their tax consultants, trying to trim their annual bill.

You'd call them misers, but that suggests a level of devious venality they generally do not have. They simply are lifestyle-fabulousness vacuums. They live very much like regular middle-class Americans—visiting the kids, going to soccer games—it's just that they work harder, started successful companies, and have a lot more money in the bank; and somewhere inside, they've got the little burn, the little engine that, as Abraham Lincoln's law partner once said of him, knows no rest.

If a novelist or an academic sociologist set out to capture their ethos, he would probably get them wrong. He might describe them, Sinclair Lewis–style, as narrow-minded Babbitts. Or he might describe them, William Whyte–style, as Organization Men, the soulless corporate cogs who lose their identity within the company machine. However, that doesn't come even close to describing what these people are like and what motivates them. American writers are famously ignorant of American business, but they are especially ignorant about success. Even Tom Wolfe, our finest contemporary writer on these subjects, usually describes businesspeople who are in the process of failing. It is nearly impossible (discounting Ayn Rand, who is off in her own world) to find a convincing portrayal of success.

That's because it is so hard to answer the mystery of motivation. What propels the quiet zealot to work so hard?

What explains his or her hunger to go from good to great? While the ranks of corporate America are dotted with midlevel managers who are terrified of change and who just want to show up in the morning and go home placidly at night, others do have that focus and need to be significant at work, even to be the best in the world. Collins hints at this trait in his description of Colman Mockler, the former CEO of Gillette: "His placid persona hid an inner intensity, a dedication to making anything he touched the best it could possibly be—not just because of what he would get, but because he simply couldn't imagine doing it any other way."

Two Work Ethics

When you start probing for the roots of this intense drive to work and rise, you realize that history is a stubborn thing. Cultural trends crest and burst, but there are some deep features of national life that are unchanging. And one of the deep features of American life is a dogged, and many would say insane, commitment to work.

A German proverb holds that in America, an hour is only forty minutes long. Indeed, it has always been this way. Benjamin Franklin called America the "land of labor." "Everybody works," Alexis de Tocqueville observed during his journey though America, "and work opens a way to everything; this has changed the point of honor quite around." George Santayana later declared that the "gospel of work and the belief in progress" constituted the two American faiths. "Works and days were offered to us," Emerson admitted in 1857, "and we chose work."

The nineteenth-century Viennese immigrant Francis Grund came to the same conclusion, in a more rueful tone, after living in Boston for a decade:

> There is, probably, no people on earth with whom business constitutes pleasure, and industry amusement, in an equal degree with the inhabitants of the United States of America. Active occupation is not only the principal source of their happiness, and the foundation of their national greatness, but they are absolutely wretched without it, and instead of the "dolce far niente," know but the *horrors* of idleness. Business is the very soul of an American: he pursues it, not as a means of procuring for himself and his family the necessary comforts of life, but as the fountain of all human felicity. . . . It is as if all America were but one gigantic workshop, over the entrance of which there is the blazing inscription, "No admission here, except on business."

Grund may have been overstating things a bit, but his tone of mixed respect, fear, and horror exactly captures the mood in which most visitors have regarded the American work ethic.

The standard historical explanation for this mentality is that it goes back to the Puritans. Every person has two callings, Cotton Mather preached, "and is a man in a boat rowing for heaven." With one oar he pulls for salvation and serves the church; with the other he pulls for usefulness, for success, for material increase. These two callings merge, uncomfortably, in the national mind, so that success is often taken as a sign of virtue.

The central thrust of this approach to life—absorbed even by those who never heard a Puritan sermon or heard of Cotton Mather—is that salvation is earned through strenuous action. Virtue is cultivated through industriousness and will. Filtered through the secularizing pen of Benjamin Franklin and a thousand eighteenth- and nineteenth-century moralists, this gospel of work came to shape American culture.

According to this ethic, it is through work, and our contribution to society, that we define ourselves. Far from being solely a thing you do, work is a way of justifying one's existence, of fulfilling one's purpose on earth, and of creating one's identity. "But do your work, and I shall know you," Emerson declared in *Self-Reliance*. "Do your work, and you shall reinforce yourself."

The lingering power of that work ethic, especially in rural America, is impressive to behold. It is not limited to farmers and well-paid executives. Sometimes you go into a Food Lion or a rural drugstore, and you notice that the aisles are meticulous and the cans are stacked on the shelf with millimeter-width precision. Someone cares about doing a good job; it is his or her source of honor. He or she may work in an apparently dead-end job, but being a good worker is what he or she is about.

Early on in American history, a different work ethic layered itself on top of the Puritan sense of calling, and character building through diligence. This later work ethic is sweeter, more optimistic, and yet more frenzied. It was born of abundance. In America, it was immediately obvious that opportunity was plentiful. The frontier beckoned, offering an open field for development, plentiful land, and the possibilities of rewards beyond all imagining. After the physical frontier closed, new frontiers were perpetually opening up—scientific and technological frontiers, new markets, new products, and new ways of doing business.

Abundance created a distinctive mentality. People came to assume that wonders must be available here, some ultimate happiness must be realizable here, if only one could go out and seize it. The abundance mentality starts with the unconscious premise that there exists, at all times, close by, a happy hunting ground, a valley where the acre of diamonds is there for the picking. In the land of abundance, fanatical work is worth it, because it can be lavishly rewarded. In the land of abundance, a person's class status is always temporary, because nearby, a complete idiot has managed to pull himself up to the realm of Lexus drivers, so someday you will, too.

The land of abundance is the land of hope. It is true that some people hang around waiting for the future to land in their laps. In *You Can't Go Home Again,* Thomas Wolfe observed:

> It is also true, and this is a curious paradox about America—that these same men who stand upon the corner and wait around on Sunday afternoons for nothing are filled at the same time with an almost quenchless hope, an almost boundless optimism, an almost indestructible belief that something is bound to turn up, something is sure to happen.

But for many others, abundance electrifies. Work is not an obligation or a duty but a fantastic chance. It's like one of those old contests—you get to keep anything you pull down from the toy store's shelves in the next two minutes. So get going!

In the land of abundance, people work feverishly hard, and cram their lives insanely full, because the candies are all around, looking up and pleading, "Taste me, taste me, taste me." People in such a realm live in a perpetual aspirational trance. They are bombarded from first waking till night-time's last thought by advertisements, images, messages, novelties, improvements, and tales of wonder. It takes a force of willpower beyond that of most ordinary people to renounce all this glorious possibility. It's easier to work phenomenally long hours and grasp at all the candies than it is to say no. It takes incredible dedication to renounce opportunity, get off the conveyor, and be content with what one is.

Dreams of future advancement dance around one's head. "Americans are born drunk," the English sage G. K. Chesterton wrote; "they have a sort of permanent intoxication from within, a sort of invisible champagne." Accordingly, they take amazing risks, for that is the paradox of the business types. They seem dull, selfish, and sober. But inside, they are naive, childlike, and hungry. They believe everything! There is no management fad so stupid that you can't get some senior executives to buy in to it. You get these engineers who have spent their whole lives studying metallurgy, and then you feed them some dumbed-down version of Jungian psychology, and it is all brand-new to them. They think you are unlocking the mysteries of the human soul. This is the insight, they fervently believe, that will enable them to climb to the promised land. They pay you hundreds of thousands of dollars to probe the unconscious mind of the consumers of micro-wave ovens and discover the magical source of their mysterious tastes. These executives believe—desperately want to believe—that the answer to all the mysteries, the secret to market dominance, the key to their glowing transformation and earthshaking success, is just out there, just out of reach, just beyond the next door, if they could only seize it. At a builders' conference not long ago, I saw a man standing at the podium, practically screaming at the audience of five hundred people to "Be the Purple Cow!" He had been sent a copy of an article in *Fast Company* magazine called "In Praise of the Purple Cow." Brown cows are boring, the author had pointed out. But if you saw a purple cow in a field, you would notice it. So in your job, you should be the purple cow. This insight was amazing! the speaker declared. A colleague had sent him the piece with the commandment: Drop everything! Before you do anything else, read this article! It will change your life!

He'd been converted. It was fantastic! He was delirious! Now he wanted to share the secret with everyone! Be the Purple Cow! Two years before, he was probably wanting everyone to move their cheese. But that was old. *This* was the key! The Purple Cow! The secret to success and eternal happiness! The Purple Cow! was his Fry! The guy was practically beside himself with excitement. He was shouting into the microphone, and his words were infectious. People were writing them down. I found myself wanting to be the Purple Cow! too. Nobody could possibly claim that this atmosphere was simply the product of the Protestant work ethic; something far more intoxicating, as Chesterton said, was going on.

We have been blessed and plagued for centuries by

these cycles of hope and experience. Some group of sup-posedly sober investors and outwardly dull businesspeople fall into a sort of trance in which they come to believe they stand on the precipice of a radically glorious future, a transforming technology or business practice, whether it is the railways, nuclear power, or the Internet. They lose their heads. They throw money from the mountaintops into the valley of the future, hoping to raise a new utopia. Most of them end up going broke, whereupon the cycle of disillu-sion sets in, but they do usually lay the infrastructure—the railways or the miles of fiber-optic cable—that leads to real progress.

"Nothing remarkable was ever accomplished in a pro-saic mood," Thoreau wrote. And he would probably deny it, but his maxim applies as much to the supposedly pru-dential world of business as to anything else. These boring, obsessed business types dream of corporate greatness. They long to be famous through the ages as the one who refash-ioned the oral-hygiene industry, who became the Bill Gates of frozen bagels. They start companies knowing that most new enterprises fail. They contemplate massive schemes at night, then spend their days seeing if they can make the numbers work out. The hope and poetry are as vital to their success as the number crunching, narrowness, and restraint. The secret of success is being visionary and prac-tical at the same time. The American work ethic grows both out of the old-fashioned work ethic—creating oneself through labor—and out of the intoxication induced by plenty, the availability, all around, of opportunities to punch through and surpass one's fondest dreams.

The Consuming Challenge

Americans have always switched jobs with amazing speed. As historian Daniel T. Rodgers notes in his book, *The Work Ethic in Industrial America, 1850–1920*, the majority of industrial workers between 1905 and 1917 changed jobs at least every three years. A Bureau of Labor Statistics study using data from 1913–1914 found that a "normal" factory had turnover of about 113 percent. This was during depressed economic conditions, and it probably understated the amount of turnover. Very few of the workers who left work had better jobs in hand. They were just dissatisfied, hoping something better would turn up around the next bend.

Today, as we have noted, Americans remain the hardest-working people on the face of the earth. We work the longest hours and take the shortest vacations of any affluent people. Polls indicate that it is not all forced; far more than people in other lands, Americans choose to live this way. Nearly half of all Americans take the initiative to check in with work while they're supposedly on vacation: Six in ten people earning over $85,000 a year do so, according to a survey done for *American Demographics*. As the sociologist Seymour Martin Lipset observed in his book *American Exceptionalism*, "The recent comparative studies of work behavior indicate that Americans are more inclined to be workaholics than other industrialized populations."

Those Americans with the most discretion over how hard to work are precisely the ones who have chosen the longest hours. For most of human history, people at the bottom of the income ladder worked longer than people at the top. But that's no longer true. According to former labor secretary Robert Reich, over the past two decades, the percentage of American executives and professionals who work over fifty hours a week has grown by a third; their number now includes nearly 40 percent of male and nearly 20 percent of female college graduates. In a hothouse environment like Manhattan, 75 percent of the college-educated twenty-five- to thirty-two-year-olds work over a forty-hour week, whereas in 1975, only 55 percent did.

That doesn't measure the emotional intensity many Americans invest in their work lives. Many of these genial but intense workers are up in the middle of the night, scribbling down ideas. They know they need some sleep for the next day, but their brain just will not shut down. People seem to like the stress, or at least fear boring work more than stressful work. Decade after decade, in poll after poll, 80 or 90 percent of respondents say they are satisfied with their jobs. In a 1997 survey done for the Department of Labor, 69 percent of Americans told researchers they would take the same job again "without hesitation." Just 6 percent of the respondents said they would definitely not accept the same job. Yet these people still switch jobs with amazing frequency, in search of something better.

Today a phenomenal 8 percent of Americans have started their own businesses. There's a vast literature on entrepreneurship, and most of it displays an admirable grasp of the obvious (people who want to be their own boss are more likely to become entrepreneurs than people who don't). A study published in 2000 by Anisya S. Thomas and Stephen L. Mueller, in the *Journal of Interna-*

tional Business Studies, compared entrepreneurialism across cultures. They found that innovative people are spread fairly evenly over the globe. But they also found that people in the United States are more likely to feel they can control their own destinies than people in Britain, Australia, Venezuela, Colombia, and elsewhere. Entrepreneurs in America also felt more comfortable with risk than those in any of the twelve nations studied. Most of all, and most puzzling to the researchers, the study found "the likelihood of high energy level decreases with cultural distance from the United States." In other words, the farther one gets from the culture of the U.S., the less likely people are to live at the same thyroidally charged pace.

Far from wanting a comfortable, easy life, as bourgeois humans are supposed to do, the Fry! followers want a consuming challenge. They want a task that will occupy all of their faculties, temporarily blotting out everything else. According to Thomas J. Stanley's research for *The Millionaire Mind*, only 55 percent of millionaires went into their profession because of some intrinsic love of the product line, but about 80 percent went into it because they felt they would be able to realize the full potential of their abilities in this sphere.

In this way, the pursuit of gain is etherealized into a pursuit of something larger and holy, the pursuit of the fully completed self.

The Dark Side of the Fry!

You see the modern workaholics coming down the airplane aisles during boarding. They've got hands-free wires clipped to their shirt; they're trying to shimmy out of their suit coat and get their carry-on bag into the overhead rack without interrupting their cell-phone conversation. And they're talking faster and faster, because they know that in just a few minutes, the door of that plane is going to close, and they'll be ordered to turn off their phones and it'll be like someone ripped out their trachea. Cut off! Severed from the information superhighway! Restricted to the tiny capsule of their own immediate experience!

As the plane fills up, and the order to turn off the phones approaches, you can hear the tone of rising panic, like drowning people trying to get those last few gulps of life. What is it they'll miss so much? It can't be the substance of their conversations, because when you overhear them you realize this is not exactly dialogue on the order of Plato's *Republic*. Much of the time they are just narrating their own lives: "Yeah, I'm boarding a plane to Atlanta. Hold on. I'm just putting my stuff in the overhead rack . . ." You imagine that the person on the other end of the conversation is doing the same thing: "Uh-huh. I'm driving by the hardware store. I'm turning left onto Maple."

But they need it. They need the stimulation, the rhythm, the connection to the world of work, productivity, the hive of information. Somewhere in this world of roughly six billion people, there might be someone trying to reach them, with some vital bit of data that only they— indispensable as they are—can handle. And what if that person can't get through!

A few hours later, you can watch the infoholics as the plane begins its final descent. They slide their cell phones surreptitiously out of their pockets. They finger the buttons. You can see them wrestling with a moral quandary.

At five hundred feet, they are tempted to turn on the phones, because they are pretty sure they can get coverage at that altitude. On the other hand, the pilots say cell-phone use disrupts the plane's navigational system.

Usually, exercising the sort of willpower that would make a Prussian officer proud, they wait until the wheels hit the tarmac and then, all up and down the plane, you can hear the trilling of the message-alert chimes, and seconds later, all the wireless men and women are restored to life: "Yeah, I've just landed. I'm unbuckling my seat belt, and I'm going to get my travel bag from the rack . . ."

If you opened up their rolling luggage, you'd be amazed by how close these business Bedouins have come to achieving perfect wirelessness, that magical state of total freedom in which all of human experience can be replicated without once resorting to a landline. The Wireless Woman's phone has voice-dial-recognition capabilities, because who has time to press the buttons? She has an Internet-access PDA, the Web clipping service, a RIM pager (whatever that is), a stowaway keyboard, and a thong clip, in case she wants to do business by the hotel pool. Her portable DVD screen allows her to watch videos and sales presentations in the van to the car-rental lot, which was formerly unproductive time, and if she swallowed all the lithium batteries in her accessories bag, that would be enough to cure depression for life.

The Wireless Man has a ruggedized Panasonic Toughbook 27 with a magnesium case, a TreePad 2.8 Freebyte Software personal organizer, a Rage Mobility AGP video controller, and full hibernation and standby modes. If it came with special helium cavities, it would be lighter than air, and if it had a disk drive that could turn into an inflatable sex doll, he wouldn't ever have to return home. He could stay out there on the road his whole life, communing with his fellow IT junkies about the CRM solutions on his mobile and how many WAP gateways he can access from his ISP. (The tragedy of his life is that while he can talk to anybody, anytime, almost nobody understands what he is saying.)

In a decentralized business age, the wireless wanderers realize, you have to be fully gadgetized. You must be at one with the huge swirling loop of communication, the living, breathing life force of digitally harmonized human interfaces. As a result, you have so many electronics on your person that if they went off all at once, with all the beepers, buzzers, vibrators, and lights, you would look like the inside of a pinball arcade.

It is this constant sense of being connected, of novelty, of relentless if low-level stimulation—this is what the infoholic can't live without. He needs to be connected to his all-consuming challenge. His brain has adapted to rhythms of wireless life. He's become an eating, breathing network server. He knows it's given him attention-deficit disorder. He acknowledges that he has a little rhythm machine in his brain; like a nursery school teacher, he's used to having his attention ripped over to something new every forty-five seconds. He can't read ten pages of a book without stopping to do something else; part of his attention is always distracted. He answers his e-mails fast and sloppy. Even as he's working on a document on his computer, he can't help himself, the new-mail alert beeps, and he toggles over just in case it's something important. His patience is totally shot. Waiting for something feels like a moral affront. His brain has shifted to handle the incessant demands of the time-maximization ethic.

He knows that it's not healthy to live so entangled in the thicket of communication, so absorbed in the bombardment of the trivial. There are too many messages, too many websites, too many reports, too many bytes screaming for his attention. He knows there's something dehumanizing about the way he has become a deft machete wielder in the jungle of communications, ruthlessly cutting away at all the extraneous but potentially interesting data forever encroaching upon him. He never allows himself to explore some curiosity. He's never at peace. Never lost in a creative fog, never mentally at play.

Occasionally, he fantasizes about life beyond the network, a life in which his mind can wander and reflect, in which he can stop for days on end to gaze at the mountains. But that is just a dream, because the Wireless Man and the Wireless Woman are headed somewhere. They are in the grip of these twin work ethics, the Puritan obligation to justify one's existence through productivity, and the abundance-induced fever to seize all the goodies. This work ethic is not without its costs and temptations. It is relentless, and it has made the Fry! follower relentless.

On the Road

Indeed, the Fry! follower is not merely on the road, he is master of the road. Every American considers him- or herself an unusually gifted driver, a masterly commuting route strategist. Go back 150 years, and there were probably streams of Conestoga wagon drivers volubly proud of their steering capacities, amazed by how many idiots there were out on the trails that day. Today air travel is the field of competition where the wireless wonder can demonstrate his or her mastery of pointless but ego-inflating life skills. The Wireless Man has his seven frequent-flier numbers memorized. He is careful to drop a bit of knowledge on 767 design so the ticket agent will be aware he is a member of the Important People Who Fly Places club. He is insanely impressed by his own ability to almost never set off the metal detectors, and he knows which shoes will keep his winning streak going. He never stands still on the moving conveyor belts, because he feels like an airport superhero to be walking at double the normal speed. He knows never to board the plane first or second, because that person often gets pulled aside for an extra bag check. He knows that on red-eye flights, you want a window seat if you have a strong bladder and an aisle seat if you don't. He knows that on morning flights, his reading material can tax 80 percent of his IQ capacity, but on evening flights, the recirculated air is fortified with special moron enzymes, and his spy thriller had better reflect that.

If Wireless Man had an orgasm every time he was reminded the luggage may have shifted in the overhead bins during flight, he would be the happiest man on the face of the earth. He is proud of his discerning taste in rental-car companies. He is pleased with his ability to reset all the car's rearview mirrors and radio station buttons by the time he's on the access road to the highway. He can find his way in every city, even though he has never once rented a luxury car in which the OnStar navigation system actually worked.

Because of his prowess, he is recognized as something of a deity by the corporations who move people. Every piece of plastic in his wallet affirms his elevated place on the Olympus of capitalism. His American Express Card is Platinum. His American Airlines Advantage card is Double Diamond. With United he is Premier Plus. His Avis Wizard is Oriental Despot, and with Hilton Honors he is Sun God. There is no arena of modern life more subtly stratified than the world of travel.

He has access to all the thick-carpeted airport clubs with sliding doors, pretty hostesses, and plentiful mimosas, a drink he would never touch off airport property. He knows that in the world of the travel lords, you never say you are flying first class. You say you are flying up front, which sounds casual and assumed. He knows that when he settles into his wide seat, 2C, he should never make eye contact with the proles trudging back to 17F. There are more of them, and if incited, they could revolt. He knows how to slide the little mini ledge out of the first-class armrest, which is the perfect place to put his pre-takeoff nut bowl. He knows the ultimate secret of the frequent traveler, which is that all the luxuries and amenities going to the top rung of corporate fliers—the airport clubs, the first-class cabins, the express security lanes—are actually shabby and disappointing, but you must never let the folks back in coach suspect this. All that matters is that you have access—testimony to the vital role you play in the turbo of American capitalism—and others do not.

Enrichment

Off they go in the relentless pursuit of their Fry! They go to sales meetings, industry conferences, and learning seminars in sanctified pursuit of perpetual advancement. A few times a year, they find themselves at a golf resort hotel in a place like Scottsdale, Arizona, or Monterey, California, at some trade-association learning conference with a name like Leading Edge or the Leadership Seminar. They check in at the registration desk, get a canvas bag with corporate tchochkes—a company-logo baseball cap, a simulated-leather binder, complimentary popcorn—as well as an ID badge that has little ribbons down the front denoting the person's importance, so that the really big shots look like Guatemalan generals with their multicolor Speaker, Sponsor, Seminar Leader, Board of Directors, and Hall of Fame ribbons stretching down their tummy.

Such is their genuine commitment to learning that in between the closest-to-the-pin contests, the spousal spa sessions, and the Range Rover driving lessons, they will force themselves to confront the greatest evil of modern times: PowerPoint presentations.

Like the soldiers in Pickett's charge, they will march straight into the hail of bullet points. They will endure hour upon hour of jargonics, the unique sales-conference language, receiving valuable advice on how they can prioritize their cost-effective operational performance and increase network functionality while magnifying their brand power through strategic B-to-B partnering in ways that will leverage their competitive-advantage matrixes without sacrificing any of their core-competency components or their multiple-vendor, mission-critical supply-chain service-provider solution resources.

The slides flow by on the screen like one of those May Day Soviet missile parades, so that after forty-five minutes of Leadership, Quality, Change, and Excellence, the speaker could have his girlfriend's sex diary up on the screen and nobody would even notice.

Business leaders *do* go to these conferences, and they sit there hoping to learn. They don't go just for the golf and the schmoozing and the chance to wear Four Seasons terry-cloth robes down to the massage center. They go to absorb, with high hopes of having their minds expanded and their optimism refurbished. While they have been pursuing their Fry!, the whole world has been going on outside, and a speaker might let them know what they've been missing. Sometimes a speaker, if his hair is historically significant enough, and if his teeth are cosmically bright, and if his tales of winning Olympic gold are sufficiently inspiring, will cause the adrenaline to pump, the old intensity to get recharged.

A speaker may offer one of those precious takeaways, a snippet of data: a consumer trend, a quotation from Marcus Aurelius or Jack Welch, that they can clasp to their chests. Hope for the future will be reinflamed. A new tool! A new concept! A new understanding or a new opportunity! The fire will flicker a little higher in the furnace of the belly. They begin to feel again that power, that drive. They begin to feel the joy of discovery, the pleasure of creating something new, the thrill of embarking on some new project, which is the most delicious sensation in professional life.

Business learning isn't mainly about knowledge and the wisdom of the past. It's not like university lecture-hall learning. Business learning is about offering glimpses of the future and getting everybody excited enough to lunge toward the horizon again.

The Soul of the Fry!

"I hail with joy the oceanic, variegated, intense practical energy, the demand for facts, even the business materialism of the current age," Walt Whitman wrote in "Democratic Vistas." "The one thing in the world of value," Emerson echoed, "is an active soul."

The redeeming fact about American business life is that it is a stimulant. It calls forth boundless energy. Even in those boring office parks, even among those narrow workaholics who have never had a philosophical self-reflection in their lives, the successful ones are driven by some inner intensity. They must relentlessly improve, perpetually grow.

In this way, the American business class has reversed the conventional moral formulae. In classical morality, money enervates and corrupts. The Roman empire illustrated the life cycle of great nations. As the historian John Anthony Froude put it: "Virtue and truth produced strength, strength dominion, dominion riches, riches luxury, and luxury weakness and collapse." It's as inevitable as death. Nations, and individuals, grow to adulthood by virtue of their simplicity, and fall to decay because they get spoiled by comfort and ease.

But in the land of abundance, money and wealth do not enervate, spoil, and corrupt. Success is never good enough. No matter how rich you are, no matter how comfortably you live, those opportunities are still out there beckoning, calling forth more work and industry. The competition never stops.

Of course, the tragedy of the Fry! followers is that the

virtues cultivated are means, and there is a near-vacuum when it comes to ends. Many successful Fry! followers work hard, aim skyward, and treat people fairly, yet ultimately, all this effort and cultivation are still dedicated to nothing more than a fast-food item. The quest may be epic, but the goal is trivial.

The endemic temptation in the Fry! life is to become so obsessed with the process of producing a better fry or a better widget that you may stop thinking about the ultimate purpose of your life. You become enmeshed in the arduous pursuit of the unimportant. You develop a furrow mentality, driving to push the plow farther down the furrow to achieve your goal and your excellence. Eventually, you become oblivious to the fact that your whole life is lived down in the furrow. Your horizon is far but narrow.

In that furrow, your personality becomes a mere selling device. Friendships become contacts. The urge to improve deteriorates to mere acquisitiveness. Money becomes the measure of accomplishment. So much intellectual energy is devoted to outward market research that there is none left for inner observation. The language of commerce obliterates the vocabulary of morality. The imagination becomes professionalized, so you find yourself budgeting your thoughts on the useful tasks at hand, rather than letting your mind roam over the landscape and into the unexpected gullies. You live by the clock, so when you pull up to the gas station, you are impatient over the three minutes you'll have to waste while the pump slowly fills up the tank.

Throughout American history, there have always been writers who looked at the vulgarities of business life and urged their readers to renounce commerce, material striving, and that bitch goddess success. But most Americans rejected that advice, concluding that commerce, for all its obvious flaws, is the instigator that electrifies and propels. A business culture is a dynamic culture. Enterprise calls forth a vitality that is the antidote to stagnation, enervation, and mediocrity. It demands certain skills and disciplines, it forces people to pay attention to others' needs, to face reality, and to avoid retreating into the realm of self-indulgence.

Many of the best people have embraced commerce while knowing it is insufficient. They adopt a gradational ethic that begins with material striving and is meant to lead to higher aims. They start with the fry, the sincere passion for taking one little corner of the universe and making it excellent. Some take the talents, skills, and virtues that have been cultivated while pursuing their fry, and they dedicate them to things loftier even than really fine fast food.

CHAPTER NINE

A History of Imagination

SO NOW WE'VE completed our hopscotch drive around middle- and upper-middle-class America, touching down in the exurbs, among the Ubermoms, on college campuses, in the office parks, into the inner-ring suburbs, the big-box malls, and the magazine racks. What we've seen at each stop is this distinctive American energy expressed in different ways: highly programmed kids being churned through the Achievatron; ambitious college students hooking up because they don't have time for real relationships; shoppers in the thrall of advertising-inspired heavens; Fry!-following businesspeople looking for that all-consuming challenge; suburbanites moving and sprawling across the landscape.

In my travels reporting for this book, I've continually been struck by how much of American life is an attempt to live out a dream. Albert Einstein famously said that imagination is more important than knowledge, and anybody can see that Americans have a talent for fantasy. The suburbs themselves were built as conservative utopias. Children are raised with visions of ideal lives. This is the nation of Hollywood, Las Vegas, professional wrestling, and Disney, not to mention all the other fantasy factories. This is the land of Elvis impersonators, jazz improvisationalists, *Penthouse* letters, computer gamers, grown men in Michael Jordan basketball jerseys, faith healers with bouffant hair, and the whole range of ampersand magazines (*Town & Country, Travel & Leisure, Food & Wine*) that display perfect parties, perfect vacations, and perfect meals—ways of living that couldn't possibly exist in real life. This is the land of Rainforest Café theme restaurants, comic-book superheroes, Shangri-La resort hotels, Ralph Lauren WASP-fantasy fashions, Civil War reenactors, gated communities with names like Sherwood Forest Grove, and vehicles with such names as Yukon, Durango, Expedition, and Mustang, as if their accountant-owners were going to chase down some cattle rustlers on the way to the Piggly Wiggly. This is the land in which people dream of the most radical Walter Mitty–esque personal transformations, in which one in three women *admits* to changing her hair color, amid all the other lifestyle alterations and fabrications that are a normal part of daily life.

This is a country in which every suburban high school has its collection of goths and chaperoned gangsta rappers and the boardrooms are filled with men and women who go to work in cowboy boots and then return home to Tudor estates, dreaming of software solutions that will revolutionize their industry and make them Sun Gods of the corporate-accounting universe. This is a land conceived in advertising, in which sneakers have personalities, and hamburgers and pizza chains have mascots. This is the land that perfected the celebrity culture, far above the realities of everyday mortal life. America is a land rife with make-believe.

Americans—seemingly bland, ordinary Americans—often have a remarkably tenuous grip on reality. I have come to think that the human longing for transcendence, spiritual depth, and moral cohesion has not perished in the sprawls of suburbia, it has just taken a different form, because Americans live so much of their lives in the imagined land of the future.

I suspect that to really understand America and the American suburb, you have to take seriously that central cliché of American life: the American Dream. You have to see that beneath the seeming flatness of American life, there is an imaginative fire that animates us and propels us to work so hard, move so much, invent so much, and leap into so much that is new and different—not always to our benefit.

The historian Sacvan Bercovitch observed that the United States is the example par excellence of a nation formed by collective fantasy. Despite all the claims that American culture is secular, pragmatic, and materialist, what is truly striking about this country is how material things are shot through with enchantment.

A History of Imagination

America, after all, was born in a frenzy of imagination. A newly discovered continent begs to be fantasized about, and from the moment they stumbled upon it, Europeans projected their hopes, utopian dreams, and paradisiacal visions onto this place. It was the biblical Eden, the Israelite's land of milk and honey, the Fortunate Islands of the Romans, the Elysium, the wish-image utopia of the medieval mind. In America, Europeans imagined, they could find Eldorado, the City of Gold, and the Fountain of Youth. The America they imagined was the virgin continent that would redeem the corruptions of the Old World.

These dreams of perfectibility had powerful effects on people from the first. During his voyage of 1497, Columbus perceived that the water grew sweeter as one approached the New World. The elevation seemed to grow higher. He concluded that the world was not in fact round, but was in "the form of a pear, which is very round except where the stalk grows, at which part it is most prominent; or like a round ball, upon which is a prominence like a woman's nipple, this protrusion being the highest and nearest the sky."

Soon Europeans were seeking this nipple of the earth for bounty, salvation, and utopia. In a letter home, Amerigo Vespucci described a communal paradise in which the natives existed naked, healthy, and free: "They live amongst themselves without a king or ruler, each man being his own master, and having as many wives as they please." All property was shared, he continued. The women were "libidinous, but comely." The natives often lived 150 years.

Almost immediately, America was established as the richest neighborhood in the world's imagination. By 1605, Europeans were already satirizing these lavish descriptions of American wealth and grandeur. A character in the English play *Eastward Ho!* declares:

> I tell thee, gold is more plentiful there than copper
> is with us. . . . Why, man, all their dripping pans are
> pure gold; and all their chains with which they
> chain up their streets are massy gold . . . and for
> rubies and diamonds they go forth on holidays and
> gather 'em by the seashore to hang on their chil-
> dren's coats.

The early settlers were aware of, and must have been oppressed by, the obvious potential of this land. They saw the possibility of plenty everywhere, yet at the start, they lived in harsh and primitive conditions. They knew and felt that heaven would be realized in this place that was God's greatest gift, but at that moment, they faced starvation. Their lives took on a slingshot shape—they had to pull back in order to someday shoot forward. Through the hardship of their present life, they dwelt imaginatively in the grandeur that would inevitably mark their future, that would make their sufferings and daring sacrifices worthwhile.

The American continent itself encouraged this dreaming by making the glorious future seem inevitable. The land stretched on infinitely, so paradise surely would be realized here. The abundance aroused the visitors' capacity for wonder.

As John Harmon McElroy has noted, the early settlers saw flocks of geese so large that it would take a half hour from when the leader bird took off to when the last bird was aflight. The settlers would shoot cannons into these clouds of birds just to see if they could change the flock's direction, but they could not. They saw untouched forests, thick vines of wild grapes, valleys of oaks, walnuts, pines, beds of oysters and clams bigger than any they had ever seen, and the abundance stretched on for miles and miles. They saw new crops, new animals, and above all, endless mountains and valleys terrifying but promising.

There were, of course, about a quarter million or more Native Americans living on the continent, but what the Europeans perceived was emptiness—vast room for them to move and move again, create a home, and then create another. John Smith's manual for colonists declared that in America, every family could "plant freely without limitation so much as he can," and that for every acre he planted, his heirs—the future generations—would realize "twenty, thirty, forty, or an hundred" additional acres.

This pattern recurred decade after decade. Each time pioneers pushed west, they found virgin land and perceived it as paradise. Indeed, their writings begin to run together, whether the new land is Virginia, Massachusetts, Wisconsin, Oregon, or California. The mood is exalted wonder. The joy is always the same, the potential is always limitless. "Let us speak of Elkhorn Creek," one farmer wrote about a spot in Kentucky. "The lands that it waters are so fertile and so beautiful, the air there is so pure, so serene almost all the year, that this country is veritably a second terrestrial paradise."

Many of these writers were marketing their discoveries; there was a bit of a sales job going on. Still, the mood of ecstasy was genuine, and the promises were not implausible. Progress in America really was incredible. Even in the seventeenth century, New England enjoyed a low infant-mortality rate that was not matched in Britain until the 1890s. In that century, over 90 percent of those who came to America as indentured servants—sacrificing their present for some free but distant future—eventually became landowners. Hundreds of new towns were created. Despite a widening gap between rich and poor, farm laborers enjoyed wages that were far higher than those in Europe, and they ate food, including meat, that was cheaper and more nutritious. Americans in the eighteenth century were on average three inches taller than their European counterparts, owing to their superior diet.

And they were well aware of their good fortune. As the Reverend Francis Higginson of Salem, Massachusetts, exulted in 1629:

> It is scarce to be believed how our [cows] and goats, horses and hogs do thrive and prosper here and like well of this country. In our plantation we have already a quart of milk for a penny; but the abundant increase of corn proves this country to be a wonderment. Thirty, forty, fifty, sixty are ordinary here. Yea, Joseph's increase in Egypt is outstripped here with us.

By 1740 the American population as a whole enjoyed a higher standard of living than the population of any European country, a lead that has never been surrendered. By 1770, the historian Jon Butler argues, America had become "the first modern society," with its own commercial farmers, multicultural trading centers, and a distinct secular-material culture producing its own furniture, clothing, and housing styles. Land speculation was feverish. Ministers complained that they could not keep their congregations together; families would spy some distant sixty acres available for tillage and pick up and move. Enveloping it all was a tremendous sense of opportunity. "We have been pros-pered in a most wonderful manner," exalted the Reverend Samuel West.

In his 1954 book, *People of Plenty*, historian David Potter argued that the mentality fostered by abundance is at the core of the American character. Indeed, the American example forces us to reverse our conventional notions of the psychological and spiritual effects of wealth. Classical thinkers tended to believe that abundance inevitably led to decadence and decline. The course of empires was clear: Nations grew because they were poor and hungry. Their ambition produced wealth. Wealth produced ease. Ease produced softness, and softness produced collapse.

But in America, abundance led to a different set of responses. It produced an ethos of availability. Risk-taking was rational because it so often paid off. Restlessness was natural because you knew that somewhere over the next horizon, there was a richer destiny waiting. Individualism was the norm because each person or family had the space to carve out a distinct mode of life. Progress was inevitable because each year saw an increase. Education was sacred because each generation could learn new skills to surpass the one before. An aristocracy and its habits of social def-erence were obsolete because you never needed to live under someone else's thumb; you could just move away. The universe was benevolent because it offered such bounty, and all present problems could be solved plausibly in the ever more abundant future. In short, abundance didn't seem to produce corruption and decline. It produced work, mobility, self-reliance, energy, and liberation.

Hector St. John de Crèvecoeur was a Norman cartog-rapher who fought with the French in the French and

Indian War. He married an Anglo-American wife, settled on a farm twenty-five miles west of the Hudson River in New York, and soon became one of the most appreciative chroniclers of how American conditions altered the European mind. Distances mattered less, Crèvecoeur famously observed:

> A European, when he first arrives, seems limited in his intentions as well as in his views; but he very suddenly alters his scale; two hundred miles formerly appeared a very great distance, it is now but a trifle. He no sooner breathes our air than he forms schemes and embarks on designs he never would have thought of in his own country.

In his middle age, Crèvecoeur recalled a journey he took around 1767 along the upper Ohio River: "I never before felt myself so much disposed for meditation: my imagination leaped into futurity. I consider the settling of these lands, which are watered by this river, as one of the finest conquests that could ever be presented to man. . . . It is destined to become the source of force, riches, and the future glory of the United States."

It didn't take a Crèvecoeur to see that America's present good fortune was nothing compared to what lay ahead. The present was pleasant, but from the start, Americans, and many around the globe, realized that the future was dazzling. "It requires but a small portion of the gift of discernment for anyone to foresee," Samuel Adams wrote in 1775, "that providence will erect a mighty empire in America." Adam Smith predicted that the British Parliament would someday move to the New World, since the economic and political weight of the colonies would obviously overwhelm the motherland. At a time when the United States was a scraggly stretch of colonies along the Atlantic seaboard, Alexander Hamilton declared that the country would soon become a mighty empire, "in many respects the most interesting in the world," and would be stronger than all the great empires of the day, "able to dictate the terms of the connection between the old and the new world!"

Noah Webster, who began work on his dictionary of American English just after 1800, observed a need for a standard guide to a language that he predicted would one day be spoken by three hundred million people. America is today closing in on that mark, but when Webster made the forecast—as John Harmon McElroy has also noted—the United States possessed only 4 percent of that total.

America's future greatness was a large glimmering fact hanging over the heads of each American, every hour of each day. From the start, Americans were accustomed to thinking in the future tense. They were used to living in a world of dreams, plans, innovations, improvements, and visions of things to come.

Their situation aroused their spiritual aspirations as well. To give meaning to their lives, early Americans had to place their bounty in some larger historical and moral narrative. It couldn't be that they had won the lottery; that they'd stumbled upon a rich land; that they were merely the recipients of its natural resources. It couldn't be so meaningless and random. Other nations might see the New World as an Eldorado to be looted, but as Arthur K. Moore writes in *The Frontier Mind*, the English pioneers saw it as an Eden to be occupied. These new Americans saw God's hand at work. They interpreted their abundance as part of a Divine Plan, as the latest and last in a series of God's dispensations. This meant that Americans had a specific destiny, a specific role to play in the history and culmination of the universe.

They looked around and concluded that they must be God's chosen people. Colonial sermons on America were studded with references to the colonies as the New Israel, the New Jerusalem, and the New Canaan, and to Americans as the Israelites of the age. They had recreated the Exodus story and settled in the land of milk and honey.

Their minds instantaneously leaped from their charmed if difficult present life in the blessed isle to their destiny as the culmination of the human race. It is striking how many thinkers and writers at the time of America's founding believed that they were not only the chosen people, they were the *final* people, the children of prophecy. History would end with them. God had sent them on this sacred errand into the wilderness; His plan would be fulfilled through them. Paradise would be realized on this new continent, and the redemption of all mankind would spread outward from here.

As Sacvan Bercovitch has remarked, many people in Europe interpreted Bishop George Berkeley's maxim "Westward the course of empire takes its way" as an example of the vanity of human wishes, because it showed how all glory was temporary—it passed on to other nations in due course. But the American colonists interpreted it as an assignment. There had been other phases in human history, other dispensations. But this American phase was the last, the completion of God's designs.

"There are many arguments to persuade us that our Glorious Lord will have an Holy City in America; a City, the street whereof shall be pure gold," Cotton Mather preached in his 1709 sermon "God's City: America." "This new world," Jonathan Edwards later wrote, "is probably now discovered that the new and most glorious state of God's church on earth might commence there." For "When God is about to turn the earth into a Paradise he does not begin his work where there is some good growth already, but in a wilderness." Other times and other places, Edwards continued, "are only forerunners and preparatories to this." America had been discovered to prepare "the way for the future, glorious times." It would welcome the arrival of "the new heavens and the new earth." And so, Edwards concluded, "we can't reasonably think otherwise, than that this great work of God . . . will begin in America."

By the time of the Revolution, this idea had passed from pulpit prophecy into the realm of public cliché. "From their birth," Thomas Yarrow of New York argued, "the American states were designed to be the political redeemers of mankind." John Adams wrote, "I always consider the settlement of America with reverence and wonder, as the opening of a grand scene and design in providence, for the illumination of the ignorant and the emancipation of the slavish part of the earth." In 1797 the Reverend James Smith, a Methodist minister in Ohio, exclaimed:

> O, what a country will this be at a future day! What a field of delights! What a garden of spices! What a paradise of pleasures! When these forests shall be cultivated and the gospel of Christ spread through this rising republic, unshackled by the power of kings and religious oppression on the one hand,

and slavery, that bane of true Godliness, on the other.

Americans considered themselves a covenanted people. Like the ancient Israelites, their faith was promise-centered. The corruptions of Europe, of the past, would be left behind, and this new nation would be responsible for building the City on the Hill. Something original, new, and glorious would happen here. History would end with us. Humanity would be redeemed by us. The evils of the world would be purged by us. The whole train of thinking was soon summarized in the phrase quoted from on the seal of the United States: *"Annuit Coeptis, Novus Ordo Seclorum"*—God prospered this undertaking; it shall be the new order of the ages.

Last Best Hope

This sense of high mission has reverberated through the centuries, and the imaginative visions were made to seem plausible by the awareness of material abundance. The Louisiana Purchase in 1803 gave the United States a landmass over three times the size of modern France, Germany, and the United Kingdom combined. Everything seemed to be growing and expanding. Between 1830 and 1880, the population of the United States skyrocketed by 400 percent (at a time when the French population rose by only 17 percent). In the three decades after 1850, factory output in the United States rose by 600 percent (while Britain, then at the height of the industrial revolution, saw its output double). By the early 1880s, there were more miles of railway track and telegraph wire in the U.S. than in all the European nations combined. Between 1899 and 1905, America's food output grew by 40 percent. In 1890, Americans produced 32,000 pianos; ten years later, the nation produced 374,000 pianos. During the nineteenth century, in other words, the United States became a consumer wonderland. Magical baubles, mass-produced luxuries, limitless possibilities dangled before the eye.

Like a teenager becoming aware of his own muscles, each American was awestruck by his vitality and strength. "Our national birth," the *Democratic Review* editorialized in 1839, "was the beginning of a new history . . . which separates us from the past and connects us with the future." At the same time, the country was approaching its most serious crisis, the Civil War. It's not surprising that many interpreted the war as yet another opportunity to realize the nation's potential, to purge all that was corrupt and backward from the land.

"The time will surely come—the holy millennium of liberty—when the 'Victory of endurance born' shall lift the masses," the young Walt Whitman wrote a few decades before the war in the *Brooklyn Daily Eagle,* "and make them achieve something of that destiny which we may suppose God intends eligible for mankind. And this problem is to be worked out through the people, territory, and government of the United States."

Daniel Webster gave voice to this sentiment in his famous eulogy to the martyrs of Bunker Hill: "In our day there has been as it were a new creation. . . . The last hopes of mankind . . . rest with us." During the war, Abraham Lincoln summarized the strain of thought when he called the United States "the last best hope of earth."

The important word in these speeches is "last." This is the final nation, Lincoln was saying. No better system of government would ever emerge to supplant it. America would be the place where mankind's dreams were tested and possibly realized, and from here, they would radiate across the globe. Lincoln's phrase has resonated through history, and its promise is invoked in just about every presidential inauguration, in every July Fourth speech, in all the political slogans that promise a Great Society or a New Deal or a New Frontier or a New Beginning (because in America an old beginning is never good enough).

The Popular Imagination

Lincoln and Whitman had deep souls. But what is fascinating about American history is that it is the deprived and the ordinary who most often seem gripped by the fire of imagination. It is often the hungriest, the uncultivated, the most grasping people who lead the way into the future. They are the desperadoes who strike out to the West, the gold-crazed adventurers who lunge for California, the crass vaudevillians who create Hollywood, the highly educated but socially awkward computer geeks who build Silicon Valley. Time and again in American history, the pioneers have been the people who rank low on the scales of grace, manners, and cultivation. Time and again the spiritual revivals start on the frontier, among those on the margins.

We may like to think that it is the most noble and heroic who are seized by grand visions. But in America the people with the broadest perspectives and the most cultivated manners are rarely the most imagination-frenzied.

Why should they be? They already have fulfilling low-risk opportunities in front of them. They can go to law school, med school, or a prestigious investment bank. Here, it is the fantastical visions of the vulgarians that constantly amaze. It's the dreams of the uncultivated—the Donald Trumps, the Don Kings, the Henry Fords. As Ralph Waldo Emerson taught, in America everyone is average and extra-ordinary at the same time, a democrat and also a king, a regular schmo and also a new Adam, ready to strike out.

When raw immigrants come to the United States, it is their fantasies about the future that have lured them. New York, the city of dreams, inspired wonder for generations of semiliterate immigrants. Sometimes they had visions of streets paved with gold, or of glorious business empires and limitless wealth. Others imagined simply owning a house, a car, a life.

In true American fashion, immigrants live in the future, undergoing that slingshot life course, pulling back so that someday they and their children can shoot off into the richer future. In true American fashion, they live pragmati-cally and materialistically, clawing around to get money and position and a foothold in society, and their practicality is constructed on a foundation of fantasy and imagination.

When the pioneers went west, it was speculation about the future that pulled them. Guides who led (and sometimes exploited) nineteenth-century pioneers were shocked by how little the trekkers knew about the surroundings they had thrown themselves into, or what would be involved in their new lives. As so often happens in American history, masses of people leaped before they looked.

In many cases, their behavior cannot be explained by the calculus of rational self-interest. The act of moving into the wilderness meant miserable homesickness; you were essentially dead to the parents and brothers and sisters and friends you had left behind. There was a very high probability that you would lose a child or a spouse or other family member en route. The settlers endured years of grinding poverty, crippling loneliness, and uncertainty. Insane asylums quickly popped up in the West because so many people were driven mad by their ordeals (or else it was a tint of madness that propelled them westward). In short, the pioneers faced risk-reward ratios, as the economists would say, that didn't make sense from any rational perspective.

In most cases, people launched on these journeys because they felt in their bones that some set of unbelievable opportunities was out there. They could not tolerate passing out their years without a sense of movement and anticipation, even if their chances were minuscule.

Whether in 1704 or 1904 or 2004, Americans have moved to new places because they've felt, sometimes semi-consciously, that they could build some piece of heaven there. They live in that heaven of their imagination long before they ever get around to constructing it in real life.

In his novel *The Pioneers*, James Fenimore Cooper's hero, a land developer, takes his cousin on a tour of the city he is building. He describes the broad streets, the rows of houses, the bubbling metropolis. His cousin looks around bewildered. All she sees is a stubby forest. "Where are the beauties and improvements which you were to show me?" she asks. He's astonished that she can't see them. "Where! Why, everywhere," he replies. Though they are not yet built on earth, he has built them in his mind, and they are as concrete to him as if they were already complete.

Cooper was illustrating one of the features of a distinctly American cast of mind, a Paradise Spell: the capacity to see the *present* from the vantage point of the *future*. It starts with imagination—the ability to see a vision with detail and vividness, as if it already existed. Then the future-minded person is able to think backward from that vision; to ask, "What must I do to take the future that is in my head and make it exist in the world?" That person is more emotionally attached to the glorious future than to the temporary and unsatisfactory present. Time isn't pushed from the remembered past to the felt present to the mysterious future. It is pulled by the vivid future from the unsatisfactory present and away from the dim past.

Future-mindedness is a trait that repeats in the biographies of inventors, entrepreneurs, and political leaders, and it is a prominent feature in the literature of the pioneers. As John Harmon McElroy notes in *American Beliefs*, there's a particularly vivid description of the mentality in Ole Edvart Rölvaag's classic 1927 novel, *Giants in the Earth: A Saga of the Prairie*. The protagonist, Per Hansa, is a Norwegian immigrant who settles in the Dakota prairies in the 1870s. His circumstances are harsh, but in his imagination, he has already moved into the future:

> But dearest to him of all, and most delectable, was the thought of the royal mansion which he had already erected in his mind. There would be houses for both chickens and pigs, roomy stables, a magnificent storehouse and barn . . . and then the splendid palace itself! The royal mansion would shine in the sun—it would stand out far and wide! The palace itself would be white, with green cornices; but the big barn would be red as blood, with cor-

nices of driven snow. Wouldn't it be beautiful—
wasn't it going to be great fun! . . . And he and his
boys would build it all!

Like the actual pioneers he depicts, Rölvaag's characters
are, he writes, "more interested in visualizing how things
were going to turn out than in making a bare statement of
how they actually were." The novel's tragic element concerns Per Hansa's wife, who longs for her old traditions
and the family she has left behind. Per Hansa finally con-
fesses his guilt over the misery he has caused her: "She has
never felt at home here in America. . . . There are some people, I know now, who never should emigrate, because, you
see, they can't take pleasure in that which is to come—they
simply can't see it."

In both Cooper's and Rolvaag's stories, it is the man
who is future-minded. But in real life, both men and
women were propelled onward by imaginative future
worlds. In *The Land Before Her: Fantasy and Experience
of the American Frontiers, 1630–1860,* the historian
Annette Kolodny plumbs the diaries of female pioneers and
finds them rife with fantastical visions. Female fantasies
tended to have a different character than male fantasies,
Kolodny writes, owing to the expectations that young
women were raised with.

Both men and women fantasized a paradise, she notes,
but "As a result, 'paradise' implied radically different
places when used by men and women. For men the term
(with all its concomitant psychosexual associations)
echoed an invitation for mastery and possession of the vast
new continent. For women, by contrast, it denoted domes-

ticity." While the men dreamed of conquering the forest, often as solitary adventurers, the women dreamed of establishing homes and neighborhoods, of building communities in which every new family was part of an extended circle of love. They dreamed of pine-tree quilts, little gardens around their pioneer cabins, and appliquéd counterpanes with brightly colored designs. The male fantasies dominated the adventure stories and the movie westerns. But the female fantasies had more influence on real life, for ultimately, settling the West was more a matter of building homes, neighborhoods, and communities than Daniel Boone adventures.

The pioneer experience and the cowboy mythology have played such an important role in the American identity because they embodied the dream-culture character that is at the core of who we are.

This really is a deep and mystical longing. In the early nineteenth century, the writer Edwin James noted "a manifest propensity, particularly in the males, to remove westward, for which it is not easy to account." The esteemed historian Francis Parkman remembered that he, too, was gripped by this mystical longing for the horizon. Writing of his youthful self, Parkman noted, "His thoughts were always in the forest, whose features possessed his waking and sleeping dreams, filling him with vague cravings impossible to satisfy."

Timothy Flint, the nineteenth-century biographer of Daniel Boone who was himself an itinerant preacher and writer and spent most of his life in the Mississippi Valley, wrote about the forces that motivated the people he met there:

There is more of the material of poetry than we imagine, diffused through all the classes of the community. . . . I am ready to believe, from my own experience, and from what I have seen in the case of others, that this influence of imagination has no inconsiderable agency in producing emigration. Indeed, the saturnine and illiterate emigrant may not be conscious that such motives had any agency in fixing him in his purpose. But I need not observe, that those who examine most earnestly what passes in their own minds, are not always aware of all the elements of motive that determine their actions.

As Arthur K. Moore concluded in his 1957 book, *The Frontier Mind*:

Common sense dictates a coming to terms with present circumstances, for change dissipates whatever goods labor has produced; but the imagination tricks people into emigration through creating a distant life in which laws of wild and human nature are miraculously suspended. More or less consciously, they seek a lost garden, where, as Horace represented the Fortunate Islands, "yearly the earth unploughed brings forth grain, and the unpruned vine flowers continuously and buds the branch of the never-failing olive." Ironically, emigrants very often flourished because the new situation is in fact no Eden and, far from affording ease and abundance, compels extraordinary energetic responses.

Future-Mindedness Today

Our minds are still with Parkman's in the forest. Our imagination still tricks us into undertaking grand projects—starting a business, writing a book, raising a family—by enchanting us with visions of future joys. When these tasks turn out to be more difficult than we dreamed, the necessary exertions, as Moore observed, bring out our finest excellencies.

Of course, in normal times, and especially these days, few would claim that Americans are the chosen people of God. Few live strictly according to their fantasies. But the past survives in the present. The cognitive strands established early in American history and through its period of explosive growth—the sense that some ultimate fulfillment will be realized here, that happiness can be created here, that the United States has a unique mission to redeem the world—are still woven into the country's fabric. The old impulses, fevers, and fantasies still play themselves out amid the Palms, the Hummers, the closet organizers, and the travel-team softball leagues. We Americans have not abandoned the horizon mentality of our forebears.

We are a bourgeois nation, but unlike some other bourgeois nations, we are also a transcendent nation infused with everyday utopianism. This utopianism lures us beyond the prosaic world. It gives us a distinct conception of time, so we often find ourselves on some technological frontier, dreaming of this innovation or that management technique that will elevate the world—and half the time, our enthusiasms, crazes, and fads seem ludicrous to others and even to us, in retrospect. We still find ourselves venturing off into world crises, roaring into battle with visions of virtue on our side and evil on the other, waging moralistic crusades that others do not understand, pushing our movie, TV, and musical fantasies onto an ambivalent and sometimes horrified world.

Mentality matters, and in the end, perhaps mentality is all that matters. The tacit assumptions, intuitive judgments, unconscious mental categories, and inherited perceptions of time and space form what John Dewey called the shared "sense of an extensive underlying whole" that binds a people. If somehow America were conquered and its institutions erased, there would still be some future-minded group of people related to a certain way of being in the world. As James Russell Lowell commented, "Our ancestors sought a new continent. What they found was a new condition of mind."

This doesn't mean all Americans think alike, simply that there is a prevailing current to national life that one feels when one comes here from other places with other currents. Some nations are bound, in all their diversity, by a common creation myth, a tale of how they came into being. Americans are bound, in all our diversity, by a fruition myth.

Born in abundance, inspired by opportunity, nurtured in imagination, spiritualized by a sense of God's blessing and call, and realized in ordinary life day by day, this Paradise Spell is the controlling ideology of American life. Just out of reach, just beyond the next ridge, just with the next home or entrepreneurial scheme or diet plan; just with the next political hero, the next credit-card purchase, or the next true love; just with the right all-terrain vehicle, the right summer home, the right meditation technique, or the right motiva-

tional seminar; just with the right schools, the right community values, and the proper morality; just with the right beer
and a good set of buddies; just with the next technology or
after the next shopping spree, there is this spot you can get to
where all tensions will melt, all time pressures are relieved,
and all contentment can be realized. Prosperity will be
joined with virtue, materialism with idealism, achievement
with equality, success with love, the Cosmic Blonde's dream
of gleaming happiness with the Cosmic Brunette's dream of
self-fulfillment and understanding, thereby producing a new
Eden.

This Paradise Spell is at the root of our tendency to
work so hard, to consume so feverishly, to move so much.
It inspires our illimitable faith in education, our frequent
born-again experiences. It explains why, alone among
developed nations, we have shaped our welfare system to
encourage opportunity at the expense of security; and why,
more than comparable nations, we wreck our families and
move on. It is the call making us heedless of the past, disre-
spectful toward traditions, short on contemplation, wasteful in our use of the things around us, impious toward
restraints, but consumed by hope, driven ineluctably to
improve, fervently optimistic, relentlessly aspiring, spiritually alert, and, in this period of human history, and maybe
for all time, the locomotive of the world.

Most of the time, we are not even aware of how this
mentality shapes us. The worldview is so ingrained in our
culture that it doesn't even need to be passed down consciously from parent to child. Yet when you go to a place
where people do not live with a mood of radical hopefulness, where people's lives are not infused with a sense of
perpetual anticipation, where people do not assume that

they have the power to remake their own destinies and radically transform their own lives, you do feel the difference. When you go to a country where the past is more real than the future, and then you return to America, it becomes clear how distinct the American imagination really is, and how each of us in this culture is molded by our horizon dreams. It becomes clear that the eschatological impulse really does influence ordinary life, that we remain lured by the promise of total happiness. We still live under the spell of paradise.

Hope Is a Trickster

This hopeful frame of mind does not mean everything is hunky-dory, for hope is not entirely a good thing. This is what the critics of middle-American life never understand. They see the treacly optimism of Disney, the sugary comfort of Hallmark, the upbeat maxims of Successories, the burbly chirpiness of the morning talk shows, the power of positive thinking, the cheery banter of the evening newsreaders, and the whole warm bath of obligatory optimism and 24/7 good cheer, and they think, America is this bland, optimistic, and fundamentally complacent place. They don't see that hope is a trickster and a seducer and a torturer. American culture is more complicated than it seems.

The German theologian Jürgen Moltmann wrote a brilliant book, *Theology of Hope*, ostensibly about Christianity, but because he was dissecting the hopeful frame of mind, he illuminated the American experience. One of his central points was that a hopeful person lives in tension with reality. He is always ahead of himself. He "finds himself a riddle and an open question." He "does not stand harmoniously and concentrically in himself, but stands excentrically to himself." He has dreams, but they do "not yet bring him to the haven of identity." He has goals, but he has a hard time experiencing pleasure and a sense of harmony with the moment. He is constantly disturbed.

Hope induces a sort of salvation panic. Though America is the land of optimism, it is also the land of lacerating self-scrutiny, of dark foreboding, of fevered pleas for reform. From the very start, Americans have felt that the same God who selected them for their sacred mission might repudiate them if they failed to live up to their side of the covenant.

The cry is always the same. Some great possibility is realizable here, so if we as a nation and as individuals are not on the right path, then we are committing some exceptional sin. Every decade, every year, every day, new jeremiads have risen with urgent cries that we get back on track and fulfill our possibilities. The American press has always had a more earnest and moralizing tone than, say, the British press, because there is a national solemn duty to make sure the national errand is scrutinized and kept on track.

The shelves of American bookstores are stacked with descriptions of our moral, material, or spiritual decline, with hysterical attacks at the supposed enemies within who are sapping our true national virtue. As we saw in Chapter 4, the most influential social critics of the past fifty years have been relentlessly pessimistic. This pessimism grows from the deep and fundamental sense of possibility. The writers see in their mind's eye how much is out there for us to accomplish, and they despair that we aren't achieving it, or aren't on the right route toward achieving it.

The historian Perry Miller argued that it was by this very process of self-improvement and self-correction that Americans forged themselves into a people: "I suggest that under the guise of this mounting wail of sinfulness, this incessant and never successful cry for repentance, the Puritans launched themselves upon the process of Americanization."

Furthermore, hope is the breeding ground for anxiety. Americans often feel, as Tocqueville remarked, a manic need to seize their opportunities before they slip away. "It is strange to see with what feverish ardor the Americans pursue their own welfare," he wrote, "and to watch the vague dread that constantly torments them lest they should not have chosen the shortest path that leads to it."

In *People of Plenty,* David Potter also noticed that everything in America turns into an arena for advancement. He pointed out that in the United States, the word "liberty" really means the freedom to grasp opportunity, and the word "equality" also means the freedom to grasp opportunity. He needn't have stopped there. In the United States, education means opportunity, welfare means opportunity, happiness means opportunity, fairness means opportunity, morality means opportunity, and civil rights mean opportunity.

Fired by hope, Americans have built a society that opens up opportunity and undermines security. We have relatively low tax rates to encourage entrepreneurialism and the accumulation of riches, but relatively little job protection, making it easier to fire workers and close companies. We encourage venture capital but discourage—compared to most other countries—regulation that might soften the blows of the marketplace. Compared to say, Germany, we favor the desires of the consumers over the safety of the producers. There are relatively few protected industries, because the old companies must be allowed to die or move away so new growths can emerge and cheap goods can flow. It is easier to get rich here, but more miserable to be poor here.

The hopeful person is always chasing the grapes of Tantalus, which remain always out of reach. The hopeful person has trouble living in the present and savoring the moment, for she is imprudently distracted by the mirages of the future. She doesn't appreciate what she has, because she is consumed by the thought of what she might have.

The hopeful person dreams of being liberated from the future. She dreams of experiencing, just once, a world in which the future is not always right over the horizon, beckoning and luring. She dreams of arriving at that resting spot where time does not exist and all striving ceases. In fact, the American Dream is the dream of finding a place where one will feel liberated from the burden of the future, though that place is always in the future. The American Dream devours its own flesh.

Throughout history, Americans have worried about their own rat-race existence. Certain countercultures have erected systems meant to serve as antidote to the ever upward nature of mainstream commercial life. In the pre–Civil War South, cavaliers tried to build a semifeudal aristocracy in which one's identity would be determined by birth, honor, race, and a chivalric code. The agrarians tried to build changeless pastoral communities rooted in the soil, immune to industrial progress. In the North, artists and intellectuals tried to create little bohemias, enclaves where people could reject the bitch goddess success and serve beauty and truth. Around the country, socialists and other utopians tried to build communities where harmony would replace competition and communal solidarity would replace climbing. In the 1960s, hippies and yippies tried to build a civilization in which we could be free to drop out and just be. At West Point and Annapolis, some tried to create a warrior code in which duty, courage, and honor would be more important than success, riches, and ascent.

All of these countercultures were eventually devoured by the voracious hunger of hope. The southern cavaliers were crushed by northern commerce. Almost all the bohemians have been co-opted. The hippies wound up founding organic salad dressing companies. The military has turned into a profession as much as a calling. In the United States, it is very hard to maintain a creed based on the renunciation of advancement. The dazzling lights of opportunity lure the young; the ethos of achievement undermines stasis and simplicity. There is virtually no escape.

By and large, Americans are utter failures when it comes to leading the simple life, which we profess to desire. You may start the day with noble intentions in your heart and one of those simplicity magazines by your side. You may tell yourself that today you are going to renounce material things. You're going to slow down and savor the moment. So you break out the seaside-scent candles, fill up the claw-foot tub with fluoridated water and tub tea, and soak with a volume of Robert Frost in your hand and some almond-scented body wash on the shelf. But then the bathroom-renovation fantasies start crowding into your brain, and along come the second-home longings.

To clear your mind, you realize, you need a country

place in the mountains where you can get away from it all, and just a couple more big financial scores so you can carry that soul-saving second mortgage. And before long, you are back in the land of desire. You've been sucked in by the alluring availability of increased earnings and the narcotic of potential capital gains. You have returned to the realm of buying and selling and earning and investing. The sheer wealthiness of American life has swallowed you back up. You turn back to the Simplicity Bible in one last desperate effort to escape from the whole chorus of buying and getting, the world of goods whispering, "Taste me . . . taste me . . . taste me." But you find that the magazine is nothing but a series of tips on how you can be a better simplifier. It has merely taken the achievement ethos and applied it to the goal of simplification. And that is no respite at all.

Even if you win the race, there is no rest. There is no position you can be awarded that will guarantee you status and respect regardless of your behavior. There is no title you can pass down to your children. Even if your own future is secure, there are still your children's futures and grandchildren's futures looming. The mentality of ascent still has you in its grip. The universe, as they say, is still pursuing its adventures, and you must work to keep your place. We must all, as the Puritans said, continue rowing for heaven.

The Provisional Life

Hope tortures and incites in other ways. In the land of the future, one's relationship to a place, to a job, to a lifestyle is provisional, because at any juncture, you might move on in pursuit of the horizon. But more fundamentally, a relationship to beliefs is provisional, because they are always being renovated and improved. George Santayana observed that Americans tend not to believe in eternal and absolute truth. Instead, ideas are always in motion, and people are always progressing on to new opinions and beliefs.

Under the influence of pragmatism, truth does not inhere absolutely in an idea; truth happens to an idea. An idea is held to be true when it turns out to be useful and good, when it serves its purpose in making life better at that moment and for that individual.

One saw this phenomenon in the nineteenth-century age of the transcendentalists, and one sees it today in the age of Oprah. What is most absolute is not truth and falsehood, virtue and vice; what matters most absolutely is the advancing self. The individual is perpetually moving toward wholeness and completion, and ideas are adopted as they suit that mission. Individual betterment is the center around which the entire universe revolves.

This is a brutal form of narcissism. The weight of the universe is placed on the shoulders of the individual. Accordingly, in modern American culture, the self becomes semidivinized. People feel free to pick and choose their own religious beliefs, because whatever serves the self-journey toward happiness must be godly and true.

This means that each individual must be the locus of values. It means that the central question of life is not "What does God command and love?" but rather "What is my destiny and fulfillment?" It is not our duty to humbly obey God's law and submit to the universal order. It is our duty to create and explore our self, to realize our own inner light. It is up to each of us to justify our own existence.

The obligation of life, in this vein, is not to hew to the straight-and-narrow course. It is to lead the richest, fullest, and broadest possible life, so as to realize as many potentialities as possible. As Oliver Wendell Holmes put it, "The chief worth of civilization is just that it makes the means of living more complex. Because more complex and intense intellectual efforts mean a fuller and richer life. That means more life. Life is an end in itself, and the only question as to whether it is worth living is whether you have enough of it."

Only a radically hopeful nation would pile so much complexity and richness onto individuals, or would believe that individuals are capable of bearing such a weight. There are, of course, many orthodox believers in America, people as rooted in absolute truth as a mountain is rooted in earth. But most Americans know very little for certain except that whatever works for me is valid, and whatever works for you probably is, too. There are few rules, this mentality holds, that apply at all times in all situations. What may be true for you may not be true for me. What may be true for me now might not be true for me later. Therefore, it is important not to judge others too harshly, because we are all pursuing our own horizons. Americans are inclined, as Henry Adams observed, to relax severity.

The sociologist Alan Wolfe has called this nonjudgmental state of mind moral freedom, because we are each free to choose our own ideas and virtues as we see fit, and we hope to be tolerant toward those who have chosen differently. Others have been alarmed by this state of belief and its radical openness.

Such a mentality puts incredible pressure on the individual. All belief is challenged by ambiguity and impermanence. Everything is provisional and instrumental. The future-minded person must perpetually be advancing, because the bridge under his or her feet evaporates as the phases of life and the needs of the moment come to an end. It is necessary to move on to the next stage or lose the presence of hope, which is life itself.

Moreover, the future-minded person is discouraged from crashing his progress on the rocks of principle. On the contrary, he is encouraged to be a little fuzzy in his principles for the sake of perpetual advancement. He is not likely to be unprincipled, exactly, just flexible. Hope is a lawyer, not a martyr.

America Is the Solution

So hope instigates, but it also lures. It arouses the most amazing energies, but it produces its own set of awful temptations. More than in most places, American life is an obstacle course demanding relentless energy and work. Whitman was right when he wrote in "Democratic Vistas" that political democracy, as it exists in America, and "with all its threatening evils," nonetheless "supplies a training school for making first class men. It is life's gymnasium, not of good only, but of all." Life in the United States is so demanding and so full of possibility that the best Americans—and by this he meant regular middle-class Americans—become "freedom's athletes." They attain "the experiences of the fight, the hardening of the long campaign," and they come to throb with the currents of their expectations. America strives to be a powerful nation so that it can bring about the full flowering of individuals.

Writing after the Civil War, Whitman lamented the materialism and crassness all about him. "Never was there, perhaps, more hollowness at heart than at present, and here in the United States. Genuine belief seems to have left us," he wrote in one dark mood. Yet no matter how disgusting his neighbors appeared superficially, he always saw down to their nobility. "Shams, etc., will always be the show, like ocean's scum," but the American people are "the peaceablest and most good-natured race in the world, and the most personally independent and intelligent."

Americans are reliable in emergencies, he continued, and possess "a certain breadth of historic grandeur, of peace and war" surpassing the citizenry of any other great nation. The behavior of the average American during the Civil War, he added, proved beyond all doubt "that popular democracy, whatever its faults and dangers, practically justifies itself beyond the proudest claims and wildest hopes of its enthusiasts."

Whitman understood that whatever the nation's problems, America, and the idealism present in that word, are the solution. America is the solution to bourgeois flatness, to materialistic complacency, to mass-media shallowness, because America, with all its utopian possibilities, arouses the energies and the most strenuous efforts. America is the answer to insularity, to balkanization, to complacency, to timidity, because America is a set of compulsions pulling people out of their narrow and trivial concerns and lifting their sights to the distant hopes.

For the past century, radicals, intellectuals, artists, revolutionaries, and dissidents have assumed that the way to see truth, to realize their highest selves, and to promote social change is to rebel against the supposed complacency of middle-American life. But those rebels only managed to send themselves off into a cul-de-sac of alienation, and they find themselves repeating the same stale gestures as their fathers and grandmothers and great-grandfathers and great-great-grandmothers. They failed to see what Whitman saw, that America is the permanent revolution, that deep in middle-American life, even in the most placid-seeming suburb, there is an unquenchable longing and hope, and it is in committing to far-off dreams that we fight the insularity and the trivialization that threaten to swallow us up every day.

Whitman, too, was gripped by the possibility before him, and before his nation. "It seems as if the Almighty had spread before this nation charts of imperial destinies, dazzling as the sun," he wrote. America will someday, he forecast, be "the empire of empires . . . making a new history, a history of democracy, making old history a dwarf . . . inaugurating largeness, culminating time."

Even in his darkest mood, Whitman radiated a spirit of radical optimism and inspired hopefulness. "Far far indeed, stretch, in distance, our Vistas," he sang. "Thus we presume to write, as it were, upon things that exist not, and travel by maps yet unmade, and a blank. But the throes of birth are upon us."

Today we wear different clothing. We live in different sorts of houses. We work at different sorts of jobs and buy different sorts of appliances. In these pages, I have described aspects of everyday American life that are tawdry, inspiring, and comic. But I think for all his overblown rhetoric, Whitman was still essentially right. America is not a perfect country. It is often an embarrassing country. But it is a great country, and it is greatly different from other countries. It is infused with a utopian fire that redeems its people, despite the crass and cynical realities.

At the start of this book, I asked, What motivates Americans to work so hard and move about so feverishly? We are motivated by the Paradise Spell, by the feeling that there is some glorious destiny just ahead. Then I asked if we are as shallow as we look. No, we are not. We are an imaginative people, a dreaming people. Middle Americans may not be contemplative or dark and brooding. We may not be rooted in a deep and mysterious past. But we do have our heads in a vast and complicated future, and that gives the American mind a dimension that is not easily understood or dismissed. In Saul Bellow's novel *The Adventures of Augie March,* one of the characters says to Augie, "You have a nobility syndrome. You can't adjust to the reality situation."

That's a pretty good description of life as we see it around us today. Americans have a nobility syndrome. We have trouble adjusting to the reality situation.

Bibliographical Essay

I really should dedicate this book to CVS, Walgreens, and Eckerd. In the stationery sections of those drugstores, they always sell these three-by-five-inch memo pads, often produced by the Mead Company in Dayton, Ohio, or the Carolina Pad Company of Charlotte, North Carolina. I would fly somewhere, stop in at a drugstore, buy a dozen of these pads, and then go out and take notes on how people live.

I spent many days in big-box malls, in housing developments, and on college campuses, watching ordinary behavior. When I conducted interviews, I found that people are really good at describing certain things about their lives, but they are generally not good at seeing broad patterns. They do not think sociologically, because they don't walk around with notepads in their hands. The pads are like little barriers that force you to see everyday life from the outside. They encourage a certain sort of observation.

Of course, observation has to be backed up by data, so that you know your impressions are not wildly unrepresentative. I've benefited enormously from the work of demographers such as William Frey and Robert Lang. I've become a fanatical devotee of the magazine *American Demographics,* which packs its pages with reliable statistics about everyday American life. I make weekly visits to the website of the University of Michigan's Institute of Social Research. I've learned a lot at conferences sponsored by the Urban Land Institute and the International Council of Shopping Centers. I've tried to use the data supplied by such individuals, magazines, and organizations to buttress my firsthand reporting. In many cases, data from different sources conflict—for example, on how much homework the average student actually does. In those cases I've tried to use the safest, least controversial findings, but there is no way to please everybody.

For broader historical perspective, I dove in to the vast literature on the American character. As always, I found that some of the most provocative books were written during the 1950s and 1960s, the golden age of American nonfiction. If I were teaching a course on this subject, I would assign David M. Potter's *People of Plenty*, R.W.B. Lewis's *The American Adam*, Arthur K. Moore's *The Frontier Mind*, Louis Hartz's *The Liberal Tradition in America*, William R. Taylor's *Cavalier & Yankee,* and Henry Steele Commager's *The American Mind.*

There are other, more recent authors I would put on my reading list. Seymour Martin Lipset has explored American exceptionalism as exhaustively as anyone. Sacvan Bercovitch has commented brilliantly on the ideas that animate this country, especially in *The Puritan Origins of the American Self*. Alan Wolfe has contributed a series of superb books on American moral belief. Michael Kammen has written beautifully on the texture of American life, especially in *People of Paradox*. John Harmon McElroy's *American Beliefs* accomplishes the impossible task of capturing the entire national mind-set without dissolving into vague generalities. I have done very little primary historical research. I have relied upon the quotations and observations found in these and other similar books to guide me as I tried to make sense of contemporary culture.

Finally, I'd like to take the opportunity to recommend a few more books that I enjoyed reading while working on this one: Jürgen Moltmann's *Theology of Hope*, Reinhold Niebuhr's *The Irony of American History*, Wilfred M. McClay's *The Masterless*, Luigi Barzini's *The Europeans*, Gregg Easterbrook's *The Progress Paradox*, Leszek Kolakowski's *The Presence of Myth,* and Colin Campbell's *The Romantic Ethic and the Spirit of Modern Consumerism*. Put all those books together, and you've got a great, if demanding, summer reading list.

Acknowledgments

Some parts of this book grew out of reporting I did for *The Atlantic Monthly, The Weekly Standard,* and *The New York Times Magazine*. Therefore, I'd like to thank David Bradley, Cullen Murphy, Amy Meeker, and the late Michael Kelly from the *Atlantic*; Bill Kristol, Fred Barnes, Richard Starr, and Claudia Winkler from the *Standard*; and Dean Robinson, Hugo Lindgren, and others from the *Times Magazine*.

I'd also like to thank my parents, Lois and Michael Brooks, for reading and commenting on the manuscript; Erich Eichman for his wise advice; Glen Hartley and Lynn Chu, my agents; Reihan Salam for his careful reading; and my editor, Alice Mayhew, for her thoughts and suggestions.

Finally, props go out to my wife, Jane, whose design for our new house made this book necessary. Just kidding.

Index

About the Author

DAVID BROOKS is a political journalist and "comic sociologist" who writes a biweekly Op-Ed column for *The New York Times*. He appears regularly on PBS's *The NewsHour with Jim Lehrer* and NPR's *All Things Considered*. Formerly a senior editor at *The Weekly Standard,* he has also written for *The Atlantic Monthly, Newsweek, Reader's Digest, Men's Health,* and other publications. He lives in Bethesda, Maryland.

About the Author

David Brooks writes a biweekly column for *The New York Times* and appears regularly on *PBS's The New Hour with Jim Lehrer* and NPR's *All Things Considered*. He lives in Bethesda, Maryland.